The What, Where, When, How & Why
Of Gardening In Indiana

Indiana
GARDENER'S
GUIDE

TOM TYLER
JO ELLEN MEYERS SHARP

COOL
SPRINGS
PRESS

Tyler, Tom and Sharp, Jo Ellen Meyers
    Indiana Gardener's Guide: the what, where, when, how & why of gardening in Indiana / Tom Tyler and Jo Ellen Meyers Sharp

    p.   cm.
    Includes bibliographical references (p.   ) and index.
    ISBN 1-888608-40-4
    1. Landscape plants -- Indiana 2. Landscape gardening -- Indiana
    3. Gardening -- Indiana I. Title
635.9--dc20
Tyl/Sha

635.9
TYL

Cool Springs Press, Inc.
206 Bridge Street
Franklin, Tennessee 37064

First printing 1998
Printed in the United States of America
10 9 8 7 6 5 4 3 2 1

On the cover (clockwise from top left): Carolina Allspice, Peony, Water Lily, Tulip.

Map (p. 9) provided by Agricultural Research Service, USDA

Visit the Cool Springs Press website at: www.coolspringspress.com

DEDICATION

⚜

FOR MY MOTHER, Pat (February 6th, 1924 to January 10, 1998), whose goodness lives in every garden. With love . . .

—T.T.

⚜

IN HONOR OF MY GREAT-GRANDPARENTS, John and Anna Kempe Heidenreich, and grandparents, Arthur and Helen Staub Heidenreich, who made their living in the nursery, greenhouse and florist business; my uncle, Bill Heidenreich, who taught me the basics; my parents, Frank and Joann Heidenreich, who taught me about nurturing all living things; and my son, Benjamin, a gardener in the making.

—J.E.M.S.

ACKNOWLEDGMENTS

WE WISH TO THANK ALL WHO SHARED with us their knowledge of gardening and horticulture as well as their technical assistance: Doug Akers, Russ Anger, Bill Brink, Dick Crum, Mike Dana, Mike Griffith, Wayne Kreuscher, Ruth Krulce, Rosie Lerner, Steve Mayer, and Sarah Palmatier.

CONTENTS

INTRODUCTION

Indiana Gardening

*I*NDIANA'S GARDENERS ARE IN GOOD COMPANY. Gardening is America's most popular outdoor activity; the majority of us spend several hours a week cutting the lawn, weeding, watering, or picking the fruits of our labor. Gardening is a dynamic process, influenced by the changing forces of nature and by the plants we use. One of Indiana's blessings is its long growing season; there is usually enough natural rainfall to guarantee that a wide variety of plants will do well in our state. In this book, we provide gardeners with information on more than 175 ornamental plants that we think will do best in the Hoosier landscape. We talk about the basics: how to grow, use, and maintain the plants, as well as how to enjoy them for a lifetime full of seasonal pleasures.

The *Indiana Gardener's Guide* includes both native and adaptive plants in twelve chapters by type: annuals, bulbs, groundcovers, herbs, lawn grasses, ornamental grasses, perennials, roses, shrubs, trees, vines, and water garden plants. The plants are listed by common name, which is the name they are usually called here in Indiana. The Latin, "scientific," or "botanical" name of each plant follows its common name. Botanists have assigned a scientific name to each plant for the purpose of universal identification. This prevents confusion in identifying plants, since different regions or countries often use various names for the same plant. For instance, some people call the August-blooming resurrection lily a "surprise lily." Others refer to it as a "naked lady." Using a plant's Latin or botanical name at all times will ensure that you purchase the plant you want.

Indiana gardening also means contending with hot, dry, humid summers and the fluctuating temperatures of winter and spring that seem to freeze and thaw the ground every other day. Another factor is the ground itself, which often is hard-packed clay or a boggy site with poor drainage. While there's little we can do about the weather, we can make the best of what we have by knowing our sites, carefully choosing our plants, and improving our soil.

Introduction

You will get much better results if you pick the right plant for the right place, which means researching light, soil, moisture, and other requirements. Pay attention to how much sun or shade a particular area of the yard gets, for instance, or which sites stay wet longer than others in the landscape.

Full Sun   Partial Sun   Shade

"Full-sun" plants need at least six hours of direct sunlight a day; "partial-sun" plants should receive about four hours of sunlight a day and prefer dappled light or shade in the hottest time of the day; and a "shade" plant can live with little or no sunlight. Reflective light and general brightness are also factors to consider.

Don't be afraid to try new plants. Check with neighbors, relatives, and friends about what has worked well in their yards. Visit public gardens and parks to see what the experts have planted; along with commercial sites, these gardens and parks are often the first places to use new plants in the landscape. An example of this is *Verbena bonariensis*, an annual with purple flowers on 3- to 4-foot stalks. It was used in public and commercially planted settings for several years before home owners started planting it in their yards.

Indiana's challenging weather requires us to use those plants that do well in the Hoosier climate. We make reference to plant "hardiness" throughout the *Indiana Gardener's Guide*. Hardiness refers to a plant's "useful range" and is determined by its ability to survive average low temperatures in the winter months and grow satisfactorily the following spring.

Daily temperatures have been recorded across the continent for many years and are used to build the hardiness zone map. The map referred to in this book is the USDA Hardiness Map published by the U.S. Department of Agriculture (see page 9).

Introduction

All of Indiana lies in Hardiness Zones 5 and 6. There is a ten-degree Fahrenheit difference between these zones and the other zones on the USDA Map. Each zone is divided into sub-zone "A," the lower portion of the zone, and sub-zone "B."

For the most part, the plants selected for this book are adapted to both Zones 5 and 6, though there are some exceptions. While a species may be adapted to your zone, a favorite variety may not. Be sure when planning your landscape to choose plants that are adapted to the hardiness zone you live in; otherwise, they may not survive the winter. In central Indiana, for instance, plants that may be hardy in Johnson County may not be winter hardy in Hamilton County.

Hardiness is affected by other factors as well. Evergreens that are not well watered or mulched in late fall may experience severe drying out, or desiccation, when winter temperatures fluctuate.

Plants that are stressed from summer drought or other environmental factors may not tolerate as low a temperature as those that are healthy. Protection from prevailing winds will improve hardiness to a limited extent, as will a plant's exposure to sun or shade.

Soil type and planting time also influence plant hardiness. For example, "hardy mums" purchased in full bloom and planted in the fall have limited chances for survival since the plants will not have sufficient time to establish a good root system before the onset of winter's killing cold.

MAKING BEDS

The ideal time to plant permanent plants such as trees, shrubs, groundcovers, and perennials is usually in the spring or fall. Transplanting may also be performed in summer if the gardener is vigilant about keeping new stock well watered. Spring-flowering bulbs are planted in fall; summer-flowering bulbs may be planted in the spring or fall; annuals are usually planted in the spring after the last frost. Though the gardening bug bites most of us in the spring, fall is actually the best time to prepare the landscape; at that time, the soil is more evenly moist and the temperature is more consistent.

U S D A   H A R D I N E S S
Z O N E   M A P

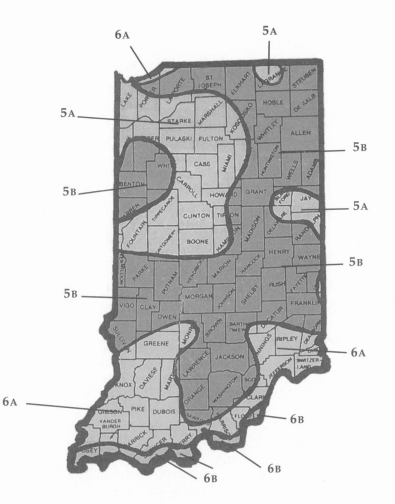

AVERAGE ANNUAL MINIMUM TEMPERATURE

Zone	Temperature
5A	-15° F TO -20° F
5B	-10° F TO -15° F
6A	-5° F TO -10° F
6B	0° F TO -5° F

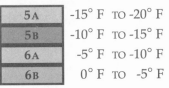

9

Introduction

Beds prepared in the fall may be planted in the fall, or they may be allowed to settle for spring planting. Fall-prepared beds usually heat up more quickly and can be planted earlier in the spring.

Improving the soil, which means digging it up and adding organic matter, is an important basic task. The *Indiana Gardener's Guide* gives specific how-to's in each chapter according to plant type. Soil testing is another important step in gardening. Gather samples of the soil every three to five years in the fall (or spring). Take samples throughout the yard, or from specific beds, to send to a lab for an analysis of the soil's nutrient values and pH. Tests reveal the nitrogen, phosphorus, and potassium levels as well as the mineral content of the soil. The baseline reading from the soil analysis is a guide for determining what additives need to be mixed into the soil in order to create an optimum environment that will help plants thrive.

GARDENER'S GOLD

The best way to enrich the soil and improve its drainage and consistency is to add compost. No backyard should be without a compost pile. Most landfills in Indiana have banned plant debris, so composts are the perfect place to dispose of what we pull from the yard. Plant debris can also be mixed with biodegradable "trash" from the house, such as lint; carpet and floor sweepings; many kitchen scraps, such as vegetable peelings, coffee grounds and filters, and egg shells; pet and human hair; and paper towels. Kitchen scraps should be buried in the pile rather than left on top. Because kitchen scraps can attract rodents, they may be banned in some municipalities or neighborhoods; check the ordinances or covenants for your area.

Materials NOT to be used in your compost pile include cat or dog waste, grease, fat or meat products, coal or coal dust or ashes, charcoal briquettes, synthetics, street sweepings, bulky materials that are slow to decompose, and sewer sludge. Grass clippings and other plant material that have been treated with pesticides and/or herbicides should be set aside to allow the chemicals to break down before they are mixed into the pile.

Introduction

The ideal size for a compost pile is about three feet by three feet by three feet. Build a compost pile in the sun or shade. The pile should be enclosed in a bin that you construct yourself, or you can purchase a bin from retailers, garden centers, or mail-order catalogs.

Making a compost pile is a lot like making lasagna. We add layers of ingredients and when it is cooked, the result is a nutritious food: compost. At the base of the compost pile, place about three inches of rough stuff such as twigs, small branches, or stalks. Add a six-inch layer of dry plant material such as chopped leaves. Add a two-inch layer of green material such as grass clippings, kitchen scraps, or fresh livestock manure. Add a one-inch layer of soil, composted manure, or compost. Water the layers as you go and repeat with layers of brown material, green material, and soil until the pile reaches the desired height. Fertilizers high in nitrogen can be used in place of grass clippings or livestock manure. Use about one-quarter to one-half cup for each layer.

For the best and fastest compost, grind or chop the ingredients before adding, keep the pile in the sun, turn it at least once a month, and keep the materials moist but not soggy wet.

ENRICHING THE SOIL

When we suggest that you add organic material to the soil, we're talking about compost or peat moss. Compost can be spread about one inch thick around plants in spring and fall. The compost works its way down into the soil and improves it along the way. You can also mix compost or peat moss in beds when preparing for planting. Spread a two-inch layer over the soil and mix it into the top layer. Pile compost and peat moss higher and deeper around shrubs and trees to provide a nutritious mulch that moderates soil temperatures and helps retain moisture.

Another good additive is a natural, slow-release nitrogen fertilizer, or an all-purpose chemical-based fertilizer. These are good products to mix in the soil when preparing a bed for the first time.

Introduction

They can also be sprinkled around plants or in flower beds. Always follow label directions when using any product.

Hoosier Gardening Heritage

Native Americans were Indiana's first gardeners, growing many of the staple crops of today—corn, beans, squash, and sunflowers. They used the barks, branches, berries, and seeds of trees and shrubs for food, medicine, and household items. Their woods and fields were rich with purple coneflowers, black-eyed Susans, serviceberries, bluebells, redbuds, birches, and maples. Today we rely on many of these plants or their close relatives (mixed with some friendly exotics) to beautify our own landscapes.

Hoosiers have been working the soil for generations. Over the years, immigrants added to the existing variety of plants. Wine grapes were grown along the Ohio River as early as 1802 by Swiss settlers in Vevay; German immigrants moved here in great numbers during the mid to late 1800s, establishing nurseries and greenhouses all over the state.

The northern part of the state was once filled with blueberry and cranberry fields that were eventually drained to make farmland. Northern Indiana celebrates the state's blueberry history with annual festivals.

Johnny Appleseed (born Jonathan Chapman in 1774) took on the role of missionary nurseryman and spent a great deal of time in Indiana. He was quite a sight traveling the frontier with bare feet, tattered clothing, and a pan turned upside down to protect his long hair from the rain. Appleseed gave seeds to everyone he met, stressing the importance of growing one's own food. When the plantsman died in the 1840s, he was buried in what is now Appleseed Park in Fort Wayne. Every year Fort Wayne celebrates his work with a festival that keeps his legendary legacy alive.

The "grandfather" of Indiana plants, Charles C. Deam, was born in 1865. He cataloged trees, shrubs, grasses, and other plants, and

Introduction

wrote *Shrubs of Indiana* in 1924, *Grasses of Indiana* in 1929, *Trees of Indiana* in 1931, and *Flora of Indiana* in 1940. Deam spent his career with the Indiana Division of Forestry, where he was a state forester and a research forester. After a long life of service to horticulture, this esteemed researcher died in 1953.

In 1931, the Garden Club of Indiana was formed. It had its first meeting at the John Herron Art Museum in Indianapolis. Garden Club members promoted victory gardens during World War II and continue their education efforts today by working with fifteen junior garden clubs, or children's groups, throughout Indiana. The Garden Club now has over 3,200 members in more than 300 clubs across the state.

A recent trend has been the growth of the state's Master Gardener Program, where participants are trained in gardening basics and given a certificate after completing a set number of hours volunteering to help others learn about horticulture. Several counties have Master Gardener Programs through their local offices of the Purdue Cooperative Extension Service. Look in the blue government pages of the telephone book for your local number.

Helping others is as much a part of gardening as is growing plants. We've learned about gardening by doing it ourselves and from others who have shared their growing experiences. We hope that through this book you will come to enjoy getting your hands dirty as much as we do—and that your life will be filled with earthly delights.

Annuals

NNUALS ARE PLANTS THAT SPROUT FROM SEED, mature, flower, set seed, and die all within one growing season. They are programmed to grow and are valued for their sustained flowers and color. Many are low maintenance and require little care once planted.

Plants grown as summer annuals here in Indiana are often perennials (geranium, or *Pelargonium*, is one such plant), but they may be too tender to survive the cold of our winters or the heat of Hoosier summers. The plants in this chapter are a good representation of the many annuals which grow well here.

Gardeners can purchase annuals either as bedding plants from nurseries or garden centers, or as seeds from mail-order catalogs or other retailers. Self-sowing annuals such as flowering tobacco or gloriosa daisies are easily acquired from friends and neighbors.

Bedding plants are sold in plastic packs, peat pots, or other containers. Look for full squatty plants with good foliage color. Plants are usually in bloom so that the buyer will know what color the flowers are. If the transplants are tall and leggy, cut them back to encourage branching and new growth. It doesn't hurt to pinch off the flowers, but it is not necessary except to shape the plant and to encourage branching. Roots on healthy transplants should be white or light brown. Be sure the soil is moist when you remove a seedling from its container. Force the plant from its pack by gently pushing from the bottom. Gently grasp the leaves and wiggle the plant loose. If the seedling is growing in a peat pot or other organic fiber, plant it pot and all. Break off any material that sticks above the soil surface, as this material could act as a wick, drawing necessary moisture away from the soil and into the atmosphere.

Many annuals are easy to grow from seeds. Some can be sown directly in the garden. Others may need more time to grow before flowering, so starting seeds indoors is sometimes a better option. Most packets and catalogers offer precise information about sowing

Chapter One

seed so follow those directions. We have given a few basic hints but by no means were we able to be inclusive in discussing each plant.

Since soil and seeds are inexpensive, growing plants from seed is less costly than buying bedding plants. But seeds need a controlled environment to grow successfully; some require cool temperatures while others need warmth. Some seeds need light to germinate and others sprout in the dark. If you purchase lights or plant-heating pads, for example, creating that special environment can be costly, but the results can be rewarding. The cost of sowing seeds indoors should be tallied against the convenience of and better chance for success with bedding plants.

It is essential that you use moistened soilless potting mix or sterilized soil to start seeds. Don't use soil taken from the garden as it may harbor diseases or insects that could kill seedlings. The second most important factor in growing annuals from seeds is the light source. Rather than starting seeds on a windowsill, use fluorescent lighting such as shop lights; these are available at hardware stores, home centers, and other retailers. Use one forty-watt warm fluorescent and one forty-watt cool fluorescent lightbulb in each two-lamp holder to give the best spectrum of light. "Grow lights" are also recommended. Lights should always be about two inches above the seedlings. This means raising the lights as the plants grow. Water freshly sown seeds and seedlings from below.

It is important to pick the right site for your plants. Shade-loving plants will probably not do well when planted in full sun, and plants that require full sun will not survive if planted in shade. You should also consider the condition of the soil. Is it well drained or does it retain water? Paying attention to all these factors will help you select the right plant for the right place. Finally, all plants do better when planted in a site that has been well prepared. Dig the soil eight to twelve inches deep and amend it with organic material such as compost, peat moss, or finely chopped, rotted leaves.

Growing annuals is an easy and inexpensive way to try new colors, textures, or looks in the landscape before investing in the more permanent perennials. Many mix well in perennial flower beds and offer color when other plants are resting or still preparing to bloom.

Ageratum

Ageratum houstonianum

Other Name: Floss Flower
Zones: 5, 6
Height: 6 to 30 inches
Bloom Period: June to frost
Flowers: Blue

Light Requirement:

*A*geratum makes an excellent edging plant in the front of the flower bed, or you can plant it in a cluster for a fuzzy patch of blue. Ageratum also does well in windowboxes or containers. The most common variety is a compact type that rarely gets taller than eight to ten inches. There are taller varieties that make excellent cut flowers; you can also dry them for floral arrangements.

WHEN TO PLANT

Plant container-grown bedding plants in the spring after all danger of frost has passed. Ageratum is a warm-weather annual; transplants often sit in the soil until the weather warms up, so don't lose patience with their slow start. Sow seeds indoors about 8 weeks before the last frost.

WHERE TO PLANT

Plant ageratum in containers, windowboxes, or in the front of the flower garden. It is easy to grow in average soil.

HOW TO PLANT

Plant bedding plants at the same depth they were growing in their containers. For a nice, full look within a few weeks, space the compact varieties about 8 inches apart. Firm the soil around plants, and water well. Mulch lightly, if you wish, but don't allow the mulch to come in contact with the plants. Sow seeds in pots or seedling trays filled with a moistened, soilless mix. Gently press the seeds into the soil surface, but don't cover the seeds with soil; they need light to germinate. Place them in a bright area out of direct sunlight where the temperature is about 70 degrees Fahrenheit. Germination may take up to 2 weeks. Transplant seedlings outdoors when all danger of frost has passed.

ADVICE FOR CARE

You may pinch ageratum once to make the plants bushier, but this is not required. Fertilize regularly with a water-soluble mixture or compost tea throughout the growing season. Water plants if the weather becomes very dry.

OTHER SPECIES, CULTIVARS, OR VARIETIES

There are several compact varieties that are readily available. 'Blue Blazer' is 8 inches tall and has blue-mauve flowers. 'Blue Danube' is 6 inches tall and has lavender-blue flowers. 'Blue Mink' grows 8 to 10 inches tall and has lavender-blue flowers. 'Pink Powderpuffs' grows about 9 inches tall and has rosy-pink flowers. 'Summer Show' is about 6 inches tall with white flowers. 'White Cushion' is about 12 inches tall with white flowers. 'Bavaria' has 18- to 20-inch-tall, light-blue flowers tipped in dark blue. 'Blue Horizon' grows up to 30 inches tall and has lavender-blue flowers that are frequently dried for arrangements. Both varieties make excellent cut flowers.

Begonia

Begonia × semperflorens-cultorum

Other Names: Wax Begonia,
  Wax-Leaf Begonia, Fibrous Begonia
Zones: 5, 6
Height: 6 to 10 inches
Bloom Period: May to frost
Flowers: Red, pink, white

Light Requirement:

*W*ax-leaf begonias are very adaptable plants. They work well for edging a flower bed, and they provide a ball of color in a container. As the name implies, begonia leaves are waxy; they have slightly fringed, or ragged, edges that are frequently tinged in red or bronze. Some varieties have green leaves; others have reddish-bronze leaves, a color that is intensified by sunlight. The prolific flowers have disk-like petals and fuzzy yellow centers. For years, begonias were popular houseplants; they are easy to dig in the fall, pot up, and bring inside for flowers in winter. The hybrids discussed here have a naturally rounded growing habit that blends well in many locations.

WHEN TO PLANT
Plant container-grown transplants in the spring, after all danger of frost has passed. Sow seeds indoors at least 12 weeks before the last frost.

WHERE TO PLANT
Wax-leaf begonias do best in partial shade. They will tolerate sun as long as they receive adequate moisture. They will also tolerate full shade, but this may make them a little leggy. Plant begonias under trees, in the front of flower beds, in windowboxes, or in other containers.

HOW TO PLANT
Begonias do best in moist, well-drained, organically rich soil. They will tolerate a wide range of conditions, but they do not do well in soil that is constantly wet. Space plants 8 to 10 inches apart. The seeds are extremely small; mix them with sand for sowing. Sprinkle

the seed-sand mixture on the surface of moistened, soilless mix in pots or seedling trays. Begonia seeds need light to germinate, so don't cover the seeds. Place them in a bright, warm area out of direct sunlight. It may take at least 2 weeks for seeds to germinate. Transplant seedlings outdoors when all danger of frost has passed. Starting seeds indoors can be difficult; transplants or bedding plants are recommended.

ADVICE FOR CARE

Begonias benefit greatly from both regular watering and applications of a water-soluble fertilizer or compost tea. They have a compact growing habit that requires no deadheading or pinching, except for a rare errant stem.

ADDITIONAL INFORMATION

Flowers are single or double. Begonias may be wintered over by taking a cutting from a growing tip and rooting it in a soilless potting medium. The easiest way, however, is to dig the plant up, trim it back, pot it, and place it in a bright window.

ADDITIONAL SPECIES, CULTIVARS, OR VARIETIES

'Cocktail Mix' series has white-flowered 'Vodka', red-flowered 'Whiskey', and pink-flowered 'Gin'. All have bronze leaves that make an excellent contrast to the flowers. 'Wings' is a hybrid with larger flowers and green leaves. 'Olympia Salmon Orange' is a relatively new introduction, as is 'Red and White Picotee', which has white flowers edged in pink. Don't confuse the fibrous-rooted *Begonia semperflorens* with *Begonia tuberhybrida*, a tuber that is discussed in the chapter on bulbs.

Browallia

Browallia speciosa

Other Name: Bush Violet	**Light Requirement:**
Zones: 5, 6	
Height: 10 to 15 inches	
Bloom Period: May to frost	
Flowers: Blue	

*B*rowallia is one of those plants that is not used nearly enough, probably because people don't know what it is. It has one-inch-wide, blue, trumpet-shaped flowers; oval green leaves; and is naturally bushy. It works well both in the front of a semi-shady bed, and in windowboxes or other containers. Blue browallia makes a nice combination with salmon-colored impatiens.

WHEN TO PLANT

Plant browallia in the spring after all danger of frost has passed. Sow seeds indoors 6 to 8 weeks before the last frost.

WHERE TO PLANT

Browallia does best in a partially shaded spot with well-drained soil. The soil can be average.

HOW TO PLANT

Plant container-grown transplants at the same depth they were growing in their pots. Space them 10 to 12 inches apart, water well, and mulch lightly if you wish. Browallia seeds are very small; sow them on the surface of pots or seedling trays filled with a moistened, soilless mix. Place them in a bright, warm area out of direct sunlight and keep them moist. Germination may take up to 2 weeks. Transplant to larger pots or thin the seedlings out so there is enough space for individual plants to grow. Transplant seedlings outdoors after the last frost.

ADVICE FOR CARE

Browallia will develop a lot of green growth if you water or fertilize it too much. Pinch the plant back when it is small to encourage bushiness.

ADDITIONAL INFORMATION

You can plant browallia in full sun, but it must be watered regularly and mulched well. You can mix it in containers in full sun, especially where it will be shaded by larger plants.

ADDITIONAL SPECIES, CULTIVARS, OR VARIETIES

Browallia speciosa comes in many shades of blue and in various heights, though none are too tall. 'Major' grows up to 14 inches tall and has 2-inch lavender flowers. 'Marine Bells' grows 10 inches tall and has 1$^{1}/_{2}$-inch indigo-blue flowers. 'Sky Bells' grows up to 10 inches tall and has 1$^{1}/_{2}$-inch sky-blue flowers. 'Vanja' reaches 14 inches tall and has 2-inch blue flowers with white centers. 'Blue Troll' grows up to 10 inches tall, and has 1$^{1}/_{2}$-inch violet-blue flowers. 'Jingle Bells' hybrids range from 9 to 14 inches tall, with 1$^{1}/_{2}$-inch blue, white, or lavender flowers. 'Silver Bells', 'White Bells', and 'White Troll' are white varieties.

Cockscomb

Celosia argentea

Zones: 5, 6 **Height:** 6 to 36 inches **Bloom Period:** Midsummer to frost **Flowers:** Various	**Light Requirement:** 

*T*he most common celosia varieties, *Celosia argentea* var. *cristata*, look like the lead in a movie called *The Plant with Big Brains*. These crested flowers take on a rounded shape with ridges; the result more closely resembles a colorful velvety brain than it does a cockscomb (the plant's common name). There is another variety, *Celosia argentea plumosa*, which has feathery, or plume-like, flowers. The brainy celosia is an acquired taste, but it makes a strong color statement in the flower bed when planted en masse. The plume types are becoming increasingly popular as gardeners learn more about them. Both varieties do well in containers and windowboxes. You can cut the flowers for indoor bouquets or dry them for arrangements.

WHEN TO PLANT

Plant transplants in the spring after the danger of frost has passed. Sow seeds indoors about 6 to 8 weeks before the last frost.

WHERE TO PLANT

Celosia prefers well-drained, average soil in a sunny or partially shaded spot.

HOW TO PLANT

Plant transplants at the same depth they were growing in their containers. Celosia doesn't like to be disturbed, so handle the roots carefully. Water well. If you are starting from seed, sow the seeds in individual pots or six-packs that have been filled with a moistened, soilless mix. Barely cover the seeds and place them in a warm, bright location out of direct sunlight. Germination may take up to 2 weeks. Transplant seedlings outdoors when the danger of frost has passed.

ADVICE FOR CARE

Celosia is drought tolerant; be careful not to overwater. Since it thrives in hot weather, celosia is apt to be a fairly slow grower when you first plant it in the spring. Once it is established, fertilize it lightly throughout the season.

ADDITIONAL INFORMATION

Celosia may self-sow, returning the next growing season.

ADDITIONAL SPECIES, CULTIVARS, OR VARIETIES

There are several popular crested varieties. 'Chief' hybrids grow to 40 inches tall; the combs may grow to 8 inches across and produce red, scarlet, rose, pink, or yellow flowers. 'Empress' grows 12 inches tall; it has reddish-green foliage and deep-red combs that grow to 10 inches wide. 'Fireglow' grows about 2 feet tall and has 6-inch reddish-orange combs. 'Prestige Scarlet', an All-America Selection in 1997, has a large, central, red flower and smaller combs along its branches; it grows about 20 inches tall and wide. Recommended feather, or plume, celosia varieties are 'Apricot Brandy', which grows about 15 inches tall; the 'Castle' series, which reaches 12 inches and has yellow or pink flowers; and 'Century', which has 6-inch plumes on 20-inch plants. *Celosia argentea spicata* is another variety that is gaining in popularity. Its flower spikes resemble wheat, so much so that it is sometimes called "wheat celosia." 'Flamingo Feather' grows about 40 inches tall and has flowers in shades of pastel pink. Late in the growing season, 'Amazon' has silvery flowers with purple or reddish highlights. 'Pink Candle' has 3-foot-tall, rose-pink flowers.

Coleus

Coleus × hybridus

Zones: 5, 6 **Height:** 6 to 24 inches **Flowers:** Foliage plant	**Light Requirement:**

*C*oleus is grown for its leaves, which come in a rainbow of colors and a variety of textures. It is equally at home as a bedding plant and in flower boxes or other containers. It comes in creamy white to crimson, and the foliage may be solid-colored, mottled, banded, puckered, highly scalloped, or serrated. Coleus is easy to grow and requires little maintenance. Don't hesitate to cut a branch for a striking addition to an indoor flower arrangement.

WHEN TO PLANT
Plant transplants in the spring, after all danger of frost has passed. Sow seeds 8 to 12 weeks before the last frost.

WHERE TO PLANT
Plant coleus in a well-drained, moist spot in full sun or partial shade.

HOW TO PLANT
Don't plant transplants any deeper than they were growing in their containers. Space them about 12 inches apart, water well, and mulch. If you are starting from seeds, sow them in pots filled with a moistened, soilless potting mix. Do not cover seeds; place them in a bright, warm area out of direct sun. It may take 3 weeks for seeds to germinate. Seedlings will start out green; transplant them outdoors when the danger of frost has passed.

ADVICE FOR CARE
Don't let coleus dry out. If the plants get too large or leggy, or begin to produce flowers, pinch them back. Coleus colors intensify in partial shade.

ADDITIONAL INFORMATION

You can take cuttings in the fall, or you can dig coleus up for an indoor houseplant. Coleus is slow to grow from seed, but not too difficult; it is frequently used for children's gardening projects. The flowers are usually removed, but you may leave them on the plants if you wish.

ADDITIONAL SPECIES, CULTIVARS, OR VARIETIES

'Rainbow Mix' grows about 15 inches tall and has medium-sized leaves. 'Wizard Mixed' grows 10 to 12 inches tall and has large leaves. 'Fashion Parade' is about 8 inches tall with smaller leaves. 'Dragon Sunset' has deeply carved leaves. Coleus sometimes may be listed as *Solenostemon scutellariodes*.

Cosmos

Cosmos bipinnatus

Zones: 5, 6
Height: 1 to 6 feet
Bloom Period: Midsummer through
  several frosts
Flowers: Various

Light Requirement:

---

*C*osmos is a Greek word for harmony and order; the flower lives up to its name. All summer long, cosmos produces colorful, daisy-like flowers and fern-like leaves on spindly, branched stems; it easily towers over or blends with companion plants in the garden. Cosmos is a native wildflower. Birds, especially goldfinches, eat the seeds; the flowers attract butterflies, hummingbirds, praying mantises, and bees. It is very easy to grow and readily self-sows, coming back year after year with no effort.

WHEN TO PLANT

Plant transplants in the spring after the danger of frost has passed. Start seeds indoors about 4 weeks before the last frost. Sow seeds outdoors after the last frost.

WHERE TO PLANT

Cosmos prefers full sun and average soil. It will tolerate light shade.

HOW TO PLANT

Plant transplants no deeper than they were growing in their contain-ers. Space them about 12 to 18 inches apart, water well, and mulch lightly if you wish. Sow seeds 1/8 inch deep in pots filled with a moistened, soilless potting mix. Place them in a bright, warm area out of direct sunlight. Germination may take up to 10 days. Trans-plant seedlings outdoors after the last frost.

ADVICE FOR CARE

Too much fertilizer, especially nitrogen, causes cosmos to develop leaves and delay flowering until late in the season. Water occasion-ally through long periods of drought.

ADDITIONAL INFORMATION

You will need to stake taller varieties, or you may pinch them to shorten the plants and make them bushier.

ADDITIONAL SPECIES, CULTIVARS, OR VARIETIES

'Sensations' hybrids grow about 3 feet tall; they have 3-inch-wide red, pink, or white flowers. 'Sonata' grows about 3 feet tall; it has 3-inch-wide red, pink, or white flowers that bloom earlier than other varieties. 'Sea Shells' grows 6 feet tall; it has 4-inch-wide pink or white flowers with tubes that flare red or white. 'Candy Stripe' grows 6 feet tall with 3$1/2$-inch white or light-pink flowers with red stripes and edges. 'Early Wonder' grows about 4 feet tall, with 3$1/2$-inch red, pink, or white flowers that are early. 'Hot Chocolate' has a chocolate color and scent. *Cosmos sulphureus* hybrids are shorter, with 2-inch red, yellow, or orange flowers; some are double. 'Bright Lights' grows about 3 feet tall and has 2-inch-wide orange flowers that vary from reddish to yellow. 'Ladybird' grows about 1 foot tall with 2-inch-wide semi-double orange or yellow flowers. 'Sunny' hybrids grow about 18 inches tall with 2-inch-wide single or semi-double orange, yellow, or red flowers. 'Lemon Twist' reaches a height of 30 inches with 2-inch-wide semi-double yellow flowers.

Dusty Miller

Cineraria maritima

Other Names: Silverdust, Ragwort **Zones:** 5, 6 **Height:** 6 to 24 inches **Flowers:** Foliage plant	**Light Requirement:**

usty miller is a name given to a group of annuals and perennials that are grown for their hairy, silvery-green foliage, which can be bold and deeply cut, or lacy like snowflakes. Dusty miller's color and texture make a nice relief in a mass of bold flowers; it cools down the scene or provides a complementary contrast. Most have a mounding habit and grow ten to fifteen inches tall; a few may reach a height of two feet.

WHEN TO PLANT

Plant container-grown plants in the spring after all danger of frost has passed. Sow seeds indoors about 10 weeks before the last frost.

WHERE TO PLANT

Dusty miller does best in full sun but is tolerant of shadier locations with well-drained, ordinary soil.

HOW TO PLANT

Plant transplants at the same depth they were growing in their containers. Space them 8 to 10 inches apart. Water well, and mulch if you wish. If you are starting from seeds, sow them on the surface of moistened, soilless potting mix in pots or seedling trays. Place them in a warm, bright area out of direct sun. Water seedling trays from below as dusty miller may be susceptible to fungus diseases. Germination may take 3 weeks. Transplant seedlings outdoors when the danger of frost has passed.

ADVICE FOR CARE

Dusty miller tolerates heat and drought. It may wilt in prolonged dry spells, but it usually responds well to a good soaking.

ADDITIONAL INFORMATION

Some varieties are quite tolerant of cold and will flower in late autumn or early winter. The daisy-like flowers are yellow, which seems odd for a plant with gray foliage. Some varieties have been known to winter over outdoors in Zone 6, but you should probably not count on this happening.

ADDITIONAL SPECIES, CULTIVARS, OR VARIETIES

There are several botanical names for the plants called dusty miller, including *Cineraria maritima, Senecio maritima, Senecio cineraria, Centaurea cineraria, Pyrethrum ptarmiciflorum,* and *Chrysanthemum ptarmiciflorum.* 'Silver Feather' or 'Silver Dust' has lacy or deeply cut foliage. 'Cirrus' has oval, slightly serrated leaves. 'White Diamond' grows about 15 inches tall and is less silvery than the others.

Flowering Cabbage

Brassica oleracea

Other Names: Ornamental Cabbage, Flowering Kale, Ornamental Kale	Light Requirement:
Zones: 5, 6 **Height:** 12 to 18 inches **Flowers:** Foliage plant	

*F*lowering cabbage and kale come into their own in late summer and fall, when there is little else going on. Cool temperatures intensify the colors of these foliage plants, making them standouts in the landscape. Flowering cabbage and kale aren't really flowers at all. They belong to the same family as cabbage and kale, and the flowers come when the plant bolts, just like their vegetable cousins. Flowering cabbage has broader leaves than flowering kale, and it forms what looks like a loose head of cabbage. The colors are green, white, purple, or pink, depending on the variety. Flowering kale has deeply cut, or more sword-like, leaves in many of the same colors.

WHEN TO PLANT
Plant transplants in very late summer or early fall—the later the better. Sow seeds in pots or a nursery bed in July.

WHERE TO PLANT
Plant in a moist, well-drained spot in full sun.

HOW TO PLANT
Plant transplants slightly deeper than they were growing in their pots so that the lower leaves are just above the soil surface. Sow seeds indoors about 1/4 inch deep in moistened, soilless potting mix in pots or seedling trays. You can also sow them in a cool, bright, protected area outside; a small nursery bed is ideal. Seeds germinate quickly, especially when the air temperature is between 55 and 65 degrees Fahrenheit. Space the seedlings about 18 to 24 inches apart, and mulch well to keep the soil cool and moist.

ADVICE FOR CARE

Flowering cabbage and kale are susceptible to cabbage worms and other pests that bother their vegetable cousins. Don't plant them in the same place year after year. The later you plant them in fall, the less likely they are to be bothered by cabbage pests.

ADDITIONAL INFORMATION

Flowering cabbage and kale are edible but have a very bitter taste. The leaves are frequently used to display foods on buffets or on trays of cold cuts. The leaves start turning color in the fall, as frosty nights become more regular.

ADDITIONAL SPECIES, CULTIVARS, OR VARIETIES

Available flowering cabbage varieties include 'Pink Beauty', which has a medium, purplish-rose center and white outer leaves with green tips; 'Rose Bouquet', which has a deep-red center with reddish-green outer leaves; and 'White Pigeon', which has a white center with medium-green outer leaves. 'Color Up Improved Hybrid' is slower to bolt, or flower, and go to seed; it has white, pink, or red centers with white and dark green outer leaves. Flowering kale varieties include 'Nagoya' hybrids, which are red, white, or rose with dark, greenish-purple to green outer leaves; 'Peacock' has deep-red or white centers with reddish-green outer leaves and grows about 12 inches tall and wide.

Flowering Tobacco

Nicotiana alata, Nicotiana sylvestris

Zones: 5, 6	**Light Requirement:**
Height: 12 inches to 6 feet	
Bloom Period: Summer through frost	
Flowers: White, red, pink, salmon, purple	

*F*lowering tobacco is an annual that need only be planted once; it will continue to reseed year after year with no effort on the gardener's part. The tubular flowers attract hummingbirds, and some varieties will knock your socks off with evening fragrance. Certain nicotiana varieties close their flowers during the day and open up at night; white ones of this type look and smell spectacular in the night garden. Nicotiana does well in the landscape, in windowboxes, or in other containers.

WHEN TO PLANT

Plant transplants in the spring after the danger of frost has passed. Sow seeds indoors about 6 weeks before the last frost. You can also sow seeds directly outdoors after the danger of frost has passed; these plants will not begin to bloom until late in the season.

WHERE TO PLANT

Well-drained ordinary soil in full sun or partial shade is best. Plant fragrant varieties where you will be able to smell them at night, such as by a bedroom window, porch, patio, or deck.

HOW TO PLANT

Plant transplants the same depth they were growing in their containers. Water well. Seeds are very small; sow them on the surface of moistened soilless potting mix. Place them in a warm, bright area out of direct sunlight. Germination may take up to 20 days. Transplant seedlings outdoors when the danger of frost has passed.

ADVICE FOR CARE

These plants require almost no maintenance. Water occasionally during long dry periods. Deadheading encourages blooming and cuts down on self-sowing, but it is not necessary. Too much nitrogen fertilizer will result in more foliage than flowers.

ADDITIONAL INFORMATION

Nicotiana readily self-sows and will come back year after year. The flowering nicotianas are in the same family as the smoking types, so the bottom leaves can get fairly large. Transplant smaller starts to keep them from getting too crowded. Shorter varieties are almost always less fragrant than taller ones. You may need to stake very tall varieties, or plant them far enough back in the flower beds so that shorter plants can help prop them up. They are not heavy and will not crush nearby growth. Nicotiana is fairly tolerant of cold; it will frequently last well into fall and early winter.

ADDITIONAL SPECIES, CULTIVARS, OR VARIETIES

'Sensation Mixed' has very fragrant, white, pink, and rose flowers that stay open during the day. 'Nicki Mix' has scented 18-inch-tall bright- and dusty-pink, rose, white, and lime-green flowers. 'Lumina' grows 3 to 4 feet tall; it has 3-inch-long, 2-inch-wide, white flowers with a jasmine scent. 'Domino' hybrids have crimson, salmon, lime-green, white, red, and purple flowers; they are compact growers and have more heat tolerance. 'Heaven Scent' grows about 24 inches tall; it has fragrant flowers ranging from crimson to white. Nicotiana sylvestris has 3- to 4-inch-long fragrant white trumpet-like flowers that grow about 1^1/2 inches wide. These plants may reach a height of 6 feet.

Geranium

Pelargonium × hortorum

Other Name: *Pelargonium peltatum*	**Light Requirement:**
Zones: 5, 6	
Height: 1 to 3 feet	
Bloom Period: Summer	
Flowers: White, red, pink, salmon, purple	

A geranium is one of those plants that just says "summer." Geraniums require little care, other than the pinching off of dead flowers. They are easy to grow in the landscape, in window-boxes, or in other containers. Geraniums are native to South Africa and are among the best-known flowers in the world. The botanical name, *Pelargonium*, is Greek for "stork," and describes the shape of a geranium seed. It used to be that geraniums were grown only by cuttings, but new seed-grown hybrids are becoming much more common. *Pelargonium × hortorum* is sometimes called "zonal geranium"; it is identified by zones, or rings, of color on its leaves. *Pelargonium peltatum* is called "ivy-leaved" or "vining geranium," and is distinguished by its glossy, waxy leaves. These are recommended for use in containers due to their vining characteristics. Some gardeners use vining geraniums as a summer groundcover.

WHEN TO PLANT
Plant container-grown transplants in the spring after all danger of frost has passed. Sow seeds indoors 12 to 14 weeks before the last frost.

WHERE TO PLANT
Geraniums do best in well-drained soil. Ivy-leafed geraniums tend to do better with a little shade, especially from the hot afternoon sun.

HOW TO PLANT
Plant transplants the same depth they were growing in their containers. Water well and mulch lightly if you wish. If you are starting from seeds, sow them in moistened, soilless potting mix in pots or seedling trays. Barely cover them and place in a light, warm area out

of direct sunlight. Germination may take 3 weeks. Give seedlings as much light as possible or they will get leggy. Pinch plants when they are small to encourage bushiness. Transplant seedlings outdoors when the danger of frost has passed.

ADVICE FOR CARE

Zonal geraniums are fairly drought tolerant, so water only when they are dry. Ivy-leafed geraniums tend to need a little more water, especially if you plant them in full sun. Don't overfertilize; too much fertilizer will cause geraniums to produce more foliage than flowers.

ADDITIONAL INFORMATION

Zonal geraniums are fairly easy to winter over. Dig the plants up in the fall, before a frost. Plant them in pots and cut back their tops to a height of about 6 inches. Place them in a sunny window and the geraniums will bloom. There are all kinds of stories about gardeners digging geraniums and storing them bare-rooted or in paper bags for planting next spring. For best results, remove the stems from the bag on a monthly basis, soak them in water for 30 minutes, let them dry, and return to the bag.

ADDITIONAL SPECIES, CULTIVARS, OR VARIETIES

There are dozens of selections. Make choices based on color, size, and use. *Pelargonium × domesticum* are called "show geraniums"; these include 'Martha Washington' varieties, which have azalea- or pansy-like flowers. Because they prefer a growing season with cool nights, they don't do as well in Indiana as they do along the coasts or in cooler climates. There are several geraniums prized for their scented leaves rather than for their flowers, which are not usually showy. There are rose-, peppermint-, lemon-, apple-, and nutmeg-scented leaf plants, just to name a few. These are best planted where the leaves will be brushed by passersby.

Globe Amaranth

Gomphrena globosa

Zones: 5, 6 **Height:** 6 to 24 inches **Bloom Period:** Summer **Flowers:** Various	**Light Requirement:**

*G*lobe amaranth looks like clover and lasts a very long time on and off the plant. It is a staple in the cutting garden for indoor bouquets or for dried flower arrangements. The plant grows in a mound and has oblong, medium-green leaves. The one- to two-inch rounded flowers can be white, pink, red, or purple; they are actually modified leaves, or bracts, that grow at the tips of the stalks that rise above the plant. Globe amaranth holds its color for a long time and does especially well in hot, dry locations. "Amaranth" comes from the Greek word *amarantos*, which means "everlasting," or perhaps from the Greek *amaranton*, which means "unfading flower." It is part of the *Amaranthaceae* family, as is *Amaranthus*, another group of ornamental annuals which includes love-lies-bleeding and summer poinsettia. There is also a group of amaranths made up of grain plants.

WHEN TO PLANT

Plant transplants in the spring after all danger of frost has passed. Sow seeds indoors about 6 weeks before the last spring frost. You can also sow seeds directly in the garden after the last frost.

WHERE TO PLANT

Plant in well-drained soil in a sunny location. Globe amaranth also does very well in hot, dry spots with ordinary soil.

HOW TO PLANT

Plant transplants at the same depth they were growing in their containers. Space plants 8 to 10 inches apart and water well. If you are starting from seeds, soak them in warm water overnight, then sow in containers filled with a moistened soilless potting mix. Barely cover the seeds with the mix and place them in a warm, dark location until they sprout. Germination takes 1 to 2 weeks.

Move seedlings to a bright location out of direct sunlight. Seeds to be sown directly in the garden should also be soaked first.

ADVICE FOR CARE

Because globe amaranth is drought tolerant, it will require watering only during long dry periods.

ADDITIONAL INFORMATION

You can pinch out the centers of the plants to encourage bushiness. Check the annual and everlasting sections of mail-order catalogs and garden centers for gomphrena seeds and plants.

ADDITIONAL SPECIES, CULTIVARS, OR VARIETIES

Shorter varieties of globe amaranth for the front of the border include 'Buddy', which grows 6 to 8 inches tall and has purple flowers. 'Gnome' hybrids grow 6 inches tall and have pink, purple, or white flowers. 'Lavender Lady', 'Strawberry Fields', 'Bicolor Rose', 'Blushing Bride' (pink), 'Professor Plum', and 'Innocence' (white) are taller, ranging from 15 to 24 inches. *Gomphrena haageana* has 1$^{1}/_{2}$-inch reddish-orange flowers and grows about 18 inches tall.

Gloriosa Daisy

Rudbeckia hirta

<table>
<tr><td>

Other Name: Black-eyed Susan
Zones: 5, 6
Height: 2 to 3 feet
Bloom Period: Mid- to late summer
Flowers: Yellow, orange, mahogany

</td><td>

Light Requirement:

</td></tr>
</table>

*I*f ever there was a confusing annual it's *Rudbeckia hirta*, or the black-eyed Susan. It is frequently thought to be the same as *Rudbeckia fulgida*, a short-lived perennial cousin that is also known as black-eyed Susan. To make things even more complicated, *Rudbeckia hirta* and *Rudbeckia fulgida* are sometimes referred to as yellow cone-flowers! This North American wildflower has been hybridized into various cultivars, such as 'Gloriosa Daisy' and 'Goldilocks'. Their daisy-like flowers are wonderful additions to the landscape because they bloom from mid- to late summer when there isn't a lot of other color. The single or double flowers range from yellow to mahogany; they can also be reddish brown or bicolor. Most have dark eyes, or centers, but a few varieties have green in the middle.

WHEN TO PLANT

Sow seeds directly in the garden or plant transplants in the spring as soon as you can work the soil (approximately 2 weeks before the last frost). Sow seeds in pots indoors about 4 to 6 weeks before the last frost.

WHERE TO PLANT

Rudbeckia hirta prefers well-drained, average soil in full sun. It some-times benefits from a little afternoon shade. The shorter varieties mix well in containers or windowboxes.

HOW TO PLANT

Plant transplants at the same depth they were growing in their con-tainers. Plant them about 12 to 18 inches apart and water well. Sow seeds in the garden by scattering them on the surface of the soil and covering them lightly. You can also sow them on moistened, soilless potting mix in pots indoors. Place them in a warm, bright place out of direct sunlight until they germinate. Germination takes 1 to 2 weeks. Thin seedlings and transplant them to larger containers if necessary. For best results, grow them under fluorescent lights until large enough to transplant outside. Transplant seedlings outdoors when you can work the soil.

ADVICE FOR CARE

Apply a water-soluble bloom-booster fertilizer. Choose one where the middle number is highest, such as a 10-20-10, and follow label directions. You can also apply a ring or light layer of compost around the plant. *Rudbeckia hirta* is fairly drought tolerant.

ADDITIONAL INFORMATION

Since you can easily sow these seeds directly in the garden, starting them indoors is unnecessary work. *Rudbeckia hirta* frequently self-sows, coming back year after year. This probably explains why it is sometimes mistaken for *Rudbeckia fulgida*. Pull up unwanted plants, or dig them when they are small to transplant elsewhere. Goldfinches like to sit on the cones and eat the seeds.

ADDITIONAL SPECIES, CULTIVARS, OR VARIETIES

There are many popular selections from which to choose. 'Gloriosa Daisy' has 2- to 3-foot-tall, 5-inch-wide flowers; the flowers are usually yellow, but may sometimes have rays of red or brown at the center. 'Goldilocks' and 'Double Gold' have 2- to 3-foot-tall, 2- to 4-inch-wide, double or semi-double flowers. 'Marmalade' is 18 to 24 inches tall and has 3- to 4-inch-wide orange flowers with a purple-black cone. 'Autumn Leaves' grows 2 to 3 feet tall and has 4-inch-wide yellow flowers with orange, red, or brown rays. 'Nutmeg' reaches 24 to 30 inches tall and has 3- to 4-inch-wide double flowers that range from red to reddish brown. 'Irish Eyes' or 'Green Eyes' has a green center, or cone, but reaches the same height as the more traditional *Rudbeckia hirta*. 'Toto', 'Becky', and 'Sonora' are dwarf varieties, ranging from 8 to 12 inches tall.

Impatiens

Impatiens wallerana

Other Name: Busy Lizzie
Zones: 5, 6
Height: 8 to 15 inches
Bloom Period: Summer
Flowers: White, orange, pink, red, purple

Light Requirement:

Impatiens wallerana is one of the top-selling annual bedding plants in America. For years, impatiens were grown only inside greenhouses and conservatories because northern zones were too cold for the plants, which are tender perennials in their native Tanzania and Mozambique. Then hybridizers developed dozens of new varieties that thrive in shade, making impatiens a much-sought-after plant for areas where few things bloom. It also does well in windowboxes, hanging baskets, and other containers. The succulent stems and small, slightly serrated dark-green leaves grow naturally in mounds that rarely need pinching. Impatiens blooms constantly; the one- to one-and-one-half-inch-wide flowers have an iridescent quality about them. Some varieties produce flowers with picotee, or contrasting color on the edge of the petals; some grow double flowers that resemble roses; and some varieties are bicolor, with star-like markings.

WHEN TO PLANT
Plant container-grown bedding plants in the spring after all danger of frost has passed. Sow seeds indoors 8 to 10 weeks before the last frost.

WHERE TO PLANT
Impatiens prefer a well-drained, moist location in part shade to full shade.

HOW TO PLANT
Plant bedding plants the same depth they were growing in their containers. Space them 8 to 12 inches apart. Water well and mulch lightly to keep the soil moist and cool. Keep the mulch 3 or 4 inches away from the plant's stem. If you are starting with seeds, sow them on the surface of pots filled with moistened soilless potting mix.

Place them in a warm, bright area out of direct sunlight until they germinate. Germination takes 2 to 3 weeks. For best results indoors, grow them under fluorescent lights until large enough to transplant to the garden. Transplant seedlings outdoors when the danger of frost has passed.

ADVICE FOR CARE

Impatiens don't require regular fertilizing if they are planted in good soil. However, container-grown plants will require monthly feeding. Too much nitrogen fertilizer may cause the plants to stop flowering. Water impatiens when they wilt, or when the soil surface feels dry.

ADDITIONAL INFORMATION

Several resource materials, catalogs, and garden centers suggest that *Impatiens wallerana* can be planted in full sun; gardeners are apt to be happier, however, if these flowering jewels have a little shade. Impatiens are shallow-rooted plants that lose moisture quickly; they will survive in full, hot sun only if you give them plenty of moisture, perhaps watering once or twice a day and mulching well. They do better in sunny conditions if they are shaded by larger plants. Impatiens planted in full sun may not flower as prolifically as those planted in some shade.

ADDITIONAL SPECIES, CULTIVARS, OR VARIETIES

Gardeners should select *Impatiens wallerana* according to particular colors, styles, and uses. 'Super Elfin' has large flowers but is a very compact grower. *Impatiens balsamina* is taller and more upright than its *I. wallerana* relative. It self-sows and can become a nuisance. The flowers are borne along succulent stems or clustered at the top; they are not particularly showy. New Guinea impatiens is a new hybrid that tolerates a bit more sun than *I. wallerana*, but still seems to do better when given some shade; it doesn't do as well in deep shade. The leaves on New Guinea impatiens may be green, variegated, or bronze; some have red veins. New Guinea flowers are frequently larger than the flowers of *I. wallerana*; they are perhaps a little more intense in color, but are just as iridescent.

Lobelia

Lobelia erinus

Zone: 5	**Light Requirement:**
Height: 4 to 8 inches	
Bloom Period: Summer	
Flowers: White, blue, red, pink, white	

The intense blue of lobelia 'Crystal Palace' is hard to beat in the annual garden or windowbox. This is an excellent edging plant for the front of the flower bed, especially in locations protected from hot afternoon sun. Lobelia grows in clumps or trails. It has one-half-inch-wide tubular flowers on spindly stems. The narrow leaves are sometimes bronzy-purple.

WHEN TO PLANT

Plant container-grown transplants in the spring after all danger of frost has passed. Sow seeds in pots indoors 8 to 12 weeks before the last frost.

WHERE TO PLANT

Plant lobelia in a well-drained spot with average soil. Lobelia does not like hot, dry weather; it does best out of the afternoon sun or in a partially shaded area.

HOW TO PLANT

Plant bedding plants at the same depth they were growing in their containers. Space them 4 to 6 inches apart, water well, and mulch lightly if you wish. Lobelia seeds are tiny. If you are starting with seeds, sow them on the surface of pots filled with moistened soilless potting mix. Don't allow seed trays to dry out; keep them in a clear plastic bag or under a clear piece of glass or plastic until the seeds sprout. Germination may take 3 weeks. For best results indoors, grow seedlings under fluorescent lights until large enough to transplant to the garden. Thin or transplant them to individual containers if necessary. Transplant seedlings outdoors when the danger of frost has passed.

ADVICE FOR CARE

Cut lobelia back about halfway if it starts to look leggy or fried during the summer. Give it a shot of bloom-booster fertilizer or a drenching of compost tea, and keep it watered but well drained. Lobelia will often stop blooming in the height of the hot summer, even in Zone 5. The plant usually responds with new, better-looking growth when summer has cooled down.

ADDITIONAL INFORMATION

For an intense spot of blue, cut lobelia and use it in floral arrangements. Don't eat the plants; lobelia contains lobelia acid, a poisonous alkaloid.

ADDITIONAL SPECIES, CULTIVARS, OR VARIETIES

Some recommended clump-growing *Lobelia erinus* include 'Crystal Palace', 4 to 6 inches tall with dark-blue flowers and bronze leaves; 'Mrs. Clibran Improved', 6 inches tall with dark-blue flowers with white centers, or eyes; 'Blue Stone', up to 9 inches tall with sky-blue flowers; 'Rosamund', 6 inches tall with carmine-red flowers with white eyes; 'White Lady', 6 inches tall with white flowers; and 'Riviera' hybrids. Trailing hybrids to consider include 'Cascade', which ranges from light blue to ruby; 'Sapphire', which has dark-blue flowers and white eyes; 'Regatta', which comes in a wide range of blues, including 'Blue Splash', which has white flowers with splotches of blue in the throat and edges, or margins. There also are perennial lobelias.

Marigold

Tagetes spp.

Zones: 5, 6
Height: 6 inches to 3 feet
Bloom Period: Summer
Flowers: Yellow, orange, red, white

Light Requirement:
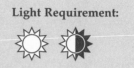

*M*arigolds may be labeled as French or African, but they originated in Mexico; in fact, the plant's history dates back to the time of the Aztecs. This easy-to-grow summer staple is equally at home in the landscape, in windowboxes, or in other containers. Most marigolds are compact growers, but African and American varieties can reach heights of up to three feet. The leaves are deeply cut and fern-like. Marigold flowers are usually in the yellow to orange range, but a white variety was introduced a few years ago that is a standout when planted en masse, and resembles a carnation in cut-flower arrangements. Marigolds are solid color, bicolor, or picotee in dozens of variations; flowers may be single or double.

WHEN TO PLANT

Plant bedding plants in the spring after all danger of frost has passed. Sow seeds in pots indoors 6 to 8 weeks before the last frost.

WHERE TO PLANT

Taller varieties prefer full sun. Shorter marigolds will take full sun, but they do best with some shade from hot, summer afternoon sun.

HOW TO PLANT

Plant bedding plants the same depth they were growing in their containers. Space them 6 to 24 inches apart depending on the variety. Larger types should be planted farther apart. Water them well. If you are starting from seeds, sow them in moistened soilless potting mix. Barely cover them and place in a warm, bright area out of direct sunlight until they germinate. For best results, grow them under fluorescent lights until large enough to transplant outdoors. Water from below as marigolds are sometimes susceptible to fungus disease. Transplant seedlings outdoors when the danger of frost has passed.

ADVICE FOR CARE

Apply an all-purpose water-soluble fertilizer throughout the growing season, or drench marigolds with compost tea. Remove dead flowers to keep the plant blooming.

ADDITIONAL INFORMATION

Marigolds have a distinct odor that some people like while others do not. It has the reputation of keeping bugs away from people and gardens, but that trait actually belongs to the native species, which has a very pungent odor. Pinch marigolds to encourage better branching.

ADDITIONAL SPECIES, CULTIVARS, OR VARIETIES

Tagetes erecta is the African, Aztec, or American marigold. It is more upright than the others and the flowers are double or semi-double, more like a pom pon. *T. patula* is the French marigold, which grows 6 to 18 inches tall; its flowers are anemone-like, single, double, or carnation-like. *T. tenuifolia pumila* or *T. signata pumila* is a dwarf variety with single flowers that only grows to about 8 inches tall. Select varieties according to color and height requirements.

Mexican Sunflower

Tithonia rotundifolia

Other Name: Mexican Hat, Tithonia, Torch Flower	Light Requirement:
Zones: 5, 6	
Height: 3 to 6 feet	
Bloom Period: Summer	
Flowers: Yellow, orange, red	

Tithonia, the Mexican sunflower, loves hot and dry conditions. It comes into its own when the temperature is similar to that of its native Mexico and Central America, where tithonia grows as a perennial. It is easy to grow and is not too fussy about location. Tithonia's two- to three-inch-wide flowers and dark-green spear-shaped leaves complement other late-summer plants, including black-eyed Susans. It looks best in the back of the flower garden and makes an excellent cut flower. The name "tithonia" is from Tithonus, a character of Greek myth who was loved by the goddess Eos. She appealed to Zeus to make Tithonus immortal, but forgot to ask that her lover not age. Zeus eventually turned Tithonus into a grasshopper as a reminder to all mortals that their time is limited and should be put to good use.

WHEN TO PLANT

Bedding plants may not be available, but tithonia is very easy to start from seed. Sow seeds directly in the garden in the spring when all danger of frost has passed. You can also sow seeds in pots indoors about 6 weeks before the last frost.

WHERE TO PLANT

Pick a spot with average soil in full sun. Give this bushy, quick growing plant plenty of room: It has a 3- to 4-foot spread. A group planting will make a good summer screen or hedge.

HOW TO PLANT

If you can find transplants, plant them the same depth they were growing in their containers. Space plants about 2 feet apart and water well. If you are starting with seeds, sow them on the surface of pots filled with moistened soilless potting mix. Place them in a bright, warm area out of direct sunlight. Germination may take 2 weeks. Transplant seedlings outdoors when the danger of frost has passed. Tithonia may take a few weeks to recover from transplanting. For best results, keep plenty of soil around the roots and water them well.

ADVICE FOR CARE

Tithonia is very tolerant of hot, dry conditions. It will not start flowering in earnest until the weather gets hot. Apply an all-purpose water-soluble fertilizer according to label directions; water deeply if dry periods become extended.

ADDITIONAL INFORMATION

Tithonia attracts hummingbirds, butterflies, and bees. Wayward monarchs sometimes flock to this plant in the late summer.

ADDITIONAL SPECIES, CULTIVARS, OR VARIETIES

'Torch' is a recent All-America Selection; it has fiery, bright-orange flowers about 3 inches wide on 4- to 6-foot-tall plants. 'Goldfinger' grows 3 to 4 feet tall. 'Sundance' has 3-inch-wide scarlet-orange flowers on plants that grow 4 to 6 feet tall.

Moss Rose

Portulaca grandiflora

Other Name: Rose Moss, *Portulaca*	**Light Requirement:**
Zones: 5, 6	
Height: 3 to 6 inches	
Bloom Period: Summer	
Flowers: Various	

*M*oss rose is an easy-to-grow plant that makes an excellent addition to a rock garden or any hot, dry location with poor soil. Moss rose is a Brazilian native with succulent, reddish-green stems and narrow, pointed leaves. Its sprawling habit keeps it low to the ground; this makes a few plants go a long way. The single, semi-double, or double bright or pastel flowers resemble one- to two-inch-wide roses as they unfurl. The flowers open in sun and close in late afternoon or in shade. They come in shades of red, yellow, orange, rose, purple, pink, or white.

WHEN TO PLANT

Transplant bedding plants in late spring. Sow seeds directly in the garden after the last frost or start them indoors 6 to 8 weeks before the last frost.

WHERE TO PLANT

Be sure you plant it in full sun if you use moss rose as an edging plant, or if you plant it in clusters to form a mat of color or summer groundcover. Moss rose won't bloom unless it is in the sun. It also does well in windowboxes or containers.

HOW TO PLANT

Moss rose is a bit finicky about being transplanted, so the less disruption the better. Plant bedding plants no deeper than they were growing in their containers. Space them 6 to 12 inches apart; the closer you plant them the more mat-like the planting will be. Water well. Sow seeds outdoors on the surface of soil where the plants are to grow. Keep seedbeds moist until the seedlings appear, then allow the soil to become a little dry; moss rose seedlings may be susceptible to fungus disease if they are kept too wet. Indoors, surface-sow

48

seeds in pots filled with a moistened soilless potting mix. Place pots in a warm, bright location out of direct sunlight. Germination may take 2 weeks. Transplant seedlings outdoors when the danger of frost has passed.

ADVICE FOR CARE

Moss rose does not like wet soil. The plant requires almost no maintenance and will bloom until frost. Cutting moss rose back about halfway at midsummer and fertilizing will renew the growth and thicken up the plant. Moss rose frequently self-sows but is not considered invasive.

ADDITIONAL INFORMATION

Moss rose is a member of the purslane family, which includes an obnoxious weed, *Portulaca oleracea* (sometimes called pigweed), which is edible.

ADDITIONAL SPECIES, CULTIVARS, OR VARIETIES

'Calypso' hybrids grow 6 to 8 inches tall and spread about 1 foot wide. 'Sundial' hybrids are 5 inches tall with a 1-foot spread; they have more succulent foliage. The 'Sundial Peppermint' hybrid has light-pink flowers with fuschia specks. 'Doubled Mix' has double flowers, and 'Sunnyside Mix' has semi-double or double flowers. 'Sundance' and 'Cloudbeater' are said to bloom more readily on cloudy days. 'Minilaca' grows only about 4 inches tall.

Nierembergia

Nierembergia hippomanica

Other Name: Cupflower
Zones: 5, 6
Height: 6 to 12 inches
Bloom Period: Summer
Flowers: Blue, white, purple

Light Requirement:

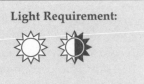

*T*his charming plant has one-inch cup-like flowers on stems with fern-like leaves. The plant has a mounding, sprawling habit, which makes it a good annual for windowboxes, hanging baskets, or other containers; it also makes a good edging plant in a flower bed. Nierembergia is a perennial in its native Argentina, and it is fairly frost tolerant in Indiana. It may survive mild winters in Zone 6, but is not reliable.

WHEN TO PLANT

Plant bedding plants a few weeks before the last frost in the spring. Sow seeds indoors 8 to 10 weeks before the last frost.

WHERE TO PLANT

Like many tropical natives, nierembergia loses its vigor in hot, dry weather. It prefers well-drained, moist (but not wet) soil. Plant it where it will have some protection from the hot afternoon sun. It also does well in partial shade.

HOW TO PLANT

Plant bedding plants the same depth they were growing in their containers. Space them 6 to 8 inches apart and water well. If you are starting from seeds, sow them in pots filled with moistened soilless potting mix. Barely cover them, and place in a warm, bright area out of direct sunlight. Germination takes 2 to 4 weeks. Transplant seedlings outdoors a few weeks before the last frost.

ADVICE FOR CARE

Apply a compost tea or an all-purpose water-soluble fertilizer throughout the growing season; follow label directions. Do not let nierembergia dry out. Shear back after the first flush of flowers to encourage new growth.

ADDITIONAL INFORMATION

Nierembergia flowers and fern-like leaves are attractive in floral arrangements.

ADDITIONAL SPECIES, CULTIVARS, OR VARIETIES

'Mont Blanc' is a recent All-America Selection; it has pure-white flowers with yellow eyes. 'Purple Robe' has lavender-blue flowers. *Nierembergia hippomanica violacea* or *N. h. caerulea* grows up to 15 inches tall with purple flowers; it is considered the hardiest of these plants, but may be hard to find. The same goes for *N. repens*, a low grower with white flowers.

ANNUALS

Pansy

Viola × wittrockiana

Other Name: Viola
Zones: 5, 6
Height: 4 to 12 inches
Bloom Period: Spring and fall
Flowers: Various

Light Requirement:

*T*he pansy has about as many names as it has faces and color combinations. *Viola × wittrockiana* is a hybrid of several viola species and is sometimes listed as *Viola tricolor hortensis*. Its leaves are oval shaped with scalloped edges; its flowers are large and five-petaled. These pansies are mildly fragrant short-lived perennials; they come in dozens of colors and are usually treated as annuals in our Indiana climate. Hoosier winters may be too severe for pansies, which are marginally hardy in Zone 5; our summers, especially in Zones 5 and 6, may be too hot for these plants, which prefer cooler temperatures. Pansies' preference for cool weather makes them difficult to grow from seed; most gardeners cannot produce the particular growing conditions that are required. Pansies are excellent plants for windowboxes or other containers; you may also cut them for floral arrangements. Because they are lightly scented, plant them where passersby can enjoy the fragrance. Pansies' popularity has expanded to fall, where they have begun to rival chrysanthemums for autumn color. Pansies last longer than mums, holding their color well into late fall and early winter. In some protected locations, especially in Zone 6, pansies may flower off-and-on throughout winter and make a spectacular comeback in the spring.

WHEN TO PLANT

Plant in the spring as soon as you can work the soil, or in late summer and early fall when temperatures begin to cool. Pansies are available in garden centers in spring and late summer. Start spring pansies 12 weeks before the last frost; start fall pansies at midsummer.

WHERE TO PLANT

Pansies do best in well-drained soil where they are protected from hot afternoon sun.

HOW TO PLANT

Plant pansy seedlings the same depth they were growing in their containers. Water well. Seeds need a dark, moist, cool climate to germinate. Sow seeds in a moistened soilless potting mix; barely cover them. Germination may take up to 3 weeks. Transplant.

ADVICE FOR CARE

Apply an all-purpose water-soluble fertilizer according to label directions throughout the growing season, or use a compost tea. Deadheading keeps pansies blooming. You can also pinch them to encourage bushiness. Pansies will lose vigor when it gets hot; water them when conditions are dry.

ADDITIONAL INFORMATION

In mild winters in Zone 6, or on the south side of the house with a nice straw mulch, pansies may winter over. The leaves turn purple and the plants flatten to the ground. If it gets warm enough, a flower or two may blossom throughout the winter. When spring arrives, pansies come out of their semi-dormant stage ready to flower for the season. You can cut pansies back to about 4 inches tall in summer to help them withstand the hot temperatures. Keep them well watered. Plants will sometimes bloom again in the fall, and may self-sow.

ADDITIONAL SPECIES, CULTIVARS, OR VARIETIES

There are dozens of color combinations to choose from including solid, bicolors, and tricolors. Select according to your color preferences. There are several All-America Selections, including 'Imperial Blue', 'Maxim Marina', and 'Padparadja'. Some heat-resistant hybrids include 'Imperial', 'Flame Princess', 'Maxim', and 'Viking'. *Viola tricolor*, or Johnny-jump-up, is a smaller plant that self-sows freely. Flowers may be solid or bicolor.

Periwinkle

Catharanthus roseus

Other Names: Madagascar Periwinkle, Vinca **Zones:** 5, 6 **Height:** 4 to 15 inches **Bloom Period:** Summer **Flowers:** Pink, purple, white, red	**Light Requirement:**

*V*inca is a workhorse in sunny locations, much as impatiens is in the shade. Vinca requires little or no care and will bloom continuously throughout the summer. The small, oval leaves are glossy and dark green with light-colored veins. The one-inch-wide flowers have five petals and open flat; some varieties have contrasting centers, or eyes. Vinca works well in a perennial flower bed, as a mass planting in the landscape, or in windowboxes and other containers.

WHEN TO PLANT

Plant bedding plants in the spring after all danger of frost has passed. Sow seeds in pots indoors 10 to 12 weeks before the last frost.

WHERE TO PLANT

Periwinkle does best in well-drained loamy soil in full sun. It is one of the best annuals for hot and dry locations. It also tolerates ordinary soil and a little shade, but the size of the plant and the number of flowers may be reduced.

HOW TO PLANT

Plant bedding plants at the same depth they were growing in packs. Space them 10 to 12 inches apart and water well. Apply an all-purpose granular or water-soluble fertilizer according to label directions, or ring the plants with compost when you plant them. Sow seeds 1/4 inch deep in pots or packs filled with moistened soilless potting mix. Place them in a warm, dark location. When seedlings sprout, move them to a brighter area that is out of direct sunlight. Transplant seedlings outdoors after threat of frost has passed.

ADVICE FOR CARE

Apply an all-purpose granular or water-soluble fertilizer in mid-summer; follow label directions. Deadheading periwinkle is not necessary. It may self-seed and return in the spring but is not reliable. Water as needed throughout the growing season.

ADDITIONAL INFORMATION

You can cut periwinkle for indoor floral arrangements; however, it has an unusual odor some people do not like.

ADDITIONAL SPECIES, CULTIVARS, OR VARIETIES

Sometimes this plant is listed as *Vinca rosea. Catharanthus roseus* 'Pretty In...' hybrids are All-America Selections that grow about 12 inches tall with rose, pink, or white flowers. 'Magic Carpet' or the 'Carpet' series of white, pink, or rose flowers grow 4 to 6 inches tall. 'Tropicana' grows 12 inches tall with 2-inch-wide flowers. 'Cooler' hybrids are 6 to 8 inches tall with 2 to 2^1/$_4$-inch-wide flowers; 'Peppermint Cooler' has white flowers with red centers. 'Little' hybrids such as 'Little Pinkie' or 'Little Bright Eyes' grow up to 10 inches tall with flowers that can be 2 inches or larger. 'Morning Mist' grows about 15 inches tall and has white flowers with rose centers.

Petunia

Petunia × hybrida

Zones: 5, 6
Height: 10 to 15 inches
Bloom Period: Summer
Flowers: Various

Light Requirement:

The petunia is one of nature's most rewarding and easy-to-grow annuals. It is among the top three bedding plants, probably because it requires little care and thrives in full sun from late spring until a hard freeze. Petunias often continue flowering long after frost has killed impatiens, the shade-loving annual that is the number-one-selling bedding plant. Scientists have developed an incredible palette of color and an impressive array of styles to suit a variety of uses. There are five types of petunias: *Multiflora* petunias do well in hot or wet spells and bloom freely all summer. Flowers may be single or double, and from one-and-one-half to three inches wide; they often have contrasting centers or stripes. *Grandiflora* are single- and double-flowering types that are excellent for mass plantings or in containers. Flowers come in many colors, including solid, bicolor, veined, striped, or edged in a contrasting shade; they may grow up to four inches in diameter. New cultivars are more compact and more tolerant of rain and diseases than their older relatives. *Spreading* petunias are low-growing plants that may spread up to four feet wide but reach only four to six inches tall. These plants do well in hanging baskets or in a flower bed. 'Purple Wave' is one of the first varieties in this category. Flowers grow to three inches in diameter along the length of each stem. Petunias of this type are prolific bloomers that do not have to be trimmed back. *Floribunda* are single- or double-flowering hybrids of improved multiflora varieties. The flowers are slightly larger and as abundant as the multiflora types. Floribunda petunias flower earlier and are more weather tolerant than grandiflora. They perk up after a rain. Floribunda does well in mass plantings or in containers, includ-ing hanging baskets. *Milliflora* petunias are tinier still, require little maintenance, and do not have to be pruned back. 'Fantasy' is a new class that was introduced in 1996; it is about two-thirds the size of a normal petunia. The flowers get up to one-and-one-half inches in diameter and literally cover the plant.

WHEN TO PLANT

Transplant bedding plants in the spring after all danger of frost has passed. Sow seeds indoors 8 to 10 weeks before the last frost.

WHERE TO PLANT

If you are planting them in the landscape, petunias prefer full sun in well-drained soil. They also do extremely well in hanging baskets, windowboxes, or other containers. If the site is too shady, they will get leggy and produce few flowers.

HOW TO PLANT

Plant bedding plants the same depth they were growing in their containers. Space them 8 to 10 inches apart. Seeds are tiny. Sow seeds on the surface of moistened soilless potting mix in pots. Place them in a light, warm area. Germination may take 3 weeks. Keep seedlings a bit on the cool side and transplant outdoors when the danger of frost has passed.

ADVICE FOR CARE

Petunias do not like to get wet, so watering them from beneath the plants is recommended. Though they are somewhat drought tolerant, water petunias during long dry spells.

ADDITIONAL INFORMATION

Sticky leaves and stems are natural for petunias, and do not indicate insects or disease. Cut petunias back to about 6 inches tall at mid-summer; this will stimulate new growth and flowering that will last well into fall. Many petunias are pleasantly scented, especially when planted in masses; members of the 'Madness' series are particularly fragrant. Select a site where people can enjoy the fragrance, such as near a bedroom window or around a deck, patio, or porch.

ADDITIONAL SPECIES, CULTIVARS, OR VARIETIES

Select petunias for their color and type of flowers.

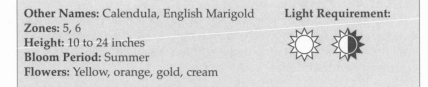

Pot Marigold

Calendula officinalis

Other Names: Calendula, English Marigold	Light Requirement:
Zones: 5, 6	
Height: 10 to 24 inches	
Bloom Period: Summer	
Flowers: Yellow, orange, gold, cream	

*I*f you need a quick spot of color in your flower bed, this easy-to-grow annual makes a great fill-in; it is also an excellent cut flower. Calendula is not a picky plant; it does well in any type of soil. You can easily grow it in pots, windowboxes, or other containers. The two- to four-inch-wide, daisy-like flowers may be single or double. This is an easy plant for children to grow from seed for a classroom project or in the home garden. The seeds resemble dried, comma-shaped worms. Calendula prefers cooler temperatures, and it makes a nice companion plant for pansies in the spring and fall.

WHEN TO PLANT

Plant bedding plants in the spring after all danger of frost has passed. Sow seeds indoors 6 to 8 weeks before the last frost.

WHERE TO PLANT

Spots in full sun or light shade are ideal for this plant. Though calendula prefers well-drained, organically rich soil, it tolerates ordinary soil.

HOW TO PLANT

Plant transplants at the same depth they were growing in their containers. Space them 12 to 18 inches apart depending on the variety. Mulch the plants to help the soil retain moisture and to keep the roots cool. If you are starting from seeds, sow them in individual pots or packs filled with moistened, soilless potting mix, and barely cover them. Water only from below as seedlings are susceptible to fungus diseases. Place them in a warm, bright area. Germination may take up to 2 weeks. Transplant seedlings outdoors when the danger of frost has passed.

ADVICE FOR CARE

Calendula loses vigor when the weather turns hot. If the plants are in pots, move them to a cooler location. Mulch the plant to keep the roots cool and moist. Apply an all-purpose water-soluble fertilizer according to label directions, or use a compost tea 2 or 3 times during calendula's growing season.

ADDITIONAL INFORMATION

Deadheading prolongs the flowering period. Pinch plants to encourage bushiness. Sow seeds directly outdoors as soon as you can work the soil in the spring; you can also sow them in midsummer for fall-flowering plants. Calendula frequently self-sows in the garden and sometimes becomes a nuisance. The flowers are edible in salads, soups, and other dishes.

ADDITIONAL SPECIES, CULTIVARS, OR VARIETIES

Calendula officinalis 'Bon Bon', 'Coronet', 'Dwarf Gem', 'Fiesta Gitana', and 'Sunglow' are dwarfs, growing 10 to 12 inches tall. 'Pacific Giant Mix' grows up to 2 feet tall and has $2^1/2$-inch-wide, yellow, semi-double flowers. 'Prince Mix' has stems up to $2^1/2$ feet tall with 3-inch double orange-and-yellow blooms. 'Touch of Red' is about 18 inches tall; its flowers are tinged with red. *Calendula muselli* has lemon-yellow, 2-inch flowers with silver-green foliage.

Salvia

Salvia farinacea, Salvia splendens

Other Names: Mealycup Sage; Scarlet Sage	**Light Requirement:**
Zones: 5, 6	
Height: 18 to 24 inches	
Bloom Period: Summer	
Flowers: Blue, purple, red, coral, white	

*T*here are two common salvias we use in the annual garden. Scarlet sage, *Salvia splendens*, has been a staple for years. *Salvia farinacea* is newer to Midwestern gardens, but has fast become a regular. *Salvia farinacea*, sometimes called mealycup sage, is an excellent plant for its ability to fill in sparse plantings. It is as welcome in the flower bed as it is in containers. *Salvia farinacea* has spikes of small blue or white cuplike flowers. The plant gets its common name, "mealycup," from the stems which seem to be dusted with a whitish powder. Also called "blue salvia," mealycup sage makes good cut flowers for indoor arrangements, or you can cut and dry the flowers for everlastings. In late summer and fall, goldfinches sit on the flower stems to eat the seeds; the yellow bird on the blue flowers makes a striking picture. Scarlet sage's flowers are more tubular in shape. Red is a very popular color for this variety, which may attract hummingbirds. Newer varieties have coral, white, orchid, burgundy, or purple flowers. *Salvia splendens* does not make a good cut flower because it quickly loses its color.

WHEN TO PLANT
Plant bedding plants in the spring after all danger of frost has passed. Sow seeds indoors 8 to 10 weeks before the last frost.

WHERE TO PLANT
Both *Salvia farinacea* and *Salvia splendens* tolerate ordinary soil and somewhat dry conditions. They look best in the landscape when planted in a mass. Two or three plants clustered in a perennial bed also make a nice showing.

How to Plant

Plant transplants at the same depth they were growing in their containers. Space them 10 to 12 inches apart and water well. If you are starting with seeds, sow them on the surface of pots or seed packs filled with moistened soilless potting mix. Place them in a warm, bright location out of direct sunlight. Germination takes 2 to 3 weeks. Water from below. Transplant seedlings outdoors when the danger of frost has passed.

Advice for Care

Deadheading is not necessary. Pinch to encourage bushiness when the plants are small. A periodic dose of water-soluble fertilizer throughout the growing season is all right, but don't overfertilize; follow label directions.

Additional Information

Both types do well in hot, dry conditions and also tolerate cool temperatures; *Salvia farinacea* is more cold tolerant. These plants may make it through a mild winter in Zone 6 if you plant them in a protected area and give them a little mulch.

Additional Species, Cultivars, or Varieties

Salvia farinacea 'Victoria Blue' has dark-blue, 8-inch-tall flower spikes; 'Argent White' has white spikes; and 'Strata', a recent All-America Selection, has white spikes with dark-blue flowers. *Salvia splendens* 'Sizzler' hybrids are about 12 inches tall and come in a variety of colors. 'St. John's Fire' is about 10 inches tall with bright, scarlet-red flowers; 'Vista Red' has dark-green foliage and is said to hold its color well; and 'Flare' has scarlet spikes over plants that grow about 18 inches tall and fill out nicely. *Salvia coccinea* 'Lady in Red' is another recent All-America Selection. It grows about 12 to 14 inches tall and does well in a hot, dry landscape or in a container. Its bright red flowers have a whorled appearance. *Salvia × superba* includes several hybrid perennials such as 'East Friesland' and 'May Night', a recent Perennial Plant Association's Plant of the Year. *Salvia officinalis* is garden sage, an herb that also does well in the perennial flower bed. It is a perennial with attractive, slightly bumpy silvery-green, green-and-yellow, green, or white-and-purple leaves. It has spikes of purple flowers in early spring.

Snapdragon

Antirrhinum majus

Zones: 5, 6 **Height:** 6 to 36 inches **Bloom Period:** Summer **Flowers:** Various	**Light Requirement:**

napdragons are reliable bloomers in a wide range of colors. They are equally at home in the perennial border, in the cutting garden, or in mass plantings in the landscape. They also do well in windowboxes and other containers. Mildew and other fungus diseases plagued snapdragons for decades, making them undesirable in the garden, but newer varieties are resistant to these problems. Snapdragons are divided by their height: dwarf, six to twelve inches; intermediate, twelve to twenty-four inches; and tall, three or four feet. Snapdragon gets its name from its flowers, or florets, which resemble miniature dragon heads. Gently squeeze the throat or sides of a floret and it snaps open and shut. Children get a big kick out of this trick! The florets range from these snapping types to a more open, trumpet-like flower that is double and bicolor.

WHEN TO PLANT

Snapdragons tolerate cool weather better than most annuals. Plant bedding plants a few weeks before the last frost in the spring. Sow seeds indoors about 8 weeks before the last frost.

WHERE TO PLANT

Snapdragons prefer rich, moist, loamy, well-drained soil in full sun for best flowering, but they will tolerate partial shade. They do not do well in wet soil. Provide snapdragons with good air circulation.

HOW TO PLANT

Plant transplants the same depth they were growing in their containers. Space plants at least 6 inches apart, farther if the varieties are intermediate or tall. If you are starting with seeds, sow them on the surface of pots filled with moistened soilless potting mix. Place seeds in a warm, bright area out of direct sunlight. Germination may take up to 2 weeks. Pinch plants when they are 3 to 4 inches tall to encourage bushiness. Transplant seedlings outdoors in late spring, a few weeks before the last frost.

ADVICE FOR CARE

Pinch transplants after the first flowering to encourage bushiness. Tall varieties will probably need to be staked. Deadheading or cutting keeps snapdragons blooming. In hot weather, snapdragons sometimes stop flowering or slow down drastically. Cut them back and feed them with a water-soluble fertilizer; they should recover when temperatures cool. Snapdragons are susceptible to rust and other fungus diseases, so try to plant resistant varieties.

ADDITIONAL INFORMATION

Snapdragon's fine roots do not do well in compacted, dry, or heavy clay soil. Snapdragons frequently self-sow. They do better when the weather is cool and moist, and they frequently make a strong comeback in the fall.

ADDITIONAL SPECIES, CULTIVARS, OR VARIETIES

'Floral Carpet', 'Magic Carpet', 'Bells', 'Floral Showers', and 'Tahiti' are dwarf varieties. Smaller snapdragons make excellent summer groundcovers. They are also great for containers and windowboxes. 'Coronette' hybrids, 'Sprite', 'Liberty', 'Cinderella', 'Sonnet' hybrids, 'Monarch', 'Popette', 'Rainbow', and 'Lipstick' are intermediates; they are a good size for containers. 'Rocket', 'Black Prince', 'Giant Ruffled Tetra', and 'Double Madam Butterfly' are tall varieties. If you are planting snapdragons for a cutting garden, select intermediate or tall varieties.

Spider Flower

Cleome hasslerana

Zones: 5, 6	**Light Requirement:**
Height: 3 to 4 feet	
Bloom Period: Midsummer to frost	
Flowers: White, pink, purple	

These tall, unusual-looking plants can be used as a summer shrub or hedge if you cluster them in the back of the flower border, or plant them in a bare spot in the landscape. They get their name from their stamens, which look like spider legs dangling from the flowers. The ball-type flowers appear at the ends of leafy, thorny stems. They are airy and open, and they look exotic bobbing above the plants. Cleome has a distinctive scent that some people dislike.

WHEN TO PLANT

Plant outdoors after the danger of frost has passed. Sow seeds indoors 6 to 8 weeks before the last frost.

WHERE TO PLANT

Give cleome a lot of room; these plants have a 3-foot spread. They do best in a rich, well-drained spot in full sun or partial shade, but they will tolerate ordinary soil and dry conditions. Cleome looks ratty at the base of the plant once it begins to bloom, so plant shorter plants around it or plant it at the back of the flower bed.

HOW TO PLANT

Plant bedding plants at the same depth they were growing in their containers. Space them 2 to 3 feet apart; if you plant them too close together, they will get leggy. Water them well. If you are starting with seeds, chill them overnight in the refrigerator. Sow them on the surface of pots filled with moistened, soilless potting mix. Place the seeds in a warm, bright location out of direct sun, and keep them moist. Germination takes 1 to 2 weeks. Transplant seedlings outdoors after the last frost.

Advice for Care

Apply a water-soluble all-purpose or bloom-booster fertilizer throughout the growing season; follow label directions. Water as needed.

Additional Information

Cleomes don't start flowering until they get fairly tall, so don't be concerned if bedding plants don't show color at the garden center. Give them time; they are usually in full flower by midsummer. If the scent doesn't bother you, cut cleomes for indoor floral arrangements; they continue to open for at least a week. Cutting the flowers encourages cleomes to branch even more. When it's hot, the flowers close up a bit during the day; they open later in the afternoon and through the night. Cleomes self-sow with abandon, but their hairy, palm-like leaves make them easy to recognize. You can easily dig them out, transplant them, give them to friends, or toss them in the compost pile. If you pick off the seedheads before they break you will reduce self-sowing. Keep the thorny stems in mind when you are cutting or removing the plants. Cleomes tend to lose vigor in late summer; you can pull them out when they do.

Additional Species, Cultivars, and Varieties

British resources sometimes refer to spider flowers as *Cleome spinosa*. The 'Queen' series has rose, pink, white, and violet flowers. 'Helen Campbell' is white. *Cleome lutea,* or yellow bee plant, is an annual wildflower in the western United States.

Sunflower

Helianthus annuus

Zones: 5, 6 **Height:** 2 to 12 feet **Bloom Period:** Midsummer to frost **Flowers:** Yellow, orange, red, white	**Light Requirement:**

*T*he common sunflower has been refined from a too-tall annual with a too-heavy flower head to shorter, more manageable varieties that are standouts in the perennial bed or cutting garden. You can still choose the twelve-foot varieties, such as 'Russian Mammoth' with its twelve-inch-wide heads; but now there are also smaller plants such as 'Sunspot', which grows only eighteen to twenty-four inches tall and has ten- to twelve-inch-wide flower heads. Sunflowers are easy to grow from seeds; you can sow them directly outdoors after the last frost. Starting seeds indoors is not necessary. Plants are also readily available at garden centers. Some varieties are bicolor; some have the traditional "sunflower" seedhead while others do not.

WHEN TO PLANT

Transplant seedlings after the last frost in the spring. If you want seeds to start indoors, sow them 6 to 8 weeks before the last frost. Sow seeds directly outdoors after the last frost.

WHERE TO PLANT

Sunflowers do best in average, well-drained soil. They tolerate light shade, but as their name suggests, sunflowers perform best in full sun.

HOW TO PLANT

Plant bedding plants the same depth they were growing in their containers. Mound soil up around the base of the taller varieties to help keep them upright; you may also have to stake them. Space the plants 12 to 36 inches apart depending on the variety. Water them well. Sow seeds about $1/4$ inch deep in peat pots filled with a moistened soilless mix. Place them in a warm area. Germination may take 2 weeks. If sowing directly outdoors, plant seeds about $1/4$ inch deep in moistened soil. You can sow 3 or 4 seeds to a small "hill," or mound of soil. Cut off the weakest seedlings, leaving one to grow.

ADVICE FOR CARE

Apply a water-soluble all-purpose or bloom-booster fertilizer when sunflowers first begin to bloom. Water during dry spells or as needed. Cutting the smaller-flowered cultivars encourages branching and more flowers.

ADDITIONAL INFORMATION

Children love to grow sunflowers. Shorter varieties do well in containers and windowboxes. Sunflower heads turn to stay with the sun; north-facing sites may not be the best location as the heads would always be turned away. Birds find sunflower seeds as edible as humans do; keep this in mind if you are planning to harvest the heads. Many gardeners cover maturing seedheads with netting to keep birds out.

ADDITIONAL SPECIES, CULTIVARS, OR VARIETIES

'Russian', 'Tall Single', 'Giant Yellow', 'Giant Single', 'Giganteus', and 'D131' are tall varieties with large heads. More intermediate-sized varieties are 'Autumn Beauty', 6 to 7 feet tall with a mix of yellow, bronze, and red flowers; 'Italian White', 4 to 5 feet tall with creamy white flowers with black centers; 'Valentine', 5 feet tall with pale lemon-yellow flowers with black centers; 'Moonwalker', up to 6 feet tall with pale-yellow flowers; and 'Sunbeam', 5 feet tall with 4-inch yellow flowers with green centers. Shorter or dwarf named varieties include 'Teddy Bear', 2 feet tall with double gold flowers on a bushy plant; 'Big Smile', 12 to 14 inches tall with bright-yellow flowers with a black center; and 'Music Box', 24 to 30 inches tall with solid and bicolor flowers ranging from cream and yellow to bronze and red.

Sweet Alyssum

Lobularia maritima

Zones: 5, 6	Light Requirement:
Height: 6 inches	
Bloom Period: Late spring to frost	
Flowers: White, pink, purple, rose	

*S*weet alyssum is one of those indispensable edging plants that help define flower beds or other landscape characteristics. It is easy to grow and flowers throughout the growing season, usually producing a second and frequently more dense flush of blooms in late summer or early fall. It forms a mat as it ambles along the ground or spills from windowboxes and containers. Flowers are clustered in a globe atop weak stems; leaves are small. The flowers have a faint honey scent that is most noticeable when sweet alyssum is planted in a mass, in a confined area, or where people sit or walk. Sweet alyssum is a good plant to use in a rock garden or along a garden path. It frequently self-sows, coming back year after year with little effort on the gardener's part.

WHEN TO PLANT

Plant bedding plants after the last frost in the spring. Sow seeds indoors 6 to 8 weeks before the last frost. You can also sow seeds directly outdoors in early spring; prepare the site before sowing.

WHERE TO PLANT

Sweet alyssum takes full sun and light shade. For the best blooms choose well-drained, moist, loose soil. Alyssum will tolerate average soil and dry conditions.

HOW TO PLANT

Plant bedding plants the same depth they were growing in their containers. Space them about 6 inches apart and water well. If you are starting with seeds, sow them on the surface of pots filled with moistened soilless potting mix. Place them in a bright, warm area out of direct sunlight and keep them moist. Germination may take up to 2 weeks. Transplant seedlings outdoors in late spring.

ADVICE FOR CARE

Water regularly. Sweet alyssum sometimes loses its vigor when the weather gets very hot. Cut plants back about halfway, water well, and apply an all-purpose or bloom-booster water-soluble fertilizer. They should come back in full force when the weather cools down.

ADDITIONAL INFORMATION

You can cut sweet alyssum for small indoor floral arrangements.

ADDITIONAL SPECIES, CULTIVARS, OR VARIETIES

'Carpet' hybrids grow about 4 inches tall. 'Rosie O'Day' has rose-colored flowers on plants that spread about 10 inches wide but get only about 3 inches tall. 'Oriental Night' is about 4 inches tall with very fragrant purple flowers. 'Wonderland' hybrids grow 3 to 4 inches tall and have purple, rose, red, or white flowers. 'Carpet of Snow' grows up to 6 inches tall with white flowers.

Verbena

Verbena × hybrida

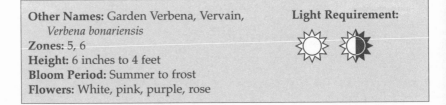

Other Names: Garden Verbena, Vervain,	Light Requirement:
Verbena bonariensis	
Zones: 5, 6	
Height: 6 inches to 4 feet	
Bloom Period: Summer to frost	
Flowers: White, pink, purple, rose	

erbena × hybrida is the more familiar garden verbena, a worthy addition to the landscape that also does well in containers. *V. bonariensis*, a newer introduction, is often seen in commercial plantings and is slowly making a niche for itself in the home landscape as well. The garden verbena is a low-growing plant that forms clusters of flowers which resemble primroses. Some varieties have an upright growing habit; others trail or creep. The serrated leaves are dark green. Garden verbena is an excellent cut flower. So is *Verbena bonariensis*, which has three- to four-foot-tall stems topped with flattish clusters of small purple flowers. Butterflies and bees love this plant. Because the flowers are at the top of the stems, *Verbena bonariensis* looks best with a lower-growing plant in front of it.

WHEN TO PLANT

Plant bedding plants after the last frost in the spring. Sow seeds indoors 8 to 10 weeks before the last frost; garden verbena seeds may be difficult to start.

WHERE TO PLANT

Garden verbena prefers a loamy, fertile soil in sunny or partially shady spots. It tolerates dry conditions. *Verbena bonariensis* does fine in average soil. Neither does well in wet conditions.

HOW TO PLANT

Plant transplants the same depth they were growing in their containers. Space garden verbena 10 to 12 inches apart; *Verbena bonariensis* can be planted 12 to 15 inches apart. Water well. If you are starting from seeds, sow them in pots filled with moistened soil-less potting mix. Barely cover them and place in a warm, dark

location. Keep seeds moist. Germination may take up to 2^1/$_2$
months. Move to light when the seedlings appear. You can sow
Verbena bonariensis directly in the ground, about ^{1}/$_4$ inch deep, or
follow the directions on the seed packet.

ADVICE FOR CARE

Deadhead to prolong flowering, especially with the garden
verbena. Apply a water-soluble all-purpose or bloom-booster
fertilizer throughout the growing season; follow label directions.
Even though verbena tolerates dry conditions, it does better
with regular watering. If the weather is very dry, garden verbena
may be attacked by spider mites. It may also stop blooming in the
height of summer.

ADDITIONAL INFORMATION

Some garden verbena is fragrant. Some varieties are solid-colored;
others have yellow or bright centers, or eyes. *Verbena bonariensis*
begins blooming in July. It may sometimes be hard to find as bedding plants, but more and more garden centers are offering them.
Seeds are readily available from mail-order catalogs; plants grown
from these don't bloom until they are fairly tall. *Verbena bonariensis*
readily self-sows and will probably come back each year.

ADDITIONAL SPECIES, CULTIVARS, OR VARIETIES

'Peaches and Cream' is a recent All-America Selection; it is approximately 8 inches tall with a 12-inch spread. 'Dwarf Jewels' is about
10 inches tall and comes in dark colors. 'Blaze' is red with white
eyes. 'Showtime' hybrids grow about 15 inches tall. *Verbena* × *speciosa* 'Imagination' is an All-America Selection with a 2-foot height
and spread and violet-blue flowers which makes a wonderful
container plant. 'Romance' is about 6 inches tall. 'Tapien' is a
trailing variety.

Zinnia

Zinnia elegans

Other Name: *Zinnia angustifolia* **Zones:** 5, 6 **Height:** 6 inches to 4 feet **Bloom Period:** Summer to frost **Flowers:** Various	**Light Requirement:** 

ith its wide variety of shapes, colors, and textures, *Zinnia elegans* says "summer garden." These annuals are native to Mexico and produce flowers that bloom all season long. Zinnias are easy to grow; seeds planted outdoors in late May and early June will be in flower by late July. Shorter varieties do well in containers or windowboxes, while taller ones blend well in the perennial bed. They are a *must* in the cutting garden. Flowers are solid, bicolor, or tricolor; they may be cactus-like, ruffled, or resemble pompons. If zinnias have a drawback, it is their tendency to get powdery mildew. That doesn't happen to *Zinnia angustifolia*, an excellent annual that mixes well with perennial flowers or in containers and windowboxes. This zinnia has one- to two-inch-wide daisy-like flowers with orange centers that form small cones as they age. It too can be cut for floral arrangements, where it provides a nice, airy texture.

WHEN TO PLANT
Plant bedding plants after the last frost in the spring. Sow seeds indoors 6 to 8 weeks before the last frost, or sow seeds directly in the garden, after all danger of frost has passed.

WHERE TO PLANT
Zinnia elegans does best in full sun but will tolerate light shade. Soil should be fertile and well drained. *Zinnia angustifolia* tolerates light shade and prefers a moist soil until it is established.

HOW TO PLANT
Plant bedding plants at the same depth they were growing in their containers. Space dwarf varieties 6 inches apart and taller ones 10 to 12 inches apart. Water well. If you are starting from seeds, sow them in pots filled with moistened potting mix. Barely cover them and

place in a warm, bright location. Germination may take up to
3 weeks. Transplant seedlings outdoors after the last frost. If you
choose to sow seeds directly in the garden, barely cover them
with moistened soil; thin as needed.

ADVICE FOR CARE
Apply an all-purpose water-soluble or bloom-booster fertilizer when
you are transplanting zinnias outdoors, and again when they begin
to bloom; follow label directions. Zinnias, especially *Zinnia elegans*,
benefit from a dose of fertilizer periodically throughout the growing
season. Deadheading and cutting *Zinnia elegans* keeps it flowering.

ADDITIONAL INFORMATION
If you avoid wetting the leaves when you water, especially with
Zinnia elegans, you will cut down on mildew problems.

ADDITIONAL SPECIES, CULTIVARS, OR VARIETIES
Select *Zinnia elegans* according to color, height, and other requirements. Popular tall varieties include 'Giant Flowered' or 'California
Giants', 'Ruffles', 'State Fair', and 'Zenith'. These range from 24
to 40 inches tall. Intermediate-size zinnias range from 18 to 24
inches and include 'Whirligig', 'Splendor', 'Cut and Come Again',
'Candy Cane', and 'Lilliput'. Shorter varieties ranging from 6 to
18 inches include 'Pulcino Double', 'Marvel', 'Peter Pan', 'Dasher',
'Dreamland', 'Small World', 'Sombrero', and 'Thumbelina'. *Zinnia
angustifolia* varieties include 'Classic', 'Crystal White' (a recent All-
America Selection), and 'Star', and come in white, orange, or gold.
Zinnia haageana, or Mexican zinnia, is bicolor and thrives in hot,
dry locations. Varieties to look for include 'Persian Carpet' and
'Old Mexico'.

CHAPTER TWO

*B*ULBS ARE "PROGRAMMED TO PERFORM." Just add water and, as if by magic, their fleshy layers transform into leaves and flowers that delight the senses. In late winter and early spring, scilla, snowdrops, crocus, and daffodils affirm another growing season, while they warm the heart and brighten the landscape with color and fragrance. By midsummer lilies, begonias, and cannas are holding court. They are followed by fall-blooming crocus just before the weather chills and the process begins all over again.

The term "bulb" commonly refers to a group of bulbous plants, and may include bulbs, corms, tubers, and rhizomes. Lilies, daffodils, and onions are true bulbs. Crocuses and gladioli are examples of corms. Begonias, anemones, and potatoes are tubers. Here are some definitions:

- True bulbs have fleshy leaves attached to a short stem, or basal plate. Leaves and stems grow from the top of the plate; roots grow from the bottom. A scaly bulb, such as lily or garlic, has fleshy leaves attached to a base. A tunicated bulb, such as hyacinth, daffodil, or onion, wears tunic-like fleshy layers or rings. Usually, the bigger the bulb, the better. Bulbs should be firm and without bruises, cuts, or mushy spots. It's okay if the outside, paper-thin layer is loose or peels away. Bulbs frequently have pointed tops (which you should plant facing up) and small, dry roots at the base.
- Corms are squat stems covered by a layer of leaves that tend to be thin and scaly. Corms are flatter than bulbs. They frequently have a sunken place at the top; you should plant them with this sunken spot face up. The flatter side is the bottom, or basal plate, which is where roots form. Some corms benefit from an overnight soaking in water before you plant them. Corms should be firm and without bruises or cuts.
- Tubers are swollen, irregularly shaped stems that grow underground. Like above-ground stems, tubers have nodes. Growth

Chapter Two

points, or "eyes," are the flower buds. These are at or near the
surface. Look for firm, healthy tubers with two or more eyes.
Many tubers should be soaked in room-temperature water
overnight, or for a few hours before planting. Tubers frequently
are meant to be placed horizontally; plant them with the eyes
facing up.

- Rhizomes are fleshy stems that creep underground or near the
surface. The stems store food and produce leaves. Select rhizomes
that are firm and without bruises. Soak rhizomes in room-temperature water for a few hours to overnight before planting.

Bulbs are hardy or tender. Tender bulbs must be dug in the fall,
wintered over, and planted again in the spring—or you may treat
them as annuals and allow them to die in winter.

Each season, bulbs process and store nutrients that will help
them perform again the following year. That is why it is important
to allow the foliage to remain on the plant until it ripens, turns
yellow or brown, and falls to the ground. Although bulbs produce
their own food, it doesn't hurt to give them a helping hand. Apply a
thin layer of compost around the plants when new growth emerges,
and again at the end of the growing season.

Many gardeners add a little bonemeal to the hole when they
plant bulbs. Bonemeal is a slow-release natural phosphorus that
encourages root development. Always water a newly planted patch
of bulbs. During dry periods in the fall and winter, continue to supplement rainfall for bulbs and other plants. Plants will be better
prepared for their winter survival if you give them several good
soakings before the ground freezes. Bulbs, like most plants, don't
like to sit in soil that drains poorly.

Here's how to plant spring-flowering bulbs in drifts or clusters:

- Dig a hole ten to twelve inches deep, and as wide as you wish.
Work the soil to break up dirt clumps, and remove roots, rocks,
and other debris. Return two to three inches of soil to the bottom
of the hole, and amend it by mixing in a heavy dusting of peat
moss and/or an inch or two of compost, finely chopped leaves, or
dried grass clippings. Following label directions, mix a slow-

release, all-purpose granular fertilizer and bonemeal in the soil, if you wish. Smooth out the three to four inches of soil in the hole.

- Place the largest bulbs (such as daffodils and tulips) in the hole so that they are six to eight inches deep; adjust the amount of soil in the hole to get the correct depth. Cover with just enough soil to plant the next layer of bulbs. Plant hyacinth, crocus, and smaller daffodils in the second layer, placing them around the larger bulbs. The second layer should be about four to six inches below ground level. Cover with just enough soil to plant the third layer. Scatter the smaller bulbs (such as Dutch iris, scilla, and snow drops) around the larger ones you have already planted so that they are about two to four inches below ground level. In general, plant bulbs approximately two to three times deeper than they are in diameter. A two-inch bulb should be planted six to eight inches deep. With many spring-flowering bulbs, it is better to plant them more deeply than to err by planting them too close to ground level.

The best time to divide or move spring-flowering bulbs is in early summer, after their foliage has died back, but while there is enough left to identify where the clump is located. Carefully dig with a garden fork or spade, beginning some distance from the clump so that the bulbs don't get speared. Gently raise the clump and remove it from the hole. Separate the bulbs, keeping as many of their roots intact as possible. Trim off foliage and replant using the directions given above as soon as possible, preferably in a bed you have already prepared. Water well. The bulbs may also be separated, dried, and stored in a cool, dry place where they won't sprout until fall, and then plant them as soon as possible.

Digging bulbs in the spring is "risky business" but sometimes unavoidable. Dig bulbs in the spring after they flower and before their foliage has ripened. Using a spade, begin digging some distance away from the clump; dig carefully so that you won't slice any of the bulbs. It's essential to keep as much soil around the roots as possible. Replant the clump immediately in its new location, preferably in a bed you have already prepared. You may also place the clump in a temporary bed, or in a large container out of direct sun.

Chapter Two

Replant as soon as possible, or allow the foliage to ripen and the bulbs to dry. Store the bulbs in a cool, dry place (such as a refrigerator) where they won't sprout. Replant in the fall, following the directions given above. This method may disrupt the food-storage process, which will reduce flowers—and possibly vigor—the next year.

You can divide and move bulbs in the fall, but finding them can be a challenge. Be sure to mark the clumps you wish to divide in the spring by outlining them with short twigs from the yard, wooden ice cream sticks, metal stakes, a ring of jute, or the bamboo sticks that are sold at many garden centers as plant stakes.

Some bulbs, particularly summer-flowering lilies, begonias, and lycoris, have gaps between their flowers and foliage and you may wish to use companion plants to help fill that space. Think about the foliage that must remain on the bulbs when you are deciding where to plant them. Daylilies, chrysanthemums, and several other perennials make good companion plants, because as they grow, they hide the bulbs' ripening foliage.

You can force hardy, spring-flowering bulbs to bloom indoors. Tender bulbs, such as freesias, can also be forced to bloom indoors. For the best and most satisfying results, select bulbs that say "ideal for forcing" or "ready for forcing." These have gone through a necessary cold, dormant period, and they can be potted up or placed on water and pebbles for a wonderful indoor display.

Most people recommend discarding hardy, spring-flowering bulbs forced to bloom indoors. Some of the bulbs may flower, however, if transplanted outdoors—so it may be worth the effort. Plant them as soon as possible in the spring after the flowers die and after a proper "hardening off" or adjustment phase. Plant them in a well-prepared, nutrient-rich bed, and water them well. Apply a layer of compost again in the fall—and hope for the best. They may bloom the following spring—or they may produce only foliage the first year, with flowers following during the second year. Fertilize or apply compost in the spring and fall.

Allium

Allium spp.

Zones: 5, 6	**Light Requirement:**
Height: 4 to 48 inches	
Bloom Period: Spring and summer	
Flowers: Various	
Type: Hardy	

*O*rnamental alliums are in the same family as garlic, onions, and chives—which is why they smell like their flavorful cousins if you crush or cut them. Alliums are easy to grow, and there are nearly 400 allium species from which to choose. Many have long-lasting, fragrant flowers; you can use them in floral bouquets, or dry them for arrangements. Allium flowers form atop leafless stalks that shoot up from the base of the plant. Alliums have two types of flower heads: ball-type and tufted. *Allium giganteum* is an example of the ball-type flower; it is a dramatic, purple-headed, early summer bloomer that looks like a giant drumstick. *Allium moly* (called golden garlic or lily leek) is an example of the tufted flower; it has loose upright or drooping clusters.

WHEN TO PLANT
Alliums may be planted in September, October, or November—or until the ground is too frozen to work.

WHERE TO PLANT
Alliums prefer full sun but will tolerate light shade.

HOW TO PLANT
Plant an allium bulb about 3 times deeper than its circumference. For example, if you have a 2-inch bulb, plant it 6 inches deep—or plant a 3-inch bulb 9 inches deep. Plant bulbs 4 to 12 inches apart— smaller bulbs should be closer together than larger bulbs. Water well. Mulch lightly with compost or wood chips, if you wish.

ADVICE FOR CARE
Apply a granular, all-purpose fertilizer after blooming and until the

foliage dies back. Ring the emerging clump with compost. It is fine to cut the flower stems for arrangements, or remove them as the blossoms die, but the foliage *must* remain on the plant after the flowers have gone. Foliage helps to store food the bulb needs to flower again next year. Wait until foliage turns yellow or brown, then remove it by cutting it at ground level.

ADDITIONAL INFORMATION

Plant alliums in the fall with other spring-flowering bulbs. The larger alliums bloom in early summer, however. When you are making your selections, be sure to check blooming times, as well as height and color.

ADDITIONAL SPECIES, CULTIVARS, OR VARIETIES

Allium giganteum grows about 4 feet tall; its 6-inch-wide, purple, drumstick-shaped flower heads can be quite impressive in the back of the perennial bed. These bloom in June or July, and they last several weeks. Another midsummer bloomer is *A. sphaerocephalon*, which grows about 2 feet tall and has dark-red, cone-shaped flowers. *A. christophii*, or 'Star of Persia', blooms in late spring or early summer; it grows about 3 feet tall and has 10-inch-wide lavender flowers. *A. azureum* or *A. caeruleum* grows about 18 inches tall, and has 1½-inch-wide, sky-blue flowers. *A. bulgaricum* is a tufted type with green, purple, and white bell-shaped flowers that grow about 30 inches tall. *A. moly* grows about 12 inches tall, and has small, yellow, star-shaped flowers; this plant can be invasive. Chives, *A. schoenoprasum*, make a lovely, edible, low-growing allium for the front of the flower border. See chives in the herb section.

Caladium

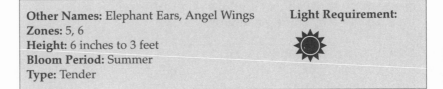

Caladium × *hortulanum*

Other Names: Elephant Ears, Angel Wings
Zones: 5, 6
Height: 6 inches to 3 feet
Bloom Period: Summer
Type: Tender

Light Requirement:

*C*aladiums provide spectacular foliage in flower beds or containers. They set off shade-loving perennials (such as hostas and ferns), and they are standouts when mixed with a bed of impatiens under trees. Caladium is a tropical, clump-growing plant with an insignificant flower (called a spathe). Caladiums are similar in shape to calla lilies, or jack-in-the-pulpits, to which they are related. Potted plants are readily available at garden centers in the spring, but it is fairly easy to start tubers indoors. Using caladiums in containers makes it easier to bring them indoors in winter.

WHEN TO PLANT
Plant container-grown transplants in the spring, after the danger of frost has passed. Start tubers indoors in March or April.

WHERE TO PLANT
Whether you plant them in the landscape or in containers, caladiums prefer a shady, moist, well-drained location. They will tolerate partial sun.

HOW TO PLANT
Don't plant caladiums any deeper than the transplants have been growing in their containers. If you are planting tubers, fill a 4-inch clay or plastic pot until it is $2/3$ to $3/4$ full of a moistened, soilless mix. Place the tuber horizontally on the soil surface, and cover it with about 2 inches of the moistened potting mix. You can plant several tubers in larger containers. Place in a warm, bright spot, but not in direct sun. Keep moist. When new growth appears, apply fish emulsion or an all-purpose, water-soluble fertilizer. When the caladiums are at least 4 inches high, you can transplant them to your desired location outdoors.

ADVICE FOR CARE

Fertilize caladiums with fish emulsion or an all-purpose, water-soluble solution throughout the growing season. If you plan to dig the tubers to winter over for next year, discontinue fertilizing and watering when the leaves begin to die at the end of the growing season.

ADDITIONAL INFORMATION

To winter over the tubers, dig them after the foliage has been killed by frost, but before a ground-hardening freeze. Remove any dead foliage from the tubers and dry them. You may dust tubers with a fungicide before you store them. Store them in dry peat moss or vermiculite in a cool, dry place that is safe from freezing. Examine the tubers regularly and discard any that get soft. Divide tubers by cutting them into sections of one or more "eyes," or growth spots.

ADDITIONAL SPECIES, CULTIVARS, OR VARIETIES

Named varieties of fancy-leaf caladiums (*Caladium × hortulanum*) grow 12 to 18 inches tall. These include 'Candidum', which has white leaves edged and veined in green; 'Frieda Hempl', which has red leaves with green borders; and 'Pink Symphony', which has pink-and-green leaves and veins. The red-centered leaves of 'Rosebud' are rimmed in white and green; the leaves of 'Pink Beauty' have pinkish-red centers, fringed by green with pink spots; 'Fanny Munson' has pink leaves with red veins; and 'Aaron' has white leaves with green fringes and veins. 'Candidum Junior', a dwarf variety of its namesake, and 'Miss Muffet' grow only about 8 to 10 inches tall. *Caladium bicolor* is the species plant used to develop *Caladium × hortulanum*. *Colocasia esculenta* is a related plant, often called elephant ears. This has very large heart- or arrow-shaped green leaves. It definitely lends a tropical look to the landscape, but give it room. The leaves may reach lengths of 6 feet, and the plant itself may grow 6 feet tall and wide.

Canna

Canna × generalis

Other Name: Indian Shot **Zones:** 5, 6 **Height:** 18 inches to 6 feet **Bloom Period:** Mid- to late summer **Flowers:** Various **Type:** Tender	**Light Requirement:**

Cannas are considered old-fashioned flowers, but they are hard to beat in the mid- to late summer, when most other plants have stopped blooming. These easy-to-grow plants are dramatic in the landscape, adding stately structure and exotic foliage. Cannas are native to South America, South Africa, and a few other tropical climates. Their rhizomes are tender in Indiana—or almost anywhere outside Zone 8. They were a staple in the Victorian garden, and are enjoying a revival.

WHEN TO PLANT

Plant container-grown transplants in the spring, after all threat of frost has passed. Canna rhizomes should be started indoors in March or April. Rhizomes planted in the garden after the threat of frost has passed will bloom later in the summer.

WHERE TO PLANT

Cannas prefer full sun in well-drained, moist soil that has been amended with organic material. Dwarf varieties do well in containers.

HOW TO PLANT

Don't plant cannas any deeper than transplants have been growing in their containers. If you are planting rhizomes, fill 6-inch clay or plastic pots 2/3 to 3/4 full of a moistened, soilless mix. Place the rhizomes horizontally in the pots, and cover with 2 inches of the moistened potting mix. Put them in a warm, bright area, and keep moist. Once new growth appears, use a fish-emulsion or all-purpose, water-soluble fertilizer regularly. Transplant to your desired location when cannas are at least 6 or 8 inches tall. Plant 18 to 24 inches apart.

ADVICE FOR CARE

Cannas don't like to dry out, so keep the soil moist. Apply a water-soluble fertilizer throughout the growing season. If you are planning to winter over the rhizomes for transplanting next year, allow frost to kill the foliage. Remove all but 4 to 6 inches of the foliage, and dig the rhizome. Rinse off the soil, allow the rhizome to dry for a few days, and store in a cool, dry place through the winter. You can divide rhizomes in the spring; cut them into sections with 2 or more "eyes," or growth points. You can start cannas from seed, but it takes a long time for them to germinate. Notch or nick seeds before planting. 'Tropical Rose' is a fairly recent introduction that is easier to sprout.

ADDITIONAL INFORMATION

Canna indica is a wild type from the West Indies; it grows up to 6 feet tall and has small, bright-red flowers. Its seed was used for shot—thus, the name Indian Shot.

ADDITIONAL SPECIES, CULTIVARS, OR VARIETIES

Taller varieties include 'The President', 3 to 5 feet tall, with red flowers and green foliage; 'King Humbert', 5 to 6 feet tall, with red flowers and bronze foliage; 'City of Portland', 3 to 4 feet tall with pink flowers and green foliage; 'Rosamond Cole', 3 to 4 feet tall, with red flowers tipped in gold; 'Pretoria', 4 feet tall, with creamy yellow-and-green, zebra-striped foliage and melon-orange flowers; and 'Wyoming', 4 feet tall, with orange flowers and bronze leaves. Dwarf varieties include 'Pfitzer's' and the 'Futurity' series; these range from 18 to 24 inches tall. Other named dwarfs include: 'Lucifer', 24 inches tall, with red flowers tinged in gold; 'Angel Pink', 24 inches tall, with apricot-peach flowers with yellow throats, and green foliage; and 'China Lady', 24 to 30 inches tall, with coral-pink flowers and green foliage.

Crocus

Crocus spp. and hybrids

Zones: 5, 6	**Light Requirement:**
Height: 3 to 8 inches	
Bloom Period: February to April	
Flowers: Various	
Type: Hardy	

With purple, white, blue, yellow or variegated flowers, these harbingers of spring harken another growing season and tell us all is right with the gardening world. Crocus grow from corms, and although hardy enough to withstand the coldest Indiana winter, they are treated like annuals in many yards because squirrels will gobble them up. Squirrels often will eat them as fast as you plant them or as they bloom, so plant a lot. Dusting the soil surface with blood meal after planting sometimes deters squirrels and other animals from digging in the bed. Interplanting crocus with daffodils (*Narcissus*) may help, too. Rodents avoid narcissus because they are poisonous to animals and humans. Some gardeners plant crocus in specially made mesh baskets, or they make their own "metal stockings" with hardware cloth or screen with a three-fourth- or one-inch grid. The basket is placed in the soil and covered. The corms send stems through the grid, which keeps out squirrels and other bulb-eating rodents. Because crocus are small, they should be planted where they can be seen, such as in a patch by the mailbox, along the walk from the house to the garage or at the very front of a flower bed. Crocus can be planted in groundcover that is not too dense, such as myrtle (*Vinca minor*) or pachysandra. They also mix well with *Iris reticulata* and early blooming daffodils. The seasoning saffron comes from the orange stamens of *Crocus sativus*, or saffron crocus, one of several varieties that bloom in the fall.

WHEN TO PLAN
Plant crocus after the middle of September until the ground freezes. Corms may be moved or divided in early summer after the foliage has died back.

WHERE TO PLANT

Crocus corms should be planted in full sun or partial shade. Those in the sun will probably bloom earlier than the ones in the shade. Soil should drain well and be amended with compost or other organic material.

HOW TO PLANT

Plant corms flat side down about 3 or 4 inches deep. Rather than dig individual holes for each corm, consider digging one larger hole and cluster the corms 2 to 3 inches apart. Water them well. Mulch lightly with compost or wood chips, if desired.

ADVICE FOR CARE

Apply a granular all-purpose fertilizer in early spring when new growth breaks ground, or ring the emerging plant with compost. Flower stems may be removed as the blossoms die. Sometimes the flowers will get nipped by a hard freeze in the spring. Cut them off to keep the plant looking tidy. The foliage must remain on the plant until it ripens, turning yellow brown. The foliage is part of the food manufacturing process needed for the corm to flower again next year. Remove by cutting at ground level.

ADDITIONAL INFORMATION

Fall-blooming crocus are ordered in spring and should be planted as soon as they arrive. They start blooming in September and last for several weeks. The foliage also needs to remain on the plant until it turns yellow or brown.

ADDITIONAL SPECIES, CULTIVARS, OR VARIETIES

Crocus flavus (sometimes *Crocus aureus*) are called Dutch crocus or Dutch yellow crocus, and are among the earliest, sometimes breaking ground in January; *Crocus vernus* also is called Dutch or common crocus. Dutch crocus tend to have large flowers. Select on color, height and blooming period. *Crocus speciosus* is an easy-to-grow fall-blooming variety. Another plant called autumn crocus is *Colchicum*, or meadow saffron, including *C. autumnal, C. byzantinum* (hardy to Zone 6), and *C. Speciosum*.

Daffodil

Narcissus spp. and hybrids

Zones: 5, 6	**Light Requirement:**
Height: 4 to 20 inches	
Bloom Period: February to April	
Flowers: Yellow, gold, white, cream, peach, or pinkish	
Type: Hardy	

The name "Narcissus" comes from Greek mythology. Narcissus was cursed to fall in love with himself, which he did when he saw his image in a pool. He drowned trying to reach the person he loved. The names "narcissus," "daffodil," and "jonquil" are frequently used interchangeably to refer to the whole group, but experts classify this plant into twelve divisions. These divisions generally describe the flowers or cups, and include Trumpet, Large-Cupped, Small-Cupped, Double-Flowering, Triandrus, Jonquilla, Tazetta, Cyclamineus, Poeticus, Species, Narcissus with Split Coronas (Butterfly), and Miscellaneous. There are also some miniatures. If I could have only one type of spring-flowering bulb, I would choose daffodils. They come back year after year with little or no fuss, can be intoxicatingly fragrant, and are an excellent value for your money. Early-blooming daffodils often flower before trees or large shrubs get leaves, so you can plant them in very shady locations. Although the yellow daffodil is most common, hybrids come in many colors, including gold, white, cream, peach, or pale pink. You can find daffodils with single or double flowers, or even multiple flowers on the same stem. Many varieties are good for naturalizing the landscape, especially 'February Gold', 'King Alfred', 'Mount Hood', 'Barrett Browning', and 'Ice Follies'.

WHEN TO PLANT
Plant narcissus bulbs from mid-September until the ground is frozen. You can move or divide bulbs in early summer, after the foliage has died back.

WHERE TO PLANT
Narcissus prefers full sun to partial shade. Choose a well-drained

spot, and amend it with compost or other organic material. Avoid planting bulbs in areas that get wet because they may rot. Daffodils mix well with many groundcovers and perennials, including daylilies (*Hemerocallis*), which grow to camouflage the ripening foliage of the narcissus.

HOW TO PLANT
Plant narcissus at least 3 times deeper than the circumference of the bulb. A 2-inch bulb should be planted 6 to 8 inches deep; a 1-inch bulb should be planted 3 to 4 inches deep. Water well and mulch lightly.

ADVICE FOR CARE
Apply a granular, all-purpose fertilizer after blooming and until the foliage dies back. Ring the emerging plants with compost. You may cut the flower stems for arrangements, or remove them as the blossoms die, but the foliage *must* remain on the plant after the flowers have gone. Foliage helps to store food the bulb needs to flower again next year. Wait until foliage turns yellow or brown, then remove it by cutting it at ground level.

ADDITIONAL INFORMATION
Narcissus releases a fluid that frequently clogs the stems of other plants in cut-flower arrangements. Changing the water daily helps, but other flowers may die quickly if you place them in a vase with narcissus.

ADDITIONAL SPECIES, CULTIVARS, OR VARIETIES
Favorites are 'Dutch Master', 'Peaches and Cream', 'Salome', 'Cheerfulness', 'Hawara', 'Jack Snipe', 'Tete-a-Tete', and 'Actaea'. Make selections based on color, blooming times, and height. It's hard to make a bad choice.

Dahlia

Dahlia hybrids

Zones: 5, 6	**Light Requirement:**
Height: 1 to 5 feet	
Bloom Period: Mid- to late summer	
Flowers: Various	
Type: Tender	

Dahlias are native to Mexico and South America, where they grow wild at altitudes of 5,000 and 10,000 feet. In the eighteenth century, the tuber was given its European name by the first man to grow dahlias successfully on the continent. He named the plant after Andreas Dahl, a Swedish botanist and student of Carolus Linnaeus, the Swede credited with devising the modern system of plant naming. By the 1830s, Europe raged with "dahliamania." Countries fought over the plant's name, and the gardening elite experimented with growing it. Marie Antoinette hoarded her supply behind a fence, and reportedly told those who asked for cuttings, "Let them grow roses!" In 1789, a single dahlia tuber was said to have been swapped for a diamond. A bed of tubers reportedly sold for 700,000 francs. A Polish aristocrat bribed one of the queen's consorts to steal some of the tubers, and with propagation, the dahlia became less expensive—but not less popular. There are some excellent, bedding-type dahlias that are grown from seed; these require less care, and they also develop tubers. Dahlia aficionados pride themselves on growing dinner-plate-sized flowers on stalks that must be staked. Dahlia colors are brilliant.

WHEN TO PLANT

Transplant bedding plants in the spring, after the danger of frost has passed. Plant tubers or clumps in a prepared bed a week or two before the last frost in the spring.

WHERE TO PLANT

Dahlias prefer full sun and well-drained soil that has been amended with compost or other organic material. They tolerate light shade. Bedding types do well in containers and flowerboxes.

How to Plant
Plant bedding types at the same depth they were growing in containers. Plant tubers or clumps 4 to 6 inches deep; dig a wide hole that allows roots to spread out. Lay each tuber horizontal in the planting hole. If you are planting a tall variety, place the stakes at this time to avoid injuring the plant later.

Advice for Care
Pinch plants for bushier growth, and remove side shoots to make the flowers larger. Fertilize and water throughout the growing season.

Additional Information
You can lift dahlia tubers and clumps to winter them over. After frost has killed the top foliage, cut the stems to about 6 inches, and gently lift the rootball. Trim back the roots and allow the plant to dry slightly. Store the plant in a bin of peat moss; choose a cool, dry place that will protect the tubers from freezing and from rodents. You can divide clumps in the spring by cutting them into sections with at least one "eye," or growth spot.

Additional Species, Cultivars, or Varieties
Dahlias have many different flower types. These include single, anemone, collarette, water lily, decorative, ball, pompon, cactus, semi-cactus, and Lilliput (a bedding variety). There are hundreds of varieties.

Dutch Iris

Iris reticulata

Zones: 5, 6 **Height:** 3 to 6 inches **Bloom Period:** Early spring **Flowers:** Various **Type:** Hardy	**Light Requirement:**

These miniature irises bloom in February and March, and the flowers last several weeks. Because they are small, you should plant them close together in drifts or large clusters; this will ensure a good show. The flowers come in purple, blue, yellow, white, and pink. Some are solid colored; others have throats with attractive contrasting colors or tiny flecks on the petals. *Iris reticulata* makes a good companion plant for crocus and early-flowering, short narcissus. Don't confuse *Iris reticulata* and other Dutch, English, or Spanish irises with bearded flowers, which are sometimes called "old-fashioned irises" or "flags." The former grow from bulbs, while the latter grow from rhizomes.

WHEN TO PLANT
Plant *Iris reticulata* bulbs in the fall, up until the ground is frozen.

WHERE TO PLANT
Iris reticulata is not fussy about soil, but prefers full sun and a well-drained spot. Plant it along the edges of walkways or flower beds.

HOW TO PLANT
The bulbs are small. Plant them about 3 inches deep and about 1 inch apart. Water well, and mulch lightly with compost or shredded bark.

ADVICE FOR CARE
Apply an all-purpose granular fertilizer after the flowers fade and until the foliage dies back. Dust some compost around the emerging plants. You may cut the flower stems for arrangements, or remove them as the blossoms die, but the foliage *must* remain on the plant after the flowers have gone. Foliage helps to store food the bulb

needs to flower again next year. Wait until foliage turns yellow or brown, then remove it by cutting it at ground level.

ADDITIONAL INFORMATION

Dutch iris and *Iris reticulata* send up grassy leaves in late fall or winter. Divide clumps then or in late spring or early summer, after the foliage has died back. They rarely need dividing, and they will spread rapidly without becoming invasive.

ADDITIONAL SPECIES, CULTIVARS, OR VARIETIES

Iris xiphium is usually 16 to 18 inches tall; it flowers in May and June. You can frequently find it in bouquets of cut flowers at florist shops. Good varieties include: 'Blue Ribbon', purple-blue flowers with yellow throats; 'Romano', light-blue flowers with white-and-yellow falls; 'White Perfection', white with a touch of yellow in the throat; 'Oriental Beauty', lavender flowers with white and pale-yellow falls; and 'Purple Sensation', dark-purple flowers with yellow throats. *Iris danfordiae* has yellow flowers with dark dots on the throat. It grows about 6 inches tall, and should be planted 5 or 6 inches deep. *I. reticulata* 'Harmony' has deep-blue flowers and flecked throats. 'Cantab' has light-blue flowers, and 'Joyce' has sky-blue flowers and red markings. *I. r. histrioides* 'Major' has deep-blue flowers and white spots.

Gladiolus

Gladiolus × hortulanus

Zones: 5, 6	**Light Requirement:**
Height: 18 inches to 6 feet	
Bloom Period: Summer	
Flowers: Various	
Type: Tender	

Gladioli, or "glads," add stalks of color to the landscape, and they make excellent long-lasting cut flowers. If only they were fragrant! Glads have sword-like, green leaves, and their flowers open from the bottom up. They continue to unfurl after being cut, and they come in nearly all colors except blue. Glads are easy to grow, although you will have to dig them up in the fall and replant them next year. The tender corms occasionally survive the winter and flower the second year—but don't count on it. Plant taller varieties along a fence row or wall to help them stay upright. You can also plant them in clusters or stands in the middle or back of the flower bed; use stakes or other supports if necessary. Miniature varieties have smaller flowers, but they reach only two to three feet in height; they do not need staking.

WHEN TO PLANT

Begin planting glad corms in the spring, after all danger of frost has passed. For continuous blooms and cut flowers throughout the growing season, continue planting until midsummer.

WHERE TO PLANT

Glads do best in full sun, but will tolerate light shade. Plant corms in a well-drained spot that has been amended with compost or other organic material.

HOW TO PLANT

Plant corms flat side down and 3 to 8 inches deep. Those smaller than an inch should be planted 3 inches deep; those larger than 1$^{1}/_{4}$ inches should be planted 8 inches deep. Cover and water well. Apply an all-purpose granular fertilizer when growth breaks ground, or add a thin layer of compost. Mulching is not necessary.

ADVICE FOR CARE

Water well during dry periods. Fertilize as described above when the flowers first show color. When you are cutting the flowers, make sure to leave a portion of the stalk and foliage so that the plant can send nutrients back to the corm. This will enable the corm to build up reserves for next year's flowers. You can help keep glads upright by mounding soil around the base of the plants as they grow taller.

ADDITIONAL INFORMATION

The foliage *must* remain on the plant if you plan to replant the corm next year. Remove foliage about 6 weeks after the plant blooms, or after foliage turns yellow or brown. Leave a few inches of foliage to identify where the corms are located. Carefully dig the corms after the first frost, and allow them to dry out of direct sunlight. Place corms in paper or mesh bags, or place them in single layers in shallow bins or boxes and cover them with dry soil, sand, or vermiculite. Store them in a cool, dry, ventilated area. Buy corms from reliable nurseries or mail-order catalogs to make sure they are disease free. Discard soft, mushy, or rotted corms. Visit the "glad show" at the Indiana State Fair each year to see some outstanding glad specimens!

ADDITIONAL SPECIES, CULTIVARS, OR VARIETIES

Select glads for color and height. *Gladiolus nanus* is hardy to Zone 5; you can find varieties with red, pink, white, and rose-colored flowers. These grow to 2 feet tall, and bloom in midsummer. Plant *G. nanus* corms about 4 inches deep and 4 inches apart in the spring.

Grape Hyacinth

Muscari spp.

Other Name: Muscari
Zones: 5, 6
Height: 6 to 10 inches
Bloom Period: Spring
Flowers: Blue/purple
Type: Hardy

Light Requirement:

Grape hyacinth is a very reliable bloomer—once you plant it, you can pretty much leave it alone. If these lovely blue or purple flowers have a drawback, it is that some varieties may self-sow too freely; they may send new plants to other parts of the landscape where you don't want their grass-like fall foliage. Grape hyacinth can have a very long foliage period; it frequently sends up foliage in the fall. The flowers rise from these grassy clumps in the spring. It has very fragrant spikes of ball- or grape-like flowers; it makes sweet cut-flower bouquets. Grape hyacinth does well under trees and shrubs; it also makes an excellent marker for perennials that may be hard to locate in the garden.

WHEN TO PLANT

Plant bulbs in the fall as early as possible, before the ground freezes. You can divide plants in early summer, when the foliage has died back.

WHERE TO PLANT

Muscari does best in full sun, but it will tolerate a little shade, especially in areas where it gets a chance to flower before deciduous trees and shrubs leaf out.

HOW TO PLANT

Plant bulbs 3 inches deep and apart, with their pointed ends up. Instead of digging small individual holes for the tiny bulbs, dig several large ones to plant muscari in drifts or clusters; this will ensure the best show. Cover and water well. Mulching isn't necessary, but a light layer of shredded bark, compost, or chopped leaves is okay.

ADVICE FOR CARE

Apply an all-purpose granular fertilizer in the fall or spring when foliage appears—or spread a thin layer of compost over the clumps in the spring and fall. Allow foliage to remain on the plant until it dries. If muscari is naturalizing the lawn, do not cut your grass until the foliage has ripened.

ADDITIONAL INFORMATION

Try to plant grape hyacinth where the flowers can be seen easily. It looks—and smells—best when densely planted. It is also very attractive in the front of the flower border. If you enjoy a traditional spring-flower combination, try planting it with yellow daffodils and red tulips; it provides the perfect blue to accompany them. Grape hyacinth *Muscari* is different from the *Hyacinthus orientalis* (commonly referred to as Dutch hyacinth or hyacinth), which is discussed elsewhere in this chapter.

ADDITIONAL SPECIES, CULTIVARS, OR VARIETIES

Muscari botryoides is the common grape hyacinth. It is the hardiest of the hyacinths, and is also most likely to send up fall foliage; it produces blue flowers. 'Album' is a white variety. *M. armeniacum* blooms in April; it has dark-purple flowers with a lower white edge. 'Blue Spike' is a popular variety; in early spring, it produces double, blue flowers, 4 to 6 inches tall. *Muscari azureum* is an early bloomer with bright-blue, low-growing flowers. *M. comosum plumosum*, or feather hyacinth, has fringed, pale-purple flowers about 6 inches tall. *M. latifolium* has 10-inch-tall spikes; the flowers shade from a grape-hyacinth blue in the top third to a deep purple or blue on the bottom two-thirds. These tend to bloom a little later, in April or May.

Hyacinth

Hyacinthus orientalis

Other Names: Dutch Hyacinth, Common Hyacinth **Zones:** 5, 6 **Height:** 6 to 12 inches **Bloom Period:** Spring **Flowers:** Various **Type:** Hardy	**Light Requirement:**

*E*veryone should have a cluster of Dutch hyacinths somewhere in the landscape—if only to provide cut flowers that will perfume a room. Hyacinths are easy to grow, and they will produce large, tightly packed flowers the first year. In subsequent seasons, they will produce looser, more airy blossoms. Hyacinths sometimes seem a bit stiff and formal; they do well mixed with plants that soften their shape. They work particularly well with groundcovers like *Vinca minor* and *Pachysandra*; these plants help hide hyacinth's foliage, which must ripen before you can remove it. Plant hyacinths where they can be seen; choose a spot you pass every day, such as on the way to the garage or mailbox. Planting them in large clusters or drifts intensifies their fragrance. These fat bulbs can also be potted in a container and forced to bloom indoors.

WHEN TO PLANT
Plant hyacinth bulbs as early as possible in the fall, or up until about a month before the ground freezes.

WHERE TO PLANT
Hyacinths do best in full sun, but will tolerate light shade. Choose a moist, well-drained spot, and amend the soil with organic material.

HOW TO PLANT
Plant hyacinth bulbs about 6 inches deep and 6 to 8 inches apart. Instead of digging several small holes, dig one larger hole and place hyacinths, tulips, and daffodils several inches apart in the bottom. Be sure to plant the bulbs with the pointed ends turned up. Cover,

water well, and mulch with shredded bark or a thick layer of chopped leaves. Winter cycles of freezing and thawing may push newly planted bulbs out of the soil.

ADVICE FOR CARE

Apply an all-purpose granular fertilizer after the blooms fade in the spring, and until the leaves die back. Spread a thin layer of compost around and over the clump. You can help the bulb replenish itself for next year's growth by removing the hyacinth flower after it fades, but before seeds are formed. Don't remove the foliage until it turns yellow or brown.

ADDITIONAL INFORMATION

Hyacinths are not as long-lived as other bulbs, especially daffodils. If you fertilize them correctly, you will increase their chances of lasting several years in the garden. Cut the blooms to fill a room with a truly heady fragrance.

ADDITIONAL SPECIES, CULTIVARS, OR VARIETIES

Grape hyacinths (*Muscari*) are a different species and are covered elsewhere in this chapter. Some Dutch hyacinths to consider: 'Delft Blue'; 'Ostara', violet-blue; 'Blue Jacket', blue and purple; 'City of Haarlem', yellow; 'Anna Marie', light pink; and 'Carnegie', white. Roman hyacinths (*Hyacinthus orientalis*) are hardy to Zone 6. *Camassia leichtlinii* is called Indian hyacinth; in late spring, it has starlike flowers on stalks up to 3 feet tall. *C. l.* 'Alba' is white. *Endymion hispanicus*, *Scilla hispanicus*, or *S. campanulata* are known as wood hyacinths or Spanish bluebells. *Scilla non-scriptus*, *S. nutans*, or *Endymion non-scriptus* are known as English bluebells. Both types are hardy to Zone 4, and they are much better for naturalizing than the Dutch hyacinths. In the fall, plant bluebell bulbs about 3 inches deep. The 12-inch-tall plants have strap-like leaves and loose, funnel- or bell-shaped flowers from mid- to late spring. The bluebells develop clumps, which you can dig and divide in the fall. Because the foliage will have ripened and gone, mark the location of the clumps in the spring.

Lily

Lilium hybrids

Zones: 5, 6
Height: 18 to 48 inches
Bloom Period: Summer
Flowers: Various
Type: Hardy

Light Requirement:

*L*ilies are exquisite plants. They produce lovely flowers, and many are intoxicatingly fragrant. Lilies are classified in six categories, depending on the shape of their flowers: trumpet, chalice, pendant, reflexed, bowl, and sunburst. They are also sorted into ten divisions, including Oriental, Asiatic, Candidum, American, and Longiflorum hybrids. Improved hybrids of Oriental and Asiatic lilies have made growing them easier than ever, although they can still be a bit fussy about their location. Asiatic lilies (such as 'Turk's Cap', 'Connecticut King', and 'Enchantment') bloom in early summer. Orientals (such as 'Star Gazer', 'Casa Blanca', and 'Mona Lisa') bloom later and are the most fragrant.

WHEN TO PLANT

Plant lilies in the spring or fall. You can also divide bulbs in the spring or fall.

WHERE TO PLANT

Plant lilies in a well-prepared bed that has been amended with compost or other organic material. Lilies prefer full sun or partial shade. Pick a spot where the lily bulbs will not compete with other perennials or with shrubs or plants. Because lilies bloom at the top of the plant, consider placing lower-growing herbaceous perennials or small shrubs at the base. Many lilies prefer to have hot heads and cool feet.

HOW TO PLANT

Plant lily bulbs 6 to 8 inches deep. Lilies don't really become dormant, so don't let the bulbs dry out. Try not to bruise or break any of the scales, or layers, that form on the outside of the bulb. Plant the bulbs with the pointed sides turned up. Cover, water well, and mulch lightly. Tall varieties frequently need to be staked.

ADVICE FOR CARE

Apply an all-purpose granular fertilizer in the spring or early summer, when the new growth breaks ground—or spread a layer of compost around the plants. Lilies look like little crowns of pointed leaves when they break ground. Too much fertilizer may weaken the stems. Apply either an all-purpose, water-soluble fertilizer or fish emulsion regularly after the blooms fade and until the foliage dies back. When you are cutting lilies, allow some of the stalk to remain on the plant; this will nourish the bulb for next year's growth. Remove the stem when it turns brown or yellow, or at the end of the growing season—whichever comes first.

ADDITIONAL INFORMATION

Lilies shouldn't have to compete with the deep roots of other plants, so don't plant them too close to large plants. It is helpful to mark where you plant them so you remember where they are. Lilies also benefit from a good mulching to get them through the winter. Remove mulch in the spring when new growth appears.

ADDITIONAL SPECIES, CULTIVARS, OR VARIETIES

Species native to North America include *Lilium canadense*, which blooms in the summer and has red or yellow flowers on 5-foot-tall stalks; *Lilium philadelphicum*, or wood lily, which grows about 3 feet tall and has orange flowers; and *Lilium superbum*, or native Turk's cap, which grows approximately 10 feet tall. *Lilium speciosum*, or Japanese lily called 'Rubrum', is frequently found in floral arrangements. The lilies sold at Easter are *Lilium longiflorum*; they may not be winter hardy in Indiana.

Scilla

Scilla siberica

Other Names: Squill, Siberian Squill,
  Bluebells
Zones: 5, 6
Height: 6 to 10 inches
Bloom Period: Late winter and early spring
Flowers: Blue, white, pink
Type: Hardy

Light Requirement:

This is probably one of the best spring-flowering bulbs to natu-ralize in the lawn. The bell-shaped flowers hang from stems, and they create a sea of blue, white, or pink against the grassy green of the lawn. The bulbs' ripening foliage is easily camouflaged by the lawn well before it needs its first cutting. Both scilla and snowdrops (*Galanthus nivalis*) bloom in February, creating an attractive show. *Scilla siberica* 'Spring Beauty' readily self-sows, but the plants are unobtrusive and have no nuisance qualities; you can leave them to grow where they land. For the fastest show, plant scilla in large masses. The flowers may be cut for sweet little arrangements indoors.

WHEN TO PLANT

Plant scilla bulbs as early as possible in the fall, but before the ground freezes.

WHERE TO PLANT

Scilla prefers full sun or partial shade, but avoid hot, dry places. It looks great under both deciduous and evergreen trees and shrubs.

HOW TO PLANT

Plant bulbs 2 to 3 inches deep in well-drained soil that has been amended with compost or other organic material. To make planting easier, there are special augers that you can attach to an electric drill. Funnel-shaped bulb planters work best in well-prepared beds where the soil is easy to dig. If you are trying to naturalize the lawn, con-sider cutting and lifting sections of sod, planting the bulbs, and covering the bulbs by replacing the sod. Keep the bulbs well watered as winter approaches. Mulching isn't necessary.

ADVICE FOR CARE

Apply an all-purpose granular fertilizer or a thin layer of compost around the plants in late winter or early spring, when new growth breaks ground. You *must* leave the foliage on the plant until it turns yellow or brown. The foliage is unobtrusive, and scilla blooms so early that the foliage is usually camouflaged by other plants as they begin to grow.

ADDITIONAL INFORMATION

Do not confuse *Scilla siberica* with *Scilla hispanicus (Endymion hispanicus)*, which is known as wood hyacinth or Spanish bluebell or with *Scilla non-scriptus (Endymion non-scriptus)*, which is known as English bluebell. These are excellent plants for naturalizing and are discussed in this chapter's section on hyacinths.

ADDITIONAL SPECIES, CULTIVARS, OR VARIETIES

Scilla siberica 'Alba' has white flowers. *S. bifolia* has 6-inch stalks of blue, starlike flowers. *S. tubergeniana* has several 4-inch spikes of light-blue flowers with dark-blue stripes. *Puschkinia libanotca (P. scilloides)*, sometimes called striped squill, has clusters of fragrant, pale-blue or almost-white flowers; 'Alba' is a white variety.

Snowdrop

Galanthus nivalis

Zones: 5, 6 **Height:** 4 to 6 inches **Bloom Period:** Late winter/early spring **Flowers:** Blue, white **Type:** Hardy	**Light Requirement:**

nowdrops bloom while there is still snow on the ground—hence their name. These bulbs may be small, but with their long-lasting, white, bell-shaped flowers, they produce a lovely show in late winter and early spring. If you plant them in a sunny spot, they may bloom in early February; in a shadier spot, they will bloom later. Snowdrops mix well with the groundcover *Vinca minor*; the early flowering, blue *Iris reticulata*; and yellow winter aconite *Eranthis hiemalis*.

WHEN TO PLANT
Plant bulbs as soon as possible in the fall, but before the ground freezes.

WHERE TO PLANT
Snowdrops will grow almost anywhere, so cluster them where you can see them—or where their white flowers can brighten up a distant spot. They naturalize nicely under both deciduous and evergreen trees and shrubs.

HOW TO PLANT
Snowdrops are most attractive if you plant them in large clusters or drifts. Instead of digging dozens of small holes, dig larger ones and cluster the bulbs. Plant the bulbs about 3 inches deep and 2 inches apart. Cover and water well. Mulching is not necessary.

ADVICE FOR CARE
Apply an all-purpose granular fertilizer in late winter or early

spring, when new growth breaks ground, or spread a layer of compost in the area. Leave the foliage on the plant until it turns yellow or brown; it is usually unobtrusive and goes away quickly.

ADDITIONAL INFORMATION

Because snowdrops bloom so early in the season, mark them so that you don't lose track of them when you are digging in the beds for other plantings.

ADDITIONAL SPECIES, CULTIVARS, OR VARIETIES

Galanthus nivalis 'Flore Pleno' blooms very early in the spring; it is a 4-inch-tall double white. *G. nivalis* 'Viridapicis' has green-edged outer petals. *G. elwesii* has larger flowers, with stems that reach 8 inches.

Surprise Lily

Lycoris squamigera

Other Names: Magic Lily, Resurrection Lily, Naked Lady **Zones:** 5, 6 **Height:** 18 to 30 inches **Bloom Period:** August **Flowers:** Pink **Type:** Hardy	**Light Requirement:**

These lovely plants, native to Asia, are named for Lycoris, a Roman actress who reportedly had an affair with Marc Antony. They send up their strap-like leaves early in the growing season, then the leaves disappear. Several weeks later, as if by magic, lovely, fragrant, lilac-pink, trumpet-like flowers rise from the ground. Lycoris develops clumps with several stalks; one stalk can have several flowers. Even though lily is part of the common name, lycoris is really part of the amaryllis family; only *L. squamigera* is winter hardy in Indiana. Plant surprise lilies among groundcovers, in the middle of the flower bed, between shrubs, or mixed with daylilies.

WHEN TO PLANT
Plant in early spring or in the fall.

WHERE TO PLANT
Plant in full sun or light shade. Choose a well-drained spot.

HOW TO PLANT
Plant bulbs so that their tops are approximately 6 inches below the soil surface. Place them about 6 inches apart in clusters. Cover, water well, and mulch lightly if you wish.

ADVICE FOR CARE
Allow the foliage to die back naturally, and remove it when it turns yellow or brown. Apply an all-purpose granular fertilizer in

early spring, when the foliage breaks ground, or add a light layer of compost.

ADDITIONAL INFORMATION

These are delightful plants at a time when there are few flowers blooming in the landscape. They naturalize nicely, too. Their foliage is sometimes confused with daffodil leaves which begin their growth at the same time.

ADDITIONAL SPECIES, CULTIVARS, OR VARIETIES

Lycoris radiata is known as red spider lily. It is not winter hardy in Indiana, but plant it about 6 inches deep in the spring if you want summer flowers. The flowers resemble pink, red, or white spiders; they hover over narrow leaves on 15-inch stalks. *L. albilora* is a white spider lily, and *L. africana* is gold.

Tuberous Begonia

Begonia × tuberhybrida

Other Name: Begonia **Zones:** 5, 6 **Height:** 12 to 24 inches **Bloom Period:** Summer **Flowers:** Various **Type:** Tender	**Light Requirement:** 

*T*uberous begonias are wonderful plants in a semi-shady border or in hanging baskets, where they bloom from early summer until frost. They work best in windowboxes, containers, and in the front of the flower border. Their camellia-like flowers mix well with annuals, such as impatiens, asparagus ferns, or ivy-leaf geraniums. They also mix well with perennials, including hostas and ferns. They make lovely cut flowers.

WHEN TO PLANT

If you buy begonias from a garden center, plant container-grown transplants in the spring, when all threat of frost has passed. If you are growing them from tubers, plant in containers indoors in February or March.

WHERE TO PLANT

Begonias do best in a moist, semi-shady, well-drained spot where the soil is rich in organic material. They will not flower if it is too shady or hot, and the leaves will burn in hot sun.

HOW TO PLANT

Don't plant begonias any deeper than the transplants were growing in their containers. Begonias have two sides; flowers and foliage are directed toward the front. If you are planting tubers, set them on top of 2 or 3 inches of moistened, soilless mix in early spring. Cover them lightly with the potting mix, and place them in a warm, brightly lit area. Water when the soil gets dry. Once new growth appears, fertilize with fish emulsion or other water-soluble, all-purpose fertilizer. Transplant to flower beds, windowboxes, or hanging baskets when the shoots are 4 to 6 inches tall.

ADVICE FOR CARE

Tuberous begonias have fragile stems and leaves. You can frequently root broken stems or leaves to make new plants. Sometimes the flowers drop just as they are about to open, but there is little that you can do about this. Fertilize regularly throughout the growing season. Soil that is too moist will cause the plants to rot. To winter over the tubers, trim foliage to a height of 8 to 10 inches before the first frost. Dig the tubers, and store them in a dry, frost-free area until the foliage dries. Once the foliage is dry, remove it. Store the tubers in paper bags, or in a box of dry peat moss or cedar shavings; be sure they are in a dry place that is cool but safe from freezing. Inspect the tubers periodically and throw out any that get soft.

ADDITIONAL INFORMATION

Taller varieties may need to be supported with stakes or hoops. Tuberous begonias are a bit on the fussy side; under the right conditions, however, they offer weeks of jewel-like blossoms that are hard to beat. You may divide them by cutting the tubers into pieces; be sure that each cutting has at least one "eye," or growth point. You may also propagate tuberous begonias from stem cuttings; root them in sand or soilless potting mixture.

ADDITIONAL SPECIES, CULTIVARS, OR VARIETIES

'Non-Stop' varieties are hybrids of *B. tuberhybrida* and *B. multiflora* that do indeed bloom "non-stop" from spring to frost. *B. tuberhybrida* has flowers that may be as large as 10 inches wide and 24 inches tall. *B. multiflora* is shorter and bushier, with smaller flowers. *B. pendula* is a trailing-type begonia. Do not confuse these with *Begonia semperflorens cultorum*, which is sometimes called a wax-leaf or fibrous-root begonia; this plant is discussed in the Annuals chapter. *B. tuberhybrida*, *B. multiflora*, and *B. pendula* may have ruffled flowers, singles, doubles, or picotee (where a contrasting color edges the petals). They come in almost every color except blue. *Begonia grandis* is a hardy perennial that blooms in late summer in Zones 5 and 6.

BULBS

Tulip

Tulipa spp. and hybrids

Zones: 5, 6
Height: 4 to 30 inches
Bloom Period: Early to late spring
Flowers: Various
Type: Hardy

Light Requirement:

Tulips are like dots of color on a stick—only dahlias come in more colors. Tulips can have single, double, frilly, fringed, lily-, parrot-, or starlike flowers. Many are fragrant. Tulips are classified and sold as hardy bulbs, but they are short-lived in most Indiana landscapes. Hoosier summers are too warm for them to retain their vigor and most of the soil is too heavy and compacted. Even in Holland, the tulip capitol of the world, the bulbs are dug in the spring, summered over in a controlled environment, and planted again in the fall. After their first flowering, tulips seem to decline about thirty-three to fifty percent each year. They will produce fewer flowers in the second year than they did in the first; fewer flowers in the third year than they did in the second; and so on. To compound the problem, tulip foliage seems to thrive, returning year after year—but without the floral rewards.

WHEN TO PLANT
Plant bulbs in the fall, until the ground freezes.

WHERE TO PLANT
Tulips prefer sunny, well-drained, loamy soil. They also bloom in partial shade, such as under trees before they leaf out.

HOW TO PLANT
Plant tulip bulbs in a hole that is approximately 3 times deeper than the bulb is in circumference; for example, a 2-inch bulb should be planted 6 inches deep. Some gardeners believe that tulips are longer-lived when they are planted rather deeply. Consider digging large holes and placing tulips and daffodils about 4 inches apart in a suitable arrangement. Cover and water well. Mulch lightly with shredded bark, compost, or chopped leaves, if you wish.

ADVICE FOR CARE

Apply an all-purpose granular fertilizer when the flowers fade and until the foliage dies back. Spread a layer of compost in the bed in the spring and fall. You *must* leave the foliage on the plant until it turns yellow or brown; this can take quite a while. Avoid planting tulips where the soil stays wet.

ADDITIONAL INFORMATION

Plan on replanting most garden tulips every 2 or 3 years. Early-flowering tulips or species tulips, on the other hand, are much longer-lived; they return year after year with little effort on the part of the gardener. Tulips are susceptible to botrytis, a fungal disease that lives in the soil. It causes the tulip leaves to streak red and the flowers to wither before opening. There is no way to control this disease so it is best to pull out all of the plants and destroy them.

ADDITIONAL SPECIES, CULTIVARS, OR VARIETIES

Tulipa greigii, T. kaufmanniana, T. tarda, T. praestans, and *T. fosteriana* are good selections for early-flowering tulips. Darwin hybrid tulips are mid-season bloomers; 'Apeldoorn' varieties, which produce a number of colors, are included in this group. Mid-season tulips last for quite a while in the garden; many range between 20 and 30 inches tall. Darwin tulips, which are different from Darwin hybrids, are late bloomers. One example is 'Black Diamond', which has a striking dark-purple flower. *T. viridiflora* 'Greenland' also has staying power in the landscape; it has pale- to medium-pink petals with a green stripe. The flower grows about 30 inches tall and is fragrant. 'Angelique' is another late bloomer; it has a pink, peony-like flower.

CHAPTER THREE

Groundcovers

WHETHER YOU CHOOSE A CREEPING VINE, low-growing shrub, or solid stand of perennials, groundcovers add definition, color, and texture to the landscape. They moderate soil temperature and moisture, reduce weeds, and provide shelter and food for birds and wildlife. Some of them form carpets of flowers, making them even more valuable. They unify the landscape—coordinating trees, shrubs, and the borders of perennial beds.

The groundcovers in this chapter are readily available and easy to grow. While good for starters, they are the first on a list limited only by a gardener's imagination. You should consider several factors when you choose groundcovers, including the look you want and the amount of time you have to maintain the plants. Ivies, vines, clump-growers, and ground-hugging shrubs are the most common types. Some scamper across the soil, sending down roots; others form underground runners that send up shoots for above-ground growth.

There are deciduous groundcovers, which drop their leaves in winter—and evergreen groundcovers, which do not. There are also semievergreen groundcovers, which—depending on the weather—may retain their leaves in winter. Daylilies (*Hemerocallis*) can be used as a groundcover, and so can clematis (*Clematis*), thyme (*Thymus*), shrub roses (*Rosa rugosa*), and climbing hydrangea (*Hydrangea anomala petiolaris*). These are discussed elsewhere in this book.

A perfect place for groundcovers is where grass won't grow, such as the shady, root-bound, nutrient-competitive areas under trees and shrubs. Groundcovers do well on difficult-to-mow hills or slopes, where they also prevent soil erosion.

PLANTING GROUNDCOVERS

The best way to ensure success is to plant groundcovers in a well-prepared bed. Dig the soil to a depth of at least twelve inches; break

Chapter Three

up clumps and remove rocks, roots, and other debris. Smooth out the bed. Add a slow-release nitrogen fertilizer and organic material (such as peat moss, compost, composted cow manure, humus, or chopped-up leaves) to the top two to three inches of soil, and smooth out again. In most cases, groundcover transplants should be planted no deeper than they are growing in plastic packs or peat pots. If the transplant is in a peat pot, break off any part of the container that shows above the soil line; then plant the groundcover, pot and all. If it is in a plastic pack, remove the transplant from the cell before planting. Try not to disturb the rootball. Backfill with the soil removed from the hole.

If you are planting bare-rooted plants, such as those that come from many mail-order companies, soak the roots in water overnight before transplanting. Prepare the soil in the same manner as described above. Form small mounds of soil in the center of the planting hole to get the right height. Gently spread the roots over the top of the mound and backfill the hole.

Digging deeply to prepare beds is not always possible, especially under well-rooted trees and shrubs. Dig as deeply as possible, even if it is only a couple of inches. Don't worry about disturbing or breaking some of a tree's or shrub's surface roots in the process. Add a two-inch layer of topsoil (mixed with organic material) to the area. This amount of soil will not smother the roots of established trees and shrubs. However, it is not advised to add more than two inches as the roots may suffocate. Plant groundcover, bulbs, or other plants. Instead of planting in rows, consider staggering the plants by placing them in triangles with equal spacing between, for a better, more uniform look.

Bugleweed

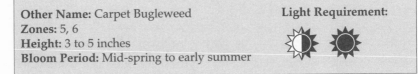

Ajuga reptans

Other Name: Carpet Bugleweed	**Light Requirement:**
Zones: 5, 6	
Height: 3 to 5 inches	
Bloom Period: Mid-spring to early summer	

*C*arpet bugleweed is a good moniker for this flowering ground-cover. It spreads fairly quickly by stolons, or runners, which can be quite aggressive, escaping into lawns or flower beds. When tamed, however, *Ajuga* is a lovely groundcover that forms a dense mat at the soil surface. It retains its colorful, textured leaves well into freezing weather, providing three seasons of interest in the landscape. In late April, May, and early June, *Ajuga* sprouts spikes of flowers to form a striking drift of color, usually blue. *Ajuga* can be used as a cut flower in vases with other spring blossoms.

WHEN TO PLANT
Container-grown plants may be planted spring through fall. Keep newly transplanted material well watered.

WHERE TO PLANT
Ajuga prefers a semi-shady spot with well-drained, moist soil enriched with organic matter. Too much moisture can cause the plant to rot at the crown or roots; too little, however, can cause the plant to dry out. Too much sun can burn the plant. If it is too shady, the plant will be smaller and less vigorous; flowering may also be diminished.

HOW TO PLANT
Space 8 to 10 inches apart. Water well. Always make sure newly planted material receives an inch of rain or water every 7 to 10 days. Water *Ajuga* during dry spells. Mulch to help retain moisture.

ADVICE FOR CARE
Use a balanced slow-release fertilizer in early spring and summer. Cut off dead flowers or mow the groundcover, using the highest

setting on the lawn mower. Plants may also be trimmed back and tidied up for a better appearance.

ADDITIONAL INFORMATION

Ajuga is grown for its foliage as well as its flowers. Depending on the variety, the leaves range from green to bronze-purple to a variegated green-and-cream. The leaves and flowers complement spring-flowering bulbs that can grow through the groundcover, including daffodils and tulips. *Ajuga* looks good, too, under spring-flowering trees and shrubs, including viburnum, dogwood, and redbud. *Ajuga*'s small, scalloped leaves make a nice contrast to hostas and iris. *Ajuga* is not recommended for areas adjacent to lawns or flower beds because it is invasive—but it is an excellent plant where it can be contained by sidewalks or other permanent borders.

ADDITIONAL SPECIES, CULTIVARS, OR VARIETIES

A. reptans 'Purpurea' has dark-bronze leaves. 'Variegata' has green leaves edged in creamy yellow. 'Burgundy Lace' has wine-colored leaves with white and pink variations; 'Alba' has dark green leaves and white flower spikes.

English Ivy

Hedera helix

Other Name: Ivy
Zones: 5, 6
Height: 6 to 8 inches
Bloom Period: Insignificant flowers
    in September

Light Requirement:

*E*nglish ivy is a woody, evergreen vine that can reach a length of fifty feet or more. It spreads quickly once established, setting down shallow roots as it creeps along the ground or up a house or tree. As *Hedera* establishes itself, the roots get more woody and can reach a depth of three feet. Leaves are dark green, glossy, and veined. Young leaves have three points; mature leaves have one. English ivy can be invasive, so it needs to be trimmed back regularly—otherwise, it is a very low-maintenance plant.

WHEN TO PLANT

Container-grown plants can be planted any time during the growing season. Cuttings with at least three aerial roots may be taken any time during the growing season, rooted in a growing medium (such as peat moss, vermiculite, or soilless potting mix), and transplanted later. The cuttings will also root quickly when planted directly in loamy, moist soil.

WHERE TO PLANT

English ivy can be planted in sun or dense shade; remember, how-ever, that the leaves can be burned by the winter sun and winds. It can be planted under trees and shrubs, around the foundation of a home, or on hills or banks. Allowing the ivy to climb houses or other structures is usually not recommended; the aerial roots dam-age wood, brick, stone, stucco, and other materials, causing them to leak or crumble.

HOW TO PLANT

For best results, the soil should be prepared and amended with organic material. If the ivy is in a peat pot, break off any part of the pot that shows above the soil line; then plant the ivy, pot and all. If the transplant is in a plastic pack, remove it from the plastic; try not to disturb the rootball. Don't plant it any deeper than it was already growing in the cell-pack. Plants spaced about 12 to 18 inches apart should fill in and form a solid mass in about two years. Water deeply and mulch lightly to retain moisture. Always make sure newly planted material receives an inch of rain or water every 7 to 10 days. Mulch should not be required once plants are established.

ADVICE FOR CARE

English ivy needs to be trimmed 2 to 3 times a year to keep it within its boundaries. It can be sheared with hedge trimmers to keep it neat and tidy, to thicken growth, and to remove leaves from winter or summer kill. English ivy may be affected by fungus, especially leaf spot and canker.

ADDITIONAL INFORMATION

Apply a slow-release high-nitrogen or all-purpose granular fertilizer in early spring as new growth appears. You can also spread or sprinkle a thin layer of compost over the ivy bed in early spring and late fall.

ADDITIONAL SPECIES, CULTIVARS, OR VARIETIES

'Thorndale' and 'Baltica' are more resistant to cold weather and are readily available in Indiana. These varieties are recommended in more exposed planting sites.

Epimedium

Epimedium grandiflorum

Other Names: Barrenwort, Bishop's Hat
Zones: 5, 6
Height: 8 to 12 inches
Flowers: Various
Bloom Period: April, early May

Light Requirement:

Epimedium may be slow to take hold, but it is well worth the wait. It holds its own against roots and shade, which makes it an excellent choice to plant in small masses at the base of trees and shrubs. Its flowers and heart-shaped, leathery, dark-green leaves have wiry stems. The tiny, waxy flowers have spurs and resemble columbine; they can be used as cut flowers. Depending on the variety, *Epimedium* flowers come in several colors. They usually bloom from early to mid-April into early May.

WHEN TO PLANT

Plant container-grown plants in spring and early fall.

WHERE TO PLANT

Epimedium is a woodland plant, so it does best in a shady or partially shady spot with rich, organic, moist soil. It will also do well in the dry, competitive zone under trees, however. The better the soil, the faster it will grow.

HOW TO PLANT

Space plants about 12 inches apart. Don't plant them any deeper than they were growing in the containers.

ADVICE FOR CARE

Clumps may be divided in early spring, as soon as the soil can be worked and new growth appears on the plants. Make sure newly planted material receives an inch of rain or water every 7 to 10 days. *Epimedium* may also need extra moisture until it gets established—especially if it is planted at the base of trees and shrubs, where there is a lot of competition for moisture and nutrients. Sprinkle an all-purpose fertilizer in early spring when new growth appears. Mulch to help retain moisture.

ADDITIONAL INFORMATION

Epimedium is usually pest- and disease-free. Depending on the variety, its foliage changes color in fall, making it interesting even as it dies back. The foliage may be left on through the winter, but for the best show, cut it back in late winter or early spring before new growth begins.

ADDITIONAL SPECIES, CULTIVARS, OR VARIETIES

Epimedium grandiflorum is the most common species. It has rose, lavender, or white flowers. 'Rose Queen' and 'White Queen' are recommended named cultivars. *E. pinnatum* grows about 15 inches tall; it has red and yellow flowers. *E. rubrum* grows about 12 inches tall; its leaves have red edges and veins, and its flowers are yellow, red, or white.

Juniper

Juniperus horizontalis, J. chinensis or *J. procumbens*

Other Names: Rug Juniper or
    Creeping Juniper
Zones: 5, 6
Height: 8 inches to 3 feet
Bloom Period: Evergreen

Light Requirement:

*R*ug and creeping junipers and other low-growing *Juniperus* are very adaptable and versatile in the landscape, providing year-round color, texture, and structure. Low-growing junipers form a rug, or carpet, of greens or blues that makes an excellent groundcover for other shrubs. In the winter landscape, juniper's colors and textures complement or show off the bark on many trees and shrubs. Usually the mats are so dense that other plants won't grow through them, which makes juniper an excellent weed barrier.

WHEN TO PLANT

Plant container-grown transplants any time the soil can be worked. Balled-and-burlapped specimens should be planted in spring or fall.

WHERE TO PLANT

Junipers are not picky about their location, as long as they have plenty of sun and good drainage. Spots that are too wet may cause root rot and kill the plant. They tolerate hot spots with clay, sandy, or dry soil, as long as they are watered regularly.

HOW TO PLANT

Transplant balled-and-burlapped or container-grown specimens of juniper by preparing a planting hole that is up to 4 times the width of the pot or rootball. Dig deep enough so that the top of the rootball is level with the ground around it. Remove any twine or wire that is wrapped around the trunk of the shrub and cut away the burlap or wire basket to half the height of the rootball. For container-grown juniper, gently tap the sides of the pot on a hard surface to loosen the rootball. Carefully remove the plant from the container and tease out any roots that appear to be growing in a circular pattern. Finally, backfill the hole with the original soil and water deeply. Spread a 2- to 3-inch layer of organic mulch over the entire planting area.

ADVICE FOR CARE

Junipers are very low-maintenance plants. They rarely need to be pruned, except for an errant branch now and then. Mulch new and mature plantings to retain moisture. Gently scratch the soil with an all-purpose granular fertilizer in early spring, or apply a thin layer of compost around the plant in spring and fall. Junipers may be affected by a moth-carried blight, called *Phomopsis juniperovora*, which attacks the tips of branches; cedar-apple rust; or bagworms. Pick off bagworms or spray with *Bacillus thuringiensis* v. *kurstaki* in early spring. Cut off tips affected with blight and remove the galls of cedar apple rust.

ADDITIONAL INFORMATION

Container-grown juniper planted in heavy clay often suffer from the "bathtub" effect. This essentially drowns the roots because the planting hole will not drain well. In heavy clay, be sure to provide ample drainage or plant juniper 2 inches higher than the ground around it.

ADDITIONAL SPECIES, CULTIVARS, OR VARIETIES

There are several popular *J. horizontalis* varieties. 'Blue Mat' is a 6-inch-tall, dense, slow grower with blue-green foliage that becomes purple-green in winter. 'Bar Harbor' is a 1-foot-tall variety, with a spread of up to 8 feet, and blue-green foliage that turns purple in winter. 'Emerald Spreader', a 7-inch-tall spreader, has a more feathery appearance and a mound in its center. 'Wiltoni' ('Wiltonii'), or 'Blue Rug', which is 4 to 6 inches tall with a 6-foot spread, bears silvery blue cones. *J. procumbens* varieties include 'Greenmound', 8 inches tall with an 8-foot spread, a mounded center, and light-green foliage; and 'Nana', up to 2^1/$_2$ feet tall with a 12-foot spread, and blue-green foliage that turns purple in winter. *J. chinensis* varieties include 'Kallays Compacta', a flat-top grower that gets up to 3 feet tall with a 6-foot spread; and 'Glauca', about 18 inches tall with a 6-foot spread.

$\mathscr{L}amium$

Lamium maculatum

Other Names: Dead Nettle or
   Spotted Dead Nettle
Zones: 5, 6
Height: 6 to 8 inches
Bloom Period: Spring and early summer

Light Requirement:

$\mathscr{L}amium$ is referred to as dead nettle because it does not sting like its wild nettle cousin. It adds brightness to low-light spots because its leaves are variegated or splotched with white. Depending on the cultivar, *Lamium's* long-lasting flowers are white, pink, or purple. Leaves may persist into early winter in more northern areas, but they die back eventually; *Lamium* is an evergreen in Zone 6. Some gardeners consider *Lamium* weedy or aggressive because it spreads rapidly by above-ground runners, but it is easily controlled. It doesn't do well when there is a lot of root competition. With a bit of trimming here and there, *Lamium* forms a colorful carpet under hostas, pulmonaria, and spring-flowering bulbs.

WHEN TO PLANT
Plant container-grown transplants any time, but they do best in spring, late summer, or early fall. Divisions may be made in spring.

WHERE TO PLANT
A shady, well-drained, moist spot is best for *Lamium*. If you plant it in full sun, be sure to water it regularly.

HOW TO PLANT
Plant 10 to 12 inches apart. Plant transplants only as deep as they were growing in their pots. Water them well. Always make sure newly planted material receives an inch of rain or water every 7 to 10 days. Mulch them lightly. Mulching usually won't be necessary after plants are established.

ADVICE FOR CARE

Apply an all-purpose fertilizer in early spring when new growth appears—or spread a thin layer of compost in spring or fall. Water, especially in hot periods, if it is planted in a dry area, such as under the eaves of a house.

ADDITIONAL INFORMATION

Shear it back after it flowers—or in the summer if it gets too leggy or thin. *Lamium* will thicken up and form a dense mat.

ADDITIONAL SPECIES, CULTIVARS, AND VARIETIES

'Album' has white flowers and green leaves marked with white. 'Beacon Silver' has silver leaves and pink flowers. 'White Nancy' has white blooms. 'Chequers' has marbled leaves and pink flowers. 'Variegatum' has a silver strip on green leaves. *Lamiastrum galeobdolon*, or yellow archangel, is sometimes confused with *Lamium maculatum*. This is a much taller and more invasive plant; it is not recommended, except in controlled areas.

Lily Turf

Liriope spicata, Liriope muscari

Other Name: Liriope
Zones: 5, 6
Height: 8 to 10 inches
Bloom Period: Late summer

Light Requirement:

Liriope spicata has one-fourth-inch to one-half-inch-wide, strap-like, evergreen leaves that resemble grass. It is sometimes called Creeping Lily turf, reflecting its tendency to spread rapidly by underground rhizomes; some gardeners consider it invasive. *Liriope muscari* is not considered invasive. Sometimes called big blue lily turf, it grows in clumps with one-half-inch to three-fourths-inch-wide, two-foot-long arched, evergreen leaves. Both mix well with spring- and fall-flowering bulbs. They bloom in late summer through early fall. *L. muscari* has purple-violet flowers that resemble grape hyacinths; *L. spicata* has pale purple, lavender, or nearly white flowers. The latter is considered less showy. Both tolerate poor soil and dry conditions.

WHEN TO PLANT

Transplant container-grown plants in spring or fall. Plants may be divided in spring and fall.

WHERE TO PLANT

Lily turf does well in the dry, competitive, shady places under trees and shrubs. The clump variety can take more sun, making it useful in the front border of a perennial bed.

HOW TO PLANT

Plant transplants at the same depth they were growing before purchase. Water them well. Always make sure newly planted material receives an inch of rain or water every 7 to 10 days. Mulch them lightly to help retain moisture. Once established, mulching probably won't be necessary.

ADVICE FOR CARE
Lily turf does best when watered periodically, especially through dry spells, though it will tolerate hot, dry settings. For the best-looking plants, shear them off in late winter or early spring. This encourages new growth and gets rid of leaves killed by winter winds.

ADDITIONAL INFORMATION
Don't confuse lily turf with mondo grass, *Ophiopogon*, which looks similar, but is not hardy here.

ADDITIONAL SPECIES, CULTIVARS, AND VARIETIES
L. muscari varieties to consider are 'Big Blue', about 12 inches tall with green foliage and dark violet flowers in July and August; 'Majestic', slightly shorter with green leaves and violet flowers; and 'Variegata', which is hardy in Zone 6, and has yellow-striped, green leaves and lilac flowers in early to midsummer. 'Silver Dragon' is a common variety of *L. spicata* in Indiana. It has white and green variegated leaves, and is hardy in Zone 6.

Pachysandra

Pachysandra terminalis

Other Name: Japanese Spurge
Zones: 5, 6
Height: 8 to 10 inches
Bloom Period: Spring

Light Requirement:

*L*ike its counterparts English ivy and myrtle, *Pachysandra* is an excellent choice for shady areas that are difficult to mow. Of the three, *Pachysandra* takes the longest to get established—but once it does, it forms a delightful, noninvasive evergreen mat. It is compatible with spring-flowering bulbs and shade-loving perennials such as hostas, ferns, and pulmonaria. *Pachysandra* has dark-green, glossy leaves with scalloped or jagged edges. In the spring, it sports white, slightly fragrant, fuzzy flowers that last for several weeks.

WHEN TO PLANT

Plant container-grown transplants at any time. Transplants from division may be made in spring or early fall.

WHERE TO PLANT

Pachysandra does well under trees and shrubs, or in other shady areas. Full sun is not recommended because it can burn or yellow the leaves and slow the groundcover's growth. If you plant it in full sun, you must keep *Pachysandra* watered. Soil should be moist but well drained with plenty of organic matter.

HOW TO PLANT

The closer together *Pachysandra* is planted, the faster the slow-growing plant will fill in. If transplants are in peat pots, remove the part of the pot that is above the soil line. Remove plants from plastic packs, being sure not to disturb the rootballs. Plant *Pachysandra* slightly deeper than it has been growing. Water them well. Always make sure newly planted material receives an inch of rain or water every 7 to 10 days. A light mulch will keep new transplants moist and weeds down. Once the plants are established, mulching should not be necessary.

ADDITIONAL INFORMATION

Pinch or cut off leaves that have been damaged by winter. Apply an all-purpose fertilizer in early spring as new growth appears, or add a thin layer of compost in spring and fall. *Pachysandra* may get leaf blight, or brown splotches, especially when stressed or neglected. Remove and discard diseased plants and reduce or eliminate any heavy mulch buildup. *Pachysandra* may also be affected by euonymous scale. Cut out infested plants and treat those remaining with a dormant oil spray (follow label directions) before new growth begins in late winter or early spring. If *Pachysandra* looks bad, shear it off and it should improve.

ADDITIONAL SPECIES, CULTIVARS, OR VARIETIES

Pachysandra terminalis varieties that are popular in Indiana include 'Green Carpet', which grows about 8 inches tall; and 'Variegata', which can brighten deep shade with its white-edged leaves. You might also consider a botanical cousin, *Pachysandra procumbens*, a native plant sometimes known as Allegheny pachysandra or Allegheny spurge. Although similar to *P. terminalis*, the Allegheny variety is taller with pinkish-purple, fragrant flowers in early spring; its leaves are also more gray or blue-green than dark green. *P. procumbens* may behave more like a deciduous plant than an evergreen in colder areas.

GROUNDCOVERS

Purple Winter Creeper

Euonymous fortunei 'Coloratus'

Other Name: Winter Creeper
Zones: 5, 6
Height: 4 to 12 inches, if used as a groundcover;
    vines will climb 20 feet or more
Bloom Period: Evergreen, semi-evergreen

Light Requirement:

Winter creeper is an easy-to-grow groundcover. It rambles along the ground, climbing walls or forming small hedges with little effort. The shiny, well-veined leaves are only about an inch long; depending on the variety, the leaves may be variegated. Purple winter creeper (*E. fortunei* 'Coloratus') is so named because its green foliage turns coppery-purple in winter, giving it additional interest in cold weather. When immature, winter creeper has smaller roots and seems to trail more. The more mature the plant, the more woody the roots. Although winter creeper forms a dense mat, it is usually open enough to allow spring-flowering bulbs to flourish.

WHEN TO PLANT

Plant container-grown transplants any time the soil can be worked. Plants can be divided and transplanted in spring or early fall.

WHERE TO PLANT

Winter creeper will grow nearly anywhere, because it tolerates most soil and light conditions, including wet areas and full sun. Winter creeper isn't considered as destructive to masonry and wood exteriors as English ivy. Avoid planting on a south-facing wall because winter kill of the leaves and stem tips may be more severe.

HOW TO PLANT

Space plants 18 inches to 2 feet apart. Don't plant any deeper than the transplants were growing. Plants will root at nodes as they trail along the ground. Water well and mulch lightly to retain moisture. Always make sure newly planted material receives an inch of rain or water every 7 to 10 days. Mulching probably won't be necessary once the plants are established.

ADVICE FOR CARE

Trim, cut, or shear as desired, especially any leaves that have been damaged by winter winds and sun. Apply an all-purpose fertilizer in spring as new growth appears—or spread a thin layer of compost in spring and fall.

ADDITIONAL INFORMATION

Winter creeper is not as perfect as it sounds. It is notoriously susceptible to leaf spots, mildews, and scale. The latter can be a killer. Prune heavily infested growth and spray with a dormant oil in late winter, followed by a horticulture oil in summer. Sulfur sprays may be used to control mildew, but good cultural conditions are the best remedies for diseases and insects.

ADDITIONAL SPECIES, CULTIVARS, AND VARIETIES

Euonymous fortunei also describes vines and shrubs, so make sure you look at the plant label to see how your selection grows. Groundcover varieties may be called *E. f.* var. *radicans*, 'Variegatus', 'Emerald 'n Gold', 'Emerald Gaiety', and 'Azusa'.

Sweet Woodruff

Galium odoratum

Other Name: *Asperula odorata*
Zones: 5, 6
Height: 6 to 10 inches
Bloom Period: May and June

Light Requirement:

*R*eferences to sweet woodruff can be found in Shakespeare; it is also a prime ingredient of May wine. A delicate-looking deciduous plant with starlike whorls of green leaves, it forms a dense cover under trees and shrubs, or throughout a flower bed. Though it may look delicate, sweet woodruff will take a little foot traffic, giving off its fragrant sweet smell when the leaves are crushed. The white, four-petaled flowers are fragrant, too. It mixes well with spring-flowering bulbs, summer perennials, and other groundcovers. You can remove it easily if it travels where it isn't wanted.

When to Plant

Plant container-grown transplants any time the soil can be worked. The plant may be divided and transplanted in spring or early fall.

Where to Plant

Sweet woodruff does best in a moist, well-drained, shady area; it tolerates dry shade well, however, making it a plant that can thrive under shallow-rooted trees and shrubs. It prefers a slightly acidic soil.

How to Plant

Space plants 10 to 12 inches apart. Don't plant transplants any deeper than they were growing previously. Water well and mulch lightly to retain moisture. Always make sure newly planted material receives an inch of rain or water every 7 to 10 days. Mulching will not be necessary once plants are established.

ADVICE FOR CARE
Apply an all-purpose granular fertilizer in early spring as new growth begins—or spread a thin layer of compost around the plants in spring and fall. Water weekly with 1 to 1$^1/_2$ inches per week throughout the summer for best results.

ADDITIONAL INFORMATION
Sweet woodruff does well in cracks and crevices, and around stones, walkways, and other areas where brushing the leaves releases their fragrant scent.

ADDITIONAL SPECIES, CULTIVARS, OR VARIETIES
There are no improved varieties of sweet woodruff.

Vinca

Vinca minor

Other Names: Periwinkle, Myrtle
Zones: 5, 6
Height: 6 to 8 inches
Bloom Period: Spring, with flushes
throughout the growing season

Light Requirement:

Myrtle is desirable because it flowers, is an evergreen, grows fairly easily, and is a good all-around groundcover. Although classified as a vine, it does not climb. Instead, it trails along the ground, rooting where it finds a desirable spot. This gives it an open growing habit, making it ideal for planting near spring- and fall-flowering bulbs. The oval leaves are shiny, dark green, and well veined. The most common varieties have one-inch periwinkle blue flowers in April and May, and occasional flushes throughout the summer and fall (depending on how much sun and moisture they get). Don't confuse this perennial groundcover with the annual vinca, also called periwinkle or *Catharanthus*. *Vinca major* has larger leaves and flowers and an even more open way of growing, but it is not winter hardy in Indiana.

WHEN TO PLANT

Plant container-grown plants any time the ground can be worked. Myrtle is easy to divide.

WHERE TO PLANT

Myrtle does best in dappled or partial shade, although it tolerates full sun well. Blooms may be diminished and growth slowed in deep shade. It does well under trees and shrubs, or on slopes or hills.

HOW TO PLANT

Plant container-grown plants 12 to 18 inches apart. If transplants are in peat pots, break off the top of the pot to the soil level. If in plastic packs, remove them from the pack, but keep the rootball intact. Don't plant any deeper than it was growing. If dividing the plant, dig up the clumps and transplant. Always make sure newly planted material receives an inch of rain or water every 7 to 10 days.

ADVICE FOR CARE

Myrtle is a very low-maintenance groundcover. Apply a slow-release high-nitrogen or all-purpose general fertilizer in early spring when new growth appears—or apply a thin layer of compost in early spring and fall. If you plant *V. minor* in full sun, be sure to water it during droughts.

ADDITIONAL INFORMATION

Vinca minor frequently benefits from a shearing with hedge trimmers or a lawn mower set on the highest setting. This may be done in spring to get rid of dead foliage or to thicken up the mat of growth. It may also be trimmed with shears or snips to keep it under control. Vinca "dieback" or "blight" frequently causes the stems to turn brown in established plantings. This can severely thin and sometimes wipe out entire beds. Contact your local office of the Purdue Cooperative Extension Service for specific control recommendations.

ADDITIONAL SPECIES, CULTIVARS, OR VARIETIES

'Alba' has white flowers. 'Atropurpurea' and 'Flore Pleno' have purple flowers; the latter has a double flower. 'Variegata' has dark-blue flowers, with variegated yellow and green leaves.

*M*OST HERBS ARE EASY TO GROW, not demanding at all. You can plant them with your annuals and perennials, in containers, in their own garden, or on a sunny windowsill.

Herbs have many different uses. The leaves are easy to dry and store in the pantry for use later. They may also be used fresh; they are particularly good in summer salads. In addition, many herbs will provide beautiful cut flowers.

Herbs may be annuals, perennials, or biennials. Annuals go from seed to flower in one growing season; perennials come back every year. Biennials usually develop foliage the first year and flower the second. Some herbs may be perennial, but we treat them as annuals because they are not winter hardy in Indiana gardens. Herbs may be evergreen or semi-evergreen and retain most of their foliage through the winter—or they may be herbaceous and lose leaves or top growth when cold weather hits.

Some herbs can be invasive, but many are worth growing anyway because of their flowers, foliage, or fragrance. Herbs that spread into unwanted territory can be pulled up as soon as they appear.

BED PREPARATION BASICS

As with any planting, the best results come from a good base, and that means adequate soil preparation—particularly if you are planting perennials. Perennial herbs last several growing seasons, so they need a good bed in which to start, as do annuals and biennials.

Dig a bed that is twelve to eighteen inches deep. Break up clumps of dirt and remove stones, roots, sticks, or other debris; smooth out the bed. Amend the top two to three inches of soil by mixing in compost, peat moss, rotted manure, or other organic material;

Chapter Four

you can add a granular all-purpose fertilizer as well. Dig holes and plant transplants. It is also possible to sow seeds directly in the prepared bed.

Starting seeds indoors can be fun, but it is very challenging. It is hard to duplicate ideal growing conditions by controlling light, heat, humidity, and other factors indoors. Seedlings generally need very good light to keep from getting scrawny or leggy; place them directly under and nearly touching growth lights. This can be as easy as using shop-lites equipped with one cool and one warm, 40-watt fluorescent tube. These items are available at your local garden center or hardware store. They grow best in a greenhouse, or in a room nearly surrounded with light. Some seeds need light to germinate while others require darkness, so be sure to follow label directions or instructions in this book.

It is possible to have more herbs by dividing plants or by taking cuttings, rooting them, and transplanting them. Spring is usually the best time to divide herbs. Dig up the plant you want to divide, and separate portions by hand; you can also cut sections with a sharp knife or spade. To get the best idea of where to make a cut, look at the plant to see how it is growing. Some plants grow in such a way that it is easy to see where to divide them.

To root a cutting, cut off a three- to four-inch-long stem or soft wood branch early in the growing season. Strip off the lower leaves and dip the cut end in a hormone-rooting powder or liquid. Allow the cutting to root in a growing medium such as vermiculite or a soilless potting mix. Once the plant has rooted, you can transplant it to a larger container or into the ground, depending on its size and hardiness.

Most herbs do not need a lot of fertilizer or rich soil. Too much richness may inhibit growth.

Basil

Ocimum basilicum

Other Name: Sweet Basil **Zones:** 5, 6 **Height:** 8 to 36 inches **Bloom Period:** Summer **Type:** Annual	**Light Requirement:**

asil is as much a staple for the gardener as it is for the gourmet cook. This square-stemmed annual dresses up the front or midsection of the ornamental garden with as much ease as it spices up an Italian dish. *Ocimum basilicum* is so strongly associated with Mediterranean cooking that it is surprising to know basil is a native plant of the Pacific islands—and that it is at home, too, in Asian cuisine. The All-America Selections (a not-for-profit trade organization of seed merchants and growers) named a Thai basil, 'Siam Queen', an award winner in 1997. Basil's botanical name comes from the Greek *Ocimum*, which means "fragrant," and *basilikon*, which means "of the kings," or "royal." In various cultures, basil was a sacred plant, a symbol of love, a sign of witchcraft, or a great healing agent. At one time, people thought the seed needed to be planted with a curse in order to ward off evil and ensure the plants would be healthy. The idea was so prevalent that the French developed a phrase, *semer le basilic* ("seeding the basil"), to mean ranting and raving. Fortunately, ranting and raving are not required to produce lusciously fragrant plants with green, purple, or splotched leaves and white, pink, or purple flowers. Basil leaves can be smooth, puckered, or ruffled.

WHEN TO PLANT

Plant container-grown transplants in the spring, after the danger of frost has passed. Basil is easy to start from seed. Sow seeds in pots indoors about a month before the last frost; you can also sow seeds directly outdoors in spring, after the danger of frost has passed. The warmer the soil the better, and it should be at least 50 degrees Fahrenheit. Seeds may not germinate in cold, wet soil.

WHERE TO PLANT

Basil does best in full sun, but it will tolerate light shade. Depending on the variety, basil can be planted in the front or middle of a flower garden. Basil also does well in flower boxes or pots.

HOW TO PLANT

Plant transplants in the soil at the same depth they were growing in packs or peat pots. Sow seeds $1/8$ to $1/4$ inch deep; it takes about 7 to 10 days for the seeds to germinate. Thin seedlings as recommended—usually 10 to 12 inches apart, or one to a pot. Transplant outdoors when frost dangers have passed. Mulch lightly to conserve moisture and reduce weeds. Keep soil moist but not wet.

ADVICE FOR CARE

Pinch back or harvest basil regularly to keep plants bushy. Pinch off flowers to keep plants producing green leaves. The sweetest leaves are usually the smaller ones at the top of the plant.

ADDITIONAL INFORMATION

The richer the soil, the deeper the color of the leaves. Basil is one of the first plants to be killed by frost, which turns it black and renders it useless. Pull dead plants from the garden and compost them. You may want to collect the tiny black basil seed produced when the flowers brown in late summer or fall. Save it in a cool, dark and dry place until planting time next spring.

ADDITIONAL SPECIES, CULTIVARS, OR VARIETIES

Basil comes in a variety of flavors, colors, and textures. Thai basil, 'Siam Queen', grows about 3 feet tall and 2 feet wide; it has purple stems and flowers. Lettuce leaf basil (*Ocimum basilicum* var. *crispum*) comes from Japan; it has white flowers and bright-green leaves. Purple basil ('Purpurascens', 'Dark Opal', or 'Purple Ruffles') has purple leaves and pink flowers. Miniature bush, or French, basil 'Minimum' is very compact, with tiny green leaves and white flowers. Lemon basil, 'Citriodorum', has a lemon scent, green leaves, and white flowers. 'Cinnamon' has a clove or cinnamon fragrance and taste. 'Anise' has purple stems and licorice-flavored leaves with purple veins.

Borage

Borago officinalis

Other Name: Star Flower **Zones:** 5, 6 **Height:** 1 to 2 feet **Flowers:** Blue/pinkish-violet **Bloom Period:** July through September **Type:** Annual	**Light Requirement:**

*D*espite the fact that it is hairy to the touch and self-sows freely, borage has so many blooms during its short life that it makes a worthy addition to the flower garden. Its foliage and hollow stems are gray-green and covered with stiff hairs, which glisten when holding moisture or in certain light. The leaves are oval and slightly serrated. Crush the leaves and they emit a cucumber scent. The leaves can be sprinkled in salads or dips; they are high in minerals and can be used as a flavoring in salt-free diets. The bright and plentiful flowers appear from midsummer until the first frost. The five-petaled, star-shaped flowers can be frozen in ice to add color to drinks, or sprinkled on cakes or other foods. The petals and leaves can also be crystallized and used for food decorations.

WHEN TO PLANT

To have a succession of flowers, sow seeds every 10 to 14 days from spring through midsummer.

WHERE TO PLANT

Borage prefers a sunny location. Like many herbs, it tolerates poor soil and drought conditions, but it does best with regular watering in soil that is rich in organic material. Borage will tolerate filtered sun.

HOW TO PLANT

Borage has a taproot, which makes it difficult to transplant—but it grows easily from seed sown directly in the garden. Sow seeds about 1/2 inch deep directly in the garden when all danger of frost has passed, and the soil has warmed to at least 60 degrees Fahrenheit. Thin seedlings to about 12 inches apart.

ADVICE FOR CARE

"Volunteers" are plants that grow from seed that falls from the parent plant—or is carried by wind, birds, or other wildlife. Borage freely self-sows, sending volunteers throughout the garden. Volunteers can easily be pulled from the ground if they sprout where you do not want them.

ADDITIONAL INFORMATION

Borrach is a Celtic word for "courage," and borage has long been associated with that virtue. The association with courage probably occurred because the leaves contain high levels of potassium, calcium, and mineral salts—a mixture believed to stimulate the production of adrenaline. The Old Masters reportedly relied on borage flowers to mix the right blue for painting the Madonna's clothing.

ADDITIONAL SPECIES, CULTIVARS, OR VARIETIES

There are no improved varieties of borage.

Chives

Allium schoenoprasum

Zones: 5, 6	**Light Requirement:**
Height: 12 to 24 inches	
Flowers: Mauve/violet	
Bloom Period: Spring and early summer	
Type: Perennial	

hives belong to the same family as onions, garlic, and several other spring- and summer-flowering ornamental bulbs. This easy-to-grow perennial works well in the front border of the flower garden because its smaller, drumstick-like flowers mix well with other plants that bloom in early summer. You can use the hollow leaves as a mild-tasting garnish for dozens of dishes, and the flowers are as decorative and edible as they are attractive. You can dry or freeze the leaves and flowers for later use. Be sure to wash leaves and flower heads well to remove any insects or grit.

WHEN TO PLANT
Plant container-grown transplants from early spring through the growing season. You can sow seeds directly outdoors when all danger of frost has passed. Plants may also be divided in the spring.

WHERE TO PLANT
Chives do best in well-drained soil in full sun, but they will tolerate poor soil, dry conditions, and a little shade. You can grow chives in containers for outdoor enjoyment in summer—or in small pots for a windowsill garden in winter.

HOW TO PLANT
About 6 weeks before the last frost in spring, sow seeds 1/2 inch deep in small pots indoors, growing them until they are ready to be transplanted; if you purchase small plants, remove them from their plastic packs to plant. In either case, plant them outdoors no deeper than they were growing in their containers. Space plants about 10 inches apart.

ADVICE FOR CARE

Chives require little or no care. When you harvest the leaves, cut them off close to the base to keep the plant looking tidy. You may also cut chives back to the ground throughout the growing season; this will encourage new growth. Cut dried, or spent, flowers when they start to look ratty. Apply an all-purpose fertilizer in early spring when new growth appears—or spread a thin layer of compost in the bed in spring and fall. Divide clumps every 3 to 4 years to keep growth vigorous.

ADDITIONAL INFORMATION

The leaves will die back in winter and can be cut off and tossed in the compost pile; new growth appears in early spring. Chive flowers form black seeds which easily self-sow; to prevent this, remove the flowers before seeds are formed. If you keep them too wet, chives may develop root or crown rot.

ADDITIONAL SPECIES, CULTIVARS, OR VARIETIES

'Ruby Gem' has red flowers and gray foliage.

Lavender

Lavandula angustifolia

Zones: 5, 6
Height: 12 to 24 inches
Flowers: Purple, white, pink
Bloom Period: Late spring and early summer
Type: Perennial

Light Requirement:

*E*nglish lavender leaves, flowers, and stems are very fragrant. For centuries, people have been using lavender to scent linens, bath water, perfumes, and the air. Flowers can be sprinkled on salads, or frozen in ice to add color to drinks. You can also dry the flowers and leaves for sachet or potpourri. Because it has silvery green leaves that make a nice contrast for other plants, this shrubby evergreen is excellent in the front of the perennial garden.

WHEN TO PLANT
Plant container-grown transplants from spring through the growing season. Seeds may be sown in pots indoors, about 10 weeks before the last frost in spring.

WHERE TO PLANT
Lavender prefers a sunny, well-drained, average soil. Choose a spot with good air circulation that isn't too wet, especially in winter.

HOW TO PLANT
Don't plant transplants any deeper than they were growing in their containers. Remove from plastic containers before planting, being careful not to disturb the rootball. Seeds may be difficult to germinate, and seed-grown plants take about 2 years to reach maturity. Sow 1/8 inch deep in a sterile, soilless mix that is at least 70 degrees Fahrenheit; germination may take up to 3 weeks. Space plants about 2 feet apart. Mulch to retain moisture and reduce weeds. Water new transplants well. Once established, they usually don't have to be watered.

ADVICE FOR CARE

Apply an all-purpose fertilizer in early spring when new growth appears—or spread a thin layer of compost in spring and fall. Even though most garden books recommend it, do *not* cut English lavender back in the fall. Last year's flowers and foliage act as buffers or insulation against winter winds and temperatures. Lavender is supposed to be hardy to Zone 5, but it may freeze in severe winters. Wait until spring, when new growth will appear as fresher and greener growth down the stem. Then cut back to the new growth. Plants are about 1 foot wide.

ADDITIONAL INFORMATION

Lavender derives its name from *lavare* which is Latin for "to wash." The word lavatory has the same origin. Another source suggests the word comes from the Medieval Latin word *livere* which means "to make blueish."

ADDITIONAL SPECIES, CULTIVARS, OR VARIETIES

Lavandula angustifolia 'Hidcote' grows about 18 inches tall, and has dark-purple flowers and silver-gray leaves. 'Jean Davis' also grows about 18 inches tall, but has pink flowers. 'Alba' has white flowers, grows about 10 inches tall, and may not be winter hardy. 'Munstead' is 18 inches tall, with dark-lavender flowers. French lavender (*Lavandula dentata*) has greener leaves and dark-purple flowers, but it is not winter hardy in Indiana.

HERBS

Oregano

Origanum vulgare, Origanum majorana

Other Name: Marjoram	**Light Requirement:**
Zones: 5, 6	
Height: 12 to 24 inches	
Flowers: White or purple	
Bloom Period: Mid- to late summer	
Type: Annual/Perennial	

regano grows wild in Greece, and it perfumes the summer air throughout the Mediterranean region. In fact, the word "oregano" comes from Greek words meaning "joy of the mountains." The Greek goddess Aphrodite is supposed to have created the plant as a symbol for happiness. There are two common varieties. *Origanum vulgare* is a perennial that is hardy in Zone 5. It has a slightly sprawling growth habit, and dark-pink or white flowers in late summer. The dark-green, oval leaves are a pungent staple of Italian, Greek, and Mexican dishes. The flowers are also edible, or you can cut them for floral arrangements or potpourri. *Origanum majorana*, sometimes known as sweet marjoram, is an annual with pale-green leaves; it has white or purple flowers that form fragrant, edible clusters, or knots, at the tips of stems in mid- to late summer. Its flavor is sweeter and milder than its perennial cousin. You can also use the flowers for floral arrangements or potpourri. Oregano is easy to start from seed in the garden.

WHEN TO PLANT

Plant container-grown transplants in spring, after the danger of frost has passed. Sow seeds at the same time.

WHERE TO PLANT

Both types do best in full sun with well-drained, moist soil. Once established, they do well in dry soil. They tolerate partial shade and drought conditions.

HOW TO PLANT

Origanum vulgare should be spaced about 2 feet apart. Plant transplants the same depth they were growing in their container. The plants may be divided in spring. Keep newly planted transplants well watered. *Origanum majorana* does best in full sun with well-drained soil that has been amended with organic material. Plant the same depth it was growing in its container. Space plants about 12 inches apart. About 6 weeks before the last frost, scatter seeds and gently press them into the surface of soil in pots indoors. The seeds need light to germinate, and the soil should be at least 70 degrees Fahrenheit. It may take 3 weeks for the seeds to germinate. For best results, buy transplants from the local garden center. Keep transplants well watered.

ADDITIONAL INFORMATION

Heavy frost will kill the tops of *Origanum vulgare*. Cut away and compost the dead foliage.

ADDITIONAL SPECIES, CULTIVARS, OR VARIETIES

Origanum vulgare 'Compact' is a shorter variety that has dark-green leaves and dark-pink flowers. 'Variegatum' is a gold marjoram with a mild flavor, yellow-and-green leaves, and pink or white flowers; it is not winter hardy in Indiana. *Origanum onites* (also known as pot marjoram or Cretan) grows about 1 foot tall, and has dark-green leaves and lavender flowers; it is not winter hardy. Greek oregano is *Origanum heracleoticum*; it grows about 9 inches tall and has spicy, fragrant leaves and pink flowers. Greek oregano is very invasive.

Parsley

Petroselinum crispum

Zones: 5, 6
Height: 12 to 15 inches
Flowers: Greenish yellow
Bloom Period: Spring
Type: Annual

Light Requirement:

This is the one herb most people recognize, since it comes with almost every plate of food served in restaurants. Parsley has been used for many things other than as a garnish. The Greeks used it to decorate tombs, and fed it to their horses in the belief that it would make them run faster. The Romans believed that it enabled them to consume more wine without drunken after-effects. Curly-leafed parsley is the most popular variety sold in the United States, although it has less flavor than the flat-leafed varieties.

WHEN TO PLANT

Plant container-grown transplants in spring, after the danger of frost has passed. You can sow seeds directly in the ground about a month before the last frost—or indoors about 8 weeks before the last frost. You can also sow seeds in the fall for foliage the following spring.

WHERE TO PLANT

Parsley prefers full sun or partial shade, and a well-drained spot that is rich in organic material. It does well in flower pots or containers outdoors in summer—or in a small pot for a windowsill garden in winter. It also makes a nice border of dark-green clumps when planted in the front of the flower garden.

HOW TO PLANT

Remove transplants from plastic containers. Don't plant any deeper than they were growing in the containers. Sow seeds 1/4 inch deep. Germination takes about 3 weeks; you can speed it up by soaking seeds in warm water for a day or two, or by freezing them overnight before planting.

ADVICE FOR CARE

Don't allow parsley to dry out. When you harvest it, snip stems close to the base of the plant. Spread a layer of compost around the plant—both when you plant it and in the fall.

ADDITIONAL INFORMATION

Parsley is rich in minerals and vitamins. It is a biennial in Zone 6, which means that it grows foliage the first year and flowers the second. It tends to lose its flavor once it starts to flower—so plan on replanting every two years, and keep the flowers cut. A severe winter may kill parsley the first season. Frost causes the top part of the plant to die; if this occurs, cut the top off and compost it.

ADDITIONAL SPECIES, CULTIVARS, OR VARIETIES

Petroselinum crispum varieties include 'Extra Curled Dwarf', 'Moss Curled', and 'Green Velvet'. Curly-leaf parsley is usually the shortest variety. Flat-leaf, or Italian parsley (*Petroselinum crispum* var. 'Neapolitanum'), grows 2 feet tall; it has a stronger flavor, succulent stems, and dark-green leaves. Hamburg parsley (*Petroselinum crispum tuberosum*) also has edible leaves—but it is prized for its root, which is used to flavor stews and soups.

Rosemary

Rosmarinus officinalis

Zone: 6
Height: 12 to 15 inches
Flowers: White, purple, and blue
Bloom Period: Winter to spring
Type: Perennial

Light Requirement:

osemary's name comes from the Latin *ros marinum*, which means "dew of the sea." English ears, however, heard "rose" and "mary" —and the English dedicated the plant to the Virgin Mary in 1440. Rosemary has been used to sweeten linens, ward off disease (including typhoid fever and bubonic plague), refresh or bring back memories, and promote fidelity. It is best known, however, as a culinary delight. You can toss the leaves in salads, use them to flavor meats, or add them to potatoes and many other vegetables. Unfortunately, this fragrant evergreen shrub will not withstand Zone 5 winters, so you will probably have to replant it each year. (The plant may make it through southern Indiana winters with a good layer of mulch, but it is not a sure thing.) Use rosemary in the front of the flower garden, where its gray-green foliage complements other plants—and where it emits a wonderful aroma when touched.

WHEN TO PLANT

Plant container-grown transplants in spring, when the danger of frost has passed.

WHERE TO PLANT

Rosemary does best in well-drained soil and full sun. It does not tolerate wet soil. Rosemary does well in containers, too. In the hopes of getting rosemary through the winter, many Hoosier gardeners grow it in containers; this enables them to carry it to a sunny location indoors. That's when one gets to see it flower.

HOW TO PLANT

Plant at the same depth the transplant has been growing. Remove it from the plastic pot, trying not to disturb the rootball. Water it well. Once established, rosemary is able to withstand drought.

ADVICE FOR CARE
Mulch to retain moisture and reduce weeds. Rosemary may be pruned for shape, especially if it has wintered over indoors.

ADDITIONAL INFORMATION
Rosemary attracts bees. Some gardeners may wish to consider this when determining whether or not to include it in their garden.

ADDITIONAL SPECIES, CULTIVARS, OR VARIETIES
'Alba' has white flowers. 'Beneden Blue' has blue flowers and a semi-erect growing habit. 'Prostratus' trails, but it is hardy only to Zone 8. 'Miss Jessopp's Upright' has broad green leaves and is one of the hardiest varieties. Remember, you'll only see the flowers if you winter it over.

Thyme

Thymus vulgaris

Other Names: Garden Thyme, Common Thyme **Zones:** 5, 6 **Height:** 4 to 12 inches **Flowers:** Pink/mauve or white **Bloom Period:** Spring and summer **Type:** Perennial	**Light Requirement:**

*T*he word "thyme" is another herb name that can be traced to the Greeks. *Thuo* is Greek for "perfume"—which certainly describes the wonderful scent this common herb gives off. Thyme is an herb that doubles as a fragrant, flowering groundcover. It is a multi-stemmed, woody plant with small, oval leaves, and flowers that cover the low-growing plant in late spring or early summer. Thyme is nearly evergreen. Depending on conditions, some varieties hold their leaves well into winter, but don't be concerned if the plant loses its foliage. It does well under roses or in the front of the flower garden. Stuff it in the cracks and crevices of steps, walkways, and rock gardens. Thyme's fragrance is released as passersby brush against it.

When to Plant

Plant container-grown transplants any time during the growing season, but spring is best. Start seeds indoors 8 to 10 weeks before the last spring frost.

Where to Plant

Thyme prefers full sun, but tolerates partial shade. Its most important requirement is good drainage. Thyme will be attacked by fungus diseases and rot if it sits in soggy soil. Thyme also does well mixed with other flowers in containers outdoors in summer—or in pots for a windowsill garden in winter.

How to Plant

Remove transplants from plastic containers. Don't plant thyme any deeper than it was growing in the pots. Sow seeds about 1/8 inch deep in indoor pots; use a soilless mix that stays at least 55 degrees Fahrenheit. Germination may take a month. Thyme may be divided every 2 to 3 years in the spring; this will ensure that it looks healthy and grows vigorously. Mulch new transplants lightly, and water well. Mulch probably won't be necessary once plants get established.

ADVICE FOR CARE
Thyme may be sheared or cut back in spring to shape it up or remove winter damage. Apply an all-purpose fertilizer in early spring when new growth appears—or spread a thin layer of compost around the plant in spring and fall.

ADDITIONAL INFORMATION
Rust fungus disease may cause brown, red, or tan spots on the leaves. Remove infected leaves or branches, and avoid watering the plant from above.

ADDITIONAL SPECIES, CULTIVARS, OR VARIETIES
Thymus serphyllum is a woody shrub-like plant called mother-of-thyme; it only grows 1 to 3 inches tall, and has purple or rose-colored flowers from June through September. *Thymus serphyllum* 'Albus' has white flowers. 'Citriodorus', or lemon thyme, grows about 1 inch tall, and has a lemony scent. 'Lanuginosus' is called woolly-mother-of-thyme.

CHAPTER FIVE

Lawn Grasses

*W*E HAVE A LOVE/HATE RELATIONSHIP WITH OUR lawns here in Indiana. We love expansive, weed-free, dark-green carpets leading up to the front door. Unfortunately, most of us hate spending the time it takes to maintain that kind of lawn. We may try to do it all ourselves or we may hire lawn care companies. Either way, we are bound to the lawn by our wallets or by the weekends we lose to mowing, raking, and speculating with the neighbors about how bad the grub problem might be this year. Of course, there are also passive lawn lovers who sleep in and don't miss a sporting event over the weekend. For them, a lawn may be pure dandelions, but at least it's something green.

The key to a good lawn is good cultural practices. A few tasks performed during the right time of the year will give hope to even the *worst* lawn. Let's look at some key ingredients in growing and maintaining a thick turf.

WHAT TYPE OF GRASS SEED SHOULD YOU USE?

Throughout the Hoosier state, bluegrass is far and away the most popular grass type. It has lush, green color and fine leaf texture. As much as we love bluegrass, however, the lawn is rarely composed of only one grass type. Instead, we plant mixtures of bluegrass, perennial "turf-type" ryegrass, and fine-leaf fescue. The wonderful thing about mixtures is that the weakness of one type of grass is offset by the strengths of another.

In sunny areas, sow a mixture of eighty percent bluegrass and twenty percent perennial turf-type ryegrass. Good mixtures use two or three varieties of each grass type. For lawns that receive a mixture of sun and partial shade, sow a mixture of fifty percent Kentucky bluegrass, thirty percent fine-leaf fescue, and twenty

Chapter Five

percent perennial ryegrass. In shady areas, the creeping fescue will dominate. In the sunny parts of the lawn, Kentucky bluegrass will be the dominant grass. For shady sites, include the shade-tolerant varieties mentioned later in this chapter. You can sow turf-type tall fescue as a 100 percent stand in the full sun or shade. Even though improved varieties of tall fescue have finer leaves, when you blend most tall fescue with the finer-textured grasses, it stands out like a clump of weeds. Always choose improved varieties of seed where possible. High-quality seed is worth the extra expense.

Zoysia grass is a popular warm season grass found throughout Indiana. It quickly forms a dense turf by sending out underground runners called "rhizomes." Zoysia grass grows so thick it sometimes squeezes out broadleaf weeds like dandelions. Unfortunately, zoysia grass is dormant most of the year throughout the Hoosier state. It turns straw colored with the first frost and does not fully green up until late May or early June. It makes a poor choice for Indiana lawns for this reason.

PREPARING THE SEEDBED

Add good topsoil to a depth of three to four inches and lightly blend it with the soil underneath. In the absence of new topsoil, rototill between four and six inches deep. In both instances, it is highly beneficial to add at least four to six inches of compost or peat moss. This will keep the soil light and well drained, and will eliminate many future problems. Check with your topsoil provider about the origins of the topsoil. Heavy clay is sometimes sold as pulverized topsoil; it will become very hard and compact unless it is mixed with organic matter. A soil test to determine pH and other nutrient levels is recommended prior to seeding. Spread a "starter fertilizer" from your local garden supplier prior to seeding.

SEEDING THE LAWN

In Indiana, the best time to sow grass seed is from mid-August to mid-September. In southern parts of the state, home owners should delay sowing for an additional two weeks. At this time, the soil is warmer, seed germination is faster, and there is much less competi-

Chapter Five

tion from weeds. For even distribution, broadcast one-half the seed through a drop spreader in one direction. Broadcast the remaining seed at right angles in a crisscross pattern to the first application. A slit seeder can also be used, especially in thin lawns. Spread clean straw over the entire seedbed until you can barely see the soil through the mulch. Keep the seedbed moist at all times. This may require light watering two or three times a day. Coarse grass will sometimes grow in the new seedbed; this is usually the result of wheat seedlings that came from seed in the straw. The coarse textured seedlings will die after two or three passes with the mower.

MOWING

For the general-purpose lawn mixture of cool-season grasses in Indiana, mowing heights between two-and-one-half and three inches tall are recommended. This allows the grass plant to develop a deeper root system that is more able to find valuable nutrients in the soil and to withstand drought stress.

Always keep the lawn mower blade as sharp as possible. Grass blades with frayed ends give the lawn a light brown, whitish color, and cause the grass plants to lose more water than they should.

Mow frequently, never removing more than one-third of the grass blade at one time. The first cut of the year is an exception to this rule, and should be around one-and-one-half inches tall. When the heavy rains of spring or an extended period without mowing cause the grass to get too tall, set the mower blade at its maximum height for the initial cut. Gradually lower the blade for subsequent cuts until it reaches the regular height.

Always leave grass clippings on the lawn, except when they are so long that they mat together and block light from the turf below. Mow frequently enough that the cut blades are short and able to filter into the turf. They will return valuable nutrients to the soil and help cut down on fertilizer costs. Studies show that the time you spend emptying mower bags is greater than the time spent mowing more frequently.

Chapter Five

FERTILIZING

A lush lawn requires three, and sometimes four, applications of fertilizer each year. Depending on the kind of lawn desired, home owners have to decide how many applications of fertilizer to make. Whether you apply fertilizer once, or four times per year, you should apply the majority of the nutrients in the fall. Applying fertilizer in the fall helps the grass plant develop a more extensive root system that stores necessary nutrients for use the following spring. Fall fertilization keeps the lawn nice and green late into the year and encourages early spring green-up.

If you want a low-maintenance lawn, the best time to fertilize is in mid-September. Apply a lawn fertilizer with at least twenty to thirty percent slow-release nitrogen according to the instructions on the label. For a moderately green lawn, fertilize in mid-September and in early November. A third and light application in May will help the lawn stay green throughout the summer, provided there is ample moisture. A lighter application of fertilizer in July would be the fourth time to fertilize; this may only be necessary for those who will spare no expense to have the greenest lawn on the block (you know who you are!). This should only be done in instances where the lawn is regularly watered. Otherwise, home owners risk burning the turf. Fertilizing in early spring causes rapid growth of the grass blades at a time of the year when they grow fast naturally. This rapid growth depletes the root system of food reserves and weakens the grass plant as it prepares for the stress of summer. It also requires extra mowing. Early spring feeding is recommended only when you skipped the fall feeding, or when you apply preemergent weed control that uses fertilizer as a carrier. You have numerous options when purchasing fertilizer. Consult your local office of the Cooperative Extension Service for the appropriate application rates for the fertilizer you chose.

OTHER CULTURAL PRACTICES

Core aeration helps get air to the roots of the grass plant. It is one of the only alternatives for relieving heavy, compacted soil, and it also helps prevent the development of a harmful thatch layer. During the

Chapter Five

process of core aeration, cylindrical cores of soil from the lawn (approximately three-fourth inch in diameter and two to three inches long) are removed from the soil. The best time to core aerate is in late summer or early fall.

Lawns should receive between one and one-and-one-half inches of water per week. This can be applied all at the same time or divided in half. Deep watering promotes a deep root system. During extended dry periods, reduce the watering and allow the lawn to turn brown and go dormant. Most lawns will fully recover from as much as six weeks without rain or supplemental watering.

PROBLEMS

Although moss in the lawn can be a nice feature that requires little attention, many people want to eliminate it. Since moss grows in shaded areas that have compacted, infertile soil, you can help get rid of it by pruning the tree limbs that create the shade. Combine pruning with fertilization and core aeration, which will help relieve soil compaction.

Managing lawn insects (including white grubs, sod webworms, and others) should not be difficult. Insect populations vary from year to year according to weather patterns and other environmental factors. You can avoid many problems with good cultural practices; these give the lawn an advantage over troublesome pests. From time to time, you may need to use pesticides to control outbreaks of one insect or another. Please consult your local office of the Cooperative Extension Service or a garden center professional for recommended treatments.

Turf diseases abound in Indiana lawns. Following the proper cultural practices including proper mowing height, timing of fertilizer applications, and core aeration, will significantly reduce or eliminate disease problems in the lawn.

Broadleaf weeds (such as dandelions, plantain, creeping Charlie, etc.) will eventually be crowded out by a nice, dense turf if you follow good cultural practices. Treatment may be necessary to get ahead of the weeds, however. Treat broadleaf weeds from mid-

Chapter Five

September until early October (later in southern Indiana). Liquid applications of a combination of herbicides like 2,4-D; MCPP; and Dicamba sprayed directly on the leaves give very good results. Always read and follow the label instructions when applying any pesticide.

Crabgrass is an annual weed that usually germinates in Indiana in April. A dense turf mowed to a height of two-and-one-half to three inches will help eliminate this weed. In severe cases, you may need to apply a crabgrass preventer in late March or early April.

Fine-Leaf Fescue

Festuca spp.

Zones: 5, 6	**Light Requirement:**
Cutting Height: 1¹/₂ to 3 inches	
Color: Medium-green	
Texture: Fine, wiry	
Wear Resistance: Good	

The fine-leaf fescues include creeping red fescue and chewings fescue. They are loved for their tough composition and for their ability to tolerate drought and shadier planting sites. Both creeping red fescue and chewings fescue are low-growers, with fine, wiry, medium-green leaves. Creeping red fescue spreads by underground rhizomes and forms a dense mat similar to bluegrass. Chewings fescue is a bunch-type grass with more shade tolerance than the creeping type. The fine-leaf fescues tolerate hot, dry summer conditions as easily as they do the extreme cold of winter. Creeping red and chewings fescues are always sold as blends with Kentucky bluegrass and perennial ryegrass. Over time, the bluegrass varieties will dominate the full-sun parts of the lawn, while the fescues will dominate the shadier portions.

When to Plant

For best results, plant all grass blends, including the fine-leaf fescues, in mid-August to mid-September. The second-best time to plant is in the early spring, before the leaves emerge on the trees in late March or early April.

Where to Plant

Both creeping red and chewings fescues tolerate shade better than perennial ryegrass or Kentucky bluegrass. They prefer an average soil and don't like to be overfertilized or heavily watered. Dry sites with medium-to-low fertility are ideal. In wet sites, the bluegrass/ryegrass portion of the seed mix will dominate.

How to Plant

Prepare a seedbed by spreading high-quality topsoil or by lightly rototilling between 4 and 6 inches deep. For best results, spread a 4- to 6-inch layer of well-rotted compost or peat moss and make a second pass with the rototiller. Level the ground with a wide garden rake or a sand rake and broadcast the seed at a rate of 4 to 5 pounds per 1,000 square feet of area. Spread a starter fertilizer according to label directions. Rake over the seed and fertilizer, making sure that the soil makes direct contact with, or lightly covers, the seed. This will ensure better germination. Spread clean straw over the entire planting area so that the soil is barely visible through the mulch. Keep the seedbed constantly moist. This may require 2 or 3 light waterings per day, especially during August and September.

ADVICE FOR CARE

Although creeping red and chewings fescues tolerate lower mowing heights, they are planted as parts of a mixture. Mow them at the same $2^1/2$ to 3 inches as the rest of the lawn. The two best times to feed the lawn are in mid-September and early November. Use a lawn fertilizer that has most of its nitrogen in slow-release form and apply according to package directions. A third application of fertilizer in May will help the lawn stay green over the summer months. Water the lawn with 1 to $1^1/2$ inches of moisture each week, preferably all at the same time to encourage the development of a deep root system. Fine fescues are very tolerant of the dry conditions typical of Hoosier summers.

ADDITIONAL INFORMATION

Both creeping red and chewings fescue are vigorous growers and will germinate readily. They are slightly susceptible to leaf spot and other fungal diseases. When possible, choose new and improved varieties for better disease resistance.

ADDITIONAL SPECIES, CULTIVARS, AND VARIETIES

Improved varieties of creeping red fescue are 'Wintergreen', 'Dawson', and 'Pennlawn'. The latter two are known for their tolerance of shade. 'Agram' and 'Waldorf' are good varieties of chewings fescue. 'Banner', 'Checker', 'Highlight', and 'Jamestown' show good tolerance for shadier sites.

Kentucky Bluegrass

Poa pratensis

Zones: 5, 6
Cutting Height: 2¹/₂ to 3 inches
Color: Dark-green
Texture: Smooth
Wear Resistance: Excellent

Light Requirement:

A leisurely drive through the rolling green hills of Kentucky will give you an idea why this grass species is so popular. Bluegrass was brought to this country from Europe during colonization, but the lush dark-green calls up memories of outings in our neighboring state. Its smooth, succulent leaf blades are soothing to the eye and pleasing to walk on. When the weather is warm, this is the grass species that makes you want to take off your shoes and run barefoot through the lawn. Kentucky bluegrass is the most popular grass species in the northern growing zones, and for good reason. A vigorous underground root system enables it to bounce back quickly under foot traffic, making it a common sight on athletic fields and other heavily traveled areas. Kentucky bluegrass stays green late into the fall and "greens up" early in spring, giving us enjoyment almost all year long. It tolerates the extreme cold of the northern part of the state, and thrives in the southern tip near Evansville. Kentucky bluegrass is the most adaptable and high-quality turf species we have.

When to Plant

For best results, sow bluegrass seed any time between mid-August and mid-September. Spring sowing will be less successful due to cooler soil temperatures and the greater chance of weeds. If late summer seeding is missed however, sow seeds in late March or early April, before the leaves emerge on the trees. Bluegrass makes an excellent tightly woven sod that is best laid in spring or late summer.

Where to Plant

Bluegrass grows in practically any soil in Indiana, but it prefers organically rich soils that are light and well-drained. It will not grow well in heavily compacted clay soils. Kentucky bluegrass will thrive in 4 to 6 hours of full sun per day; in shadier sites, it is important that you use shade-tolerant varieties in a partial mixture with fine fescues. Avoid the temptation to try growing grass in heavy shade. Instead, plant a shade-loving groundcover or mulch around the area. You will save yourself a lot of time and energy.

How to Plant

Prepare the planting site by spreading high-quality topsoil or by rototilling from 4 to 6 inches deep. For best results, mix in 4 to 6 inches of commercial compost or peat moss. Remove lumps, level off low or high spots by using a sand rake, and spread a starter or organic fertilizer. Broadcast a mixture of at least three improved varieties of Kentucky bluegrass at the rate of 1 to 2 pounds of seed per 1,000 square feet of area. Rake the planting bed to ensure the seed has direct contact with the soil. Lay a thin layer of straw over the planting area. Keep the seedbed moist at all times; this may require light waterings 3 times a day, especially during late August and early September.

Advice for Care

The best defense is a good offense. On a regular basis, mow the grass between 2^1/$_2$ and 3 inches tall. Apply a slow-release lawn fertilizer with at least 20 percent nitrogen in mid-September and again in November according to the instructions on the bag. A third application the following May is advisable for those who want the greenest lawn possible. Core aerate the lawn once each year in September to help get air to the roots and reduce compaction. Water the lawn deeply with 1 to 1^1/$_2$ inches of water each week. This will keep the lawn green all summer long.

Additional Information

Bluegrass goes dormant during hot and dry weather by turning brown. It will survive up to 6 weeks with little or no moisture before permanent damage occurs. A thick, dense turf is the best way to keep weeds and fungus from attacking the lawn. You can reduce or completely avoid weed and fungus infestations if you follow the cultural practices described above on a regular basis.

Additional Species, Cultivars, or Varieties

Many new varieties with a lower growing habit and better disease resistance are now available. Some varieties recommended for Indiana include 'America', 'Merion', 'Adelphi', 'Wabash', and 'Challenger'. Varieties that should be mixed with the fine-leaf fescues in shadier sites include 'Bristol', 'Glade', 'Nugget', 'Touchdown', and 'Victa'.

Perennial Ryegrass

Lolium perenne

Zones: 5, 6
Cutting Height: 2 to 2¹/₂ inches
Color: Dark-green
Texture: Medium to fine
Wear Resistance: Good

Light Requirement:

*I*f you've ever sown grass seed, you know that something starts growing within a few days (if you've done everything right). The first thin blades to poke their tips through the soil are usually perennial ryegrass seedlings. Perennial rye helps to establish a lawn in a short time. With adequate moisture, the seedlings germinate within a week and help hold the soil in place for the more cherished Kentucky bluegrass, which can take up to three weeks to sprout. Perennial "turf-type" rye has a medium-to-fine texture and dark-green leaves. Its "bunching" growth habit causes it to grow in very small clumps as opposed to a dense mass of sod. Like bluegrass, perennial rye has good wear resistance. Newer varieties have greater immunity to problem lawn diseases. Choose improved varieties whenever possible.

WHEN TO PLANT

Always sow ryegrass as a blend with Kentucky bluegrass and fine fescue during the late summer and early fall. The ideal time is between August 15 and September 15. The second-best time is in the early spring just before tree leaves emerge.

WHERE TO PLANT

Perennial turf-type rye grows best in full sun, although some new varieties tolerate light shade. (In heavy shade, gardeners will be much more successful planting an appropriate groundcover.) It prefers moist but well-drained areas with plenty of organic matter. Like many plants, it will struggle to survive in compact, heavy clay sites. Perennial rye is not very tolerant of drought. In dry areas, bluegrass or fine fescues will predominate in the lawn.

HOW TO PLANT

Prepare a seedbed by lightly rototilling or by spreading high-quality topsoil between 2 and 4 inches deep. For the best long-term results, use the rototiller to incorporate 2 to 4 inches of well-rotted compost or peat moss into the seedbed. Level the area with a sand rake, and broadcast the seed at a rate of 6 to 8 pounds per 1,000 square feet of area. This rate will be reduced in a mixture. Spread a starter fertilizer according to the label directions. Rake over the area; make sure the seed is lightly covered and in direct contact with the soil, but avoid covering the seed with more than 1/4 inch of soil. Spread clean straw over the entire seedbed until you can barely see the soil through the mulch. Water lightly every day in order to keep the seedbed moist at all times. This may require watering 2 or 3 times a day.

Advice for Care

Although perennial rye will tolerate a slightly lower mowing height than Kentucky bluegrass, it is still best to mow it to a height between 2 1/2 and 3 inches when it is planted in a mixture. The two best times to apply fertilizer are in mid-September and early November. Use a slow-release lawn fertilizer with at least 20 percent nitrogen; follow the instructions on the bag. A third application in mid-May is also beneficial; it will keep the lawn fed during the summer. Apply at a slightly lower rate when fertilizing in May. Perennial ryegrass should receive at least 1 inch of water each week. This is especially important during the dry spells we endure in all parts of the state at some point during the summer. Water deeply, preferably all at once, to encourage a deep root system. All turf will benefit from core aeration in September, particularly those sites with compacted soils and heavy thatch layers.

Additional Information

In parts of Europe, ryegrass is used as forage for cattle and horses. When you purchase grass seed, do not confuse perennial ryegrass with its annual counterpart. Annual ryegrass is short-lived; it is used in specific situations where a quick and temporary cover is desired. Always read the seed ingredients label, or consult your garden center professional for help.

Additional Species, Cultivars, or Varieties

One of the earliest improved varieties of perennial ryegrass was collected in Central Park in New York City; it was appropriately named 'Manhattan'. Other improved varieties include 'All Star', 'Omega', 'Pennfine', and 'Derby'. Some improved varieties with reported tolerance for shadier sites are 'Citation II', 'Fiesta II', 'Manhattan II', and 'Regal'.

Tall Fescue

Festuca arundinacea

	Light Requirement:
Zones: 5, 6	
Cutting Height: $2^1/_2$ to 3 inches	☀ ◑
Color: Medium green	
Texture: Coarse	
Wear Resistance: Good	

Almost everyone who grows up in the country hears about 'Kentucky 31'. This is the old, standard, tall fescue used for pastures, roadsides, and some home lawns. This tough variety became popular after 1940. It has a deep root system, which helps it survive dry weather, and it needs little fertilizer. It survives through benign neglect in areas where you don't need the finer textures of bluegrass. Fortunately, this old standby—well-known for its coarse leaves and clump-forming growth habit—has been improved with the development of numerous varieties that create higher-quality home lawns. These new "turf-type tall fescues" have much of the same durability and drought resistance as Kentucky 31 but with finer, more delicate leaves and a lower growing height. Turf-type tall fescues have better shade tolerance than either bluegrass or ryegrass, but less than the fine-leaf fescues.

WHEN TO PLANT

For best results, seed turf-type tall fescue in mid- to late August. Seeding after the middle of September in central and northern Indiana is less successful than in areas south of Indianapolis. The second-best time to plant is in the early spring before the leaves emerge on the trees.

WHERE TO PLANT

Sow stands of turf-type tall fescue for low-maintenance areas or lawns where the lush qualities of Kentucky bluegrass are not required. Tall fescue is also useful for areas where soil erosion is a problem, and for compact, heavy clay sites. Tall fescue tolerates a wide range of soil pH. It thrives in full sun, but tolerates partial shade. Avoid planting grass seed in heavy shade; plant a ground-cover instead.

How to Plant

Prepare the seedbed by adding 2 to 4 inches of high-quality topsoil, or by lightly rototilling 4 to 6 inches of the existing topsoil. Whether you add topsoil or use the existing layer, you will achieve the best long-term results by incorporating 2 to 4 inches of well-rotted compost or peat moss. Level the area, using a sand rake to eliminate bumps or low spots. Spread a starter fertilizer according to the package directions. Sow a mixture of 80 percent turf-type tall fescue and 20 percent bluegrass seed at the rate of 6 to 8 pounds of seed per 1,000 square feet of area. Lightly rake the area so that the soil comes in direct contact with, or even slightly covers, the seed. Spread clean straw over the entire seedbed until you can barely see the soil through the mulch. Water regularly to keep the seedbed moist at all times. This may require watering 2 or 3 times a day during the late summer.

Advice for Care

Mow tall fescue to a height of 2^1/$_2$ to 3 inches. Mow regularly, so that no more than ^{1}/$_3$ of the leaf area is removed at any one time. Fertilize with a lawn fertilizer that has most of its nitrogen in slow-release form. Lawn fertilizers should have at least 20% nitrogen. For maximum results, fertilize once in mid-September and again in early November. Tall fescue is drought resistant and should not need supplemental watering during the summer.

Additional Information

Though tall fescue withstands infestations of insects that many turf species do not, improved varieties, particularly the turf-types, may develop some fungus problems.

Additional Species, Cultivars, or Varieties

Improved turf-type varieties include 'Falcon', 'Finelawn', 'Jaguar', 'Olympic', 'Rebel', and 'Rebel II'. Coarse varieties for low-maintenance sites include 'Kentucky 31', 'Alta', and 'Kenwell'.

CHAPTER SIX

Ornamental Grasses

*T*HE TERM "ORNAMENTAL GRASS" MAY SEEM REDUN-DANT—most of us have spent a good part of our leisure time manicuring acres of lawn grasses around our homes, schools, businesses, and public institutions, all for their *ornamental* effect. This term, however, describes a group of plants within the larger grass family. (The grass family is the second largest family of plants in the world. Other familiar "grasses" are the major food crops of the world such as rice, corn, wheat, millet, and sorghum, as well as all the Kentucky bluegrass, ryegrass, and the fescues we sow for lawns.)

Ornamental grasses are a unique group of plants grown for their year-round ornamental effects and freedom from pests. An integral element in the "New American Garden," they define the term "maintenance free." The "New American Garden" is the result of a shift in landscape design and plant selection toward plants that require less maintenance, as well as those that are indigenous or easily adapted to the region they are grown in.

Ornamental grasses come in all shapes and sizes, from a very short six inches to plumes more than fifteen feet tall. Most have fine textures, an upright or arching growth habit, and leaves that billow and sway in the breeze, adding a soothing effect to the garden. They offer varying shades of green, yellow, or variegated leaves, as well as interesting blooms. Most ornamental grasses turn scarlet or straw colored in cold weather, and the best varieties, like Japanese silver grass or bluestem, will stay showy throughout most of the winter. When these decorative grasses are planted next to the right selection of broadleaf plants, the effect can be dazzling, winter or summer!

Known for their ability to quickly establish themselves and spread, ornamental grasses have either a clumping growth habit or a running growth habit. "Clumpers" spread more slowly than "runners," some of which have a reputation for being invasive. Most have deep root systems, especially those that formed the solid car-

Chapter Six

pets of sod that made up the original prairie here in the Midwest and Plains. Their deep roots help them find the moisture they need to withstand drought, as well as pull up nutrients that might be lacking in the topsoil.

In this chapter, our focus is on the use of ornamental grasses in the garden. It is assumed that these plants will be growing in small containers when purchased. The majority of ornamental grasses prefer planting sites in full sun, but a few (like northern sea oats) will grow in the shade. The soil should be light and well drained. Some grasses will tolerate moisture better than others; first know your planting site, then choose an appropriate plant for the conditions.

To transplant the selected grass, dig a hole up to eighteen inches deep and three times the width of the rootball or container. Tap the container on a hard surface to loosen the roots from the sides of the pot. Return enough soil to the bottom of the hole so that the top of the rootball is level with the ground around it after planting. Gently tease the roots apart from the root mass after removing the pot, and spread them out in the hole. Backfill with the remaining soil, and water the plant deeply. Although most ornamental grasses are drought tolerant, spread a two- to three-inch layer of organic mulch around the planting area when finished. This will conserve moisture and help the plant develop more quickly, as well as keep out weeds.

Enjoy the plants as they grow throughout the year, especially as they show off their seasonal changes, first into blooming plants, then into spectacular winter specimens. Some gardeners may be tempted to cut the straw-colored leaves and flowers back in the fall. Instead, allow them to stay all winter for an effect that is unlike any other. Plant ornamental grasses near other plants that have good winter characteristics, such as winterberry holly. Cut the foliage back to within a few inches of the crown in late winter, before new growth begins. To divide an ornamental grass, slice through the crown and root mass with a sharp shovel or spade. Transplant the divisions as described above and water them deeply every few days. Since ornamental grasses have no known insect or fungus problems, these few practices will be all the care required—which will free up your time for other gardening endeavors!

Big Bluestem

Andropogon gerardii

Other Name: Turkey Foot
Zones: 5, 6
Height: 5 to 8 feet
Bloom Period: August to September
Flowers: Purplish-brown
Type: Perennial

Light Requirement:

When the pioneers first settled the prairie states, they made their way through meadows full of bluestem. This native grass was the backbone of the tall grass prairie that covered the Midwest and Plains states, including parts of northern Indiana. Most of the tall grass prairie has disappeared because of modern agricultural development. Fortunately, many original prairie plants, including bluestem, were saved and have recently started to become popular in Hoosier gardens. If it is given plenty of moisture, big bluestem can grow up to eight feet tall. Its stems have an upright and slightly arching growth habit; they are a silvery blue-green at the base, which helps give the grass its name. In the late summer, bluestem sends up many purplish seedheads that have three branches. The branching pattern of the new seedheads resembles a turkey foot, which is how it got its nickname. The foliage turns light bronze with the onset of frost in October. The plant stays upright all winter, providing food and shelter for wildlife.

WHEN TO PLANT
Transplant big bluestem into the garden in April or May, when the soil is dry enough to cultivate, or work.

WHERE TO PLANT
Big bluestem is tolerant of a wide variety of planting sites, but all must receive at least 6 hours of full sun per day. It prefers a deep, moist, well-drained soil with plenty of organic matter, but it will tolerate heavy clay. It also tolerates hot, dry locations, though it will not grow as tall. Bluestem's deep root system makes it a good plant for naturalizing and for erosion control on banks or hillsides.

How to Plant

Although bluestem can be planted as a bare-root plant or from seed, most gardeners will end up planting a container-grown specimen. Dig a planting hole up to 3 times the width of the container. Gently tap the container on a hard surface to loosen the root mass from the sides of the pot. Remove the pot and tease out any roots that are growing in concentric circles. If there is a large mass of roots concentrated at the bottom of the pot, slice the root mass vertically 4 or 5 times with a sharp knife. This will encourage better rooting after planting. Transplant the grass to the same level it was growing in the pot. Backfill the hole with the original soil, and water deeply. Spread a 2- to 3-inch layer of organic mulch over the entire planting area.

Advice for Care

Big bluestem is a durable and maintenance-free plant. During dry spells, water it deeply once a week. Maintain a 2- to 3-inch layer of organic mulch to prevent weeds and conserve soil moisture. Cut the foliage back before growth begins again, preferably in late winter. Like all ornamental grasses, big bluestem does not have any pest problems.

Additional Information

Plant bluestem in masses with other tall prairie plants such as purple and yellow coneflowers, rattlesnake master, or asters. Bluestem plumes are nice additions to dried flower arrangements.

Additional Species, Cultivars and Varieties

'Champ' is a shorter variety, and 'Pawnee' has a more weeping or arching growth habit. Little bluestem, *Schizachyrium scoparium*, has similar foliage to big bluestem but only grows to 3 feet, making it more adaptable to smaller gardens. It thrives in full sun.

Blue Fescue

Festuca ovina 'Glauca'

Other Name: Sheep's Fescue	**Light Requirement:**
Zones: 5, 6	
Height: 1 foot	
Bloom Period: June to July	
Flowers: Tan	
Type: Perennial	

This highly popular grass forms small, bluish-gray mounds about one foot in diameter; the mounds resemble perfectly round, tiny clouds in the garden. Blue fescue's leaves grow outward, and they are so thin they look like fine hair. Some gardeners think the mounds look like blue porcupines. In late June and early July, blue fescue sends up straw-colored seedheads that extend twelve to eighteen inches above the foliage. Although these "flowers" are not particularly showy, they add some seasonal interest. With the onset of frost, these blue puffs turn golden tan, making small "spots" in the garden through the winter.

WHEN TO PLANT

Plant blue fescue when the soil dries out in the early spring, preferably before new growth begins. If you are planting in the summer, cut the foliage back by at least half to prevent the plant from drying out.

WHERE TO PLANT

Blue fescue prefers soil that is moist but well drained. In fact, good drainage is essential; blue fescue tends to die out in soils that stay wet (such as heavy clay). Blue fescue also grows best in the cool temperatures of spring and fall. It prefers sites that provide afternoon shade in the summertime. Blue fescue's short stature requires that it be planted as an edging plant in the garden. The blue-gray foliage makes a nice accent.

HOW TO PLANT

Prepare a planting hole at least 2 or 3 times the width of the rootball or container. Work soil to remove clumps, rocks and other debris, and return enough of it to the hole so that the top of the rootball is level with the ground around it. It is very important that blue fescue have good drainage, so it is best to err on the side of safety by planting this grass an inch *above* grade. Tap the side of the container on a hard surface to loosen the root mass from the pot. Carefully remove the plant from the container and tease out any roots that appear to be growing in concentric circles. Backfill the hole with the rest of the original soil, and water deeply. Spread a 2- to 3-inch layer of organic mulch over the entire planting area to help keep the roots cool.

ADVICE FOR CARE

Every year, cut the foliage to a height of 3 inches in late winter, before new spring growth starts. Blue fescue often dies out in the center of the plant after a couple of seasons, especially if it is planted in heavy clay sites. To help prevent this, divide the plant every 2 or 3 years. In the heat of summer the foliage sometimes turns brown. Cut the seedheads back; then clip the foliage to at least half the original height to encourage new blue leaves to grow later in the summer. Maintain a 2- to 3-inch layer of organic mulch around the plants at all times to conserve moisture, to keep the roots cool, and prevent weeds.

ADDITIONAL INFORMATION

Blue fescue is a welcome addition to any rock garden. Mix it with other plants that have blue-gray foliage or white flowers; artemesia, dusty miller, candytuft, or snow-in-summer create a spectacular effect.

ADDITIONAL SPECIES, CULTIVARS, OR VARIETIES

'Elijah Blue' grows only 8 inches and has bright-blue, very finely textured leaves. 'Blaufuchs' is another reliable variety; it grows from 6 to 12 inches high. 'Sea Urchin' has more silvery leaves, and it also grows 6 to 12 inches high.

Feather Reed Grass

Calamagrostis × *acutiflora* 'Stricta'

Zones: 5, 6	**Light Requirement:**
Height: 3 to 5 feet	
Bloom Period: June, lasts all summer	
Flowers: Purplish bronze, fading to golden	
Type: Perennial	

*F*all is the time when many tall grasses send up their plume-like flowers—feather reed grass is the perfect ornamental grass for gardeners who can't wait that long. Feather reed grass is one of our earliest blooming grasses; its masses of slender, spike-like flowers open in June. The flowers are thin and wispy, and they have a purplish-bronze tinge which eventually fades to golden tan. The flower stalks grow two to three feet above the leaves. They have an upright, stiff habit that gives the entire plant a strong vertical effect in the garden. For this reason, feather reed grass makes an excellent accent plant; it looks especially good with a dark evergreen background. The flower spikes remain showy throughout the rest of the summer. After the first hard frost, both the leaves and the flower spikes bleach to a straw color. Like many ornamental grasses, feather reed grass holds its upright character throughout the winter. Although it may lean from the weight of heavy snow, it recovers well and will return to its upright habit.

When to Plant

Transplant feather reed grass in the early spring, after the soil dries and before the leaves emerge on the trees.

Where to Plant

Feather reed grass grows best in moist, well-drained soil enriched with plenty of organic matter. It tolerates heavy clay very well as long as it is kept moist but not wet. It prefers full sun; you can plant it in partial shade, but it will produce fewer blooms. Feather reed grass makes a powerful vertical accent in the garden. Plant it in large groups to create a sea of golden flowers in early summer.

How to Plant

Prepare the site by digging a hole up to 18 inches deep and at least that wide. Return enough soil to the hole so that the top of the rootball will be even with the ground around it. Lightly tap the side of the container on a hard surface to loosen the roots from the pot. Tease out any roots that are wound in concentric circles and lay them flat in the hole during planting, then cover them well with the soil. If the bottom of the pot is filled with masses of roots, take a sharp knife and make 4 or 5 vertical slices in the rootball. Backfill the hole with the original, well-worked soil, and water deeply. Spread a 2- to 3-inch layer of organic mulch over the planting area to conserve moisture.

Advice for Care

Like all ornamental grasses, feather reed grass is considered a low-maintenance plant. To help it grow best, however, water deeply in the summer at least once a week, and maintain a layer of organic mulch around the root zone. Cut it back to 6 to 8 inches in the late winter. Feather reed grass starts spring growth earlier than most other ornamental grasses, so you need to cut it soon enough that the tips of the new leaves will not be affected.

Additional Information

The golden flowers have a pink cast, and they mix well with other pink, purple, or blue flowers such as *Salvia farinacea*, the veronicas, or *Verbena bonariensis*. Generally, the more moisture feather reed grass receives, the taller the plant will grow.

Additional Species, Cultivars, or Varieties

'Overdam' has variegated foliage with a cream-colored stripe running the length of its leaves. 'Karl Foerster' is grown more widely than 'Stricta' because it blooms a few weeks earlier.

Fountain Grass

Pennisetum alopecuroides 'Hameln'

Other Name: Dwarf Fountain Grass	**Light Requirement:**
Zones: 5, 6	
Height: 2 to 3 feet	
Bloom Period: August through the winter	
Flowers: Golden tan	
Type: Perennial	

ountain grass is one of the most widely planted ornamental grasses throughout Indiana—and rightly so! Its narrow leaves have an upright, arching growth habit; they look exquisite when topped with their flowers, which start opening in July. These abundant blooms closely resemble foxtail. They cascade outward from the plant, opening just barely above the leaves, and giving the whole plant the look of a water fountain. The flowers open with a light tan color that fades to a pinkish brown as fall approaches. With the onset of frost, the leaves streak yellow then bleach to a straw color by November. The leaves and flowers remain upright and rigid through January, even after snowfall; they are perfect additions to the winter garden. They have no pests to speak of and are simple to care for. They may qualify as "indestructible" plants!

WHEN TO PLANT

Fountain grass transplants easily at any time of the year, but prefers spring planting. Choose a time after the ground is dry and just before the leaves emerge on the trees.

WHERE TO PLANT

This durable plant will grow in almost any moist, well-drained soil that has been enriched with plenty of organic matter. It may not grow to its full capacity during dry summers unless you water it deeply once a week. It grows best and will produce more blooms in full sun, but it will hold its own in partial shade. Plant this beautiful grass along a pathway so that the flowers appear to bow to the passersby. It looks natural planted on the edge or bank of a water garden. Plant it with chokeberry or winterberry holly for a fantastic winter combination.

How to Plant

Prepare the planting site by digging a hole that is at least 18 inches deep and 3 times the width of the rootball. Return enough soil to the hole so that the top of the rootball is even with the ground around it. Backfill the rest of the hole with the original soil, and water deeply. Spread a 2- to 3-inch layer of mulch around the entire planting area

Advice for Care

Fountain grass is a maintenance-free plant; it is a perfect choice for gardeners who have little time to invest. To help keep weeds down and conserve moisture, maintain a 2- to 3-inch layer of organic mulch around the root zone throughout the growing season. In the late winter or very early spring, cut the foliage back to 3 to 4 inches.

Additional Information

Fountain grass is closely related to pearl millet, a staple food crop of many semi-arid countries. The dwarf form, called 'Hameln', is a variety that is more useful than the species plant because its leaves and flowers remain stiff and rigid through the winter. The species, *P. alopecuroides*, grows about a foot taller, but its flowers will shatter and its leaves will break after the first snow or ice storm.

Additional Species, Cultivars, or Varieties

'Little Bunny' is a short, compact variety; it grows only 1 foot tall. In Indiana, *Pennisetum setaceum* is an annual fountain grass that grows about 3 feet tall and has longer, bottlebrush-type blooms. The variety 'Rubrum' has stunning ruby-red foliage and combines well with the pink blooms of flowering tobacco, cockscomb, or purple coneflower. It contrasts well with black-eyed Susans, especially the 'Goldstrum' variety. For something different, plant purple fountain grass in a large container for the patio or deck. Remember to keep it well watered in the summer.

Japanese Blood Grass

Imperata cylindrica 'Red Baron'

Zones: 5, 6
Height: 1 to 2 feet
Type: Perennial

Light Requirement:

The name "Japanese blood grass" sounds rather dramatic; but it *can* be described as having been dipped in red paint. Either description serves the purpose, since the tips of the leaves are a beautiful wine red. Unlike many other grasses (including maiden and fountain grasses), Japanese blood grass spreads by underground runners called rhizomes. With ample water, it will spread in large clumps, filling in any empty space around it if you give it free rein in the garden. In this way it is similar to ribbon grass, although it is not nearly as invasive. From the time they emerge, the new leaves are tinged with red from the tip to halfway down the eighteen-inch blade. The color intensifies throughout the summer, and it is especially spectacular in the fall. After the first hard frost, the leaves turn a tawny brown and stay that way until the following spring. You can appreciate Japanese blood grass best when it is backlit by early morning or late afternoon sunlight. At those times of day, it appears as if the leaves are actually glowing red.

When to Plant

Transplant Japanese blood grass in the early spring, after the ground dries out and before leaves emerge on the trees.

Where to Plant

Japanese blood grass grows best in full sun, but it will tolerate partial shade. The more sun it receives, the more intense the red will be. It will spread faster in soil that is moist but well drained; it grows poorly in overly wet or dry situations. Plant it as a border plant or as a specimen mixed with yellow-blooming flowers such as zinnia, coreopsis, or marigolds. It also mixes well with chrysanthemums in the fall garden. Japanese blood grass grows well in a pot or other large container.

How to Plant

Prepare a planting area that is 18 inches deep and up to 3 times the width of the rootball or container. Replace enough soil in the hole so that the top of the rootball is even with the ground around it. Tap the side of the container on a hard surface to loosen the roots from the pot. Remove the plant, and tease out any roots growing in concentric circles around the bottom of the pot. Spread the roots out in the hole, and backfill with the original, well-worked soil. Water deeply, and spread a 2- to 3-inch layer of organic mulch around the entire planting area.

Advice for Care

Water deeply at least once a week in the summer, especially during dry spells—but avoid overwatering. Cut the foliage down to 3 or 4 inches in the late winter. To prevent Japanese blood grass from spreading too aggressively, plant it in a large pot that has been buried in the soil. Sometimes a part of the plant will revert to a green form; this should be pruned out with a shovel or spade. These green "mutants" are usually very aggressive, and they may take over the rest of the clump.

Additional Information

Unlike the other ornamental grasses, 'Red Baron' Japanese blood grass does not produce any flowers, but is appreciated solely for its beautiful leaves.

Additional Species, Cultivars, or Varieties

There are no other important varieties.

Maiden Grass

Miscanthus sinensis 'Gracillimus'

Other Name: Japanese Silver Grass
Zones: 5, 6
Height: 5 to 7 feet
Bloom Period: July to fall
Flowers: Light brown to silvery tan
Type: Perennial

Light Requirement:

Of all the ornamental grasses, there are probably more types of Japanese silver grass than any other. This genus includes maiden grass, flame grass, zebra grass, porcupine grass, and many others. Maiden grass is one of the oldest, and most common, ornamental grasses in use today; it is often mistakenly called "pampas grass" because of its tall stems with plume-type flowers on the tips. True pampas grass, however, is not hardy in our climate. Maiden grass has showy flowers that are wonderful when used in cutflower arrangements or simply left out in the garden. They open in late September and become fluffy as they dry out in late fall. The leaves grow thick and upright but arch outward toward the ends in a classic vase shape. After the first frost in October, the graceful leaves will turn a straw color that lasts throughout the winter months. When growth resumes in the spring, the leaves will quickly reach a height of four to five feet; they can serve as a dense screen or background plant for other grasses or broadleaf plants.

WHEN TO PLANT

Transplant maiden grass in the early spring, preferably after the soil has dried out and before the leaves emerge on the trees.

WHERE TO PLANT

Maiden grass grows best in full sun or partial shade. It tends to be more spindly in the shadier sites, and it will occasionally flop over in the wind. It tolerates a wide variety of soil types, but it prefers moist, well-drained areas with plenty of organic matter. Use maiden grass and its relatives carefully in the landscape, since they all call attention to themselves for their size, flowering habit, texture, or winter interest. Maiden grass makes an excellent background or screen. Combine it with winterberry holly and the 'Goldsturm' variety of black-eyed Susan for an outstanding winter display.

How to Plant

Prepare a planting hole that is 18 inches deep and up to 3 times the width of the rootball. Replace enough soil in the hole so that the top of the rootball is level with the ground around it. Backfill the hole with the original, well-worked soil, and water deeply. Spread a 2- to 3-inch layer of organic matter over the entire planting.

Advice for Care

In the summer, water maiden grass deeply once a week, and maintain a 3-inch layer of mulch around the root zone. Cut it back to a height of 6 to 8 inches in late winter or early spring. Maiden grass tends to form clumps, with the majority of the foliage growing from the outside. Divide it every 3 years to contain its size and reinvigorate the clump.

Additional Information

Maiden grass and its relatives grow well and look superb planted near small ponds and water gardens.

Additional Species, Cultivars, or Varieties

'Morning Light' has narrow, wispy leaves with a very fine texture. The foliage of the variety 'Purpurescens', also called flame grass, turns a brilliant, fiery red in the fall; it is unmatched in late afternoon light. 'Zebrinus', also called zebra grass, has long, arching green leaves with small yellow bands that make hash marks down the length of the blade. It sprawls almost as wide as it grows tall. 'Variegatus' is the variegated maiden grass; it has silvery white stripes that run on the margins and down the center of the leaves. It spreads 6 feet wide, so give it plenty of room.

Northern Sea Oats

Chasmanthium latifolium

Zones: 5, 6
Height: 2 to 3 feet
Bloom Period: July through fall
Flowers: Silvery tan
Type: Perennial

Light Requirement:
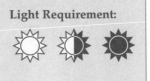

orthern sea oats closely resembles bamboo. It has erect stems with short, wide leaves that come to a quick point and are held at right angles. In midsummer, it sends up flower stalks that droop with light-green, flat seedheads that hang like spangles and shimmer in the breeze. The seedheads turn a silvery tan in the fall, and they persist well into winter. The seedheads make wonderful additions to dried flower arrangements and are much sought after in the florist trade. Northern sea oats has the unusual ability to grow both in sun and in shade, making it ideal for just about any garden.

WHEN TO PLANT

Transplant northern sea oats just about any time the ground is dry, but preferably in the early spring before the leaves emerge on the trees.

WHERE TO PLANT

Northern sea oats grows best in deep, moist, well-drained soil enriched with plenty of organic matter. These are versatile plants that grow well both in sun or partial to full shade. In sun, the leaves will be a lighter green; shadier sites produce a darker-green leaf. Plant sea oats in masses or as an accent against a dark evergreen background like yew or boxwood, where it will stand out. It is also wonderful as an edging or as container plants around a water garden.

HOW TO PLANT

Prepare the planting site by digging a hole that is 18 inches deep and up to 3 times the width of the rootball. Return enough soil to the hole so that the top of the rootball is level with the ground around it. Lightly tap the container on a hard surface to loosen the root mass, and pull the pot away from the plant. Gently tease the larger roots away from the rootball and spread them out in the planting hole. If there is a thick collection of roots growing in concentric circles at the bottom of the pot, use a sharp knife to make 4 or 5 vertical slices in the root mass. This will help the roots establish themselves better. Backfill the hole with the remainder of the original, well-worked soil. Water deeply, and spread a 2- to 3-inch layer of organic mulch over the entire planting area.

ADVICE FOR CARE

Like other ornamental grasses, sea oats requires very little care. Broadcast a tablespoon of balanced fertilizer around the root zone each spring as growth begins. Maintain a 3-inch layer of organic mulch around the root zone at all times to conserve moisture and to keep the weeds down. Cut the foliage back to 3 inches in late winter, before new growth begins.

ADDITIONAL INFORMATION

Northern sea oats is a native grass in the United States; it is highly prized for its ornamental flowers and seedheads. The plants grow in clumps, and are easily divided in the spring by cutting down through the crown with a sharp spade. Sea oats also reseeds itself in the garden, but it is not invasive. In a few years, you will have enough plants to give to friends and neighbors.

ADDITIONAL SPECIES, CULTIVARS, OR VARIETIES

There are no improved varieties of northern sea oats.

ORNAMENTAL GRASSES

Prairie Dropseed

Sporobolus heterolepis

Zones: 5, 6
Height: 1 to 3 feet
Bloom Period: July to August
Flowers: Golden
Type: Perennial

Light Requirement:

At one time, fields of prairie dropseed covered the Midwest and Plains states, but this grass disappeared with the development and spread of modern agriculture. An important component of the original tall and short grass prairies, this plant is native to northwest Indiana, where natural prairie was common. Prairie dropseed is an elegant plant that produces clumps of very fine leaves—almost like hair—that can reach to three feet. The leaves have an upright, arching growth habit; they are topped with airy, light-green wisps of blooms, eight inches long. The flowers rise two or three feet above the leaves and make a fine accent in the garden. The seeds mature in early fall and are an excellent food source for birds. Native Americans ground the seeds into flour for baking. The first hard frosts will give the leaves their golden brown "winter coat"; they will stay that color until early spring, when the cycle begins again.

WHEN TO PLANT

Transplant prairie dropseed in the early spring, after the ground dries and before the leaves emerge on the trees.

WHERE TO PLANT

There isn't a better plant for hot, dry locations that have rocky soil. Prairie dropseed also likes full-sun locations with moist, well-drained soil; it cannot tolerate wet sites. Plant it in groups or masses for a sunny groundcover, or as a specimen or accent in the perennial border. Its clumping growth habit makes a nice edging around the garden.

HOW TO PLANT

Prepare the planting site by digging a hole 18 inches deep and 3 times the width of the container or rootball. Return enough of the original soil to the hole so that the top of the rootball is level with the ground around it. Tap the side of the container on a hard surface to loosen the roots from the pot. Remove the container and tease out any of the larger roots, especially those growing in concentric circles around the pot. If there is a large mass of roots at the bottom of the pot, use a sharp knife to make 4 or 5 vertical cuts in the rootball. Place the plant in the hole, and backfill with the remainder of the original, well-pulverized soil. Water deeply, and spread a 2- to 3-inch layer of organic mulch over the entire planting area.

ADVICE FOR CARE

Prairie dropseed, like other ornamental grasses, is virtually mainte-nance-free. To help it grow best, maintain a 3-inch layer of mulch to conserve moisture and prevent weeds. Cut the foliage back to a height of 4 inches in late winter or early spring, just before new growth begins.

ADDITIONAL INFORMATION

To divide prairie dropseed, take a sharp spade and slice through the center of the clump after cutting the foliage back in the early spring. Water the divisions deeply after you transplant them. Prairie dropseed is slower to establish itself than other ornamental grasses; it may not bloom until the second or third year after you plant it. Patience in the early years will reward you with permanent satisfaction. Mixed with other native prairie grasses and wildflowers, prairie dropseed will provide excellent food and cover for wildlife.

ADDITIONAL SPECIES, CULTIVARS, OR VARIETIES

There are no improved varieties of prairie dropseed available.

Switch Grass

Panicum virgatum

Zones: 5, 6 **Height:** 3 to 5 feet **Bloom Period:** August to September **Flowers:** Light brown tinged with pink **Type:** Perennial	**Light Requirement:**

*C*ombined with other grasses and many wildflowers, switch grass was an important part of the tall grass prairie that welcomed settlers to the Midwest and Plains states. Along with bluestem, dropseed, and deep-rooted wildflowers, switch grass helped form thick sod that created the deep soils that gave rise to the corn belt. Switch grass is loved for its light and airy seedheads and its brilliant fall color that varies from yellow to red. The leaves grow to two or three feet and have a mostly upright habit, arching only slightly toward the tips. The wispy blooms open in mid- to late summer, and they have a light-brown to pink caste to them. They mature to a golden tan and have hard reddish seedheads that make a good food source for birds and other wildlife. The leaves bleach to a light straw color in the winter, making a spectacular show when massed in their natural setting.

WHEN TO PLANT

Plant switch grass in the early spring, after the ground dries out from the long winter and before new growth begins.

WHERE TO PLANT

This grass grows best in deep, moist, well-drained soils. It tolerates the dry periods of summer as well as the wet periods of winter and spring. Switch grass grows well and shows its true colors when it is massed in large natural planting fields, or when it is used on steeper slopes or banks for erosion control. In the garden, switch grass is a good background plant for shorter grasses or perennials and other wildflowers.

How to Plant

Prepare the planting site by digging a hole 18 inches deep and up to 3 times the width of the rootball. Return enough of the soil to the hole so that the top of the rootball is even with the ground around it. Tap the container on a hard surface to loosen the roots from the sides of the pot, and then remove it. Tease out the larger roots and spread them out in the planting hole. If there is a thick mass of roots growing in concentric circles at the bottom of the pot, take a sharp knife and make 4 or 5 vertical cuts to improve establishment. Backfill the hole with the rest of the original, well-worked soil, and water deeply. Spread a 2- to 3-inch layer of organic mulch over the entire planting area to help conserve moisture.

Advice for Care

Like other ornamental grasses, switch grass requires little maintenance. To encourage faster growth, water deeply once a week throughout the growing season, and maintain a 3-inch layer of organic mulch around the root zone. Cut the leaves back to a height of 6 to 8 inches in the early spring, before the new leaves emerge.

Additional Information

Its tolerance of damp soils makes switch grass a good species for planting around ponds, streams, and water gardens. The seedheads are attractive additions to dried flower arrangements in the fall and winter.

Additional Species, Cultivars, or Varieties

Red switch grass, *Panicum virgatum* 'Haense Herms', grows 3 feet tall, and has wine-red to purple-tipped leaves. The red deepens as the season progresses; the fall color is an intense orange-red. 'Rotstrahlbusch' is another popular red-leafed variety; it grows to 3 to 4 feet. 'Heavy Metal' has blue-green leaves and fine wisps of golden seedheads in the fall.

Tufted Hairgrass

Deschampsia caespitosa

Zones: 5, 6	**Light Requirement:**
Height: 1 to 3 feet	
Bloom Period: June until fall	
Flowers: Golden yellow	
Type: Perennial	

ufted hairgrass is one of the most shade-tolerant grasses there is. The clouds of dry, creamy-white seedheads open in early summer. They brighten shade gardens full of the usual hostas and ferns and give those plants a different character. Tufted hairgrass produces masses of blooms on two-foot stems that tower over the short, slender leaves, making it appear almost top-heavy. The fine, hair-like texture of the leaves is mostly concealed by the billowy masses of flowers that appear in June and last all summer. By fall, the flowers have begun to shatter; cut them back so they will not detract from the fine displays of other fall-blooming grasses. Tufted hairgrass flowers are good additions to dried arrangements if you cut them shortly after they open. Plant tufted hairgrass as an accent or a specimen plant near a water garden. The billowy tufts of flowers make a nice background for periwinkle, shasta daisies, or purple heliotrope.

WHEN TO PLANT

Plant tufted hairgrass in late fall or very early spring, after the ground is dry and before the new growth begins.

WHERE TO PLANT

Tufted hairgrass is native to wet and boggy soils, but in the garden it prefers soils that stay moist with good drainage. It grows well around water gardens, provided there is minimal flooding. It will produce more flowers in full sun; the foliage tends to burn, however, if it is planted in a dry site where it gets afternoon sun, so provide these plants with partial shade. Tufted hairgrass tolerates partial shade and makes a good companion for other shade-loving plants such as bugleweed (*Ajuga*) and coral bells. The informal feathery blooms contrast beautifully with a more formal evergreen background like yew or boxwood.

HOW TO PLANT

Prepare the planting site by digging a hole 18 inches deep and up to 3 times the width of the rootball. Return enough of the soil to the hole so that the top of the rootball is level with the ground around it. Tap the container on a hard surface to loosen the roots, and remove the pot from the rootball. Tease out any long roots and spread them flat in the planting hole before backfilling with the remainder of the original soil. Spread a 2- to 3-inch layer of organic mulch over the entire planting area.

ADVICE FOR CARE

Trim the flowers back to the height of the foliage when it starts to look ragged in the late summer or fall. Trim the dead foliage in late winter; the new foliage of this species is one of the earliest to emerge. Maintain a 2- to 3-inch layer of mulch around the plants during the growing season to conserve moisture and to help keep the weeds down.

ADDITIONAL INFORMATION

Tufted hairgrass is easy to divide. Simply slice through the middle of the plant with a sharp spade or shovel. Always keep newly planted divisions moist by watering deeply at least once or twice a week. Tufted hairgrass is a favorite of rabbits.

ADDITIONAL SPECIES, CULTIVARS, OR VARIETIES

'Bronzeschleier', also called 'Bronze Veil', has bronze-colored flowers that have a drooping growth habit. 'Fairy's Joke' produces new plantlets at the tips of the flowers. 'Goldgehaenge' produces mounds of bright, golden flowers in June.

CHAPTER SEVEN

Perennials

*P*ERENNIALS ARE TEMPTING PLANTS. The more you
have, the more you want. By definition, a "perennial" is a
plant that lives for two years or more. Some perennials (such as
daylilies) last for many years, while others (columbine, for example)
have short, spectacular lives. Most perennials are grown for their
flowers (such as veronica) while others (lamb's ear, for example)
are grown for their foliage. Many (like sedum) are grown for both
foliage and flowers; some (coneflowers, for example) are valued for
the dried flower heads that provide food for birds or decorate the
winter landscape.

In theory, it all seems easy. Buy plants that come back each year,
put them in the ground, then stand back and watch them grow! It *is*
that easy for some plants, especially the native varieties that thrive
in Indiana. Purple coneflowers (*Echinacea purpurea*) and black-eyed
Susans (*Rudbeckia fulgida*) are two natives that "strut their stuff" with
little help from the gardener. Other perennials may require more
effort on your part. As with anything worthwhile, perennials take
time, from planning the beds to selecting and maintaining the
plants. Before a spade turns soil, pencil should hit paper to sketch
out a plan. One might say "plan" is a root word of "plant."

Here are some basics to make growing perennials rewarding:

- Measure and make a sketch of the area to be planted. Show
  existing plants, shrubs, and trees; structures, such as a fence, air
  conditioner, driveway, or sidewalk; and other permanent objects
  in the landscape, like stumps or boulders.
- Indicate what sizes, colors, and textures you want in the garden.
  Research and make a list of plants that bloom in the color and at
  the time of the year you desire. Do you want an all-season garden, a summer cutting garden, or something more formal? You
  can create a cottage, English, or wildflower garden, or simple
  islands of plants that bring personal pleasure. Your perennial
  garden may be monochromatic, blooming all in one color; or it

Chapter Seven

may be an evening garden, with plants that come into their full glory at night; or you may choose to grow flowers that fill the air with their fragrant scents. Depending on your ideas, a perennial border can be created in one season, or it can be an ongoing multi-year project.

- Prepare the bed by digging at least twelve inches deep. If planting large or deep-rooted perennials such as peonies and roses, dig eighteen to twenty-four inches deep. Perennials are considered permanent plantings and their beds should be well prepared for the long stay. The deeper the bed is dug, the better.

- Mix organic material such as compost, peat moss, or finely chopped leaves with the soil in the hole to improve drainage and add nutrients. Add a slow-release nitrogen fertilizer. Work the soil until it is so loose that it can be dug by hand.

- If you don't want to dig because of hard, compacted soil, consider making raised beds. Mound additional soil up to twelve inches above the level of the ground and plant your plants there. Eventually the beds will settle closer to ground level.

- One of the easiest ways to grow perennials is to buy them already growing in containers at garden centers, retail shops, or through mail-order catalogs. You can also get transplants from neighbors, friends, or plant sales. Plant perennials in holes dug three times as wide as the rootball or container they came in and at the same depth they were growing previously.

- Another easy way to acquire plants is by dividing what you have. Some perennials should be divided every few years to keep them vigorous. Perennials may also be grown from seed. Most perennials grown from seed do not flower the first year.

- The perennial bed should be cleaned up in late fall or early winter. Cut back plant material that has been killed by frosts and remove stems, seedheads, dead leaves, and other debris. Material from diseased or insect-infested plants should be removed as soon as possible regardless of the time of year.

- Don't be afraid to change things around. If a plant is too big or requires too much maintenance, move it or pull it out.

- Finally, remember that above all else, gardening—even with perennials—should be fun!

Achillea

Achillea millefolium 'Cerise Queen'

Other Names: Yarrow, Sneezewort, *Achillea filipendulina* **Zones:** 5, 6 **Height:** 2 to 5 feet **Bloom Period:** Summer **Flowers:** Various	**Light Requirement:** 

*P*eople either love *Achillea* or hate it. Those who dislike it complain that it falls over; those who love it remind us that it blooms throughout early and midsummer, has occasional blossoms late in the season, and is a wonderful cut flower. It can also be dried for everlasting arrangements. This is a trouble-free perennial that is seldom bothered by pests or diseases. It has long had the reputation for having healing powers and is often classified as an herb instead of as a perennial. Its flowers and leaves are fragrant, and its foliage adds nice texture to the perennial bed. In France, *Achillea* is called "carpenter's herb" because it was used to heal cuts on carpenters' hands.

WHEN TO PLANT

Transplants may be planted or divided in the fall, or in spring as soon as the soil can be worked. They may also be transplanted in summer if given adequate water.

WHERE TO PLANT

Well-drained, average soil is best. *Achillea* prefers sun but will tolerate light shade. Taller varieties should be planted in the middle or at the back of a flower border. If you are not bothered by *Achillea's* floppiness, the plants look great in the front of the border, too.

HOW TO PLANT

Plant transplants, 18 to 24 inches apart, as deep as they were growing in their containers. Backfill with soil from the planting hole. Water them well. Mulch if desired, or spread a layer of compost around the plant.

ADVICE FOR CARE

Achillea is a fairly low-maintenance plant. After it flowers in summer, cut back the stems; the plant may flower again in late summer or early fall. The foliage is nearly evergreen and is frequently visible all winter. Once established, *Achillea* tolerates drought, although it does best when watered regularly. Apply an all-purpose granular fertilizer around the plant in spring when new growth appears, or spread a layer of compost in spring and fall.

ADDITIONAL INFORMATION

Soil that is too rich may cause yarrow stems to weaken and fall over. *Achillea* can be grown from seed, though it may not flower the first year. Some *Achilleas* are more invasive than others. They are easy to pull out to transplant elsewhere, give away, or compost. Tall varieties that fall over may be staked.

ADDITIONAL SPECIES, CULTIVARS, OR VARIETIES

The tallest yarrows are *Achillea filipendulina*. Popular named varieties are 'Gold Plate', which may have 6-inch heads; 'Coronation Gold', which grows about 3 feet tall and has gray-green foliage; and 'Moonshine', which grows about 18 to 24 inches tall and has creamy-yellow flowers with silvery-gray foliage. Common yarrow, *Achillea millefolium*, rarely grows taller than 3 feet. The foliage is green to gray-green, depending on the variety. Popular varieties are 'Paprika', 'Cerise Queen', 'Summer Pastels', and 'Galaxy Hybrids'. *Achillea ptarmica* 'The Pearl' grows about 2 feet tall and has small, pure-white flowers.

Anemone

Anemone × hybrida

Other Name: Japanese Anemone **Zones:** 5, 6 **Height:** 3 to 5 feet **Bloom Period:** Late summer/early fall **Flowers:** Pink, rose, white	**Light Requirement:**

*J*apanese anemones are long-lasting flowers that come into bloom in late summer or early fall. For weeks the flowers float on spindly branches well above dark-green, maple-like foliage. Eventually the flower petals fall away, leaving the seedheads, brown balls which offer late-fall and winter interest. Anemones sometimes struggle to take hold, but once established in the garden they require little care. Most anemones are planted from transplants or from corms which eventually develop a fibrous root system.

WHEN TO PLANT

Anemones do best when planted in spring as soon as the soil can be worked.

WHERE TO PLANT

Japanese anemones will do better if given a little light shade, though they tolerate full sun if given plenty of water. Plant in the middle or at the back of the flower garden, or mix them in a bed of daffodils and daylilies for 3 seasons of interest.

HOW TO PLANT

Transplants should be planted 18 to 24 inches apart, at the same depth they were growing in their pots. Backfill with soil from the planting hole. Water them well. Mulch if desired.

ADVICE FOR CARE

Apply an all-purpose granular fertilizer around the plant in spring when new growth appears, or spread a layer of compost around the plant in spring and fall. Cut back spent flowers in late winter when the plant begins to look ratty (or cut them off sooner to keep volunteer seedlings under control).

ADDITIONAL INFORMATION

Japanese anemones may be invasive or may multiple rapidly. They are easy to pull up, however, and can be transplanted elsewhere, given away, or composted. The pink varieties seem to be slightly more winter hardy, so it may be a good idea to mulch white anemones with a light layer of leaves. Remove the layer as soon as new growth appears in spring.

ADDITIONAL SPECIES, CULTIVARS, OR VARIETIES

'Alba' and 'Honorine Jobert' have single white flowers; 'September Charm', 'Bressingham Glow', 'Queen Charlotte', and 'Hadspen Abundance' have single pink or rose flowers; 'Prinz Heinrich' and 'Margarete' have double or semi-double rose or pink flowers. *Anemone tomentosa* (sometimes called *Anemone vitifolia* 'Robustissima') is one of the more invasive types. This is a very hardy plant. *Anemone blanda* are often called Grecian windflowers. These are spring-flowering plants that grow from corms that are formed from seeds.

Aster

Aster novae-angliae, Aster novi-belgii

<table>
<tr><td>

Other Names: Michaelmas Aster,
   Michaelmas Daisy, New England Aster,
   New York Aster
Zones: 5, 6
Height: 2 to 7 feet
Bloom Period: Late summer through fall
Flowers: White, violet, pink, red

</td><td>

Light Requirement:

</td></tr>
</table>

*T*he aster is another late bloomer that is indispensable in the perennial garden. Some varieties take on an almost shrub-like quality, and are literally covered with daisy-like flowers that bloom well into fall. Flowers are one to two-and-one-half inches in diameter. Asters are easy-to-grow native plants. They make excellent cut flowers for indoor arrangements. Newer varieties are shorter and more resistant to mildew.

WHEN TO PLANT

Asters are best planted in spring as soon as the soil can be worked. They may be divided in spring and early summer, too.

WHERE TO PLANT

Most asters are fairly tall, so plant them in the middle or at the back of the perennial border. Some varieties may also be used as late-flowering shrubs in a shrub border. Asters prefer well-drained soil; wet soil may cause the plants to rot. Plant asters in full sun or part shade locations.

HOW TO PLANT

Transplants should be planted the same depth they were growing at the nursery. Plant 12 to 24 inches apart, depending on the variety. Backfill with soil from the planting hole and water well. Mulch if desired.

ADVICE FOR CARE

Asters can be pinched like chrysanthemums to keep them compact and to delay flowering. Stop pinching around July 4. Tall varieties may need to be staked. Once established, asters tolerate drought, but they do better with regular watering. Apply an all-purpose granular fertilizer around the plant in spring when new growth appears, or add a layer of compost to the bed in spring and fall.

ADDITIONAL INFORMATION
Dividing plants every 2 or 3 years will keep them vigorous. Because they are susceptible to mildew, be sure the plants have good air circulation. Powdery mildew causes the lower leaves to turn white, then yellow-brown, before falling off.

ADDITIONAL SPECIES, CULTIVARS, OR VARIETIES
Varieties from *A. novae-angliae* and *A. novi-belgii* may be referred to as Michaelmas daisy. Named varieties of *Aster novae-angliae* (New England aster) include 'Alma Potschke', which grows about 3 feet tall and has salmon-pink flowers; 'Purple Dome', which grows about 2 feet tall and has purple flowers; 'Harrington's Pink', about 4 feet tall with pink flowers; 'September Ruby', about 4 feet tall with pink-rose flowers; and 'Autumn Snow', which has white flowers. Named varieties of *Aster novi-belgii* (New York aster) include 'Crimson Brocade', which grows about 4 feet tall and has semi-double, dark-red flowers; and 'Professor Kippenburg', which grows only about 12 inches tall and has lavender-blue flowers. *Aster × frikartii* is a hybrid that is bushier and blooms longer than other asters, but it tends to be killed by winter in Zone 5. Some sources suggest that if you wait until spring to cut back the plant, it will winter over more successfully. Named varieties include 'Monch' and 'Wonder of Stafa', both of which have lavender-blue flowers and range between 2 and 3 feet tall.

Autumn Joy Sedum

Sedum × 'Autumn Joy'

Other Names: Live Forever, Stonecrop **Zones:** 5, 6 **Height:** 1 to 2 feet **Bloom Period:** July to frost **Flowers:** Pink fading to reddish brown	**Light Requirement:**

'Autumn Joy' sedum is one of the outstanding fall flowers for a perennial garden. More commonly known as "live forever," it gets this name for its ability to thrive in hot, dry soils where nothing else will grow. This is a plant for "high traffic areas" if you have young (or older) children; it seems to come back stronger the more it is trampled on! Sedums are succulents that closely resemble the popular jade plant we grow indoors. They have thick, fleshy leaves attached closely to the stems. 'Autumn Joy' grows to about eighteen inches under average conditions. They begin to show masses of light-green flower buds as early as July. The flowers are produced in circular but flattened masses at the top of the plant. Eventually opening to light pink in August and September, the flowers fade to russet brown by early fall. 'Autumn Joy' is especially known for its ability to stand tall throughout most of the winter, with the brown seedheads on top of the dead stalks providing good winter interest. For a fantastic display through January and February, plant 'Autumn Joy' with dwarf fountain grass, *Rudbeckia fulgida* 'Goldsturm' (black-eyed Susans), and winterberry holly.

WHEN TO PLANT

Transplant 'Autumn Joy' and other sedums in early spring, after the soil dries. Because they tolerate drought, sedums will also tolerate planting in the summer. Avoid planting sedum in the late summer and fall, since it is at the height of its bloom and won't have time to establish a good root system before winter.

WHERE TO PLANT

Sedums like 'Autumn Joy' are the perfect plants for hot, dry, sandy soils in full sun to light shade. Plant them in masses for the best effect. Sedums can be the backbone of a rock garden.

How to Plant

Prepare the garden as described in the introduction to this chapter. Dig a hole up to 3 times the width of the rootball or container, and about 12 inches deep. Plant 'Autumn Joy' at the same depth it was growing in its container, then backfill the hole with the original soil. Water deeply and spread a 2- to 3-inch layer of organic mulch around the entire planting area.

Advice for Care

This is a reliable plant that asks only to be enjoyed, year-round. It has no serious pests in our climate. If you don't like the erect stems of brown seedheads in the winter, cut the flower stalks back to 4 inches after the first hard frost. If you like them, cut the stalks back in late winter before signs of new growth.

Additional Information

'Autumn Joy' is easily propagated after a few years by slicing through the crown of the plant in early spring with a sharp spade or shovel. Another method is to take a 2-inch cutting of the new growth in the spring, dip it in rooting hormone, stick it in a sturdy flat of moist sand, and place the flat in the shade.

Additional Species, Cultivars, or Varieties

Sedum × 'Ruby Glow' grows to 12 inches and has sprawling stems topped with deep rosy-red flowers in mid- to late summer. 'Vera Jameson' has larger flowers on shorter plants. *Sedum spectabile* 'Meteor' and 'Stardust' are upright like 'Autumn Joy' and have deep-pink flowers. *Sedum kamtschaticum* 'Variegatum' grows to 6 inches tall and has leaves edged in white and flashy yellow flowers in early summer.

Black-Eyed Susan

Rudbeckia fulgida 'Goldsturm'

Other Name: Yellow Coneflower	**Light Requirement:**
Zones: 5, 6	
Height: 18 to 30 inches	
Bloom Period: Mid- to late summer through fall	
Flowers: Yellow	

*B*lack-eyed Susan or yellow coneflower are common names given to these yellow daisy-like flowers with dark centers. Some of them are annuals and others are perennials. *Rudbeckia fulgida* 'Goldsturm' is a hybrid of the native plant often seen along highways, on the fringes of woods, and in meadows. This hybrid is very easy to grow and will frequently self-sow. Goldfinches and other birds like to sit on the cones and eat the seeds. The leaves are dark green and the flowers get about three inches wide. Some seed varieties may have color variance. Most *Rudbeckia* bloom from July through September.

WHEN TO PLANT

Transplant in spring as soon as the soil can be worked, or in fall. Plants may be divided at those times, too.

WHERE TO PLANT

Rudbeckia does best in well-drained soil in full sun. It tolerates light shade. This is a good plant for the middle of the perennial border.

HOW TO PLANT

Transplants should be planted the same depth they were growing in their containers. Space 18 to 24 inches apart. Backfill with soil from the planting hole. Water them well and mulch.

ADVICE FOR CARE

Apply an all-purpose granular fertilizer in spring when new growth appears, or spread a layer of compost around the plant in spring and fall. Spent flowers may be cut off to encourage more flowers, or they may be left on the plant to feed the birds and provide winter interest.

ADDITIONAL INFORMATION
Divide every 3 or 4 years.

ADDITIONAL SPECIES, CULTIVARS, OR VARIETIES
Rudbeckia laciniata and *R. speciosa* are called cutleaf coneflowers. These grow 6 feet tall and have slender yellow flower petals. 'Golden Glow' is a named variety that grows 6 to 8 feet tall. *Rudbeckia nitida* grows 2 to 3 feet tall with reflexed petals, more like the native coneflowers; named varieties are 'Herbsonne' and 'Autumn Sun'. 'Goldquelle' and 'Gold Drop' have double flowers and range from 4 to 6 feet tall. Some of these larger varieties may be too big and rough for small gardens.

Blanket Flower

Gaillardia × *grandifolia*

Zones: 5, 6	**Light Requirement:**
Height: 8 to 24 inches	
Bloom Period: Summer through fall	
Flowers: Red / yellow / bronze	

*B*lanket flower has a daisy-like blossom that is usually bicolor but is sometimes all one color. It gets its name from its resemblance to the colorful blankets of Native Americans. This is a steady bloomer in the garden, especially when deadheaded, but birds do like to munch on the seeds in the flower heads.

WHEN TO PLANT

Transplants may be planted in spring as soon as the soil can be worked, or in fall. Plants may be divided at these times, too.

WHERE TO PLANT

Blanket flower does best in well-drained soil in full sun. Depending on the variety, it can be planted in the front or middle of the flower border.

HOW TO PLANT

Plant transplants the same depth they were growing in their containers. Space them 12 to 20 inches apart, depending on the variety. Backfill with soil from the planting hole and water them well. Mulching is not recommended because blanket flower may develop mildew.

ADVICE FOR CARE

Clumps tend to die out in the center after a couple of years. Dig them up and discard them, and replant the side shoots that are growing vigorously. Apply an all-purpose granular fertilizer in spring when new growth appears, or spread a layer of compost around the plants in spring and fall. Blanket flowers are drought tolerant, so don't overwater them.

ADDITIONAL INFORMATION

Gaillardia make excellent long-lasting cut flowers for indoor arrangements. Sometimes plants may be killed by winter, especially if they are in wet soil. Lightly mulching plants in well-drained soil during the winter may be helpful. Blanket flowers are easy to start from seed, frequently blooming the first year.

ADDITIONAL SPECIES, CULTIVARS, OR VARIETIES

'Goblin' grows about 12 inches tall and has red flowers with yellow edges; 'Burgundy' has wine-red flowers; 'Yellow Queen' has yellow flowers. *Gaillardia aristata* is a native perennial variety. 'Monarch Strain', with variegated colors, is a good seed variety. *Gaillardia pulchella* is an annual blanket flower.

Boltonia

Boltonia asteroides

Zones: 5, 6 **Height:** 2 to 7 feet **Bloom Period:** Late summer/fall **Flowers:** White, pink, lavender	**Light Requirement:**

A lot of people mistake this plant for a Michaelmas aster because the flowers are similar, both are native plants, and they bloom about the same time. But *Boltonia* flowers are smaller than those of most asters, sometimes only one inch in diameter. *Boltonia* tends to be tall, and some varieties will fall over later in the season from the weight of the flowers. The numerous flowers literally cover the plant and last for several weeks in August and September. *Boltonias* tolerate light shade, but if there is not enough light, they will become leggy and have fewer flowers.

WHEN TO PLANT

Plant in spring as soon as the soil can be worked. Plants may be divided at that time, too.

WHERE TO PLANT

Boltonia does best in organically rich, well-drained soil. It should be planted at the back of a perennial border or used as a specimen mixed with shrubs. Boltonia prefers a sunny location.

HOW TO PLANT

Transplants should be planted the same depth they were growing in their containers. Space at least 3 feet apart and backfill with soil from the planting hole. Water them well and mulch.

ADVICE FOR CARE

To encourage bushiness, *Boltonia* may be cut back by about a third in late spring or early summer. Apply an all-purpose granular fertilizer in early spring when new growth appears, or spread a layer of compost around the plant in spring and fall. *Boltonia* is drought tolerant.

ADDITIONAL INFORMATION
Boltonia should be divided every 3 or 4 years to keep clumps a reasonable size. Division is best done in the spring. The plant grows as a clump and spreads quickly but is rarely invasive. Sometimes *Boltonia* self-sows. It makes an excellent cut flower for indoor arrangements.

ADDITIONAL SPECIES, CULTIVARS, OR VARIETIES
Boltonia asteroides 'Snowbank' is a popular variety that is readily available at garden centers and through mail-order catalogs. It grows 4 to 5 feet tall and has white flowers. 'Pink Beauty' grows 3 to 4 feet tall and has pink flowers. *Boltonia latisquama* is about 3 feet tall and has lavender flowers. 'Nana' is about $2^{1}/_{2}$ feet tall and has pink flowers.

Butterfly Bush

Buddleia davidii

Other Names: Butterfly Shrub, Summer Lilac	**Light Requirement:**
Zones: 5, 6	
Height: 2 to 7 feet	
Bloom Period: Late summer/fall	
Flowers: White, pink, lavender, blue	

This plant is a woody shrub-like specimen that is frequently found in the perennial border. It is classified as a shrub, but it acts more like an herbaceous perennial in Indiana, where winter usually kills the plant to the ground. Fortunately, *Buddleia* blooms on new growth, so the flowers are not affected by winter cold. True to its name, butterfly shrub attracts butterflies and moths in incredible numbers. Add a shallow dish of water to a muddy or sandy spot and the butterflies may never leave, they'll have it so good. *Buddleia* is fragrant to humans as well and is an excellent cut flower for indoor arrangements. Tight flowers form along the tips of branches, and the foliage is a lovely gray-green.

WHEN TO PLANT
Transplant in the fall, or in spring as soon as the soil can be worked.

WHERE TO PLANT
Buddleia does best in ordinary, well-drained soil in full sun. Plant it at the back of the perennial border. It also can be used as a specimen in a shrub border.

HOW TO PLANT
Transplants should be planted at the same depth they were growing in their containers. Space about 5 feet apart and backfill with soil from the planting hole. Water them well and mulch.

ADVICE FOR CARE
Cut back winter-damaged branches in early spring after the new leaves begin to emerge. The plant may be cut to the ground without affecting flower production. Apply an all-purpose granular fertilizer in spring when new growth appears, or spread a layer of compost

around the plant in spring and fall. *Buddleia* is fairly drought tolerant, but it does best when given water during long dry periods.

ADDITIONAL INFORMATION

Very harsh winters can kill the roots. To propagate *Buddleia*, take soft wood or new growth cuttings, root them, and transplant.

ADDITIONAL SPECIES, CULTIVARS, OR VARIETIES

Most varieties have a small orange eye in the center of their blossoms, and grow about 5 feet tall in a season. 'White Profusion' and 'Peace' are white; 'Empire Blue' has violet-blue flowers; 'Black Knight' and 'Dubonnet' have dark-purple flowers; 'Charming' and 'Fascination' are pink; and 'Fortune' is lilac. 'Nanho' hybrids are white, purple, or blue dwarf varieties. *Buddleia alternifolia*, or fountain butterfly bush, grows 15 feet tall and wide and is considered very hardy. It can be used as a shrub or small tree. The flowers are purple. 'Argentea' is a popular variety.

Chrysanthemum

Chrysanthemum × morifolium

Zones: 5, 6
Height: 1 to 3 feet
Bloom Period: Late summer/fall
Flowers: Various

Light Requirement:

*C*hrysanthemum is a confusing, beautiful family of plants that includes the summer-flowering Shasta daisy (*C. × superbum*) and the fall-flowering mum (*C. × morifolium*). Plant experts have been trying to group them together in better ways, which is why *Chrysanthemum* is frequently listed under several different names, including *Pyrethrum, Matricaria, Tanacetum,* and *Dendranthema.* The garden mum category (*C. × morifolium* and *Dendranthema × grandiflorum*) includes hardy fall-blooming varieties and the florist types. Mums are at their peak in late summer through early fall, when they form cushions of button- or daisy-like flowers that last through a frost or two. They make excellent cut flowers.

WHEN TO PLANT

The best time to plant fall-flowering garden mums is in spring. Spring is also the best time to divide them.

WHERE TO PLANT

Plant mums in well-drained, fertile soil. If used in the perennial border, they should be planted toward the front.

HOW TO PLANT

Container-grown transplants or divisions should be planted at the same depth they were growing previously. Space 1 to 3 feet apart, depending on the variety. Backfill with soil from the planting hole and water them well and mulch.

ADVICE FOR CARE

Apply an all-purpose granular fertilizer in spring and in summer, or spread a layer of compost around the plants in spring or fall. Keep mums well watered but not wet. Pinch mums back to 6 to 8 inches tall at least twice before the middle of July to keep plants compact and full flowered. Pinching also delays flowering. Mums survive Indiana winters better if we don't cut back the spent flowers and stems until early spring when new growth appears. The stems hold tiny bits of leaves and other debris which act as an insulator against the cold.

ADDITIONAL INFORMATION

Very tall varieties may need staking, but most can be pinched to a compact size. Mums are "photoperiod sensitive" plants and can be programmed to bloom just about any time of the year. Potted, spring-blooming mums may re-bloom in the fall; however, these varieties are not reliably hardy in Indiana. Most garden mums are sold in the fall, but they can be slow to establish roots at this time, as they are putting their energy into flowering. For best results, plant them as early as possible and keep them well watered into winter until the ground freezes. It will help to add a light layer of leaves around fall-planted transplants to insulate them.

ADDITIONAL SPECIES, CULTIVARS, OR VARIETIES

'Prophet' series hybrids are excellent fall bloomers, holding their flowers for several weeks. 'Cheyenne' hybrids have good cold tolerance. Other fall-blooming types are the free-flowering daisy-like *C. rubellum* 'Clara Curtis' (with pink flowers) and 'Mary Stoker' (with cream-colored flowers). In *Perennials for the Lower Midwest*, Ezra Haggard recommends *Chrysanthemum* 'Single Apricot' Korean as a new specimen to consider. It grows 18 inches tall and about 2 feet wide and does not need pinching. It has apricot daisy-like flowers in October.

Columbine

Aquilegia × hybrida

Zones: 5, 6
Height: 1 to 3 feet
Bloom Period: Spring/early summer
Flowers: Various

Light Requirement:

olumbines have some of the most exquisite, incredibly detailed flowers you can imagine. Many have three or more colors or shadings, inch-long spurs, and double flowers. If they have a drawback, it is that many of these flowers are short-lived, even the native *A. canadensis*. They can, however, survive in many gardens by self-sowing, sometimes where they are not wanted. They are easy to dig up and transplant, give away, or compost. Columbine are cool-weather plants that stop flowering when it gets hot. Some varieties will have a second flush of flowers in fall.

WHEN TO PLANT
Container-grown transplants may be planted any time throughout the growing season as long as they are well watered. Columbine are usually transplanted or divided in early spring as soon as the soil can be worked, or in fall.

WHERE TO PLANT
Columbine prefer a well-drained, moist spot with average to better-than-average soil. Although they will tolerate full sun, they may benefit from a location in filtered sun during hot summer days.

HOW TO PLANT
Container-grown transplants and divisions should be planted at the same depth they were growing in their containers. Space hybrids about 1 foot apart. Backfill with soil from the planting hole and water well. Mulch lightly if desired.

Advice for Care
Apply an all-purpose granular fertilizer in early spring when new growth appears, or spread a layer of compost around the plants in spring and fall. Cut off spent flower stems to keep the plant looking tidy and to reduce the number of volunteers. Cut the plant to the ground in fall to reduce insects or disease.

Additional Information
Columbine should be divided every 2 or 3 years to keep the plants vigorous. If they are not divided, they will become woody and have fewer flowers. Leaf miners, aphids, and mildew can be bothersome to columbine, which is why good cultural habits are necessary.

Additional Species, Cultivars, or Varieties
Named hybrids include 'McKana Giants', 'Spring Song', 'Nora Barlow', and 'Biedermeyer Strain'. *A. canadensis* is a native plant in eastern North America. It has red and yellow flowers, grows up to 30 inches tall, and is rangy on its own; it seems to mix well with other perennials that can hide its wildness. It also does very well at the edges of woody areas or in rock gardens. *A. vulgaris*, or European columbine, grows about 2 foot tall and has smaller purple, blue, red, pink, or white flowers in late spring. This plant can be an invasive self-sower.

Coneflower

Echinacea purpurea

Other Name: Purple Coneflower **Zones:** 5, 6 **Height:** 1 to 3 feet **Bloom Period:** Midsummer **Flowers:** Pink, white, lavender	**Light Requirement:** 

here are lots of reasons to like purple coneflowers in the garden. They are very easy to grow and they flower for several weeks from July into September. They are excellent cut flowers, lasting a long time in the vase. They attract butterflies and bees. They also attract American goldfinches, which live to feast on the seedheads, or cones, that rise from the center of this perennial. Purple coneflower is native to the eastern United States. Its foliage is a bit rough, a little hairy, but its dark-green color makes it an attractive foil in the perennial border. Its dried seedheads offer interest in the winter and food for birds. The flowers are two to three inches wide.

WHEN TO PLANT
Container-grown transplants and divisions can be planted in the fall, or in spring as soon as the soil can be worked. Plants may be divided at these times, too.

WHERE TO PLANT
Purple coneflowers do well in well-drained, average soil in full sun or light shade. Their natural habitat is prairie and meadowland.

HOW TO PLANT
Container-grown transplants and divisions should be planted the same depth they were growing in their pots. Space about 2 feet apart and backfill with soil from the planting hole. Water them well. Mulching is not necessary.

ADVICE FOR CARE
Apply an all-purpose granular fertilizer in spring when new growth appears, or spread a layer of compost around the plant in spring

and fall. Spent flowers, stems, and foliage may be cut to the ground in fall—or wait until spring so the birds can enjoy the seedheads over the winter.

ADDITIONAL INFORMATION

Purple coneflowers are fairly drought tolerant once established, and relatively care-free. They spread quickly but are not invasive. Unwanted volunteers are easy to dig for transplanting elsewhere, giving away, or composting. *Echinacea purpurea* is easy to grow from seed, but it may not bloom the first year. It is thought to have curative powers and is frequently included in herb books.

ADDITIONAL SPECIES, CULTIVARS, OR VARIETIES

'Bright Star', a readily available variety, has lavender-purple flowers; 'White Swan' and 'White Lustre' have white petals, though they too are called *Echinacea purpurea*. 'Bravado' and 'Magnus' are good seed varieties.

Daylily

Hemerocallis spp. and hybrids

Zones: 5, 6	**Light Requirement:**
Height: 1 to 5 feet	
Bloom Period: Various	
Flowers: Various	

aylilies may be the easiest perennial to grow. They seem to thrive in any soil and condition, except in soils that are too wet. With no effort on the part of the gardener, daylily hybrids burst forth in flower from June through early August, depending on the variety and the amount of light. The medium-green strap-like leaves appear first, followed by stalks with flowers at the top. Each individual trumpet-like flower lasts only a day—thus the name. Other flowers on the stalk will bloom the next day and for days after, frequently for two weeks or more, depending on the variety. A few of the newer varieties, such as the dwarf 'Stella de Oro', bloom off and on for most of the summer. Daylilies (*Hemerocallis*) grow from rhizomes. They are not the same plant as lilies (*Lilium*), which are bulbs (see Bulbs chapter). Daylilies offer a wide selection of color, and many are fragrant. The flowers, too, offer variety: some are simple, some have ruffled petals or fringes, and some are bi- or tricolored. The flowers range from two to six inches across. Daylilies make excellent cut flowers. Cut stems that have several buds, some close to opening and some just showing color. Snipping the spent flowers off the stem will keep the daylily flowering in the vase.

WHEN TO PLANT

Daylilies can be planted almost any time during the growing season. Most are transplanted or divided in spring as soon as the soil can be worked, or in fall.

WHERE TO PLANT

Daylilies do well in full sun or in considerable shade as long as it is not dense. The more sun, the more plentiful the flowers. Plant daylilies in the perennial border according to their size, or set them apart in their own bed for a spectacular show. Daylilies do well in a wide range of soil conditions. Once established, they will tolerate drought.

How to Plant

Container-grown transplants or divisions should be planted at the same depth they were growing. Space them about 2 feet apart; larger varieties should have more space. Backfill with soil from the planting hole and water well. Spread a thin layer of mulch.

Advice for Care

Apply an all-purpose granular fertilizer in spring when new growth breaks ground, or spread a layer of compost around the plants in spring and fall. Cut back stems and leaves in fall—or this task can wait until spring. Spent flowers can be removed every few days to keep the plants looking tidy, but this is not really necessary. They have few, if any, pests.

Additional Information

Daylilies can be left undisturbed for years, though the number of flowers may decline. Divide every 4 to 6 years to keep them vigorous. Daylilies spread fairly rapidly but are not invasive.

Additional Species, Cultivars, or Varieties

There are tens of thousands of cultivars from which to choose. Select varieties according to height, color, when they flower, and for how long. *Hemerocallis lilio-asphodelus* and *H. flava* are the old-fashioned daylilies frequently found growing by roadsides or in clumps on the old family farm.

Foam Flower

Tiarella cordifolia, Tiarella wherryi

Zones: 5, 6	**Light Requirement:**
Height: 6 to 12 inches	
Bloom Period: Mid- to late spring	
Flowers: White, pink	

*T*his is a charming little plant that looks more fragile than it is and makes an excellent perennial flowering groundcover for moist, woodsy areas. Foam flower has maple-like leaves and spikes of star-like white or purple-pink flowers. It spreads by surface (or just-below-surface) runners or grows in clumps.

WHEN TO PLANT
Container-grown transplants may be planted in early spring as soon as the ground can be worked, or in fall. Plants may be divided at those times, too.

WHERE TO PLANT
Foam flower is a woodland plant, so it does best in moist, humusy soil. It can be planted around the bases of trees or shrubs, or in a shady moist spot in the front of the flower border.

HOW TO PLANT
Container-grown transplants and divisions should be planted the same depth they were growing previously. Space about 12 inches apart and backfill with soil from the planting hole. Water well. Mulch lightly with chopped leaves or shredded bark. Once the plants are established, mulching won't be necessary.

ADVICE FOR CARE
Apply an all-purpose granular fertilizer in early spring when new growth begins, or spread a layer of compost or other organic material such as chopped leaves around the plants in spring and fall.

Spent flowers can be removed to make the plants look tidy, or they can be left to weather naturally. (Removing the flowers from a large mass planting can be time-consuming.)

ADDITIONAL INFORMATION

If planted in partial sun, the leaves of foam flower may turn a bronzy or reddish purple.

ADDITIONAL SPECIES, CULTIVARS, OR VARIETIES

Tiarella cordifolia spreads by stolons. Its roots are at ground level or slightly below ground level and quickly form a mat, or colony, of plants. *Tiarella wherryi* is more of a clump grower and is considered less invasive. Its flowers have pinkish tips.

Geranium

Geranium sanguineum, Geranium himalayense

Other Names: Cranesbill Geranium,
  Bloody Cranesbill Geranium

Zones: 5, 6

Height: 12 to 24 inches

Bloom Period: Late spring/summer

Flowers: White, pink, blue, rose, purple

Light Requirement:

This is the true geranium. (The geranium we use as a summer-flowering annual or houseplant is called *Pelargonium* and is discussed in the Annuals chapter of this book.) The true geranium is a hardy perennial that flowers in early spring and summer with flushes of color into fall, depending on the variety. Even when it's not flowering, the foliage is attractive in the front of the flower border. These are rewarding, easy-to-grow plants that require minimal care. They get their name from the long, beak-like (like a cranesbill) fruit that develops after the flowers. The flowers are about one inch wide; some varieties are double. Most geraniums grow in mounds, while some have a sprawling habit.

WHEN TO PLANT

Container-grown transplants may be planted in spring as soon as the soil can be worked, or in fall. Plants may be divided then, too.

WHERE TO PLANT

Plant geraniums at the front of a flower border in rich, well-drained soil in full sun or partial shade. They do best when shaded from afternoon sun.

HOW TO PLANT

Container-grown transplants and divisions should be planted at the same depth they were growing. Space them 18 to 24 inches apart, depending on the variety, and backfill with soil from the planting hole. Water them well. Mulch lightly if desired.

ADVICE FOR CARE

Apply an all-purpose granular fertilizer in early spring when new growth appears, or spread a layer of compost around the plants in spring and fall. Some varieties should be cut back after their first bloom to make the plants more compact, to tidy them up, or to encourage flowers later.

ADDITIONAL INFORMATION

Cranesbill geraniums seldom have to be divided, though dividing them is an easy way to get more plants.

ADDITIONAL SPECIES, CULTIVARS, OR VARIETIES

G. himalayense × *G. pratense* 'Johnson's Blue' forms a 12-inch-tall clump that blooms with violet-blue flowers in late spring or early summer; 'Plenum' grows about 2 feet tall and has large blue-violet flowers in early summer. *G. macrorrhizum*, or big-root geranium, is a low-growing plant that can be used as a groundcover for dry, shady spots. The flowers are pink or white, and they bloom in late spring and early summer. Varieties include 'Album', with white flowers, and 'Ingwersen's Variety', with pink. *G. sanguineum*, sometimes listed as 'Lancastriense', is called bloody cranesbill. It has pink or magenta flowers. 'Shepherd's Warning' has deep-rose flowers and grows only 6 to 8 inches tall. All these varieties should be divided every 3 or 4 years. *G. endressii* 'Wargrave Pink' grows up to 18 inches tall and 30 inches wide, blooming with bluish-pink flowers during summer to fall when planted in the right spot. It prefers a cool location and may be cut back after its first flowering.

Hosta

Hosta fortunei

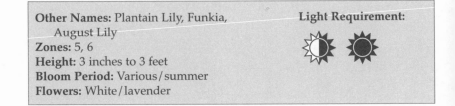

Other Names: Plantain Lily, Funkia,
   August Lily
Zones: 5, 6
Height: 3 inches to 3 feet
Bloom Period: Various/summer
Flowers: White/lavender

Light Requirement:

*H*ostas are easy-to-grow perennials that were made for flowering in a shady summer garden. Small trumpet-like flowers form along stalks that dangle above the plants, which are primarily grown for their foliage. Some gardeners don't care for the flowers at all, and they quickly cut them off. Many hostas are fragrant, however, especially *H. plantaginea*, and their flowers make nice additions to a cut-flower arrangement, bringing a graceful height to the bouquet. Hostas are clump-growing plants that come in hundreds of varieties. Leaves can be broad or narrow, solid-colored to bi- and tricolored, wrinkled or smooth. The plants tend to be wider than they are tall.

WHEN TO PLANT

Container-grown transplants may be planted in spring as soon as the soil can be worked, or in fall. Plants may be divided at those times, too.

WHERE TO PLANT

Hosta is an excellent edging plant; the larger varieties can be used to form an herbaceous shrub border. These plants are best planted in clusters or masses. They prefer well-drained, rich organic soil in shady or semi-shady locations. The hostas with gold leaves need more sun to intensify their color.

HOW TO PLANT

Container-grown transplants and divisions should be planted at the same depth they were growing. Space them according to the variety; the larger or wider plants will require more space. Backfill with soil from the planting hole and water well. Mulch, but keep it away from the base of the plant.

ADVICE FOR CARE

Apply an all-purpose granular fertilizer in spring when new growth appears, or spread a layer of compost around the plants in spring and fall. Hostas are a slug's favorite treat, so keep an eye open for telltale holes in the leaves. You may need to control the slugs that like to live in wood mulch. Cut back the hosta leaves and stems after they've been killed by a frost. Hostas do not have to be divided, but division is an easy way to get more plants. The ideal time is in spring or fall, but plants can be divided any time as long as they are kept well watered.

ADDITIONAL INFORMATION

Hosta flower stalks may be cut back after the blooms fade.

ADDITIONAL SPECIES, CULTIVARS, OR VARIETIES

There are thousands of hosta cultivars, and new ones are being introduced all the time. Select according to desired size, foliage, and flowers. Some popular named varieties are *H. fortunei* 'Francee', which has green leaves edged in white; 'Hyacinthina', with gray-green leaves with white lines; 'Albo-picta', which has yellow-green leaves edged in dark green; 'Albo-marginata', with white edges; 'Aurea', with cream leaves that turn green with age; and 'Gold Standard', which has yellow leaves with green borders. *H. sieboldiana* has puckered leaves. 'Elegans' has large, blue-gray leaves. 'Frances Williams' has blue-green leaves edged in paler green. *H. plantaginea* is a group of large August-flowering hostas. Named varieties include 'Grandiflora', 'Aphrodite', 'Honeybells', and 'Royal Standard'.

Iris

Iris spp. and hybrids

Other Names: Flags, Bearded Iris, German
  Iris, Japanese Iris, Siberian Iris
Zones: 5, 6
Height: Various
Bloom Period: Late spring/summer
Flowers: Various

Light Requirement:

here are three different kinds of plants discussed in this section, and each is worthy of inclusion in the garden. *Iris* is the general name for irises, and it also is what we call bearded iris, flags, and German irises. These are all familiar plants with blue-green sword leaves and stalks of flowers. Their flowers have an upright portion called the standard and a lower part called the fall, or beard. They bloom in late spring and early summer. They spread by means of shallow-rooted rhizomes. *Iris ensata* (sometimes referred to as *I. kaempferi*) is the Japanese iris. It has flat-topped flowers that bloom in early to midsummer, and it grows in a clump. *Iris sibirica* is the Siberian iris, which has a flower even more delicate than that of the Japanese varieties and also grows in a clump. All are easy to grow, though they grow differently.

WHEN TO PLANT

Container-grown transplants may be planted in spring as soon as the soil can be worked, or in fall. Plants may be divided at those times, too.

WHERE TO PLANT

Iris does best in full sun with a little afternoon shade. Japanese iris takes a little more shade and may need more protection in winter. Siberian iris also takes a little shade, and is very hardy. All irises need well-drained soil, but Siberian iris tolerates wetter soil.

HOW TO PLANT

Iris roots are buried, but the rhizomes are barely covered with soil. The plants grow in one direction, so point the green, leafy part the way you want it to grow. Space 10 to 24 inches apart, depending on the size of the variety. Transplanted irises may not bloom their first year. Divide them in summer every 3 to 4 years. They often do best when planted in their own beds. *I. ensata* rhizomes are clump-like. Plant them about 2 inches deep, spacing them 12 to 18 inches apart. They are best divided every 3 or 4 years. *I. sibirica* are also clump-like. Divide when the clump looks like a doughnut (with a dead center). Space 2 to 3 feet apart. Transplants may not bloom until the second year.

ADVICE FOR CARE

Apply an all-purpose granular fertilizer in spring when new growth appears, or spread a layer of compost around the plants in spring and fall. Deadheading Japanese iris will keep them blooming.

ADDITIONAL INFORMATION

Bearded iris are susceptible to iris borers or fungal infections, so keep an eye out for wilting plants or leaves with streaks. Keeping the bearded iris bed clean of debris is important. Trim iris to the ground in winter.

ADDITIONAL SPECIES, CULTIVARS, OR VARIETIES

There are many varieties of each type from which to choose. Select according to color, height, and time of bloom. *Iris cristata* is a dwarf crested iris that grows about 8 inches tall and has a 2-foot spread. It is a good woodland plant. *Iris reticulata* are bulbs that are discussed in the Bulbs chapter. *Iris pseudacorus* is called yellow flag and is used around ponds and water gardens. You can find it in the chapter on water plants.

Lamb's Ear

Stachys byzantina

Zones: 5, 6
Height: 15 to 18 inches
Bloom Period: Summer
Flowers: Purple

Light Requirement:

*L*amb's ear is an excellent edging perennial with its foliage of soft, hairy, silver-gray leaves. Children (of all ages) enjoy touching the leaves. This is a plant frequently found in sensory gardens because its foliage is fun to feel. It spreads rapidly and some people think it is invasive. Many don't like the flowers because they become heavy after a rain and fall over, causing a soggy, squishy mess. Some varieties are susceptible to rot. However, there are newer cultivars that don't flower and are resistant to rot.

WHEN TO PLANT

Container-grown transplants can be planted in spring as soon as the soil can be worked, or in fall. Plants may be divided at those times, too.

WHERE TO PLANT

Lamb's ear needs well-drained average or poor soil in full sun or partial shade. Lamb's ear looks nice as a groundcover at the front of a flower bed, where its silvery foliage can set off the pinks, blues, and greens of nearby plants.

HOW TO PLANT

Container-grown transplants or divisions should be planted at the same depth they were growing. Space them 12 to 18 inches apart and backfill with soil from the planting hole. Water them well. Mulching is not required.

ADVICE FOR CARE

Apply an all-purpose granular fertilizer in spring when new growth appears, or spread a layer of compost around the plant in spring and fall. Lamb's ear is heat and drought tolerant, but it will fade fast in humid conditions and wet weather. Trim off spent flowers and brown leaves as needed. Cut back in late winter or early spring. Foliage is killed by frost, but the plant's roots are hardy.

ADDITIONAL INFORMATION

Sometimes *Stachys* is referred to as "betony."

ADDITIONAL SPECIES, CULTIVARS, OR VARIETIES

'Silver Carpet' and 'Helene Von Stein' have few or no flowers and are fairly resistant to rot.

Obedient Plant

Physostegia virginiana

*I*f only this plant would do what it is told! As is true of many native perennials, *Physostegia* can be very invasive, spreading its clump rapidly by means of underground runners. The tall flower spikes are attractive, however, and they come at a time of year when they can blend well with companions such as sweet autumn clematis, goldenrod, and other late bloomers. With a little taming, easy-to-grow obedient plant deserves a spot in the perennial bed. It prefers moist, rich soil, so if you can keep it a little dry and in poor soil, it will grow less rampantly.

WHEN TO PLANT

Container-grown transplants may be planted in spring as soon as the soil can be worked, or in fall. Obedient plant can be divided any time of the year as long as transplants are well watered until they are established.

WHERE TO PLANT

Plant obedient plant where it can spread freely. It is stunning as a major stand or clump. In the perennial border, plant it in the back. It thrives in moist soil. Remember, the better the soil, the more this plant will grow, and the harder it will be to control.

HOW TO PLANT

Container-grown transplants and divisions should be planted at the same depth they were growing. Space 24 inches or more apart (one plant is really all one needs for most areas). Backfill with soil from the planting hole and water well. Mulching may be desired, but it is really not necessary.

ADVICE FOR CARE
Apply an all-purpose granular fertilizer in spring when new growth appears, or spread a layer of compost around the plants in spring and fall. Remember, obedient plants thrive in rich soil; a poorer soil will keep them under control. Cut the plants to the ground in late fall, early winter, or early spring. The dried seedheads offer winter interest to the landscape.

ADDITIONAL INFORMATION
Cut back in early summer to keep obedient plant from getting too tall.

ADDITIONAL SPECIES, CULTIVARS, OR VARIETIES
'Rose Banquet' has rose-pink flowers; 'Variegata' has cream-colored foliage with pink flowers; 'Vivid' has rose-colored flowers and grows about 18 inches tall. 'Alba', 'Crown of Snow', and 'Summer Snow' are white varieties.

PERENNIALS

Peony

Paeonia lactiflora

Zones: 5, 6 **Height:** 2 to 3 feet **Bloom Period:** May to June **Flower Color:** Pink, white, rose, red	**Light Requirement:**

*P*eonies' ability to tolerate a wide variety of soils and still produce a beautiful fragrant flower leaves no doubt why it was
chosen the State Flower of Indiana. The large, luscious flowers open
gradually to reveal a collection of deep-yellow and orange stamens. In
"double" varieties, an extra set of petals hides the stamens and adds a
whole new dimension to the bloom. However, peonies are not well-
liked by gardeners who have "insect phobia." Their propensity for
attracting small red ants is well known, to the point that some believe
there have to be ants present in order for the flowers to open! I must
admit that the ant stories were enough to keep this gardener away
for a very long time, until I cut some of the stems and put them in a
vase on the dining room table. There isn't a finer cut flower to enjoy
indoors, ants or no ants. When cut for indoors, peonies' heavenly
fragrance will fill the house.

WHEN TO PLANT

Transplant peony crowns in late September to early October.
Container-grown peonies should be planted in early spring.

WHERE TO PLANT

Peonies prefer soil that is moist but well drained, with plenty of
organic matter. For best results and more blooms, plant in full sun.
Peonies are part of the backbone of a perennial garden; plant them
in the middle to the rear of the garden so that the foliage will be
hidden by other plants in the foreground after the peonies have
finished blooming. Because of their huge blossoms and short
flowering period, peonies are best given their own flower bed.

How to Plant

Prepare the soil as described in the introduction to this chapter. When planting the woody peony crowns, dig a hole approximately 12 inches wide and deep. Mix the original soil with at least 1/3 organic matter before refilling the hole to within 2 inches of the top. Check the crown of the peony for next year's buds. These should appear as bright red nubs called "eyes." Plant the crown so the eyes are no deeper than 2 inches below the surface after refilling the rest of the hole. If planted deeper than this, the peony may never bloom. Space about 18 inches apart. Backfill the hole with the rest of the original soil and organic matter, and water deeply.

Advice for Care

Maintain a 2- to 3-inch layer of organic mulch around the plants to help conserve moisture and keep out weeds. Fertilize each spring after blooming with 1 tablespoon of balanced fertilizer like 12-12-12 or an organic substitute. After the stems are about 6 inches tall, stake the peonies with a basket or other supports. As they get older and the buds begin to swell, the flower stems become top-heavy and easily fall over. If peonies are in full bloom and a storm is brewing, quickly cut as many as you can, as rain will flatten the stems.

Additional Information

Deadhead spent flowers, as they are unsightly and take energy away from the plant. As peonies age, most of the flower stems are produced on the edge of a circular ring with small amounts of foliage (or no foliage) in the center. When the clumps get to this stage, divide them in late September or early October, using a sharp spade to slice through a clump in several locations.

Additional Species, Cultivars, or Varieties

There are many reliable varieties. Two good choices are 'Festiva Maxima', which has double white petals with good fragrance, and 'Sarah Bernhardt', which has large double pink blossoms.

Phlox

Phlox paniculata

Other Name: Garden Phlox **Zones:** 5, 6 **Height:** 6 inches to 3 1/2 feet **Bloom Period:** July to frost **Flowers:** Pink, red, white, rose, purple, bicolor	**Light Requirement:** 

'*P*hlox' describes many popular garden flowers, including woodland phlox (*Phlox divaricata*), creeping phlox (*Phlox subulata*), annual phlox (*Phlox drummondi*), and garden phlox (*Phlox paniculata*). Native to North America, garden phlox is an old-fashioned mainstay of the perennial border. Prized for its fragrant cloud-like blooms, the clusters of tubular flowers at the tips of three-foot stems are a favorite of hummingbirds. Garden phlox grows in spreading clumps with many upright stems. It is among the earliest to grow in the spring. Although somewhat finicky and susceptible to powdery mildew, the extra effort required to care for this plant is worth it.

WHEN TO PLANT

The best time to plant garden phlox is in early fall so the roots will have a chance to establish themselves. The second-best time is in early spring before the leaves emerge on the trees.

WHERE TO PLANT

Garden phlox grows best in full sun, in moist but well-drained soil that has been enriched with organic matter.

HOW TO PLANT

Prepare the garden soil as described in the introduction to this chapter. Garden phlox should be transplanted at the same depth it was growing in its containers. Space the plants about 2 feet apart so there is plenty of air flow around the stems. Divide them every 2 or 3 years. This will discourage the development of powdery mildew, which can completely defoliate these plants by the end of summer. Backfill the hole with the original soil and water deeply. Spread a 2- to 3-inch layer of organic mulch around the entire planting area.

ADVICE FOR CARE

Garden phlox is slightly more demanding than many perennials. Each spring, sprinkle a tablespoon of balanced fertilizer around the base of the plants and lightly cultivate. As the new foliage begins to grow, thin each clump by removing all but 4 to 6 of the sturdiest stems. This will encourage larger flowers and, even more important, it will improve air circulation and discourage mildew. Water deeply once a week, keeping the leaves as dry as possible. Maintain a 2- to 3-inch layer of organic mulch throughout the growing season.

ADDITIONAL INFORMATION

Divide each clump every 3 years, in the early spring. Use a sharp spade or shovel to slice through the crown, creating clumps of 4 to 6 stems. Transplant as described above and water well. Keep the dead flowers pruned to encourage more blooms. If mildew is a problem, spray with approved fungicides every 10 to 14 days, starting in mid-June. Be sure to follow label directions when spraying. If mildew continues to plague your *Phlox paniculata*, it is best to replace it with a mildew-resistant variety of *Phlox maculata* such as 'Miss Lingard'. This is one of the finest white phlox around. 'Omega' is another white variety of *P. maculata*. It has a pink center and good mildew resistance. 'Rosalinde' is dark pink.

ADDITIONAL SPECIES, CULTIVARS, OR VARIETIES

Phlox paniculata comes in many varieties with variable susceptibility to mildew, so try different ones in your garden to find the one that is best for your particular micro-environment. 'Bright Eyes', 'Mt. Fuji', and 'Starfire' are good pink, white, and red varieties, respectively. *Phlox subulata*, or creeping phlox, is the low-growing spring-blooming species that has brilliant flowers of white, pink, or lavender. These are excellent for a sunny bank or rock garden and are found everywhere in country gardens. If you have a shadier location, plant woodland phlox, *Phlox divaricata*.

Pincushion Flower

Scabiosa caucasica

Zones: 5, 6	**Light Requirement:**
Height: 1 to 2 feet	
Bloom Period: July to frost	
Flowers: Shades of blue; white	

The tightly packed stamens in the center of the round *Scabiosa* flowers resemble pins in a pincushion and give this plant its common name. Long, blue, fringed petals surround the "pins" and help make up the "cushion." Dark-green leaves are quick to come back each spring, and by summer, *Scabiosa* sends forth numerous thin stalks tipped with flowers in shades of blue or white. The original species bloomed a deep shade of blue, almost purple, and because of the dark color was called 'Mournful Widow'. Modern versions of *Scabiosa* are anything but mournful. When deadheaded, their cheery blooms repeat all summer long, and the fresh blossoms make excellent cut flowers. *Scabiosa* looks especially attractive near plants that have silver, white, and blue hues. For an excellent combination, plant *Scabiosa* near Russian sage, *Veronica*, *Artemesia*, dusty miller, or dwarf fountain grass.

WHEN TO PLANT
Transplant pincushion flower in early spring after the soil dries and as the leaves begin to emerge from the trees. The second-best time to plant is in late summer or early fall so the roots will have time to establish themselves before going dormant for the winter.

WHERE TO PLANT
Pincushion flower grows best in soil that is moist but well drained, with plenty of organic matter. It will produce more flowers in full sun but also grows well in very light shade. Overall, *Scabiosa* is a short plant that looks best when planted in the front of the flower garden as an edger. The blooms resemble a water fountain, opening in profusion above the basal leaves in a grand way. These blooms are not as dense as those of other perennials, so plant pincushion flowers in groups of 3 for greater impact.

How to Plant

Prepare the garden as described in the introduction to this chapter. Dig a hole up to 3 times the width of the rootball or container and at least 12 inches deep. Return enough soil to the bottom of the hole so that the top of the rootball is level with the ground around it. Pincushion flower should be planted at the same depth it was growing in its container. Backfill the hole with the original soil and water deeply. Spread a 2- to 3-inch layer of organic mulch around the entire planting area to help conserve moisture and to keep the weeds down.

Advice for Care

Pincushion plant is virtually maintenance-free. Deadhead the flowers to encourage additional blooms throughout the summer. Broadcast 1 tablespoon of balanced fertilizer around each plant early in the spring, and lightly cultivate. Maintain a 2- to 3-inch layer of organic mulch around the root zone throughout the growing season. Divide pincushion flower every 3 or 4 years or it will gradually decline. Using a sharp spade or shovel, slice through the crown of each plant early in the spring in 2 or 3 sections, and transplant as described above.

Additional Information

Sow seeds of *Scabiosa* indoors during the late winter. Transplant after the threat of frost has passed, usually by mid-May in central Indiana, but 2 weeks earlier in the south, and 2 weeks later in the north. With the proper care, *Scabiosa* may bloom during its first year.

Additional Species, Cultivars and Varieties

'Blue Perfection', a profuse bloomer with fringed petals, grows to 24 inches. 'Bressingham White' has large flowers on stems up to 3 feet tall. 'House Hybrids' have numerous blooms of blue and white, all on the same plant.

Russian Sage

Perovskia atriplicifolia

Zones: 5, 6
Height: 3 to 4 feet
Bloom Period: July to frost
Flowers: Light blue to lavender

Light Requirement:

A Perennial Plant of the Year winner, and considered one of the finest perennials around, Russian sage provides outstanding blooms from June through frost. The light-blue flowers are produced in thin, wispy spikes at the tips of light-gray stems. The leaves are a light silvery green and have a heavy sage aroma when crushed. The number of blooms and the blue color intensifies as the summer progresses, until Russian sage is at its peak in September. Slow to grow new leaves in the spring, the plant quickly makes up for that by producing numerous spiky stems that collectively give the plant a mound-like shape. Cut the blooms any time to add a delicate but fragrant touch to your garden bouquets.

WHEN TO PLANT

Transplant Russian sage in early spring after the soil dries out and as the leaves begin to emerge on the trees. The second-best time to plant is in late summer or early fall so it will have time to establish new roots before going dormant for the winter.

WHERE TO PLANT

Russian sage is the perfect plant for hot, dry locations. It is relatively intolerant of poorly drained or wet soils. If your garden has such soils, add 3 or 4 inches of organic matter, or plant the sage in a raised bed to improve drainage. It will thrive in full sun in poor-but-dry soils, and makes the perfect rock garden plant. Plant Russian sage in groups of 3 or more for the best effect, in front of ornamental grasses, purple coneflower, or butterfly bush. A favorite breathtaking fall combination is *Boltonia* 'Snowbank', Russian sage, and *Aster × frikartii*.

HOW TO PLANT

Prepare the garden soil as described in the introduction. Dig a hole that is 2 to 3 times as wide as the container and about 12 inches deep. Russian sage should be planted at the same depth it was growing in the container. Space about 2 feet apart. Backfill the hole with the rest of the original soil and water it deeply. Spread a 2- to 3-inch layer of organic mulch over the entire planting area.

ADVICE FOR CARE

Russian sage is one of the most care-free plants around, requiring only neglect! As a rule, it has woodier stems than most perennials and does not always die back completely to the ground. Leave the foliage alone in the fall and wait until growth becomes apparent in the spring. Then remove the branches that are not producing any new foliage. Sometimes the new buds are hard to identify; if in doubt, cut the whole plant back to about 8 inches. Although Russian sage produces masses of new foliage each season, it doesn't grow a large enough root system to divide. This plant is virtually pest-free.

ADDITIONAL INFORMATION

Russian sage can be easily propagated by taking cuttings from new stems in June. Cut the stems into 2-inch pieces and strip off the foliage. Moisten each piece by spraying with water, then dip each one in rooting hormone. Stick each one upright in a sturdy flat full of moist sand. Be sure at least one node of each of the stem cuttings is below the surface of the sand, and place the entire flat in the shade. Mist it a few times a day and make sure the sand stays wet but well drained. The cuttings should root in a few weeks.

ADDITIONAL SPECIES, CULTIVARS, OR VARIETIES

'Blue Haze' has lighter blue flowers and 'Blue Spire' has very finely cut, delicate leaves.

Salvia 'May Night'

Salvia × superba 'May Night'

Other Name: Salvia 'Mainacht'
Zones: 5, 6
Height: 18 inches to 2 feet
Bloom Period: June to July and sporadically
  until frost
Flowers: Deep blue to purple

Light Requirement:

*S*alvias are among the most diverse and useful groups of garden flowers, having more than 700 different species. Grown as annuals or perennials, their common attribute is a flower with numerous tubular to cup-shaped blooms attached tightly to a spike. Rising above the leaves, the flowers provide a vertical accent in the garden. The most familiar annual is the old-fashioned red salvia; most of the perennial types bloom in shades of blue and indigo. 'May Night' produces masses of deep-blue spikes above gray-green leaves in May and June. If deadheaded, 'May Night' and other perennial salvias will continue to flower throughout the summer until frost. 'May Night' establishes itself quickly in the garden, growing into an irregular mound shape. It was the 1997 Perennial Plant of the year. Planted among other spring bloomers like the hardy geraniums, cottage pinks, or catmint, salvias are stunning.

WHEN TO PLANT

Transplant 'May Night' and other *superba* varieties in early spring, after the soil is dry and when the leaves begin to emerge on the trees. The second-best time is in late summer and early fall so they will have time to establish roots before going dormant.

WHERE TO PLANT

Salvias prefer soils that are moist but well drained, in full sun. If planted in the shade, the plants will get leggy and fall over. Plant 'May Night' at the front of the flower border among plants that have a mounded or round shape. 'May Night' looks especially good when planted near the 'Silver Mound' *Artemesia* or 'Moonshine' yarrow. All three species have leaves with a silver hue, but the flowers complement each other to an outstanding degree.

How to Plant

Prepare the garden bed as described in the introduction, then dig a hole 2 to 3 times the width of the rootball or container and about 12 inches deep. Replace enough of the soil to the bottom of the hole so that the plant is growing at the same level it was in the container. Space about 18 inches apart. Backfill the hole with the remainder of the soil and water deeply. Spread a 2- to 3-inch layer of organic mulch around the entire planting area.

Advice for Care

Fertilize each spring with a tablespoon of all-purpose fertilizer; broadcast it around the plant, then cultivate it into the soil. Maintain a layer of organic mulch around the plants throughout the growing season to conserve moisture and to keep out weeds. Deadhead the flowers after they finish blooming to encourage additional blooms all summer long. After the first hard frost in the fall, cut the plant back to 3 or 4 inches. Spread a thin layer of chopped leaves over the crown to give it extra protection for the winter.

Additional Information

Salvia 'May Night' has virtually no pests other than too much moisture. Don't drown the plant with too much attention. These plants tend to sprawl after they get tall, leaving an empty spot in the center. When this happens, the plant is telling you it is time to be divided. Early the following spring, take a sharp spade or shovel and slice down vertically into the crown about 8 inches deep. Be sure to do this early in the year because salvia "greens up" early. Transplant the divisions and water well.

Additional Species, Cultivars, or Varieties

'East Friesland' has deep-purple blooms on short 18-inch plants; its short stature keeps it from sprawling. 'Rose Queen' has rose-pink spikes and grows to 20 inches tall.

Tickseed

Coreopsis verticillata 'Moonbeam'

Other Names: Threadleaf Coreopsis, Moonbeam Coreopsis **Zones:** 5, 6 **Height:** 18 to 24 inches **Bloom Period:** June to frost **Flowers:** Light yellow	**Light Requirement:**

A native of the prairies of the Midwest, lanceleaf *Coreopsis*, or "tickseed," is the standard older species in this genus of more than 100 known selections. 'Moonbeam', a variety of threadleaf *Coreopsis*, has many of the characteristics of the native that make it widely adaptable to gardens in Indiana. Its cheerful lemon-yellow daisy-like flowers cover the tips of its needle-like leaves. Like the native tickseed, 'Moonbeam' will tolerate poor, dry soils and neglect. Its ability to bloom day after day throughout the summer, right up until frost, earned it the prestigious Perennial Plant of the Year Award for outstanding character a few years ago.

WHEN TO PLANT

Transplant *Coreopsis* early in the spring after the ground is dry and as the leaves begin to emerge on the trees. *Coreopsis* is a drought-loving plant and will tolerate transplanting in the summer and fall better than the average perennial.

WHERE TO PLANT

Threadleaf *Coreopsis* thrives in full sun in a well-drained soil with plenty of organic matter. It tolerates dry locations and makes a good addition to the rock garden. For an excellent contrast all summer long, plant it in the front of the perennial garden, combined with 'Crater Lake Blue' *Veronica*.

HOW TO PLANT

Prepare the soil as described in the introduction to this chapter. Dig a hole 3 times the width of the rootball and about 12 inches deep. Water the plant well before planting it at the same depth it was growing in the pot. Space about 18 inches apart. Backfill the hole with the original soil, and water deeply again. To conserve moisture and keep the weeds out, spread a 2- to 3-inch layer of organic mulch around the planting area

ADVICE FOR CARE

Coreopsis are low-maintenance plants that make excellent choices for the weekend gardener or for anyone who does not have a lot of time. Sometimes the threadleaf varieties go through "flushes" of bloom, producing many flowers in cycles throughout the summer. As one cycle fades, the next one can be encouraged by shearing the plant about an inch below the dead blooms. After the first hard frost in the fall, cut the stems back to 3 or 4 inches and spread a layer of chopped leaves over the crown. Remove winter mulch in spring when new growth appears. To keep the weeds down, maintain a 2- to 3-inch layer of organic mulch around the plant.

ADDITIONAL INFORMATION

If given ample room and well-drained soil, threadleaf coreopsis will spread quickly by underground runners. After the foliage greens up in the spring, divide it by slicing vertically through the crown. A good division should have 5 to 10 new stems per 3-inch clump. *Coreopsis* is virtually pest-free!

ADDITIONAL SPECIES, CULTIVARS, OR VARIETIES

Coreopsis verticillata 'Zagreb' is a shorter version of 'Moonbeam' and has darker yellow flowers. 'Golden Showers' will grow to 2^1/$_2$ feet, spreading quickly. *C. rosea* is a threadleaf type that has light-pink daisy-like petals with yellow centers; it is one of the few *Coreopsis* that likes wet soils. *C. lanceolata*, or lanceleaf *Coreopsis*, has wider petals that are toothed at the tips and bloom at the end of 18-inch-long stems. It will reseed itself throughout the garden—this can be a nice feature, or a liability, depending on your preferences. 'Early Sunrise' is a lanceleaf type with double flowers also. It grows to 12 inches tall and blooms off and on all summer after a fantastic display in June. 'Early Sunrise' grows easily from seed, which should be started indoors in February.

Veronica

Veronica spicata

Other Names: Speedwell, *Veronica spicata*
Zones: 5, 6
Height: 1 to 3 feet
Bloom Period: June to frost
Flowers: Blue, pink, white

Light Requirement:

There are more than 250 classified varieties of *Veronica*, many of which make excellent additions to the perennial garden. Although each one is different, the flowers of all are typically three- to four-inch-long icicle-shaped spikes with slightly fuzzy petals that open from bottom to top. Ranging from twelve inches to three feet tall, they provide a nice vertical accent in the garden, blooming in shades of blue, pink, and white. In full bloom, they are a favorite of many different pollinators like honeybees and bumblebees, who feast on the sweet nectar. The best varieties of *Veronica* have a dense flush of bloom in late spring and early summer and continue blooming sporadically the rest of the year, right up to frost.

WHEN TO PLANT

Transplant container-grown specimens as early in the spring as possible, after the ground dries out and about the time the leaves are emerging on the trees. The second-best time to plant is in late summer or early fall so that the roots will have time to establish themselves before going dormant for the winter.

WHERE TO PLANT

Tall varieties of *Veronica* should be reserved for the middle or back of the border, while short varieties like *V. latifolia* 'Crater Lake Blue' or *V. spicata* 'Red Fox' should be planted at the front edge of the garden. Shorter varieties also make excellent rock garden plants. *Veronica* will bloom best in full sun. (In light shade, flower production will be somewhat reduced.) *Veronica* plants are easy to grow and will come back year after year in average but well-drained garden soil. When planted in wet sites they have a shorter life expectancy.

How to Plant

Prepare the soil as described in the introduction to this chapter. Container-grown *Veronicas* should bloom in the first year after transplanting, provided the soil is well prepared and the plants were in good condition at planting time. In wet sites, *Veronica* will be longer lived if the garden bed is raised 2 to 4 inches to improve drainage. Space 18 to 24 inches apart.

Advice for Care

Veronica requires the type of care given to all perennials after planting. Since the plants repeat their bloom throughout the summer and fall, deadheading old blooms will encourage additional flowers. Pinch or cut the old blooms an inch below the dead flowers. Cut the foliage back to 3 or 4 inches after the first hard frost, and spread a shallow layer of chopped leaves over the crown. Divide *Veronica* in early spring by slicing through the crown in one or two places with a sharp spade or shovel.

Additional Information

Veronicas bloom in the deepest shades of blue imaginable. For a stunning fall combination of blue, white, and silver, plant them with Russian sage, artemesia, and *Aster × frikartii*. The annual *Verbena bonariensis* as a background for veronica is also beautiful.

Additional Species, Cultivars, or Varieties

Veronica x 'Sunny Border Blue' is a hybrid with deep-blue flowers. It grows 18 inches to 2 feet tall. It blooms all summer long and was awarded the Perennial Plant of the Year award a few years ago. In some gardens, it tends to get powdery mildew in midsummer. *Veronica spicata* 'Red Fox' has deep-pink flowers and grows to 18 inches tall. *V. alpina* 'Goodness Grows' is a long-blooming medium-blue variety that grows to 12 inches tall. *V. longifolia* 'Icicle' has white blooms and grows to 2 feet. One of the best deep blues is *Veronica teucrium* 'Crater Lake Blue'; it grows only 18 inches tall and is perfect for the front of the border.

Yellow Coneflower

Ratibida pinnata

Other Name: Prairie Coneflower
Zones: 5, 6
Height: 3 to 5 feet
Bloom Period: July to September
Flowers: Pale yellow

Light Requirement:

---

oth purple and yellow coneflowers are mainstays in the
prairie wildflower garden. Blooming at the height of summer,
the yellow coneflower is a welcome friend each July when its drooping petals open to reveal a prominent greenish gray "cone." In the
wild, yellow coneflower may reach only three feet tall before blooming; in the garden, it can reach up to four or five feet tall. When it
grows this tall, it almost always needs some type of support or it may
fall over. Yellow coneflower leaves are deeply cut with three prominent lobes, resembling the footprint of a chicken or other "fowl."
Adapted to prairie living, it is best known for a root system that grows
two to three times the size of the foliage. Yellow coneflower's aggressive root system helps it establish quickly after transplanting. In its
native habitat, its extensive root system helped it survive drought and
wildfires, and allowed it to pull up nutrients lodged deep in the sub-
soil. This is a good plant for attracting birds, which feed off the drying
coneflower heads.

WHEN TO PLANT

Like many perennials, yellow coneflower can be successfully transplanted almost any time of the year if it is given the proper care.
Both container-grown and bare-root yellow coneflower will bloom
best during the first year if planted early in the spring as the soil
begins to dry and the tree leaves begin to emerge. The second-best
time to plant is late in the summer or early fall so that the roots will
have a little time to establish themselves before cold weather forces
the plants into dormancy.

WHERE TO PLANT

Yellow coneflower will grow in heavy clay or a well-drained loamy soil. Because it will get tall, plant it toward the back of the perennial border.

HOW TO PLANT

Transplant yellow coneflower into garden soil that is well prepared as described in the introduction. Backfill the planting hole with the original soil and water deeply. Spread a 2- to 3-inch layer of organic mulch around the entire planting area. Space 2 to 3 feet apart.

ADVICE FOR CARE

Yellow coneflower will thrive in most situations even when neglected, but a few regular maintenance chores will improve its appearance in the garden. To prevent weeds, maintain a 2- to 3-inch layer of organic mulch throughout the growing season. Cut the flower stalks back to the height of the foliage after blooming—unless you want to help feed hungry birds with ripening seed-heads. Cut the foliage back to 3 inches after the first hard frost, and spread chopped leaves over the crown for winter protection. The root system and crown are so dense that division is very difficult, but after a few years in the garden, the plant will be large enough to split. Division is best performed in very early spring or in late summer and fall. Bisect the crown with a sharp shovel or spade, being sure to dig deep. Then transplant and water deeply. Be sure to mulch well if dividing in the fall.

ADDITIONAL INFORMATION

Yellow coneflower looks best when mixed with other prairie wild-flowers like purple coneflower, black-eyed Susans, gayfeather, bee balm, and bluestems or other ornamental grasses. "Skippers," the name of several butterfly species, love to visit coneflower when it is in bloom!

ADDITIONAL SPECIES, CULTIVARS, OR VARIETIES

Ratibida columnaris, the Mexican hat plant, has red and yellow blooms and a "cone" that is almost twice the length of the petals. In Zone 5 in Indiana, it will need a layer of chopped leaf mulch at least 2 inches deep to protect it during the winter.

Gardening is a dynamic process, influenced by the changing forces of nature and by the plants we use.

The

Gardener

who plans

reaps

the

Greatest

Reward

COOL
SPRINGS
PRESS

The Indiana Gardener's Guide
Photographic Gallery of Featured Plants

ANNUALS

Ageratum
Ageratum houstonianum

Begonia
Begonia × semperflorens-cultorum

Browallia
Browallia speciosa

Cockscomb
Celosia argentea cristata

Coleus
Coleus × hybridus

Cosmos
Cosmos bipinnatus

Dusty Miller
Cineraria maritima

Flowering Cabbage
Brassica oleracea

Flowering Tobacco
Nicotiana alata

Geranium
Pelargonium × hortorum

Globe Amaranth
Gomphrena globosa

Gloriosa Daisy
Rudbeckia hirta

Impatiens
Impatiens wallerana

Lobelia
Lobelia erinus

Marigold
Tagetes spp.

Mexican Sunflower
Tithonia rotundifolia

Moss Rose
Portulaca grandiflora

Nierembergia
Nierembergia hippomanica

Pansy
Viola × wittrockiana

Periwinkle
Catharanthus roseus

Petunia
Petunia × hybrida

Pot Marigold
Calendula officinalis

Salvia
Salvia farinacea

Snapdragon
Antirrhinum majus

ANNUALS

BULBS

Spider Flower
Cleome hasslerana

Sunflower
Helianthus annuus

Sweet Alyssum
Lobularia maritima

Verbena
Verbena × hybrida

Zinnia
Zinnia elegans

Allium
Allium azureum

Caladium
Caladium x hortulanum

Canna
Canna × generalis

Crocus
Crocus vernus hybrids

Daffodil
Narcissus spp. and hybrids

Dahlia
Dahlia hybrids

Dutch Iris
Iris reticulata

Gladiolus
Gladiolus x *hortulanus*

Grape Hyacinth
Muscari spp.

Hyacinth
Hyacinthus orientalis

Lily
Lilium hybrids

Scilla
Scilla siberica

Snowdrop
Galanthus nivalis

Suprise Lily
Lycoris squamigera

Tuberous Begonia
Begonia x *tuberhybrida*

Tulip
Tulipa spp. and hybrids

Bugleweed
Ajuga reptans

English Ivy
Hedera helix

Epimedium
Epimedium grandiflorum

Juniper
Juniperus horizontalis

Lamium
Lamium maculatum

Lily Turf
Liriope spicata

Pachysandra
Pachysandra terminalis

Purple Winter Creeper
Euonymous fortunei 'Coloratus'

Sweet Woodruff
Galium odoratum

Vinca
Vinca minor

Basil
Ocimum basilicum

Borage
Borago officinalis

Chives
Allium schoenoprasum

Lavender
Lavandula angustifolia

Oregano
Origanum vulgare

Parsley
Petroselinum crispum

Rosemary
Rosmarinus officinalis

Thyme
Thymus vulgaris

Big Bluestem
Andropogon gerardii

Blue Fescue
Festuca ovina 'Glauca'

Feather Reed Grass
Calamagrostis x acutiflora 'Stricta'

Fountain Grass
Pennisetum alopecuroides 'Hameln'

Japanese Blood Grass
Imperata cylindrica 'Red Baron'

Maiden Grass
Miscanthus sinensis 'Gracillimus'

Northern Sea Oats
Chasmanthium latifolium

Prairie Dropseed
Sporobolus heterolepis

Switch Grass
Panicum virgatum

ORNAMENTAL GRASSES

Tufted Hairgrass
Deschampsia caespitosa

Achillea
Achillea millefolium 'Cerise Queen'

Anemone
Anemone × *hybrida*

PERENNIALS

Aster
Aster novae-angliae

'Autumn Joy' Sedum
Sedum x 'Autumn Joy'

Black-Eyed Susan
Rudbeckia fulgida 'Goldsturm'

Blanket Flower
Gaillardia × *grandifolia*

Boltonia
Boltonia asteroides

Butterfly Bush
Buddleia davidii

Chrysanthemum
Chrysanthemum × *morifolium*

Columbine
Aquilegia × *hybrida*

Coneflower
Echinacea purpurea

Daylily
Hemerocallis and hybrids

Foam Flower
Tiarella cordifolia

Geranium
Geranium sanguineum

Hosta
Hosta fortunei

Iris
Iris spp. and hybrids

Lamb's Ear
Stachys byzantina

Obedient Plant
Physostegia virginiana

Peony
Paeonia lactiflora

Phlox
Phlox paniculata

Pincushion Flower
Scabiosa caucasica

Russian Sage
Perovskia atriplicifolia

Salvia 'May Night'
Salvia × *superba* 'May Night'

PERENNIALS

Tickseed
Coreopsis verticillata 'Moonbeam'

Veronica
Veronica spicata

Yellow Coneflower
Ratibida pinnata

ROSES

'Frau Dagmar Hastrup' Rugosa Rose
Rosa rugosa 'Frau Dagmar Hastrup'

'Golden Showers' Climbing Rose
Rosa 'Golden Showers'

'Jean Keneally' Miniature Rose
Rosa 'Jean Keneally'

'Olympiad' Hybrid Tea Rose
Rosa 'Olympaid'

'Souvenir de la Malmaison' Old Garden Rose
Rosa 'Souvenir de la Malmaison'

'Sunsprite' Floribunda Rose
Rosa 'Sunsprite'

SHRUBS

'The Fairy' Polyantha Rose
Rosa 'The Fairy'

Arborvitae
Thuja occidentalis

Bayberry
Myrica pensylvanica

Bluebeard
Caryopteris × *clandonensis*

Bottlebrush Buckeye
Aesculus parviflora

Burkwood Viburnum
Viburnum × *burkwoodii*

Carolina Allspice
Calycanthus floridus

Doublefile Viburnum
Viburnum plicatum var. *tomentosum*

Dwarf Alberta Spruce
Picea glauca 'Conica'

Dwarf Fothergilla
Fothergilla gardenii

European Cranberry Bush
Viburnum opulus

Fringetree
Chionanthus virginicus

Hydrangea
Hydrangea paniculata 'Grandiflora'

Inkberry Holly
Ilex glabra

Japanese Barberry
Berberis thunbergii

Japanese Yew
Taxus spp.

Korean Boxwood
Buxus microphylla 'Koreana'

Leatherleaf Viburnum
Viburnum rhytidophyllum

Lilac
Syringa vulgaris

'Little Princess' Spirea
Spirea japonica 'Little Princess'

Potentilla
Potentilla fruticosa

Red Chokeberry
Aronia arbutifolia

Red Twig Dogwood
Cornus sericea

Summersweet
Clethra alnifolia

Vernal Witchhazel
Hamamelis vernalis

Winterberry Holly
Ilex verticillata

Amur Maple
Acer tataricum ssp. ginnala

Bald Cypress
Taxodium distichum

Beech
Fagus grandifolia

Bur Oak
Quercus macrocarpa

Flowering Crab Apple
Malus spp.

Flowering Pear
Pyrus calleryana

Ginkgo
Ginkgo biloba

Green Ash
Fraxinus pennsylvanica

Hemlock
Tsuga canadensis

Japanese Black Pine
Pinus thunbergiana

Japanese Maple
Acer palmatum

Japanese Tree Lilac
Syringa reticulata

Kousa Dogwood
Cornus kousa

TREES

Littleleaf Linden
Tilia cordata

Redbud
Cercis canadensis

Red Maple
Acer rubrum

River Birch
Betula nigra

Serbian Spruce
Picea omorika

Serviceberry
Amelanchier x grandiflora

Shingle Oak
Quercus imbricaria

Staghorn Sumac
Rhus typhina

Sugar Maple
Acer saccharum

Sweetbay Magnolia
Magnolia virginiana

White Fir
Abies concolor

Winter King Hawthorn
Crataegus viridis 'Winter King'

Boston Ivy
Parthenocissus tricuspidata

Clematis
Clematis spp.

Climbing Black-Eyed Susan
Thunbergia alata

Climbing Hydrangea
Hydrangea anomala ssp. *petiolaris*

Cup-and-Saucer Vine
Cobaea scandens

Honeysuckle
Lonicera spp.

Hyacinth Bean
Dolichos lablab

Moonflower
Calonyction aculeatum

Morning Glory
Ipomoea purpurea

Porcelain Berry
Ampelopsis brevipedunculata

Trumpet Vine
Campsis radicans

Virginia Creeper
Parthenocissus quinquefolia

Arrow Arum
Peltandra virginica

Arrowhead
Sagittaria sagittifolia

Blue Flag Iris
Iris versicolor

Pickerel
Pontederia cordata

Water Lily
Nymphaea spp.

We seek for
beauty on the
height afar;
But on the
earth it glim-
mers all the
while . . .

CHAPTER EIGHT

We seek for beauty on the height afar;
But on the earth it glimmers all the while:
'Tis in the garden where the roses are;
'Tis in the glory of a mother's smile.

—E. W. Mason

*M*Y EARLIEST MEMORIES OF ROSES are of the numerous rose beds scattered about my grandmother's compact and tidy backyard. Although I was too young to ask its name, or even realize it *had* a name, I am sure my favorite rose was 'Peace'. Having lived through and celebrated the end of the war as she did, it is logical that my grandmother would have planted this popular variety. I am sure many other gardeners have been introduced to roses in their grandparents' backyards as well. After all, roses have been one of our most popular flowers across the millennia. They have been the subject of more painting, more photography, and more writing than perhaps any other flower. The rose has been our national flower since 1986.

—T.T.

Roses are often written off by Hoosier gardeners as too finicky and prone to disease and insect problems. Many varieties are susceptible to the ever-present black spot and powdery mildew, especially the hybrid teas. Selecting the right variety can mean a greater number of blooms. Different types of roses show big differences in the number of flowers they develop through the course of a season. It is only logical to desire those that produce the most flowers and that also have the other great rose attributes like fragrance and long stems for cutting. A good book and a couple of visits to local rose society meetings will help you learn about the different types of roses and determine which varieties "throw" the most flowers or are least susceptible to disease. Many old types, like shrub roses, fell from popularity years ago, but they are regaining their place as reliable and maintenance-free plants that are perfect if you want a rose to plant and forget about. With a few exceptions, hybrid teas are still quite susceptible to disease and should be left to the gardener who has the interest and time to coddle plants with regular sprays, fertilizer, and winter protection.

SOIL PREPARATION

Whether planting disease-prone varieties or not, soil preparation should not be overlooked. Well-prepared soil is probably the single most important factor in determining success. With the exception of some of the landscape roses and perhaps the rugosas, roses generally deplore heavy clay soil. To grow healthy roses you *must* amend the planting area with at least one-third organic matter. This helps improve drainage, brings oxygen to the roots, and holds moisture during the dry spells of summer. Many roses, especially the hybrid teas, grow best when planted in raised beds, thus ensuring good drainage. A good soil mix for a raised rose bed consists of one-third soil, one-third sand, and one-third organic matter. It should be raised eight to twelve inches above the ground.

Whether the soil is raised or not, it is best to prepare an entire bed rather than individual holes. The bed should be dug to a depth of at least eighteen inches. Two feet deep is even better, and digging to this depth will reward your hard work with seasons of good roses. Mix organic matter completely with the soil that has been removed. Rich, well-prepared soil will grow healthier roses that are better able to withstand disease and insect threats.

PLANTING ROSES

Roses perform best during the first year if planted from bare-root stock. Bare-root stock are plants that have been pulled from the ground during their dormant period and held in cold storage. There is no soil around the roots, and they are always kept wrapped and damp. Plant roses in early spring, just as the forsythia begin to bloom. Remove the wrapping from around the roots and soak the

Chapter Eight

entire bush in a bucket of water for two to three hours. In the mean-time, dig a planting hole in the newly prepared bed from one- and one-half to two feet deep. Add a few inches of pure organic matter to the bottom of the hole. Continue refilling the hole, making a mound with the soil as it approaches the top. Spread the roots over the mound, then fill the rest of the hole. The rose should be planted so that the bud union is level with the soil. The bud union is the point at which the canes of one desirable plant were grafted onto the roots of a less-desirable plant. The bud union has to be protected from severe cold weather during the winter or the canes may die off completely. Space roses two feet apart in the rose bed.

Container-grown roses can be planted in much the same way as the bare-root types. A peat or paper-based container need not be entirely removed; instead, remove the bottom and score the sides with a sharp knife to help improve initial drainage. The container will eventually decompose in the ground.

MAINTENANCE

Roses grow better and will reward you with more blooms when fertilized regularly. Choose a good rose food, organic fertilizer, or complete fertilizer like 5-10-5 or 12-12-12; add one tablespoon per plant in the early spring. Continue to fertilize with a tablespoon per plant per month until August 15. With the exception of the lower-maintenance shrub and landscape types, roses cannot tolerate the dry soils that are especially common during Indiana summers. Apply one to one-and-one-half inches of water per week and always maintain a two- to three-inch layer of organic mulch. This will help moderate both soil moisture and soil temperature, while keeping out invasive weeds.

Two very common foliar diseases, black spot and powdery mildew, will attack susceptible roses in Indiana. Without the protection of regular fungicidal sprays, most canes will lose their leaves to these diseases over the course of the growing season. Sprays of Triforine® must be applied every ten to fourteen days for effective control.

Chapter Eight

Most roses are Sunday dinner for the voracious Japanese beetle which appears in late June or early July in most of the state. Vigilant hand picking or regular sprays of carbaryl are necessary to control this hungry pest. Roses are favorites of aphids, rose midges, rose slugs, and other pests. Before spraying for any insect, be sure you have properly identified the pest and have chosen the appropriate insecticide. For good diagnosis and control, contact the local office of the Cooperative Extension Service, a local garden center, or your local rosarian. Always follow label directions when applying pesticides.

One of the most commonly asked questions is "When do I prune roses?" Pruning at the correct time of year will encourage more canes and better flowers. As a rule, rose pruning should be left till spring; at this time, cut away all blackened and dead canes or damaged wood. On bush roses like hybrid teas, grandifloras, or floribundas, cut healthy canes back to green wood. Prune the roses into an open and vase-like shape, removing all canes from the center of the bush. This will help improve air circulation and reduce disease. Always cut the canes back to an outward-facing bud to encourage an open growth habit. Remove old flowers with sharp pruners as soon as they start to fade; this will encourage new blooms. Any cut canes thicker than a pencil should be sealed with white glue to prevent rose cane borers. More specific pruning infor-mation is described in the discussion for each plant.

Many roses require protection in the winter. After the first hard freeze, tie the canes together with twine or other string. Be careful that the material you use does not cut into the flesh of the canes. Slip a commercial rose collar over the canes so that it encircles the base of the plant. Homemade collars are easily made from 4 sheets of newspaper stapled end-to-end to form a circle. Chicken wire or other fencing can also be used. After the collar is set in place, mound 4 to 6 inches of soil over the crown of the plant to protect the bud union and the base of the canes. Fill the collar to the brim with chopped leaves. Remove the leaves and collars in the spring when the buds begin to swell.

'Frau Dagmar Hastrup' Rugosa Rose

Rosa rugosa 'Frau Dagmar Hastrup'

Other Name: 'Frau Dagmar Hartopp'
Zones: 5, 6
Height: 3 to 4 feet
Bloom Period: June to frost; hips, summer to fall
Flowers: Pink; hips, bright red

Light Requirement:

There couldn't be a tougher or all-around more pleasing rose than the rugosa. This shrubby rose is known for its vigorous growth habit and its ability to thrive in poor planting sites. Although rugosas have been around a long time, they were made for rose lovers who have neither the time nor the energy to care for their finicky cousins, the hybrid teas. Rugosas have an upright, bushy, slightly mounded growth habit and very thorny stems. For this reason they make a good living fence. 'Frau Dagmar Hastrup' has deep-pink blooms with yellow centers and perhaps the best fragrance of all the rugosas. An added bonus is the bright orange-red fruit, called "hips," which begin turning color in July and last through late fall. The leaves turn bright yellow-orange before falling to the ground in preparation for winter.

WHEN TO PLANT

Plant 'Frau Dagmar Hastrup' in early spring, preferably right before the leaves emerge on trees or as the forsythia begin to bloom. Fall is the second-best time to plant.

WHERE TO PLANT

Plant rugosas on banks or slopes, or as a hedge along the driveway or sidewalk. 'Frau Dagmar Hastrup' prefers good drainage and grows well in sandy soils. It is well known for its ability to tolerate salty environments, and thrives on the northeastern seashore.

HOW TO PLANT

Start by soaking the entire plant in water for 2 or 3 hours. After preparing a planting bed as described in the introduction, plant rugosas by digging a planting hole up to 2 feet deep and 18 inches wide. Add a few inches of rotted compost or peat moss to the bottom of the hole. Add $1/2$ cup of balanced fertilizer to the soil and mix well. Return the amended soil to the planting hole, making a mound toward the top of the hole. Prune any damaged or overly long roots with sharp pruning shears. Spread the roots of the plant over the mound and finish filling the hole. Plant rugosas so that the bud union is level with the ground. Water deeply and spread a 2- to 3-inch layer of mulch around the planting site to preserve moisture. To make a hedge, space plants $2^{1}/2$ feet apart.

ADVICE FOR CARE

Rugosas are practically care free. Prune dead wood in the spring and remove old, thick canes every 2 or 3 years to encourage new growth. Prune by removing approximately $1/3$ of the cane. Rugosas will not require heavy sprays like other roses. Some insects, such as Japanese beetles, feed on the blooms and the leaves. You can pick them by hand when they appear in small numbers. Apply an insecticide containing carbaryl during severe infestations. Always follow label directions when applying any pesticide.

ADDITIONAL INFORMATION

'Frau Dagmar Hastrup' and other rugosas are easily mixed in with flowering annuals and perennials. The hips are sometimes used to make jam and are prized for their high concentration of Vitamin C. This variety is extremely winter hardy and is known to grow not far from Siberia. Obviously, it does not require additional winter protection.

ADDITIONAL SPECIES, CULTIVARS, OR VARIETIES

'Blanc Double de Coubert' is an excellent white rugosa with all the attributes of 'Frau Dagmar Hastrup' except for the showy hips. 'Albo-plena' and 'Alba' are other good whites, while *Rosa rugosa* 'Rubra' is a good red variety. 'Jens Munk' has light-pink semi-double flowers.

'Golden Showers' Climbing Rose

Rosa 'Golden Showers'

Zones: 5, 6 (needs winter protection)
Height: 6 to 9 feet
Bloom Period: May, June; repeats throughout
   the summer
Flowers: Yellow

Light Requirement:

$\mathcal{C}$limbing roses stir memories of split-rail fences and trellises thick with the bright-red blooms of May and June. In the "old days," the flowers were so plentiful and satisfying that the average gardener never thought about repeat blooming, winter hardiness, fragrance, or any other important aspects of climbing roses. Today, however, climbers offer the rose enthusiast many more choices in both color and bloom period. Everblooming climbers grow on long canes that must be trained on a fence, deck rail, trellis, or pergola. Climbing rose flowers are slightly smaller than the popular hybrid tea flowers and appear as individual blooms or in clusters. The variety 'Golden Showers' offers today's gardener a large, extremely fragrant yellow flower that blooms off and on during the summer after a lavish display in May or June. In September, it rewards gardeners with a second heavy blooming period. 'Golden Showers' is one of the few climbing roses to win the prestigious All-America Rose Selection award for its outstanding bloom and luxurious, disease-resistant foliage.

WHEN TO PLANT

Climbers like 'Golden Showers' are best planted in the spring, just before tree leaves emerge or as the forsythia start to bloom.

WHERE TO PLANT

Plant climbers where they will receive at least 6 hours of full sun each day. Like most roses, they prefer light but well-drained soils and plenty of organic matter like peat moss or compost. 'Golden Showers' will do equally well planted alongside a fence or pillar, or on a trellis that is fastened to the house.

How to Plant

Prepare a planting bed as described in the introduction at least 6 weeks before planting. Dig an individual hole 2 feet deep and at least 18 inches wide. Space climbers 3 to 4 feet apart. For bare-root roses, soak the entire plant in water for 2 to 3 hours before planting. Trim off damaged or excessively long roots with sharp pruning scissors. Prune the canes back to an outward-facing bud, to about 12 to 18 inches. Add a few inches of compost or peat moss directly to the bottom of the hole and mix 1/2 cup of a balanced fertilizer like 12-12-12 or rose food to the soil that was removed. Return enough soil back to the hole in the shape of a mound so that the bud union is level with the ground around it after planting. Spread the roots over the mound and fill the hole with the remaining soil. Water deeply and spread an organic mulch at least 2 inches thick.

Advice for Care

Fertilize regularly with rose food for maximum bloom. Water regularly and maintain a 2- to 3-inch layer of organic mulch to preserve moisture and keep the roots cool. Use appropriate fungicides regularly to prevent black spot, powdery mildew, and other foliar diseases. Vigilance and an application of carbaryl will help reduce Japanese beetle infestations. Winterize 'Golden Showers' with 12 inches of soil mounded around the base of the canes to protect the graft union. Gather the canes in a bundle and fasten them to the ground with wire or wood stakes. Cover the canes with 6 inches of mulch and 6 inches of soil to protect them from sub-zero temperatures. Remove protective mulch and soil in the spring as new growth begins.

Additional Information

Prune climbers in a fan shape with many lateral canes to encourage the maximum number of blooms. Use sharp pruners in spring to remove dead, damaged, or spindly canes.

Additional Species, Cultivars, or Varieties

Other excellent climbers for Indiana include 'William Baffin', with its watermelon-pink flowers; 'Clair Matin', a pink that blooms all summer long; and 'Altissimo', an excellent red.

'Jean Keneally' Miniature Rose

Rosa 'Jean Keneally'

Zones: 5, 6
Height: 1¹/₂ to 2 feet
Bloom Period: June to September
Flowers: Apricot

Light Requirement:

When you need everblooming roses for tiny spaces, miniature roses are the answer. Modern miniatures come in different heights, but the flowers and leaves are all smaller than two inches. Some miniatures' flowers grow on single stems like hybrid teas, while others bloom in clusters or sprays. The tiniest miniatures will grow in pots as small as a jelly jar! They come in all colors except the elusive blue, and virtually all of them bloom continuously. With regular watering, miniatures grow well as container plants and are excellent for summer decks or patios. 'Jean Keneally', one of the highest rated rose varieties ever, is a medium-sized miniature that blooms throughout the summer. Its tea-like flowers open to a lush apricot color.

WHEN TO PLANT

Plant 'Jean Keneally' in the spring just before leaves come out on the trees. If moving a potted miniature from overwintering indoors, be sure to harden it off before subjecting it to the chilly air of early spring.

WHERE TO PLANT

'Jean Keneally' and other miniatures prefer 6 hours of full sun per day but tolerate as little as 4 hours per day. Plant them in the foreground of the rose garden in soil that is moist but well drained. On the patio or deck, group many pots together for a special effect.

HOW TO PLANT

Prepare a planting bed as described in the introduction. Soak bare-root plants in water for 2 to 3 hours before planting. In the meantime, prepare a planting hole 18 inches deep and 18 inches wide. Add a few inches of compost or peat moss directly to the bottom of the hole while adding $1/4$ cup of fertilizer to the soil. Mix soil and fertilizer well. Return the soil to the planting hole, creating a mound towards the top of the hole. Trim off any roots that are broken or excessively long. Spread the remaining roots over the mound and cover them with the soil mix. Plant them at the same level they were growing in the field. Water the plant deeply after planting and spread a 2- to 3-inch layer of organic mulch. Prune the canes back to $1/3$ their original height when finished. When planting miniatures into containers, be sure to use a pot that is 12 to 18 inches in diameter. Use a commercial soilless potting mix or make your own blend.

ADVICE FOR CARE

Fertilize each spring with a teaspoon of rose food or balanced fertilizer, and repeat monthly until August 15. For potted plants, use a liquid houseplant fertilizer. Keep the soil moist during the summer. Maintain a 2- to 3-inch layer of organic mulch at all times. Miniatures like 'Jean Keneally' will only need winter protection the first year. In following years, a few inches of mulch or shredded fall leaves will suffice. In early spring, prune the branches back from $1/3$ to $1/2$ their original height.

ADDITIONAL INFORMATION

Potted miniatures can be overwintered in a sunny room in the house or kept in an attached garage or basement. Left in a dark, cool basement or garage, the miniature will drop its leaves and go through a brief dormant period; water it only when the soil dries out.

ADDITIONAL SPECIES, CULTIVARS, OR VARIETIES

'Party Girl' is named for an Indianapolis rosarian and is an excellent yellow blend. 'Minnie Pearl' is a pink blend. 'Hot Tamale' is a new introduction with yellow-orange flowers that fade to pink.

'Olympiad' Hybrid Tea Rose

Rosa 'Olympiad'

Zones: 5, 6 (needs winter protection)
Height: 2¹/₂ to 5 feet
Bloom Period: June through October
Flowers: Red

Light Requirement:

*N*o other flower is as beloved or as sought after as the red rose. Long a symbol of romance, red hybrid teas are considered the "queen" of roses, the standard by which all other flowers are judged. The hybrid tea is a rose made for the gardener who likes to pamper. A well-tended hybrid tea will reward the attentive owner with a truly regal flower. A much anticipated exception to the notion that hybrid teas are fraught with disease is the relatively recent introduction 'Olympiad'. This lightly fragrant deep-red variety has a classic bush form with lovely pointed buds, and is much more resistant to rose diseases like black spot and powdery mildew than are other hybrid teas. 'Olympiad' won the prestigious All-America Rose Selection award in 1984 for its outstanding flower and foliage characteristics.

WHEN TO PLANT

Plant hybrid teas like 'Olympiad' in early spring, just before tree leaves emerge. The second-best time to plant is during the fall, but plants will need extra winter protection.

WHERE TO PLANT

For maximum bloom, plant in a location with full sun and light but well-drained soil. Reserve a special place in the garden for these particular plants since they don't mix well in the annual or perennial border. A planting bed made just for roses will make caring for them easier.

HOW TO PLANT

Prepare a planting bed as described in the introduction, then dig a planting hole 2 feet deep and at least 18 inches wide. Add a few inches of compost or peat moss directly to the bottom of the hole while mixing $1/2$ cup of balanced fertilizer or rose food with the displaced soil. Return most of the soil to the hole, making a mound as it nears the top. Spread the roots over the mound and carefully finish covering the roots with the remaining soil. The bud union, which appears as a bump or swelling at the point where the canes join the roots, should be even or slightly below ground level after planting. Water each plant deeply and spread a 2-inch layer of organic mulch over the entire planting area. In heavy clay soils or sites with poor drainage, plant roses in raised beds for best results. Space hybrid teas 18 inches to 2 feet apart.

ADVICE FOR CARE

Most hybrid teas benefit greatly from regular applications of fungicide. For disease-free plants, this means spraying every 10 to 14 days with a fungicide containing triforine. 'Olympiad' may require less spraying. After the first bloom in June, fertilize each rose plant with 1 tablespoon of rose food or a balanced fertilizer like 12-12-12. Fertilize monthly until August 15. Keep roses moist all summer by maintaining a 2-inch layer of organic mulch around the entire planting area. To protect the bud union in the winter, place a rose collar around each plant after the first hard freeze and mound 4 to 6 inches of soil over the crown, followed by 8 inches of chopped leaves. Fill the collar to the brim and remove it in the spring as the buds begin to swell.

ADDITIONAL INFORMATION

Prune roses in the spring by cutting dead canes back to the point where live growth begins. When cutting roses for indoor display, cut the stems just above a leaf with 5 leaflets to encourage more blooms.

ADDITIONAL SPECIES, CULTIVARS, OR VARIETIES

The variety 'Peace' was smuggled to the United States from occupied France during World War II. Its light pink and yellow blooms along with its dramatic history make it the world's most cherished rose. 'Peace', like many hybrid tea roses, requires regular spraying for disease control. 'Mr. Lincoln' is another favorite red variety with excellent fragrance and deep-red color. 'Marijke Koopman' is a newer pink that blooms throughout the summer. 'Uncle Joe' has huge red flowers and is considered one of the best.

ʼSouvenir de la Malmaison'
Old Garden Rose

Rosa 'Souvenir de la Malmaison'

Zones: 5, 6 (needs good winter protection) **Light Requirement:**
Height: 2 to 3 feet
Bloom Period: June through fall
Flowers: Light pink

Old Garden Roses is a special class of roses that includes all roses in cultivation prior to 1867. They make a complex and varied collection; all are forerunners of the popular roses we have today. After the development of 'Peace' and some of the other early hybrid teas, these older roses fell out of favor. Fortunately, they have experienced a resurgence and are once again "en vogue" among hobbyists. 'Bourbon' is an Old Garden class of rose known for its heady fragrance. 'Souvenir de la Malmaison' is a classic Bourbon-type and makes a super choice for Indiana gardeners who like to dote. Its pale-pink double blooms grow up to four inches wide and perfume the air with over fifty petals on each flower. Best of all, the flowers repeat themselves throughout the summer and fall, an unusual trait for the older rose types.

WHEN TO PLANT
Plant 'Souvenir de la Malmaison' and other old roses in the spring, preferably before tree leaves emerge.

WHERE TO PLANT
Fragrant roses like 'Souvenir de la Malmaison' are best planted where their sweet scent can be enjoyed as often as possible; next to a doorway is ideal. Plant them in full sun in soil that is well drained but rich in organic matter.

HOW TO PLANT
Prepare a planting bed as described in the introduction, then begin by soaking the bare-root plant in water for 2 to 3 hours. Dig a planting hole at least 2 feet deep and 18 inches wide. Add a few inches of compost or peat moss to the bottom of the hole while mixing 1/2 cup

of balanced rose fertilizer to the displaced soil. Return the amended soil to the planting hole, making a mound towards the top of the hole. Trim any broken, damaged, or overly long roots with sharp pruning shears. Plant the rose by spreading the roots over the mounded soil and fill the hole so that the bud union is even with the ground around it. Water the plant deeply and spread a 2- to 3-inch layer of organic mulch around the entire planting area.

ADVICE FOR CARE

Unlike many of the old roses, 'Souvenir de la Malmaison' is somewhat resistant to the classic rose diseases of Indiana. To ensure disease-free plants, however, a regular schedule of fungicidal sprays should be followed. Fertilize in the spring after the first bloom with 1 tablespoon of balanced fertilizer like 12-12-12 or rose food. Apply 1 to $1^1/2$ inches of water each week during the summer and maintain a 2- to 3-inch layer of organic mulch at all times. Prune to remove dead or damaged canes each spring. Cut healthy canes to half their original height to stimulate new and vigorous growth. Winterize 'Souvenir de la Malmaison' by placing a rose collar around the plant, tying up the canes, and filling the collar to the brim with chopped leaves.

ADDITIONAL INFORMATION

'Souvenir de la Malmaison' was released in 1843 in honor of La Malmaison, the rose garden of collector Empress Josephine I. Her garden was home to all of the 250 named varieties of the time. Her passion for roses was instrumental in popularizing them throughout the world.

ADDITIONAL SPECIES, CULTIVARS, OR VARIETIES

'Madame Hardy' is of the fragrant damask class and is one of the most beautiful white roses. 'Celsiana' is another fragrant white damask. 'Reine des Violettes' is a deep-pink hybrid perpetual with heavy fragrance.

'Sunsprite' Floribunda Rose

Rosa 'Sunsprite'

Zones: 5, 6
Height: 3 to 4 feet
Bloom Period: June to September
Flowers: Golden yellow

Light Requirement:

Next to the hybrid tea, the floribunda is the most widely planted rose. Floribundas are known for their shrubby character; they reach three to four feet high and a few feet wide. Floribundas produce masses of bloom throughout the summer which makes them ideal for the gardener who doesn't have time for the fussier types. Their flowers are larger than those of the polyanthas and appear as either a spray of many blooms or as single specimens, much like the hybrid teas. 'Sunsprite' is considered one of the best floribundas and perhaps the most beautiful yellow floribunda available. In Indiana it has very good disease resistance and rewards gardeners with blooms even in August when the rest of the garden seems to wane. An added benefit is the sweet and fruity fragrance that perfumes the air around it.

WHEN TO PLANT

Plant bare-root specimens of 'Sunsprite' and other floribundas in early spring, preferably right before the leaves emerge on the trees. Container-grown specimens can be planted at any time of the year provided they receive adequate moisture.

WHERE TO PLANT

Plant 'Sunsprite' in moist but well-drained soil. Amend the soil with plenty of organic matter for best results. Floribundas make excellent additions to the landscape when planted in groups. Mass them together to create "drifts" and season-long yellow color. They also add color to the cottage garden or perennial border when planted as single specimens.

How to Plant

Prepare a planting bed as described in the introduction, then dig a planting hole 2 feet deep and 18 inches wide. Soak the entire plant in a bucket of water for 2 to 3 hours to rehydrate it. Add a few inches of compost or peat moss to the bottom of the hole. Mix $1/2$ cup of rose food or balanced fertilizer like 12-12-12 to the displaced soil and return it the hole, forming a mound towards the top. Trim dead, damaged, or overly long roots with sharp pruning shears. Spread 'Sunsprite's' remaining roots over the mound and finish filling the hole. The bud union should be even with or slightly below ground level after planting. Water the plant deeply and spread a 2- to 3-inch layer of mulch around the entire planting area to preserve moisture and keep the weeds out. Prune the canes back to 6 or 8 inches tall after planting to encourage vigorous regrowth.

Advice for Care

'Sunsprite' requires very little care but will produce more flowers if fertilized with a tablespoon of an all-purpose fertilizer such as 12-12-12 or rose food for each plant, starting after the first bloom. Fertilize monthly until August 15. Maintain a 2- to 3-inch layer of organic mulch around the plants at all times; this will help keep the roots cool and moist. 'Sunsprite' is very resistant to many of the typical rose diseases in Indiana and should not require regular spraying except in very wet years. Japanese beetles love roses, and 'Sunsprite' is no exception. Vigilant handpicking or an application of carbaryl will help deter them. Always read and follow the label directions when applying any pesticide.

Additional Information

Deadheading old flowers will encourage more blooms. Floribundas were developed by crossing the smaller and continuous blooming polyanthas with the larger and more fragrant hybrid teas.

Additional Species, Cultivars, or Varieties

Other floribundas for Indiana rose gardens include 'Showbiz' and 'Europeana', two excellent red varieties; 'Apricot Nectar', which has apricot blooms; 'Angel Face', with lavender blooms; 'Iceberg', with white blooms; and 'Sexy Rexy', with pink blooms.

'The Fairy'
Polyantha Rose

Rosa 'The Fairy'

Zones: 5, 6	**Light Requirement:**
Height: 3 feet	
Bloom Period: May through frost	
Flowers: Pink	

Polyanthas are generally low growers that spread wider than they are tall. They are usually covered with sprays of small pink or white flowers. Only a few polyanthas remain popular today; most polyanthas have been replaced by the floribundas, which have a wider color range and more generous fragrance. Introduced in 1932, one selection has survived the fall from glory—and for good reason. 'The Fairy' must have been named for its magical effect in the garden. It blooms all season long with full sprays of small, hybrid-tea-like pink flowers. Bothered by few pests, 'The Fairy' is virtually maintenance free, making it a superb choice for the beginner or "weekend" gardener.

WHEN TO PLANT
The best time to plant 'The Fairy' is in the spring, preferably before leaves emerge on the trees. The second-best time to plant is in the fall.

WHERE TO PLANT
'The Fairy' should be planted in full sun, but it will tolerate light shade. 'The Fairy' (along with other polyanthas, floribundas, and shrub roses) prefers moist but well-drained soil with plenty of organic matter. Its short stature makes 'The Fairy' a perfect border or edging plant in the garden.

HOW TO PLANT
'The Fairy' does not need a special planting bed as the other roses do. Start the planting process by soaking bare-root plants in water for 2 to 3 hours. Prepare the planting site by digging a hole at least 2 feet deep and 18 inches wide. Add a few inches of compost directly

to the bottom of the hole and mix $1/2$ cup of rose food or balanced fertilizer to the displaced soil. Finish filling the hole, forming a mound as it reaches the top. Trim any dead, damaged, or overly long roots with sharp pruning scissors. Spread the roots over the mound of soil in the planting hole and finish filling the hole with soil. The bud union should be level with the ground around it after planting. Water deeply and spread a 2- to 3-inch layer of organic mulch around the entire planting area. If planting a container-grown plant, carefully remove the plant from its pot if the pot is metal or plastic. Organic pots made from a peat or paper base will decompose in a short amount of time. These pots do not have to be removed; however, the bottoms should be cut out and the sides of the container should be scored to improve initial drainage.

ADVICE FOR CARE

Encourage additional flowers by fertilizing with 1 tablespoon of balanced fertilizer like 12-12-12 after the first blooms. Fertilize monthly until August 15. Keep the plant watered with 1 to $1^1/2$ inches of water each week. Maintain a 2- to 3-inch layer of mulch to keep the roots cool and to prevent weeds. 'The Fairy', like all polyanthas, should not need extra winter protection. Prune 'The Fairy' canes back by half each spring and remove any dead or damaged wood.

ADDITIONAL INFORMATION

'The Fairy' may be bothered by spider mites. To test for spider mites, hold a white sheet of paper under a branch and tap hard. The pinhead-sized mites will be barely visible to the naked eye. Treat with an appropriate miticide, following the label directions.

ADDITIONAL SPECIES, CULTIVARS, OR VARIETIES

Other shrub and landscape roses include the red, pink, and white 'Meidilland' varieties. 'Bonica' is an excellent pink variety that was the first shrub rose to win an All-America Rose Selection award. 'Carefree Wonder' and 'Carefree Beauty' are two varieties that come in shades of deep-pink and salmon. They have single blooms.

CHAPTER NINE

Shrubs

FOR MANY GARDENERS, SHRUBS ARE JUST ANOTHER chore to add to the list of weekend yard activities, the green "meatballs" they have to clip throughout the season to keep from growing over the windows. For others, shrubs give a special gift with each passing season: springtime flowers, the glossy green leaves of summer that become fall's scarlet red, followed by brilliant berries in winter.

Whether planted alone or in calculated designs, shrubs make up the "walls" of our landscapes, much as trees form the "ceilings." Their shorter stature helps to enclose the garden, giving it shape and feeling. They also serve as living fences, screening off unsightly views and giving privacy. Shrubs provide essential food and cover for wildlife and make excellent backgrounds for flower gardens. When planted strategically, they can make small buildings look larger, and can help to soften harsh man-made views.

Shrubs come in all shapes and sizes, and include evergreen, deciduous, blooming, and non-blooming types. The most important thing to consider when planting a shrub is its appropriateness for the planting site. While many shrubs are considered "tough" or "hardy," they are more likely to thrive in the environment best suited for the particular type. When selecting a shrub, take into account its ultimate size as well as anything near the planting location that might limit the growth of the roots, such as a sidewalk, underground utility lines, or driveway. Think about how much sun the site receives, and whether it gets morning or afternoon light. It is just as important to consider soil drainage and soil type. Choosing the right plant for the right place could mean the difference between success and failure. Finally, be realistic about how much time you can spend tending your landscape. Many shrubs are low-maintenance plants, but most require pruning, watering, or some other care, especially when they are less than five years old.

Chapter Nine

Shrubs are purchased as either container-grown, balled-and-burlapped, or bare-root plants. All three types grow equally well when handled correctly. Soil preparation procedures are the same regardless of type. First, dig a hole that is up to four times the width of the rootball or container; because most of the roots grow outward from the plant rather than downward, it is important to loosen the soil as far out as possible. Always dig just deep enough so that the plant is at the same depth it was growing in the field or container. A shrub that is planted even a couple of inches too deep might easily die.

For container-grown specimens, be sure to unravel any roots growing in concentric circles around the bottom of the pot. Gently tease them apart, or in severe cases, use a pruning knife to score the roots with four or five vertical cuts. Spread the roots out in the hole and knead some soil around them for best results. Remove any twine or wire wrapped around the stems of balled-and-burlapped shrubs; if left in place, this could eventually girdle the stem. Burlap can be removed or left in the soil to decompose. There have been no harmful effects reported from leaving wire baskets around the roots. Even so, you may wish to partially cut away the burlap and any wire basket to about half the height of the rootball. Any synthetic material should be completely removed from around the roots because this will not decompose.

Bare-root shrubs have been pulled from the ground during the dormant season and stored in a cool environment. They should be planted within a couple days of purchase. Remove the protective root covering and soak the roots in water for two hours. Plant the shrub as deep as it was growing in the field.

Spacing shrubs depends on how they are being used in the landscape, and how big they will get. As a rule, plant shrubs six feet from the house or more. Plant them so that at their mature size, the branches will overlap. Shrubs planted for screening purposes or as a hedge can be planted closer together. Consult with your local nursery operator, garden center staff, or the Purdue Cooperative Extension Service for more detailed information.

Chapter Nine

Backfill the planting holes with the original soil. It is not necessary to add compost or organic matter to the soil before returning it to the hole. In fact, in some heavier soils this can eventually "drown" the plant. Loosen the soil before returning it to the hole by pulverizing with a shovel. Water deeply and spread two to three inches of mulch over the entire planting area. Mulch will help the shrubs establish themselves better and grow more quickly by keeping the roots moist and cool and preventing weed growth. During the first five years after planting, it is important to water with one to one-and-one-half inches of water per week. Adequate soil moisture is most important during the hot, dry days of summer, since this is when spring-blooming plants are setting flower buds for the following year. Poor spring-blooming can often be traced back to dry weather in the previous summer.

Pruning is a regular maintenance chore that keeps shrubs the appropriate size for their planting sites. It also stimulates growth and helps keep the plant healthy. Pruning methods depend on how the plant is used in the landscape. It's always best to start by knowing the shrub's natural growth habit and shape. Whenever possible, maintain the natural shape of the plant when pruning. As popular as the green meatball seems to be, the shape is far from natural. When the shrub is used as a background plant for a garden, as a privacy screen or specimen plant, pruning once a year should be adequate. For flowering shrubs, time pruning chores according to when the plant blooms. Prune spring blooming shrubs like vibunums and lilacs immediately after they bloom. Spring bloomers develop flower buds for the next season on the current season's growth. Pruning in the summer, fall, or winter (although not a serious health threat) removes blooms that could be enjoyed the following spring. Summer and fall blooming shrubs develop flowers on the current season's growth. Prune these types early in the spring, just as new growth begins.

Start pruning by removing any dead branches all the way down to the next living branch using sharp "scissor-type" loppers or hand pruners. Shape the shrub by removing overgrown or tall branches all the way down to the ground. It's best not to remove more than

Chapter Nine

one-third of the total branches in any one year. Shorten other branches by cutting back to a larger branch. Don't leave short stubby branches as this will cause an abundance of regrowth from these stubby tips. This practice eventually causes abundant top growth and spindly bottom growth. Instead, prune branches back to the collar or swollen area where the two branches eventually join. Remove select branches on all sides to maintain a balanced shape and so that light reaches the center of the plant. This will encourage new growth from below the branch tips. Overgrown shrubs can be rejuvenated and shortened by removing one-third of the tallest and oldest branches each year for three years.

"Shearing" removes the tips of the branches and is an appropriate pruning practice for formal hedges or when other unnatural shapes, like topiary, are desired. Evergreens like boxwood, yew, and juniper are often sheared to maintain their shape. Shear hedges in the early spring as new growth begins. In both formal and informal hedges, prune so that the bottom of the shrub is wider than the top. This will keep the lower branches green and full. With the exception of yews, *Taxus* spp., evergreens cut back to brown wood will not regrow at those pruning points.

For best results, fertilize shrubs in early November as described in the introduction to the chapter on trees. There is no advantage to fertilizing during planting time or even in the first year. Wait until the second year after planting to begin a fertilizing program.

Most of the shrubs chosen for this chapter are adaptable for any part of Indiana. When selecting a plant, pick one that gives you the most enjoyment for the price: good foliage, sweet fragrance, interesting bark, enticing flowers, winter fruit. We're always searching for more bang for the buck, so why stop when we get to the landscape?

Arborvitae

Thuja occidentalis

Zones: 5, 6 **Height:** 15 to 30 feet in cultivation; to 60 feet in nature **Type:** Evergreen	**Light Requirement:**

The story going around when I was in junior high school was that if you went to the local public golf course late at night, you could see the silhouettes of hooded monks praying in the moonlight. Never mind that the golf course was closed at night; the monks were reported to stand perfectly still, like statues. Although I never went to the golf course to verify this rumor (and I've never been cow tipping either), I am sure the alleged "monks" were arborvitae shrubs. This story is a good testament to arborvitae's densely evergreen and upright growth. These plants do resemble human figures at night—if you use your imagination. Their fan-shaped needle-like leaves never spread very far from the trunk, growing only ten to fifteen feet wide. For this reason arborvitae make excellent vertical screens and hedges. Their slow to medium rate allows them to grow for years before pruning is necessary.

—T.T.

WHEN TO PLANT

Plant arborvitae at any time of year when the ground is dry. If planting in summer, be sure to water the plants deeply at least once a week.

WHERE TO PLANT

Arborvitae prefer deep, moist, but well-drained loamy soils with high organic matter content. When young, they cannot survive drying out, which is a regular condition during our Indiana summers. Arborvitae prefer full sun but tolerate light shade. Their dense green color is a wonderful low-maintenance background for the mixed-flower border; they also make excellent accent plants or hedges.

How to Plant

Prepare a planting hole that is 4 times the diameter of the rootball. Dig the hole deep enough so that after planting the top of the root-ball is level with the ground around it. Gently slope the sides of the planting hole outward from the bottom of the hole to the surface. Remove any twine or wire that is wrapped around the trunk. Cut away the burlap or any wire baskets to half the height of the root-ball. Backfill the hole with the original soil and water deeply. Spread a 2- to 3-inch layer of organic mulch over the entire planting area.

Advice for Care

Arborvitae are relatively care-free plants. Like all evergreens, they do not require additional fertilizer. Maintain a 2- to 3-inch layer of organic mulch around the plants to help keep the soil moist, to moderate soil temperatures, and to keep the weeds down. Arborvitae should not require regular pruning unless a particular hedge size is desired; in this case, prune in the early spring.

Additional Information

Many gardeners fret that their arborvitae is dying in the fall when it regularly sheds its inner needles. This can admittedly be very dramatic. More common varieties of arborvitae will turn an ugly brownish yellow during the winter. When planting new shrubs, choose varieties that are known to retain their dark-green color throughout winter. Heavy snow and ice will sometimes cause the branches to break or its multiple trunks to spread apart. To prevent this, carefully brush off heavy accumulations of snow.

Additional Species, Cultivars, or Varieties

'Techny' and 'Emerald' are two excellent varieties that grow 15 feet tall and retain their dark-green color in the winter. 'Globosa' is a perfect globe shape, growing 6 feet high and turning light gray-green in winter. 'Hetz Midget' stays green all winter and slowly grows to a mature height of 4 feet.

Bayberry

Myrica pensylvanica

Zones: 5, 6
Height: 6 to 12 feet
Bloom Period: Fruit, fall through winter
Flowers: Insignificant (fruit, light-gray)
Type: Deciduous/semi-evergreen

Light Requirement:

I was first introduced to bayberry during childhood vacations on the eastern seashore where it grows wild and scrubby and helps to stabilize beach dunes. Bayberry's unique ability to tolerate heavy salts and high winds enables it to thrive in such locations. Since we never spent much time at the beach during cold weather, it was as an adult that I learned of the light-gray berries that cling tightly to their stems till February. After the first hard freezes of fall, bayberry's leaves give way to upright stems packed full of these summer survivors. Its berries make it a must for the winter garden. Who can help but think of bayberry-scented candles when conjuring up images of this fine shrub? Its leathery green leaves are semi-evergreen in southern Indiana, but completely deciduous in northern parts of the state. Bayberry makes an excellent plant for massing and for urban areas as well; it also works well when used as a screen.

—T.T.

WHEN TO PLANT

Transplant bayberry specimens any time the soil is dry in spring, summer, or fall.

WHERE TO PLANT

Bayberry tolerates poor, dry, sandy locations as well as heavy clay sites. Its ability to grow in salt-laden areas makes it a good choice near roads and highways where winter salt spray from passing cars can be a problem. Bayberry should also be planted where its winter berries can be enjoyed on a regular basis. It spreads by sprouting suckers, so be prepared to prune.

How to Plant

Transplant balled-and-burlapped or container-grown specimens of bayberry by preparing a planting hole that is 4 times the width of the pot or rootball. Dig deep enough so that the top of the rootball is level with the ground around it after planting. Remove any twine or wire that is wrapped around the trunk of the shrub and cut away the burlap or wire basket to half the height of the rootball. For container-grown bayberry, gently tap the sides of the pot on a hard surface to loosen the rootball. Carefully remove the plant from the container and tease out any roots that appear to be growing in a circular pattern. Finally, backfill the hole with the original soil and water deeply. Spread a 2- to 3-inch layer of organic mulch over the entire planting area.

Advice for Care

Bayberry tolerates such poor planting sites that supplemental fertilizing is not necessary. Prune in late winter when the branch structure of this shrub can be easily observed. To help contain bayberry in a specific area, remove the small root suckers that will begin to sprout around the base of the plant when it is a few years old. Always prune this shrub to retain its informal and billowy shape. Never give it a "haircut" that destroys its natural beauty. Prune taller branches all the way to the base to reduce the overall height. Prune smaller branches back to the next largest branch.

Additional Information

Bayberry are dioecious and need both male and female plants to produce a good crop of berries. The female plant produces the berries, so plant a ratio of 3 to 5 females for every male to ensure good pollination. Wax collected from the berries is used to make the popular bayberry-scented candle.

Additional Species, Cultivars, or Varieties

There are no improved cultivars.

SHRUBS

Bluebeard

Caryopteris × clandonensis

Other names: Blue Mist Shrub, Blue Spirea, Caryopteris	**Light Requirement:**
Zones: 5, 6	
Height: 2 to 3 feet	
Bloom Period: July to September	
Flowers: Blue	
Type: Deciduous	

ecently, when summer began to wane and the garden had passed its peak, the shrub 'Bluebeard' literally turned our heads. At almost three feet tall, this rather large planting was a veil of blue from the ground up. In a fashion rare for shrubs, the small clusters of dainty medium-blue flowers bloom at the base of the outermost leaves. Combine these flowers with the silvery-green leaves and it is obvious why this plant is sometimes called "blue-mist shrub." Both the flowers and the leaves have a light, sweet fragrance. *Caryopteris* has a mound-shaped growth pattern and rarely reaches over three feet tall. Its branches die to the ground each winter and must be pruned back. Other than this small chore, we consider *Caryopteris* a maintenance-free landscape plant, an excellent choice for the weekend gardener. It is the perfect plant to brighten the gardens of late summer and fall.

WHEN TO PLANT

Transplant *Caryopteris* in the early spring, preferably before the leaves emerge on the trees. These are versatile plants and with a little bit of care, can be planted at just about any time of the year.

WHERE TO PLANT

Caryopteris prefer locations with full sun or very light shade for maximum flower production. They grow in practically any soil but do best in sites with good drainage and plenty of organic matter. Plant these late-summer beauties along a walkway or as a low corner planting in front of larger evergreens. Their uniform growth makes them suitable for a low hedge or border plant. Because they die to the ground each winter, *Caryopteris* are often treated as a perennial and planted in the mixed-flower border.

How to Plant

Prepare a planting hole that is 2 to 3 times the width of the rootball. Dig the hole deep enough so that when planted at the bottom of the hole, the top of the rootball is level with the ground around it. Most *Caryopteris* are grown in containers, so gently tap the side of the pot on a hard surface to loosen the rootball from the sides. Tease any roots that are growing in a circular fashion away from the rest of the root mass. In pot-bound situations, the bottom of the pot will be thick with roots which can be cut and pulled away. Backfill the hole with the original soil and water deeply. Spread a 2- to 3-inch layer of organic mulch over the entire planting area.

Advice for Care

Caryopteris should not require special care. Fertilize in the spring by spreading $^1/_2$ cup of balanced fertilizer around the plant (spread twice as much if you use organic fertilizer). Maintain a 2- to 3-inch layer of organic mulch around the plants at all times. This will help prevent moisture loss and moderate the soil temperatures around the root zone. It also helps to keep the weeds down. Hard-prune *Caryopteris* to the ground in late winter.

Additional Information

Caryopteris was originally collected in China. The hybrid we grow today resulted from an unplanned cross-pollination between two native Chinese species in a nursery. *Caryopteris* attracts hummingbirds.

Additional Species, Cultivars, or Varieties

'Blue Mist' is the most common variety and has light powder-blue flowers that are slightly fringed around the edges. 'Dark Knight' is a deep purple-blue variety with good fragrance.

Bottlebrush Buckeye

Aesculus parviflora

Zones: 5, 6
Height: 8 to 15 feet, spreading at least
  as wide
Bloom Period: Late June to early July
Flowers: White
Type: Deciduous

Light Requirement:

With a name like 'Bottlebrush', it is only a *small* wonder that this shrub is rare in contemporary landscapes. Its name, however, does not do it justice, for this is one of our most beautiful native shrubs. Indigenous to the southeastern United States, this large shrub makes an excellent specimen plant where there is ample room for it to spread. Although it may reach a maximum height of only twelve to fifteen feet, it spreads at least that wide by sending up root suckers. Bottlebrush is related to both the Ohio buckeye and horse chestnut, but its large palm-like leaves are not bothered by any of the foliar diseases that afflict these larger relatives. Showy bristle-like blooms cover the shrub in late June and July, growing four inches wide and a foot in length. After the rush of spring-blooming plants, when larger shrubs and trees have ceased to bloom, bottlebrush buckeye is a glorious sight.

WHEN TO PLANT

The bottlebrush buckeye is most successfully planted in the early spring just before the leaves emerge on the trees.

WHERE TO PLANT

Plant bottlebrush buckeye in full sun to part shade. It is also known to grow quite well in shadier sites. It grows best in soil that stays moist but well drained and has plenty of organic matter. It grows under acidic or alkaline conditions. Because it spreads so wide, bottlebrush buckeye will make a nice corner planting, but it will need to be kept in check. When massed together, the plants make a nice screen in the back of the yard.

How to Plant

Prepare the planting site by digging a hole 4 times the width of the rootball. Dig deep enough so that when placed in the bottom of the hole, the top of the rootball is level with the ground around it. Gently tap the side of the container on a hard surface to loosen the rootball. Carefully remove the plant from the pot and tease out any roots that were growing in a circular pattern around the sides. Backfill the hole with the original soil. If planting balled-and-burlapped specimens, be sure to remove any twine or wire that is wrapped around the trunk. Cut away any burlap or wire basket to half the height of the rootball, and backfill the hole as you do with container-grown specimens. After planting, be sure to water deeply. Spread 2 to 3 inches of organic mulch.

Advice for Care

Broadcast a balanced fertilizer around the root zone in early November. Maintain a 2- to 3-inch layer of organic mulch around the roots at all times. This is especially important if the bottlebrush is planted under a large tree where it will have to compete for water. Prune the suckers to keep the plant from spreading. Like lilac and forsythia, the bottlebrush buckeye can be pruned to the ground if it gets out of hand.

Additional Information

The nectar of the bottlebrush plant is apparently toxic to bees and will poison their colonies if eaten by wayward workers. In good years, its fall color is bright yellow.

Additional Species, Cultivars, or Varieties

There are a few improved varieties which may be difficult to locate. 'Rogers' has large blooms that open a few weeks later than the original. The red buckeye, *Aesculus parvia*, is a small tree that grows to 20 feet. Its large erect red blooms open earlier in the spring and are quite a sight. There are fine specimens on the grounds of the Indianapolis Museum of Art. Red buckeye suffers from severe foliar blight from mid-summer through fall.

Burkwood Viburnum

Viburnum × burkwoodii

Zones: 5, 6
Height: 8 to 10 feet
Bloom Period: April to May; fruits in summer
Flowers: White (fruit is red, turning to black)
Type: Deciduous

Light Requirement:

The sweet smell of a burkwood viburnum in April is a sure sign that spring has arrived. While a few other shrubs bloom before the burkwood, their fragrance pales by comparison. The first time we had the pleasure of smelling this versatile shrub, we were reminded of lilac, not because the fragrances are similar, but because they are both so powerful! This is a shrub to plant near a window that you open to let the sweet, fresh spring air in and to let the musty winter air out. Burkwood viburnums have rounded clusters of tiny pink buds that open to white flowers. The leaves that follow are easily identified by their glossy green color. The shrub forms a rounded mound when left alone. In good years, the fall color is a deep burgundy red.

WHEN TO PLANT

Burkwood viburnum is a versatile plant and will tolerate planting just about any time the soil is dry.

WHERE TO PLANT

Plant the burkwood viburnum in soil that is moist but well drained with plenty of organic matter; avoid planting in overly wet sites. Burkwood viburnum tolerates both acidic and alkaline conditions. It should receive at least 6 hours of full sun per day. The less sunlight the plant receives, the fewer the blooms; it should still flower profusely with as little as 4 hours of direct sun. Plant the burkwood as a specimen near the house to enjoy its fragrance, or as a background plant in the shrub border.

HOW TO PLANT

Prepare the planting site by digging a hole 4 times the width of the rootball. Dig deep enough so that after planting the top of the rootball is level with the ground around it. For balled-and-burlapped specimens, be sure to remove any twine or wire wrapped around the trunk of the plant. Cut away the burlap and wire basket to half the height of the rootball. It is not necessary to remove all the burlap or wire basket since this will decompose or break apart. Any synthetic burlap, however, should be completely removed. Backfill the hole with the original soil and water deeply. Spread a 2- to 3-inch layer of soil around the entire planting area to help keep the roots moist.

ADVICE FOR CARE

Fertilize lightly in early spring or late fall. Maintain a 2- to 3-inch layer of mulch to help keep the roots cool and moist and to keep the weeds down. Prune burkwood viburnums shortly after they bloom in the spring. Avoid shearing the shrub into a ball; instead, remove select branches to retain the natural shape. Overall, burkwoods are very tolerant of poor planting sites as long as there is good drainage. They are sometimes bothered by foliar diseases like leaf spot, but this is rarely a serious problem.

ADDITIONAL INFORMATION

In southern Indiana, burkwood viburnum may remain partially evergreen. The fruit display can be disappointing unless planted in a group where better pollination will be assured.

ADDITIONAL SPECIES, CULTIVARS, OR VARIETIES

'Mohawk' will produce red flower buds that open very slowly and extend the effective bloom period by several weeks. The Koreanspice viburnum, *Viburnum carlesii*, has a fragrance similar to the burkwood's and is perhaps more widely grown. Nevertheless, burkwood is a superior species because of its glossy lustrous green leaves and its adaptability to a wider range of growing conditions.

Carolina Allspice

Calycanthus floridus

Other Name: Sweetshrub	**Light Requirement:**
Zones: 5, 6	
Height: 6 to 9 feet	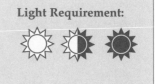
Bloom Period: May to July	
Flowers: Brownish-red	
Type: Deciduous	

*A*s its name suggests, allspice has sweet fragrant flowers; the flowers are produced in late spring and very early summer. These unusual but dainty dark-maroon to brown blooms are quietly beautiful, nothing like the loud hydrangea or ubiquitous lilac. Its light-green leaves set off the darker flowers like a picture frame, helping them to stand out in shadier sites. Their fragrance is light and sweet, very different from the strong and spicy smell of the viburnums. This is a special shrub for a special space in a plant-lover's garden. Plant allspice near the patio or other outdoor living area where its fragrance can really be enjoyed.

WHEN TO PLANT

Carolina allspice is a hardy plant and tolerates planting at any time of the year when the soil is dry. If planting in the summer, make a special effort to keep the soil moist at all times.

WHERE TO PLANT

This plant tolerates both wet and dry locations, but it prefers a deep and well-drained soil that is high in organic matter. It does not seem to have a preference for acidic or alkaline conditions. Plant allspice in the shrub border or as a background plant in a shady or woodland garden.

HOW TO PLANT

Though allspice has a medium growth rate, it will get off to a faster start if the soil is well prepared. Start by digging a hole 4 times the width of the rootball. Dig the hole deep enough so that after planting, the top of the rootball is level with the ground around it. Gradually slope the sides outward from the bottom to edge of the hole. Always remove all twine or wire that is wrapped around the trunk. Cut away any burlap or wire basket to half the height of the rootball. Any synthetic material used to wrap the rootball should be completely removed. Backfill the hole with the original soil and water deeply. Spread a 2- to 3-inch layer of organic mulch around the entire planting area.

ADVICE FOR CARE
Allspice is a care-free plant, but it will benefit from occasional applications of fertilizer. Sprinkle fertilizer around the root zone of the shrub in early November for best results. These added nutrients will be stored in the root system for growth the following spring. Maintain a 2- to 3-inch layer of organic mulch over the root system at all times. This shrub will benefit from having the roots damp but not wet. The mulch also helps moderate soil temperatures in the heat of summer and keeps the weeds to a minimum. Allspice will not require regular pruning since it grows slowly. Pruning out the root suckers will keep it from spreading too wide; do this shortly after blooming in the early weeks of the summer. Allspice is virtually pest-free.

ADDITIONAL INFORMATION
Although native to the eastern and southern states, it is not completely clear whether allspice is native to Indiana. Nevertheless, it is one of our favorite American shrubs and is quite common in the South. Allspice is a useful plant *inside* the home as well as outside. Its flowers are often found in dried flower arrangements. The name "allspice" fits its description, since various parts of the plant reportedly possess fragrances similar to strawberry, pineapple, grapefruit, and banana, as well as cider and cinnamon!

ADDITIONAL SPECIES, CULTIVARS, OR VARIETIES
There are none that are important in the nursery trade.

Doublefile Viburnum

Viburnum plicatum var. *tomentosum*

Zones: 5, 6
Height: 8 to 10 feet
Bloom Period: May (fruit, August to September)
Flowers: White (fruit, red turning to black)
Type: Deciduous

Light Requirement:

*D*oublefile viburnum is an exquisite shrub that should be used in the landscape more often than it is. This unique shrub has long horizontal branches that grow as if in layers, or rows, up to twelve feet long! When mature, this feature makes the shrub wider than it is tall with a form that is reminiscent of dogwoods, especially the *Kousa* species. Its white blooms are elegant two- to four-inch clusters produced in the leaf axils and held closely to the branch. There is a row of showy, hydrangea-like, white florets that surround an inner group of non-showy flowers. The inner flowers produce bright red berries in July and August and turn black shortly afterward. The fruit is a favorite for birds. Doublefile viburnum also has easily identifiable leaves with many parallel and furrowed veins. It makes a wonderful accent plant in the garden!

WHEN TO PLANT

Transplant balled-and-burlapped specimens in early spring before the leaves emerge, or in late fall after the leaves drop.

WHERE TO PLANT

Doublefile viburnum is less tolerant of dry sites than other viburnum species. It should be planted in soil that is moist but well drained and that has plenty of organic matter. Full sun will encourage the maximum number of flowers possible, but doublefile viburnum also grows well in partial shade. Use as an accent plant in a partly shaded corner or on the edge of a woodland garden.

HOW TO PLANT

Prepare the planting site by digging a hole 4 times the diameter of the rootball. Gently slope the sides outward from the bottom toward the top of the hole. Dig deep enough so that the top of the rootball is level with the ground around it after planting. Remove any twine or wire from around the stem of this shrub and cut away the burlap or wire basket to half the height of the rootball. It is not necessary to completely remove the burlap or wire basket, as this will decompose or break apart. Any synthetic material like plastic, however, should be completely taken off. Backfill the hole with the original soil and water it deeply. Spread a 2- to 3-inch layer of organic mulch around the entire planting area to help hold moisture.

ADVICE FOR CARE

Keep doublefile viburnums moist throughout the summer. Maintain a layer of organic mulch to help moderate the soil temperature and water level. This will also help keep weeds down. Doublefile viburnum has a medium growth rate which can be encouraged by broadcasting a granular or organic fertilizer over the root zone in early November. Prune overly long branches that throw the plant out of balance shortly after the flowers fade. When pruning, be careful not to remove the lower branches that grow close to the ground. This would destroy its natural shape.

ADDITIONAL INFORMATION

With few pests and outstanding year-round character, doublefile viburnum is considered one of the best all-around shrubs for the landscape. It may experience branch dieback from winterkill in severe weather, especially in northern Indiana.

ADDITIONAL SPECIES, CULTIVARS, OR VARIETIES

Among the best varieties is 'Mariesii', which has much larger flowers and fruit and strong horizontal branches. 'Shasta' grows only 6 feet high but spreads twice that far, with flowers 6 inches wide; it also has excellent dark-red fall color.

Dwarf Alberta Spruce

Picea glauca 'Conica'

Zones: 5, 6
Height: 10 to 12 feet
Type: Evergreen

Light Requirement:

A variety of white spruce, the dwarf Alberta spruce represents a favorite group of novelty plants generally referred to as "dwarf conifers." These shorter versions of taller "tree-size" plants are very popular among hobbyists and gardeners who are looking for something a little different. Practically all conifers, including spruce, pine, fir, arborvitae, and hemlock, have some short or irregularly shaped variant that would be considered a dwarf. Their short or irregular stature does not mix well in the shrub or flower border, so these novelties are usually planted as accent plants or in rock gardens, where they easily stand out. Hobbyists often collect them in gardens reserved just for dwarf conifers. Their diminutive size makes dwarf conifers a good choice for gardeners with small spaces. Dwarf Alberta spruce grows in a perfect cone shape with short, soft, light-green needles. Its dense foliage and naturally rigid form make it a good choice for a formal garden setting or for those gardeners who like their plants "neat and tidy."

WHEN TO PLANT

Transplant dwarf Alberta spruce and most other dwarf conifers in early spring, as soon as the ground is dry. The second-best time to plant is in late fall, after the leaves fall from trees.

WHERE TO PLANT

Dwarf Alberta spruce prefers the full sun but tolerates light shade; the foliage may not be as full in the shade. The soil should be moist but well drained with plenty of organic matter. Alberta spruce has no preference for acidic or alkaline soil, so it should grow well in most situations in Indiana except in heavy clay.

HOW TO PLANT

Prepare the planting site by digging a hole 4 times the size of the container. Gently slope the sides outward from the bottom to the edge of the hole. The hole should be deep enough so that the top of the rootball is level with the ground around it after planting. Gently remove the container by tapping it on a hard surface to loosen the root mass. Tease out any roots that appear to be growing in concentric circles and spread them out before backfilling the hole with the original soil. Water the plant deeply and spread a 2- to 3-inch layer of organic mulch. When planting in the fall, a layer of mulch as well as regular watering until the ground freezes solid is important to prevent winter burn.

ADVICE FOR CARE

Maintain 2 to 3 inches of mulch to help keep the roots moist in the summer, to moderate soil temperatures, and to keep the weeds down. This is a very slow-growing shrub, so pruning will not be necessary. Hot and dry weather in the summer predispose this spruce to attack by spider mites. To check for spider mites, hold a white sheet of paper under one of the branches and tap it hard. Pinhead-sized mites will begin moving around on the paper a few seconds after they make themselves upright. Depending on the time of the year, treatment may include a dormant or summer weight oil, or a traditional miticide.

ADDITIONAL INFORMATION

The dwarf Alberta spruce was "discovered" by two famous horticulturists while they were waiting for a train in Canada.

ADDITIONAL SPECIES, CULTIVARS, OR VARIETIES

The bird's nest spruce, *Picea abies* 'Nidiformis', has a spreading, flat, mounded shape just like its name, and is a popular dwarf variety. *Pinus mugo* 'Compacta', the dwarf form of mugo pine, has a more rounded mound shape and longer and stiffer pine-type needles. Numerous dwarfs of juniper, *Juniperus* spp., also make excellent dwarf conifers.

Dwarf Fothergilla

Fothergilla gardenii

Zones: 5, 6
Height: 2 to 3 feet
Bloom Period: May
Flowers: White
Type: Deciduous

Light Requirement:

*F*othergilla flowers float in the air like tiny white bottle brushes and send out a light and sweet fragrance when in bloom. Opening before there are any leaves on its branches, the flowers remind us of white candles lighting up a candelabra made of twigs! This handsome short version of the native large *Fothergilla* is a plant for all seasons. After the flowers fade and give way to summer, the shrub takes on a mound shape suitable for foundation planting. The leaves have prominent veins with a slightly scalloped edge. In the fall, they turn bright yellow-orange and easily compete with the burning bush for most brilliant fall color. This is a slow grower native to the Southeast; it is practically pest-free. *Fothergilla* was named after an English horticulturist, John Fothergill, who had the largest collection of American plants anywhere.

When to Plant

Plant *Fothergilla* in the early spring before the leaves emerge on the trees, or in the late fall after the leaves drop.

Where to Plant

Fothergilla grow best in moist but well-drained acidic soils that are high in organic matter. Plant them where they receive at least 4 to 6 hours of full sun per day. Dwarf *Fothergilla* plants are wonderful in the foreground of a shrub border or as a foundation planting.

How to Plant

Prepare the planting site by digging a hole 4 times as wide as the rootball. Slope the sides gently outward from the bottom to the edge of the hole. Dig deep enough so that after planting the top of the rootball will be level with the ground around it after planting. Remove any wire or twine that is wrapped around the stem or trunk, and cut away the burlap or wire basket to half the height of the rootball. Be sure to completely remove any synthetic wrapping such as plastic. Backfill the hole with the original soil and water deeply. Spread a 2- to 3-inch layer of organic mulch over the entire planting area to help preserve moisture.

ADVICE FOR CARE
Fothergilla has a slow growth rate but it can be encouraged with extra care. Broadcast fertilizer around the root zone in early November. Maintain a 2- to 3-inch layer of organic mulch at all times and keep the root zone moist with at least 1 inch of water per week during the growing season. Like all spring-blooming shrubs, *Fothergilla* develop flower buds for the next year during the summer of the current season. Prune the plants shortly after blooming in the spring to avoid removing the future flowers. The dwarf fothergilla should not require extensive pruning since it rarely grows taller than 3 feet.

ADDITIONAL INFORMATION
Plant *Fothergilla* with late-blooming daffodils for an excellent effect. The dwarf fothergilla received the prestigious Pennsylvania Horticultural Society's Gold Medal awards for outstanding performance. The showy bottlebrush effect of *Fothergilla* flowers is due to the male portion of the flower, the "stamens." The blooms themselves have no true petals, but this doesn't detract from the flower one bit. Dwarf fothergilla may not be hardy in Zone 5A, in northern Indiana.

ADDITIONAL SPECIES, CULTIVARS, OR VARIETIES
The variety 'Mt. Airy' produces numerous large flowers and grows to 5 feet. Large fothergilla, *Fothergilla major*, has a similar flower and bloom time as the dwarf species, but grows 10 feet tall and almost as wide. It is more useful as a background shrub or mass planted for screening.

European Cranberry Bush

Viburnum opulus

Zones: 5, 6	**Light Requirement:**
Height: 8 to 12 feet	
Bloom Period: May to June (fruit, September to December)	
Flowers: White (fruit, red)	
Type: Deciduous	

*T*he name 'Cranberry Bush' might lead one to believe that this plant is responsible for the ruby-red *gelatinous mass* served alongside holiday turkeys—but this is not the case! To our good fortune, the European cranberry bush is suitable for the landscape, even though the commercial cranberry type may not be. The flower is a sophisticated collection of showy sterile florets that surround smaller fertile blooms on the inside. Together they form a circular but flat mound of flowers. The resulting bloom resembles a lace doily and is quite stunning set against the background of lush green leaves. The inner fertile flowers produce bright red berries in late summer that persist well into fall and early winter. The fruit shrivel after several hard freezes, but last all winter as a reminder of warmer weather to come. Covered in snow, even these withered berries are charming.

WHEN TO PLANT

Plant balled-and-burlapped specimens of European cranberry bush just about any time of the year the ground is dry, but preferably in the spring.

WHERE TO PLANT

European cranberry bush is extremely adaptable to a wide variety of planting conditions. It will produce more flowers and fruit in full sun, but does well in partial shade also. The soil should be moist but well drained, and the plants show no preference for acidic or alkaline conditions. It may be mass planted for screening or as food for wildlife. The shorter 'Compact' variety is more suitable for foundation plantings or for smaller spaces.

HOW TO PLANT
Prepare a planting hole 4 times the width of the rootball. Dig deep enough so that after planting, the top of the rootball is level with the ground around it. Gently slope the sides outward from the bottom to the edges of the hole. Remove any twine or wire from around the stem or trunk of this shrub. Cut away any burlap or wire basket to about half the height of the rootball. Any synthetic material, like plastic, that was used to wrap the rootball should be completely removed. Backfill the hole with the original soil and water deeply. Spread a 2- to 3-inch layer of organic mulch around the entire planting area.

ADVICE FOR CARE
European cranberry bush will thrive with little care; an early November application of fertilizer, however, will encourage better growth. Maintain a 2- to 3-inch layer of organic mulch around the root zone at all times. Prune large branches all the way to the ground to allow for better light penetration to the inside of the shrub. This will help prevent a "leggy" growth habit that is typical of the European cranberry. Watch for stem borers which sometimes plague this plant in the Midwest.

ADDITIONAL INFORMATION
The fall color of European cranberry varies from brilliant yellow-orange to red and purple. This shrub is highly recommended for attracting birds and other wildlife to the garden. The sweeter fruit of the native American cranberry bush, *Viburnum trilobum*, is often used for jams and jellies.

ADDITIONAL SPECIES, CULTIVARS, OR VARIETIES
The variety 'Compactum' is the most popular form in the nursery trade since it only grows to 5 or 6 feet tall but has all the attributes of the taller species. The arrowood viburnum, *Viburnum dentatum*, grows quickly to 15 feet tall and is an excellent source of food for the birds. Another fast-growing *Viburnum* for naturalizing and attracting wildlife is nannyberry, *Viburnum lentago*. It grows to 30 feet tall and suckers freely, so it needs plenty of room to spread.

Fringetree

Chionanthus virginicus

Zones: 5, 6
Height: 15 to 20 feet
Bloom Period: May and June (fruits, August to September)
Flowers: White (fruits, blue to black)
Type: Deciduous

Light Requirement:

---

*T*he name fringetree describes these blooms perfectly: the white, pendulous petals resemble the fringe on a bedspread or pillow, but are much finer and softer. The flowers appear in very late spring in clusters up to eight inches long. Fringetree is one of our best native plants, and can be found growing in moist stream banks and ponds in the Southeast. Even though it grows perfectly well in Indiana, its slow growth rate probably explains its scarcity in Hoosier landscapes. In its native environment, fringetree grows to the size of a small tree, but as a cultivated landscape plant, it can be grown into a rounded open shrub. Its unusually delicate white bloom, light fragrance, and resistance to pests make it a choice plant for the garden.

WHEN TO PLANT

Plant balled-and-burlapped specimens of fringetree in early spring, as soon as the soil dries out and preferably before the leaves emerge on the trees.

WHERE TO PLANT

Fringetree grows best in moist but well-drained soils in full sun. Plant it as a specimen shrub or small tree, or as a screen or background in the shrub border.

HOW TO PLANT

Plant balled-and-burlapped specimens after preparing a planting hole that is 4 times as wide as the rootball. Dig the hole deep enough so that after planting the top of the rootball is even with the ground around it. Fringetree and other shrubs and trees that are planted too deep will not thrive and may eventually die. Remove any wire or twine that is still wrapped around the trunk or stem.

Cut away the burlap and any wire basket to half the height of the rootball. Be sure to remove any synthetic material such as plastic that was used to wrap the rootball. Backfill the hole with the original soil and water deeply. Spread a 2- to 3-inch layer of organic mulch over the entire planting area to conserve moisture.

ADVICE FOR CARE

Broadcast fertilizer around the root system in early November to encourage growth the following year. Maintain a 2- to 3-inch layer of organic mulch around the root system at all times to help conserve moisture and to moderate the temperature around the roots. Prune dead and broken branches as needed or shape fringetree into a small tree; it should require little additional pruning. With the exception of occasional outbreaks of scale, this plant is rarely bothered by pests.

ADDITIONAL INFORMATION

Fringetree's broad, rounded growth habit makes it a good screen. Plant some earlier blooming shrubs like dwarf fothergilla, European cranberry, and dogwood to stagger the blooming in your landscape and to prolong your enjoyment. The fringetree is dioecious, which means that there are male and female plants. The male is usually slightly showier, but the female plant develops the fruit that birds devour. Both male and female are required for good fruiting. Fringetree is reported to be tolerant of air pollution and should grow well in an urban environment, provided other cultural conditions are adequate.

ADDITIONAL SPECIES, CULTIVARS, OR VARIETIES

Fringetree is very difficult to propagate from seed; this may partially account for the dearth of improved varieties.

Hydrangea

Hydrangea paniculata 'Grandiflora'

Other Name: Pee Gee Hydrangea
Zones: 5, 6
Height: 15 to 25 feet
Bloom Period: July through fall
Flowers: White turning to green, pink, then tan
Type: Deciduous

Light Requirement:

The pee gee is the most common of all the hydrangeas and has one of the showiest flowers of all the summer-blooming shrubs. Their large, white, pompon-like blooms open in midsummer. Rather than wilting or browning immediately, the pee gee's conical-shaped blooms slowly fade to apple green, then pink, and finally to a light tan, almost straw color. This slow color change gives us months of enjoyment. The faded flowers are extremely popular for cutting and in dried arrangements, wreaths, and garlands. They also make wonderful holiday decorations and give Christmas trees a Victorian appearance. When in bloom, they are a wonderful relief in the summer shrub border when other flowering shrubs are scarce.

WHEN TO PLANT

Plant pee gee hydrangea before the leaves emerge on trees in early spring, or after the leaves drop in late fall.

WHERE TO PLANT

Pee gee hydrangea will reward its caretakers with many blooms when planted in full sun to light shade. All *Hydrangea* prefer sites that have rich, moist but well-drained soil with plenty of organic matter. They will grow in acidic or alkaline conditions. Plant the pee gee in a shrub border or as an accent plant, with *Fothergilla* or *Caryopteris* in the foreground. This will create season-long interest and hide the sometimes spindly base of the plant.

HOW TO PLANT

Prepare a planting hole that is 4 times the width of the rootball. The hole should be deep enough so that the top of the rootball is level with the ground around it after planting. Gently tap the sides of the container on a hard surface to loosen the root mass and tease out any roots that have been growing in concentric circles around the bottom of the pot. Backfill the hole with the original soil and water deeply. Spread a 2- to 3-inch layer of organic matter to help preserve moisture.

ADVICE FOR CARE
Maintain a 2- to 3-inch layer of organic mulch around the root zone at all times and broadcast fertilizer in early November. Pee gee hydrangea has few pest problems. Prune back in early spring since the flowers are produced on new growth.

ADDITIONAL INFORMATION
Pee gee hydrangea is a favorite old-fashioned shrub that is criticized by many horiculturists for its coarse texture, gaudiness, and ugly stature in winter. When properly pruned and blended with other plants in the landscape, however, it makes an outstanding plant whose usefulness as a cut flower should not be overlooked.

ADDITIONAL SPECIES, CULTIVARS, OR VARIETIES
'Tardiva' is an excellent late summer- and fall-blooming variety. It has more open and conical-shaped blooms than pee gee and tolerates partially shaded sites. The oakleaf hydrangea, *Hydrangea quercifolia*, is an outstanding species that blooms much earlier in the summer and tolerates more shade than 'Tardiva'. Oakleaf hydrangea leaves turn a superb shade of scarlet in the fall before dropping to reveal bronzish exfoliating bark that is displayed throughout the winter season. It will not survive severe winter weather in central and northern Indiana. The florist hydrangea, *Hydrangea macrophylla*, is much sought after for its large blue and pink blooms. With the exception of a couple of improved varieties, these *Hydrangea* bloom on last year's wood and are not reliably hardy in Zone 5, which covers much of the northern two-thirds of our state. It should bloom well in Zone 6 around Evansville, however. The variety 'Nikko Blue' is reported to be hardy in Zone 5B if planted in a well-protected location.

Inkberry Holly

Ilex glabra

Zones: 5, 6	**Light Requirement:**
Height: 6 to 8 feet	
Bloom Period: June (fruit, fall)	
Flowers: Not showy (fruit, black)	
Type: Evergreen	

*M*ention the word "holly," and images of bright-red berries and sharply pointed leaves come to mind. Inkberry differs from its popular holiday cousins as it lacks these attributes for the most part. Inkberry is one of the few broadleaf evergreens that can survive Indiana's harsh winters. Its narrow, dark-green leaves and mounded shape are a welcome relief from the ever-present yew and juniper that make up at least seventy-five percent of the foundation plantings in our state. The leaves have a few "teeth" at the tips, but they do not jab like other hollies, and the berries are a dark-blue-to-black color. These characteristics differ enough from traditional holly that many a rookie horticulturist has mistaken it for another plant, not a holly at all. This is a tough evergreen shrub that tolerates salt, air pollution, and other conditions found in urban areas.

WHEN TO PLANT

For best results, transplant inkberry holly in early spring after the soil has dried out, or late fall.

WHERE TO PLANT

Plant inkberry in moist but well-drained soil that has plenty of organic matter. The shrub will grow thicker when planted in full sun, but it also grows well in partial shade. Although it prefers acidic soils, it will tolerate alkaline conditions as long as the pH is not over 7.5. Use inkberry as a screen or background plant for the mixed-flower border, or trim it into a hedge.

HOW TO PLANT

Prepare a planting hole 4 times the width of the rootball. Gently slope the sides outward from the bottom to the edges of the hole.

Dig deep enough so that after planting, the top of the rootball is level with the ground around it. Be sure to remove any twine or wire that is still wrapped around the trunk or stem of the shrub. Cut away the burlap and wire basket to half the height of the rootball. Backfill the hole with the original soil and water deeply. Spread a 2- to 3-inch layer of organic mulch over the root zone.

ADVICE FOR CARE

Broadcast a balanced fertilizer in early November to help the plant store nutrients for the following year. Maintain a 2- to 3-inch layer of organic mulch around the root zone at all times, especially during the hot, dry weather of summer. Winter temperatures below -10 degrees Fahrenheit may kill some of the leaves or branches. Remove dead or broken branches in the spring with sharp pruning shears. Inkberry grows in many soil types, but does best in acidic environments. Spread sulfur after Thanksgiving to help acidify the soil.

ADDITIONAL INFORMATION

When left alone, inkberry has a tendency to grow open and airy. To renew its vigor and density, cut it to the ground in the spring. Inkberry also grows well as a clipped hedge. Like all hollies, inkberry has male and female plants. For good berry production, be sure to plant at least 1 male for every 5 females.

ADDITIONAL SPECIES, CULTIVARS, OR VARIETIES

'Compacta' is a slow-growing shorter variety that reaches only 4 to 6 feet tall. 'Nordic' is a dwarf that will tolerate temperatures below -20 degrees Fahrenheit. The other evergreen hollies suitable for Indiana are the meserve hybrids, *Ilex × meservae*. The best varieties for our area are 'China Girl' and its pollinator, 'China Boy'. They grow to 10 feet tall and have lustrous, green, traditionally spiny leaves and bright-red fruit.

Japanese Barberry

Berberis thunbergii

Zones: 5, 6
Height: 3 to 6 feet
Bloom Period: May (fruit, October to December)
Flowers: Yellow, not very showy (fruit, bright-red)
Type: Deciduous

Light Requirement:

Japanese barberry is a truly utilitarian shrub that is blessed with a few ornamental characteristics. Armed with thorns, it makes a dense "living fence" that deters pests of both the two- and four-legged variety! Children who have run-ins with this shrub tend to call it "sticker bush." The thorns are a deterrent, which is a primary reason barberry is planted. Barberry makes a wonderful hedge when clipped anywhere from three to six feet tall. Added advantages today include new varieties with red or purple leaves that provide season-long interest. The bright red berries liven up the hedge in late summer.

WHEN TO PLANT

Japanese barberry is one of the hardiest of shrubs and will tolerate transplanting any time the ground is dry.

WHERE TO PLANT

Plant this thorny workhorse in soil that stays moist but well drained and has plenty of organic matter. It prefers full sun but will tolerate light shade. Purple-leaved varieties usually do not color as brilliantly in shaded sites. Shorter varieties may be used as specimens in the foreground of shrub borders.

HOW TO PLANT

Plant container-grown specimens after preparing a planting hole 4 times the width of the rootball. The hole should be deep enough so that after planting, the top of the rootball is level with the ground around it. Tap the side of the container on a hard surface to loosen the root mass. Tease out any roots that are growing in concentric circles at the bottom. Spread the roots out in the hole and backfill with the original soil. Plant barberry 2 feet apart to form a dense hedge that will keep foot traffic to a minimum. Water deeply and spread a 2- to 3-inch layer of mulch over the entire planting area to preserve moisture.

ADVICE FOR CARE

Broadcast fertilizer around the root zone in early November of every year. This will give these tough shrubs added nutrients to store for the following spring. Maintain a 2- to 3-inch layer of organic mulch around the root zone at all times to help conserve moisture, to keep the roots cool, and to keep the weeds out. Prune in early spring to remove dead or broken branches and to open up the shrub. If they are planted as a hedge, shear the plants in spring as well. Whether you shear into a rounded or an angular shape, the base of the hedge should always be wider than the top. This will allow better light penetration, which helps grow a denser shrub. Overgrown plants can be trimmed to the ground and will success-fully regenerate themselves.

ADDITIONAL INFORMATION

Berberis vulgaris, the common barberry, had numerous medicinal uses before and during colonial days, from "purging" one's system to dyeing one's hair. Common barberry has been banned from import into the United States because it was found to harbor black rust, a virulent wheat disease.

ADDITIONAL SPECIES, CULTIVARS, OR VARIETIES

'Atropurpurea Nana', also called 'Crimson Pygmy', is the most widely grown variety today. It grows as a low mound 3 feet tall and has bright purplish-red leaves. The 4-foot-tall variety 'Aurea', also called golden barberry, calls attention to itself with its bright yellow leaves. 'Rosy Glow' has beautiful purple-and-pink variegated splotches on its leaves and grows 6 feet tall.

Japanese Yew

Taxus spp.

Zones: 5, 6
Height: 3 to 20 feet
Bloom Period: Spring (fruit, fall)
Flowers: Insignificant (fruit, bright-red)
Type: Evergreen

Light Requirement:

*T*here is hardly a landscape in Indiana that doesn't have a yew planted *somewhere*. Affectionately known as the "meatball" plant for its unfortunate resemblance to that popular spaghetti sauce companion, yews are synonymous with the word "evergreen" once home owners have finished shearing it into shape. They are perhaps the most widely planted shrub in Indiana and dot the foundations of many homes with their year-round green. With good drainage, yews are very easy to grow and provide one of the lushest green backgrounds available for flowering plants. Combine this with their ability to withstand shady locations, and the widespread use of yews in the landscape is not difficult to explain. Yews are sold in a variety of shapes and sizes, from dwarf and spreading to upright and columnar. The soft new spring leaves are a light green that fades to darker green when they mature. The yew's bright red berries are a sure sign that fall is in the air!

WHEN TO PLANT

Transplant yews in the spring when the ground is dry, or fall.

WHERE TO PLANT

Plant yew in a rich loamy soil with plenty of organic matter. Above all else, yew must have good drainage or it will die. Poor soil preparation, along with poor drainage, kills many newly planted yews each year. Plant in sun or shade. It is the perfect evergreen for the north side of a home and makes an excellent background screen or sheared hedge.

HOW TO PLANT

Prepare the planting site by digging a hole 4 times the width of the rootball. Dig deep enough so that the top of the rootball is level with

the ground around it after planting. Planting the yew too deep could
"drown" it. In heavy clay, it is best to plant the yew an inch or two
higher than the soil around it. Remove any twine or wire that is
wrapped around the trunk or stem and cut away the burlap and
wire basket to half the height of the rootball. Backfill with the original soil and water deeply. Spread a 2- to 3-inch layer of organic
mulch around the planting site.

ADVICE FOR CARE

Prune yews once a year to encourage their naturally spreading
growth habit. In more formal settings where sheared hedges or
specific shapes and sizes are desired, yews will have to be pruned
at least twice a year. In this situation, always shear the plants so
that the bottom is wider than the top to prevent shading and the
eventual thinning out of the lower branches. Remove dead or
broken branches in the spring and maintain a 2- to 3-inch layer of
organic mulch around the root zone. Though yews are very sensitive
to poor drainage, continue to water them deeply once a week
throughout the fall when rain is scarce. This will help reduce
winterkill of younger and more tender branches.

ADDITIONAL INFORMATION

Yews are dioecious, and only the female plants produce the bright
red berries. All parts of the plant are poisonous to humans and
animals. According to legend, Robin Hood used the wood from
yews to make his bows.

ADDITIONAL SPECIES, CULTIVARS, OR VARIETIES

Both *Taxus cuspidata* and *Taxus × media* produce excellent cultivars.
Among these are 'Hicksii', which has an upright and columnar
shape and is excellent for use as a screen. 'Capitata' has a conical
shape, while 'Nana' and 'Intermedia' are shorter with a rounded
habit. At maturity, 'Wardii' and 'Densiformis' are both much wider
than they are tall.

Korean Boxwood

Buxus microphylla 'Koreana'

Other Names: Boxwood, Box
Zones: 5, 6
Height: 3 to 4 feet
Type: Evergreen

Light Requirement:

*T*ours to Mount Vernon, Colonial Williamsburg, and other histori-
cal sites of the Southeast have helped to popularize this plant:
common boxwood is the evergreen shrub that is pruned into formal
hedges, topiaries, and sheared edgings around herb, rose, and other
gardens. The species used in Virginia, however, is not hardy here in
Indiana. Instead of the common boxwood, we plant the sturdier
Korean boxwood. This dainty shrub closely resembles the common
boxwood, but it grows to be only a few feet tall. Like yew, Korean
boxwood is a favorite evergreen for pruning into the popular "meatball" shape. The main difference between them is that this plant rarely
gets taller than two-and-one-half feet.

WHEN TO PLANT
Korean boxwood should be planted in early spring. Late fall planting may result in winterkill of some of the branch tips.

WHERE TO PLANT
Boxwood prefers moist but well-drained soil with plenty of organic
matter. Plant in partially protected sites with full sun or part shade.
Avoid planting boxwood in windy and exposed sites, as this may
cause the branch tips to brown and die during the winter. Korean
boxwood makes a perfect low edging around a rose or herb garden.
It is also an excellent low-growing hedge.

HOW TO PLANT
Prepare a planting hole that is 4 times the width of the rootball. Dig
deep enough so that the top of the rootball is level with the ground
around it after planting. Remove any twine or wire that is still
wrapped around the trunk or stem and cut away the burlap or wire
basket to half the height of the rootball. Backfill after pulverizing the
original soil with a shovel and water deeply. Continue deep-water-

SHRUBS

ing on a weekly basis throughout the summer. Spread a 2- to 3-inch layer of organic mulch around the planting site.

ADVICE FOR CARE
When used as a formal hedge, boxwood requires annual pruning. It grows more slowly than yew, however, and will not require shearing as often. Always trim hedges so that the base of the plant is wider than the top. This will prevent shading and the eventual thinning of the lower branches. Boxwood has a very shallow root system, so be careful when cultivating around this shrub. Always maintain a 2- to 3-inch layer of organic mulch to keep the roots moist, to moderate the soil temperature, and to keep down the weeds.

ADDITIONAL INFORMATION
Boxwood is very susceptible to salt damage. Using salt on walkways and driveways where boxwood are nearby is not recommended. Salt will cause severe dieback of the branches by late winter and early spring. In the best of years, most varieties of Korean box refute their "evergreen" title and turn bronzy yellow during the winter. Common boxwood had multiple uses in Colonial times, especially as medication. Not-so-reputable physicians used boxwood for "unmentionable" illnesses. A legitimate extract from the leaves, however, was a common sedative and narcotic during WWII.

ADDITIONAL SPECIES, CULTIVARS, OR VARIETIES
'Wintergreen' is hardy in all parts of the state, and is probably the best Korean boxwood for Indiana. It does not turn yellow during the winter, hence the name "wintergreen." 'Sunnyside' is a fast grower but is hardy only in Zone 6 in Indiana. 'Compacta' is a mound-shaped slow grower that is also hardy only in Zone 6. Hybrids of Korean and common boxwood are hardy in most of Indiana. 'Green Mountain' is the tallest of several hybrids, growing from 4 to 5 feet tall.

Leatherleaf Viburnum

Viburnum rhytidophyllum

Zones: 5, 6 with winter protection
Height: 12 to 15 feet
Bloom Period: May (fruits in August
    to September)
Flowers: Creamy-white (fruit, bright-red)
Type: Semi-evergreen

Light Requirement:

As its name suggests, the leaves of this *Viburnum* are as rugged as they come. The thick, dark-green, wrinkled upper surface complements the softer hairy underside. From a distance, the leatherleaf resembles rhododendron, but it's not nearly as finicky about soil. In southern Indiana, the creamy-white flowers open in early May in flat but circular clusters consisting of many smaller flowers, sometimes reaching eight inches in diameter. The flowers are followed by bright-red fruit in late summer that fade to black (if birds don't gobble them up first!). Leatherleaf grows fifteen feet tall in a rounded shape and is very useful when set against a brick or concrete building.

WHEN TO PLANT

Transplant leatherleaf in early spring after the ground dries out. Planting in late fall may subject it to additional winter leaf scorch.

WHERE TO PLANT

Like many viburnums, leatherleaf is not picky about soil type, but prefers a moist, well-drained location with plenty of organic matter. It likes sun but should be protected from exposed and windy locations, especially in the winter. Too much exposure will cause severe leaf dieback. In fact, leatherleaf is considered a semi-evergreen in the northern reaches of the state since it often has leaf dieback. Poor drainage will increase the amount of dieback. Fortunately, leatherleaf grows well in shade and is ideal on the north side of a building. The coarse foliage contrasts well with fine-needled evergreens such as spruce, fir, and hemlock.

How to Plant

Prepare a planting hole that is up to 4 times the width of the root-ball. Dig deep enough so that the top of the rootball is level with the ground around it after planting. Gently slope the sides of the hole outward from the bottom up to the edge. Be sure to remove any twine or wire that is wrapped around the stem or trunk before refilling the hole with the original soil. Water deeply and spread a 2- to 3-inch layer of organic matter over the entire planting area.

Advice for Care

In severe winters, leatherleaf may suffer extensive leaf dieback if it is not protected from the sun and wind. Prune out any dead or broken branches after blooming in late May or early June. Broadcast fertilizer around the root zone in early November to encourage growth the following year. Keep the root zone covered with a 2- to 3-inch layer of organic mulch to conserve moisture and keep the roots cool. Leatherleaf is seldom bothered by pests unless it is planted in poorly drained sites where it may be weakened and made more susceptible.

Additional Information

Though not as refined as other broadleaf evergreens, leatherleaf has its place in the southern Indiana landscape. It makes an excellent screen or background for the shrub and flower border. If leatherleaf becomes thin and leggy, it can be cut to the ground and rejuvenated with good success. Leatherleaf is native to China.

Additional Species, Cultivars, or Varieties

Since it tends to be hardier, the lantanaphyllum viburnum, *Viburnum × rhytidophylloides*, is a much better choice than the species leatherleaf, especially in northern Indiana. Leaf dieback will not be nearly as severe with this cultivar. The varieties 'Willowood' and 'Alleghany' repeat their bloom in late summer.

Lilac

Syringa vulgaris

Zones: 5, 6
Height: 10 to 15 feet
Bloom Period: May
Flowers: Lavender, purple, blue, pink, white
Type: Deciduous

Light Requirement:

With the exception of roses, the common lilac has no equal when it comes to captivating fragrance. For many gardeners, the strongly perfumed blooms bring back childhood memories of grandmother's house; in today's modern landscapes, lilac is often planted for nostalgic purposes. My earliest memories of lilac are of picking them from yards where I wasn't supposed to be in order to place them in a vase to honor the Virgin Mary. More than 1,600 species and varieties of lilac exist today. Of the types that are adapted to Indiana, the flowers are pink, blue, purple, or white and come in double- and single-petaled versions.

—T.T.

WHEN TO PLANT

Plant lilac in early spring before the leaves emerge on trees, or in late fall after the leaves drop.

WHERE TO PLANT

Lilac will bloom more profusely when planted in full sun. It prefers moist but well-drained soil that has plenty of organic matter; the average Indiana soil pH is fine. Because it tends to thin at the bottom, lilac should be planted as a background in the shrub border, or as a screen.

HOW TO PLANT

Prepare a planting hole that is 4 times the width of the rootball. Dig the hole deep enough so that the top of the rootball is level with the ground around it after planting. Remove any twine or wire that is wrapped around the trunk or stem and cut away the burlap or wire basket to half the height of the rootball. Backfill the hole with the original soil and water deeply. Spread a 2- to 3-inch layer of organic matter around the entire planting area.

ADVICE FOR CARE

Common lilacs should not require special care. Broadcast fertilizer around the root zone in early November. Maintain 2 to 3 inches of organic mulch over the root zone throughout the growing season. Lilac flowers are formed on growth from the previous season, so prune the thickest overgrown stems to the ground immediately after blooming. Prune a maximum of 1/3 to 1/2 of the stems at any one time, but remove *all* dead blooms before they set seed. This will encourage the best possible growth and will help prevent heavy blooming one year and lighter blooming the next. Water deeply on a weekly basis each summer to encourage good flower bud formation and to help prevent stress. Lilac borers will infest and kill plants that are under drought or other environmental stresses.

ADDITIONAL INFORMATION

The biggest drawback to growing lilacs is their susceptibility to powdery mildew. This common fungus turns most of the leaves an unattractive chalky white color by late summer but does no long-term harm to the shrub. To help discourage this problem, improve air circulation by pruning to open up the center of the shrub. Overgrown lilac can be successfully rejuvenated by cutting them completely to the ground. It may take 2 to 3 years before they bloom again.

ADDITIONAL SPECIES, CULTIVARS, OR VARIETIES

'President Grevy' and 'Belle de Nancy' are beautiful varieties with double flowers in blue and pink respectively. 'Sensation' has a deep-red-to-purple flower edged in white and is deserving of its name. *Syringa patula* 'Miss Kim' is a species with smaller, disease-free foliage covered in light-purple flowers from May to June. It is the only lilac that develops colorful leaves in the fall that turn shades of dark-red to purple.

'Little Princess' Spirea

Spirea japonica 'Little Princess'

Zones: 5, 6	**Light Requirement:**
Height: 1 to 4 feet	
Bloom Period: June to July	
Flowers: Pink or white	
Type: Deciduous	

*J*ust when the perennial garden is at its best, Japanese spirea also bursts forth with its fuzzy pink, red, and white blooms. The flat-topped, circular clusters of flowers cover the entire plant and remind us of mums in their density. When used in the foreground of a shrub border, 'Little Princess' and other *Spirea* varieties turn heads with their colorful blooms. Depending on the variety, these low-growing, rounded mounds with light-green leaves often emerge with pink, red, or golden tips. Several types, including 'Little Princess', will bloom off and on throughout the summer, especially if the old blooms are pinched off. *Spireas* are easy, low-maintenance, fast-growing plants that are seldom bothered by pests.

WHEN TO PLANT

Spireas are flexible and can be planted in either spring or fall when the ground is dry.

WHERE TO PLANT

These plants tolerate both sandy and heavy clay soil types but prefer a moist, well-drained site. They will produce more flowers when planted in full sun. *Spireas* grow best as foundation plants or as low-growing edgings in the shrub and perennial border. Brilliantly colored gold-leaved varieties serve well as accent plants.

HOW TO PLANT

Prepare a planting site by digging a hole that is 4 times the width of the rootball or container. Dig deep enough so that after planting, the top of the rootball is level with the ground around it. Gently slope the sides of the hole outward from the bottom to the upper edge. Lightly tap the side of the container on a hard surface to loosen the root mass. Carefully remove the rootball, trying not to allow the soil to fall away from the roots. Tease out any roots that appear to be growing in concentric circles around the bottom of the container and place the shrub in the planting hole. Backfill the hole with the original soil and water deeply when finished. Spread a 2- to 3-inch layer of organic mulch around the entire planting area to help conserve moisture and moderate the soil temperature.

ADVICE FOR CARE
Broadcast fertilizer around the root zone in early November to encourage growth the following year. Maintain a 2- to 3-inch layer of organic mulch around the root zone at all times. Prune away any dead or broken branches in the early spring. Pinch off dead or fading flowers to encourage intermittent blooming throughout the rest of the summer.

ADDITIONAL INFORMATION
It is recommended that you shear 'Little Princess' and other *spireas* down to the ground every 3 years or so. For the lowest-growing types, this could almost be done with a lawn mower. Prune early spring-blooming *Spireas* right after they bloom. Prune 'Little Princess' and other late bloomers like 'Goldmound' in early spring since they bloom on the current year's growth. The old-fashioned and ever-present bridal wreath *spireas* have been improved upon with numerous new species and varieties.

ADDITIONAL SPECIES, CULTIVARS, AND VARIETIES
'Anthony Waterer' is perhaps the oldest variety and grows 4 feet tall. It has deep-pink flowers that bloom against a background of blue-green foliage. This variety's leaves turn deep red in the fall, an unusual trait for *Spirea*. 'Goldflame' has brilliant yellow foliage with red tips in the spring. Both these varieties are often listed as the hybrid *Spirea × bumalda*. 'Shirobana' has flowers that bloom in rose, pink, and white all on the same plant.

Potentilla

Potentilla fruticosa

Other Name: Bush Cinquefoil **Zones:** 5, 6 **Height:** 1 to 4 feet **Bloom Period:** June to October **Flowers:** Yellow, white, and pink **Type:** Deciduous	**Light Requirement:** 

The word "happy" comes to mind when describing this low-growing hardy shrub. *Potentilla's* five-petaled buttercup flower is the shape every child draws when practicing his or her artistic skills. The yellow stamens in the center of the flower make a perfect dot, just like those masterpieces hanging on the refrigerator. *Potentilla's* flowers open in June and continue blooming until frost, making it one of our most useful summer shrubs. The flowers are borne individually and close to the leaves on narrow arching branches which give it a mounded shape. This shrub is well known for its ability to bloom continuously throughout the summer in tough urban conditions, where it has earned the reputation of being "indestructible."

WHEN TO PLANT

For best results, transplant *Potentilla* in the early spring before the leaves emerge on the trees, or in the late fall after the leaves drop.

WHERE TO PLANT

Potentilla grows best and produces more flowers if planted in full sun. It tolerates light shade, but will not produce as many blooms. Plant this shrub in soil that is moist but well drained with plenty of organic matter. Potentilla grows well in dry locations and does poorly in wet soils. Use it at the front of the shrub border, mixed in with the flower border, or as a foundation plant.

HOW TO PLANT

Prepare the planting site by digging a hole 4 times the width of the rootball. Dig deep enough so that after planting, the top of the rootball is level with the ground around it. Gently slope the sides of the hole outward from the bottom to the upper edges. Tap the sides of the container on a hard surface to loosen the roots from the walls of the pot. Tease out any roots that are growing in concentric circles around the base of the pot. Backfill the hole with the original soil and water deeply. Spread a 2- to 3-inch layer of organic mulch around the entire planting area to help conserve moisture.

ADVICE FOR CARE

Potentilla is the perfect plant for the weekend gardener with little time to spare. It blooms despite neglect and requires only occasional pruning every 2 years when it becomes leggy. Prune in early spring by cutting the stems as close to the ground as possible. Even though this plant will survive under the toughest of circumstances, broadcasting a general, all-purpose fertilizer around the root zone will encourage additional growth. For best results, maintain a 2- to 3-inch layer of organic mulch around the root zone during the growing season. In humid years, *Potentilla* is occasionally bothered by powdery mildew, which turns the leaves a chalky white.

ADDITIONAL INFORMATION

Relatives of the *Potentilla* have been grown in Britain for centuries. Its name means "small plant with great potency"; a related species was once used to drive out witches and other demons. One look at its flowers and you'll see how closely related this shrub is to our favorite June fruit, the strawberry.

ADDITIONAL SPECIES, CULTIVARS, AND VARIETIES

'Abbotswood' is considered the best white-flowered variety and grows to 3 feet. 'Goldfinger' also grows 3 feet tall with large, lemon-yellow blooms. 'Katherine Dykes' and 'Coronation Gold' are two other good yellow varieties.

Red Chokeberry

Aronia arbutifolia

Zones: 5, 6
Height: 6 to 10 feet
Bloom Period: Late April to May
Flowers: White
Type: Deciduous

Light Requirement:

The red chokeberry is another shrub for all seasons. This native Hoosier blooms in May throughout most of the state; earlier around Evansville. The subtle white blooms are tinged with pink and similar to hawthorn flowers in their subtlety. In fall, chokeberry leaves turn a brilliant red, rivaling any burning bush. The red chokeberry is most appreciated for its bright-red fruit, which turns color in the fall and lasts all winter. The 1/4-inch berries are stunning at their peak and resemble misplaced cherries. The shrub gets its name from the berries' bitter taste. It is strong enough to choke human and beast! This explains why fruit can still be found clinging to the branches as late as March.

WHEN TO PLANT

Plant chokeberries in the early spring before the leaves on trees emerge or in the late fall after the leaves drop.

WHERE TO PLANT

For best flower and fruit production, plant chokeberries in full sun. They will also grow well, but produce fewer berries, in partial shade. Chokeberries prefer moist, well-drained soil that is rich in organic matter, but they are known to tolerate fairly harsh growing conditions as well, such as very wet or very dry soil. Plant chokeberries as a screen or as a mass planting to enjoy the tremendous display of fruit all winter.

HOW TO PLANT

Prepare the planting site by digging a hole that is 4 times the width of the rootball. Dig deep enough so that after planting the top of the rootball is level with the ground around it. Gently slope the sides of the hole outward from the bottom to the outer edges. Remove any twine or wire that is still wrapped around the stem or trunk and cut away the burlap and wire basket to half the height of the rootball. Backfill with the original soil and water deeply. Spread 2 to 3 inches of organic mulch over the entire planting area.

ADVICE FOR CARE

Red chokeberries are relatively maintenance-free and are a good plant choice for the gardener with little time. Encourage faster and lusher growth by broadcasting fertilizer around the root zone in early November. Water deeply on a weekly basis and maintain a 2- to 3-inch layer of organic mulch throughout the growing season. Chokeberries tend to become leggy or spindly as they age, so prune them every 2 or 3 years to promote denser growth. Prune by cutting from 1/3 to 1/2 of the stems to the ground. This will allow more light to reach the center of the plant and encourage bushier growth with more flowers. Chokeberries are not regularly bothered by any pests.

ADDITIONAL INFORMATION

Red chokeberry has a tendency to sucker, so give it plenty of room to grow. The berries look especially beautiful when planted near or mixed with low-growing ornamental grasses that turn straw colored in the fall. Mass plantings of fruiting red chokeberry will turn the head, especially after the leaves drop.

ADDITIONAL SPECIES, CULTIVARS, OR VARIETIES

'Brilliantissima' is the best known variety, with larger leaves and brighter red fruit. The black chokeberry, *Aronia melanocarpa*, is similar to the red except for its black berries. It has more upright branches than the red chokeberry.

Red Twig Dogwood

Cornus sericea

Other Name: Red Osier Dogwood
Zones: 5, 6
Height: 6 to 10 feet
Bloom Period: May to June and intermittent
throughout the summer
Flowers: Dull-white
Type: Deciduous

Light Requirement:

ake one glance at red twig dogwood in December and you will instantly understand how it got its name: the color appears painted on its bright-red stems. This native Indiana shrub is easy to spot in the country where it grows in masses along stream banks and other wet areas. In moist locations, the shrub easily spreads through root suckers and will colonize large areas in a short time. It sends forth subtle white blooms in May and June, followed by dull-white berries that are immediately eaten by birds. For the rest of the summer this dogwood makes a nice background shrub; then, with the onset of cold weather, the twigs begin to turn red. At this time red twig dogwood stands out best against an evergreen background. The stems will stay red all winter and fade to green again with the arrival of spring. When cut, they make excellent additions to holiday greenery and other arrangements.

WHEN TO PLANT

Transplant red twig dogwood at any time of the year when the ground is dry.

WHERE TO PLANT

Red twig dogwood grows best in moist but well-drained soils with plenty of organic matter. It grows naturally in swampy areas and therefore tolerates wet landscape conditions better than most other shrubs. It prefers full sun but also grows well in partial shade.

HOW TO PLANT

Prepare the planting site by digging a hole that is 4 times the width of the rootball. Dig deep enough so that after planting, the top of the rootball is level with the soil around it. Remove any twine or wire that is wrapped around the trunk or stems and cut away the burlap and wire basket to half the height of the rootball. Backfill the hole with the original soil and water deeply. Spread a 2- to 3-inch layer of organic mulch over the entire planting area to help conserve moisture and to keep the weeds down.

ADVICE FOR CARE

The only necessary maintenance will be severe pruning every 2 years. In the early spring, use loppers to cut all the stems to the ground to encourage young and vigorous new growth. These young stems have a more intense red color in the winter than the older branches do. To encourage additional growth, broadcast fertilizer around the root zone in early November and maintain a 2-inch layer of organic mulch during the growing season. Red twig is bothered by a stem canker disease that causes random branch dieback during the growing season. It is rarely fatal, but removing these branches at the base will improve the shrub's overall appearance.

ADDITIONAL INFORMATION

Red twig dogwood was formerly known as *Cornus stolonifera*. This name is slightly more indicative of its rapid growth rate through suckers or "stolons." Branch tips will also root when they come in contact with the soil.

ADDITIONAL SPECIES, CULTIVARS, OR VARIETIES

'Cardinal' is an excellent variety for intense red color. 'Kelseyi' is a shorter, slower-growing form. 'Flavarima' has golden-yellow stems rather than red. *Cornus alba* 'Elegantissima' is a species that is similar to *sericea* and perhaps more popular; it has variegated white-and-green leaves. The pagoda dogwood, *Cornus alternifolia*, is an excellent shrub dogwood for partially shaded areas. Like red twig, it is a native shrub, but its white flowers are more attractive and it branches horizontally, much like the flowering dogwood. It is most useful for naturalizing.

Summersweet

Clethra alnifolia

Other Name: Sweet Pepperbush
Zones: 5, 6
Height: 3 to 10 feet
Bloom Period: July to August
Flowers: White or pink
Type: Deciduous

Light Requirement:

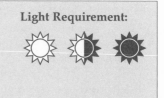

A highly adaptable shrub, summersweet is well named for the fragrant scent its flowers exude during the height of summer, when most other shrubs have "shut down." Summersweet's flowers are as loved by bees and other pollinators as they are by their owners. Numerous small white blooms open in fuzzy, six-inch long spikes on the tips of arching branches. The leaves are a thick, shiny, dark green that turn light yellow in the fall. Summersweet has a rounded mound shape that makes it wider than it is tall.

WHEN TO PLANT

Transplant summersweet in early spring before the leaves emerge on the trees or in late fall after the leaves drop.

WHERE TO PLANT

This shrub is adaptable both to sun and shade, though it may not bloom as prolifically in dense shade. Summersweet grows best in moist soil that has plenty of organic matter. It prefers slightly acidic soils, but is known to grow in alkaline sites as well. With its dense green leaves that give way to summer blooms, summersweet makes an excellent background shrub for the flower border. Shorter varieties should be planted as foundation plants or in the foreground of the shrub border.

HOW TO PLANT

Prepare the planting site by digging a hole 4 times the width of the container or rootball. Dig the hole deep enough so that after planting the top of the rootball is level with the ground around it. Gradually slope the sides of the hole outward from the bottom to the upper edges. Lightly tap the container on a hard surface to loosen the roots from the pot. Tease out any roots growing in concentric circles and backfill the hole with the original soil. Water deeply and spread a 2- to 3-inch layer of organic mulch over the entire planting area.

ADVICE FOR CARE

During dry periods, summersweet will grow better and produce more flowers if watered deeply each week. Maintain a 2- to 3-inch layer of mulch around the root zone to conserve moisture. Broadcast fertilizer in early November to encourage growth the following year. Summersweet blooms on the current season's growth, so prune it in early spring to shape or to remove dead or broken branches. Summersweet has few pests other than spider mites, which can be a problem in dry years.

ADDITIONAL INFORMATION

Summersweet is highly tolerant of salt conditions and grows naturally near the seashore on the East Coast. It should not be bothered by the salt spray used on roads and sidewalks here during the winter. In moist sites it spreads by sending up root suckers that will help give it a rounder shape; these can be transplanted if handled with care.

ADDITIONAL SPECIES, CULTIVARS, OR VARIETIES

One of the best varieties, 'Hummingbird', won a Gold Medal from the prestigious Pennsylvania Horticultural Society for its outstanding character and numerous lovely white blooms. It grows into a 4-foot mound. 'Rosea' and 'Pink Spire' have medium-pink blooms that fade to light pink. 'Paniculata' is a white-blooming variety with larger flowers; it grows faster than the species, and can reach 8 to 10 feet tall.

Vernal Witchhazel

Hamamelis vernalis

Other Name: Ozark Witchhazel
Zones: 5, 6
Height: 6 to 12 feet
Bloom Period: January to February
Flowers: Yellow, red
Type: Deciduous

Light Requirement:

or those of us who can't get to Florida or some other warm climate every winter, we can at least look forward to the witchhazel's blooming! Vernal witchhazel is easily our earliest-blooming shrub, with short, yellow, fringe-like flowers on all its branch tips. Opening as early as January, each flower has four petals that unfurl on warm days and curl up to protect themselves when the weather is chilly. This phenomenon enables the blooms to last up to four weeks. Vernal witchhazel grows into a multi-stemmed mounded shrub with thick green leaves that turn brilliant yellow in the fall. When mature, witchhazel is much wider than it is tall and makes a nice background shrub for screening. Cut some branches to force indoors during January and you will be rewarded with a sweet fragrance that will help lift you out of the winter doldrums.

WHEN TO PLANT
For best results, transplant vernal witchhazel in early spring before the leaves emerge on the trees.

WHERE TO PLANT
Vernal witchhazel will grow best in moist but well-drained soil with plenty of organic matter. It rewards the home owner with more blooms if planted in full sun; it also tolerates partial shade. Vernal witchhazel's mound shape helps soften the corners of buildings. It also makes an excellent background or screen in the shrub border. Since we spend less time outdoors in the winter, it would be best to plant this plant near an entryway to the house or office, where it will be enjoyed the most.

How to Plant

Prepare a planting hole that is 4 times the width of the rootball. Gradually slope the sides of the hole outward from the bottom to the upper edges. Dig deep enough so that after planting the top of the rootball is level with the ground around it. Remove any twine or wire wrapped around the trunk or stems and cut away the burlap or wire basket to half the height of the rootball. Backfill with the original soil and water deeply. Spread a 2- to 3-inch layer of organic mulch around the entire planting area.

Advice for Care

Broadcast fertilizer around the root zone in early November, and maintain a 2-inch layer of organic mulch throughout the growing season. After the shrub has bloomed, prune as needed to shape or to remove any dead or broken branches. Vernal witchhazel is not bothered by any serious pests, but wasps often cause unsightly nipple-like galls to appear on the leaves. These galls do not cause any long-term damage to the shrub.

Additional Information

Vernal witchhazel is not native to Indiana, but it is related to the common witchhazel, *Hamamelis virginiana*, which blooms in the fall and grows tall enough to be considered a small tree. The inner bark of the common witchhazel has been used for centuries by Native Americans and herbalists to cure various ailments.

Additional Species, Cultivars, or Varieties

The variety 'Carnea' has deep-red flowers that fade to an orange pink at the tip. 'Sandra' is a variety with excellent bright-red fall color and yellow flowers that bloom intermittently from November until February. Chinese witchhazel, *Hamamelis mollis*, also blooms in January with a more brilliant flower display than vernal witchhazel. This species is only hardy at best in southern Indiana, specifically in Zones 5B and 6.

Winterberry Holly

Ilex verticillata

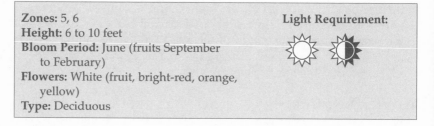

Zones: 5, 6	**Light Requirement:**
Height: 6 to 10 feet	
Bloom Period: June (fruits September to February)	
Flowers: White (fruit, bright-red, orange, yellow)	
Type: Deciduous	

*I*f an interesting winter landscape is important to you, winterberry holly *must* be part of it. Its brilliant red berries brighten the landscape from late September through February. Tiny, white, non-showy flowers open in June and are followed by pea-sized light-green fruit. Both flowers and fruit are hidden by winterberry holly's dark-green leaves, which do not resemble the "typical" thick, glossy holly leaf with spines on the tips. The berries begin turning pink in the late summer, and become bright red by the time the leaves drop in October. They cling tightly to the branches and are much sought after by commercial florists for fresh holiday flower arrangements. There is nothing as exquisite as winterberry holly branches under a fresh coating of snow. Plant them around a river birch with some ornamental grass and you'll forget how cold it is outside!

WHEN TO PLANT
Transplant winterberry in early spring before the leaves on trees emerge or in the fall after the leaves drop.

WHERE TO PLANT
In their natural habitat, winterberry hollies grow in deep, moist, organic soils typical of that found in and around a "wetland." They prefer slightly acidic soils and will develop yellow leaves if the pH goes much above neutral. In the home landscape, winterberry will grow in both wet and dry sites, and even tolerate heavy clay. In drier locations, however, it will probably not grow as large or as quickly. Plant winterberry where you can enjoy the berries the most, such as near an entryway or against an evergreen background such as spruce or yew.

How to Plant

Prepare the planting site by digging a hole 4 times the width of the rootball. Dig the hole deep enough so that after planting the top of the rootball is level with the ground around it. Gradually slope the sides of the hole outward from the bottom to the upper edges. Remove any twine or wire from around the stems or trunk of the shrub; cut away any burlap or wire basket to half the height of the rootball. Backfill the hole with the original soil after pulverizing well with your shovel. Water deeply and spread a 2- to 3-inch layer of organic mulch around the entire planting area.

Advice for Care

Broadcast fertilizer around the root zone in early November and maintain a 2-inch layer of mulch throughout the growing season. Winterberry hollies tolerate wet soil and will not be bothered by frequent flooding. Water generously during drought to keep this shrub growing vigorously.

Additional Information

Male and female flowers grow on different plants; the fruit only develops on the female plant after bees and other insects have helped pollinate it. Plant one to two males as pollinators for every five females to achieve good fruit set.

Additional Species, Cultivars, or Varieties

Be sure the nursery provides you with the appropriate pollinator for the variety you choose. 'Winter Red' is the most common and most vigorous-growing variety in our area; it is pollinated by 'Southern Gentleman'. A short, compact variety, 'Red Sprite', grows to only 4 feet tall and is pollinated by 'Apollo'. The variety 'Sparkleberry' has won several awards and is also pollinated by 'Apollo'.

CHAPTER TEN

Trees

A DRIVE THROUGH A NEW SUBDIVISION ALWAYS BEGS
the same question: What would the world be like if there
were no trees? The thought is incomprehensible! We recall Hurricane
Hugo, which decimated parts of the Carolina coast in 1989. Residents
interviewed after this natural catastrophe said that more than anything else, they missed the trees.

Trees make invaluable contributions to our daily lives. They are
nature's air conditioners, shading buildings in summer and giving
us a cool place to rest when the temperatures soar. In winter, they
serve as windbreaks and help keep heating costs down. Trees absorb
water and reduce runoff and erosion. They clean the air by removing carbon dioxide and other impurities in the city as well as in the
country. Trees also serve as shelter for birds and other wildlife. They
keep us closer to nature and replenish the human spirit.

If you think of a landscape in the same way that you think of
your house, the soil is the foundation and the trees are the ceiling
and walls. Trees help to enclose the vast outdoor space and package
it into more manageable sections such as gardens or play areas.
Trees have other functions in the landscape as well. Their shapes,
leaf colors, and imposing size serve as focal points. Trees soften
"real" buildings with their round canopies and cool green color.
Whether large or small, they give us something beautiful to look at
or, when blooming, something sweet to smell. We may be able to
survive with fewer trees, but life wouldn't be nearly as rich.

PLANTING TREES
No amount of soil preparation or "coddling" by attentive gardeners
can make up for planting a tree where it doesn't belong. Select the
appropriate tree for your planting site first, and you'll be much happier later on. Besides, a tree is a lot harder to move than a perennial.

Chapter Ten

When mature, at least two-thirds of a tree's root system is in the top two feet of soil over a wide area. Therefore, to encourage faster establishment, dig a hole that is three or four times the width of the rootball you are planting. There may be some benefit to sloping the sides of the hole outward from the bottom and up to ground level. Dig the hole deep enough so that when the rootball is sitting at the bottom of the hole, its top is even with the surrounding grade. This is very important, as planting a tree just a few inches too deep can result in its gradual death.

Whether planting a balled-and-burlapped or a container-grown tree, always handle it from its rootball. Never move a tree by grabbing its trunk and never allow a tree to drop from your hands or to drop off the back end of a pickup. It is crucial to the survival of the tree that the soil remain in contact with the existing roots. If planting a container-grown tree, gently remove the specimen from its container. Gently tease long roots from the natural mold of the container. This is especially important if you notice that they are "pot-bound," or growing in concentric circles. These roots may be pulled apart and even cut if necessary.

When planting balled-and-burlapped trees, leave the burlap in the ground where it will decompose. It is wise to tuck it under and cover it with soil so that moisture is not "wicked" from the burlap exposed above ground. It is just as easy to cut away most of the burlap with a sharp knife at planting time. Any synthetic covering such as plastic should be removed. Removing the wire basket from a larger tree is extremely difficult and awkward once the tree is in the hole. Research shows that leaving the wire basket in place should not cause any harm to the tree. Even so, you may wish to cut away at least half of the upper portion of the basket with tin snips once the tree is in the hole. Before backfilling the hole, be sure there is no twine or wire wrapped around the trunk. At the same time, remove any tags used to identify the tree. These pieces of wire or twine could eventually girdle the trunk or branches, and cause the slow death of the tree.

Chapter Ten

🐚

Many mail order companies ship bare-root plants. Bare-root trees should have their roots kept moist at all times before planting. Plant them immediately after receiving them, as deep as they were growing in the field. The original soil line should be obvious on the trunk, but if not, it is better to plant the tree too shallow than too deep. Bare-root trees usually need staking for support while container-grown trees, or those with trunks less than two inches in diameter, do not.

It is not necessary to amend the soil with organic matter before backfilling the hole unless you have very sandy soil. It is a good idea, however, to pulverize the soil well with a shovel before backfilling. It is not necessary to fertilize at planting time; in fact, it may even damage the tree. It is best to avoid fertilizing altogether during the first year.

Water deeply after planting. Continue watering deeply once a week throughout the growing season, especially during the height of summer. Avoid light watering every day or two since this will encourage the development of shallow roots. Spread a two- to three-inch layer of mulch around the planting site to help conserve moisture.

FERTILIZING TREES

Whether using organic or inorganic sources of fertilizer, a good feeding program will help the tree get off to a good start. There is no real advantage, however, to feeding a tree at planting time or at any time during the first year. Instead, focus first-year energies on mulching and watering; begin the feeding program the second year. If the tree is surrounded by lawn and you are feeding the grass two or three times per year, separate feeding of the tree is usually unnecessary. Otherwise, trees prefer to be fed in mid- to late fall. Early November, before the soil gets too cold, is an ideal time throughout all of Indiana. Early spring is the second-best time.

There is a wide variety of fertilizers available at local garden centers that homeowners can use on their own. Landscape maintenance contractors also fertilize and provide other services for a fee. Most fertilizers are sold in proportions of nitrogen, phosphorus, and potassium, which are three of the most vital nutrients for plant growth. The proportion of the nutrients in the fertilizer are listed on the outside of the bag. For instance, a 12-12-12 fertilizer contains twelve percent by weight of nitrogen, phosphorus, and potassium, in that order. Fertilizers are applied both as granulars in a dry form, or as solubles that are mixed with water.

Broadcasting dry fertilizer from a spreader over the root zone of the tree is the easiest way. The feeder roots are located by starting halfway between the trunk and the drip line, then going one to two times that distance. There are numerous fertilizers available to the home owner. The following chart developed by Purdue University will help you estimate the correct amount of fertilizer:

Fertilizer	Pounds of fertilizer needed for 1000 square feet of root zone
Urea (45-0-0)	4
Ammonium Nitrate (33-0-0)	6
10-10-10	20
12-12-12	16

When using organic sources of fertilizer, compare the percent nitrogen (the first of the three numbers) on the container with the percent nitrogen in the analyses above and apply accordingly. At these rates you may fertilize once in the fall and again in very early spring, right before the leaves emerge.

PRUNING

Pruning eliminates dead branches, helps shape the tree, and stimulates new growth. It is a routine maintenance practice that will encourage a good growth habit and possibly increase the tree's longevity.

Chapter Ten

⚘

Pruning is safe for the overall health of the tree at any time of the year, but there are more logical times to prune depending on whether the tree blooms. As a rule of thumb, spring-blooming trees should be pruned shortly after the flowers die. This encourages maximum flower production for the following year. Prune shade trees during late fall or early spring, when the leaves are absent, because it will be easier to see the branch structure. Study the natural growth habit of the tree to get a good idea of how much of a branch needs to be removed. Cut the branch back all the way to the collar, but don't actually cut into the collar. This will leave a small swelling or lump at the point of the pruning cut, which is necessary for proper healing. Pruning paint or sealant is no longer recommended for fresh tree wounds. Never leave stubby branches as is typical of the pruning practice called "topping." This is unhealthy for the tree and will cause an abundance of weak-wooded branches called "water sprouts" to develop. Topping is also a huge disservice to a tree's natural growth pattern. If a tree is growing into overhead power lines, then it would be a wise investment to remove it and replace it with a shorter species and plant a new one where it will have room to grow to its normal size.

WATERING AND MULCHING

Keep trees watered during the growing season with one to one-and-one-half inches of water per week. For best results use a "soaker hose," which lets the water seep into the ground. Mulch will keep the roots cool and reduce competition for moisture and nutrients. The larger the percentage of the root zone that is covered with mulch and is free of weeds and grass, the faster the tree will grow. It is unnecessary and may cause damage to the tree to mound the mulch up around the trunk. Instead, make a small basin with the mulch around the trunk of the tree.

TREE PROBLEMS

Diagnosing tree problems is not an easy task. A misdiagnosis can be costly to both the home owner and the environment. There is not enough room to discuss diagnosing tree problems in this short intro-

Chapter Ten

duction. You can avoid many problems, however, by following the maintenance practices previously mentioned.

Tree problems may occur even when wise maintenance practices are followed. Approximately three-fourths of all problems are caused by environmental factors such as compacted soil, cold injury, drought stress, salt toxicity, wind damage, injury to the root system, or poor planting procedures. Many disease and insect problems affecting trees are short-lived and only cause cosmetic damage. These problems are rarely life-threatening to a tree and normally don't require intervention with a pesticide. Examples of these minor but frequent foliar diseases include maple, sycamore or ash anthracnose. These diseases sometimes cause alarm among homeowners because of heavy leaf drop in the spring. Some insects lay eggs inside a leaf which cause abnormal growths called "galls." These growths are unsightly and often numerous but do not affect the health of the tree. Pesticides should only be used when a pest has been identified and there are no other alternatives for control. Consult a certified arborist, your local garden center representative, or your local office of the Purdue Cooperative Extension Service for a more accurate diagnosis.

Amur Maple

Acer tataricum ssp. *ginnala*

Zones: 5, 6	**Light Requirement:**
Height: 15 to 20 feet	
Bloom Period: April or May	
Flowers: Yellowish-white, fragrant	
Type: Deciduous	

Most gardeners in Indiana grow the Japanese maple, but the Amur has many qualities that make it preferable to its more favored cousin. The Amur maple has a fine, glossy green leaf. As its leaves unfurl each spring, it puts forth plentiful blooms with a sweet fragrance. The Amur's fall color is an outstanding fiery yellow turning to brilliant red, especially in improved varieties. The fruits, called "samaras" or "helicopters" by most youngsters, turn red in early summer while the leaves stay green, making a nice color contrast. The Amur maple remains small, reaching only twelve to eighteen feet. It makes an excellent specimen around patios and decks. It is one of the best small trees for container use since it is reliably hardy in Indiana with no protection, unlike the Japanese maple and other small trees. It can also be mass planted to form a low screen or to soften the corners of houses or other lowrise buildings.

WHEN TO PLANT

The Amur maple transplants well almost any time of the year but prefers spring. Spring planting is especially important when planting bare-root specimens. Wait until the soil has dried before digging the planting hole.

WHERE TO PLANT

Soil should be moist but well drained. The Amur maple tolerates wide ranges in soil pH. It prefers full sun but will grow well in partial shade.

HOW TO PLANT

Prepare a planting hole 4 times the width of the rootball. Dig the hole only as deep as the rootball. Gently slope the sides of the planting hole from the bottom up to ground level like a basin or shallow

320

bowl. Place the tree in the hole, being careful not to loosen any soil from around the roots. Before refilling the planting hole, be sure that the top of the rootball is level with the ground around it. Return the soil to the hole after breaking apart any clods. Water the tree, letting the water soak deeply into the ground. Spread two inches of mulch to keep the roots cool and moist, and to keep the weeds and grass away. Plant Amur maples 10 feet apart to make a dense screen.

ADVICE FOR CARE

Water tree with at least 1 to $1^1/2$ inches of water per week. This is especially important during our "hot and dry" periods that come at different times each summer, and for newly planted specimens. The Amur maple will grow faster and endure environmental stresses better if fertilized each year, especially in the first 5 to 10 years after transplanting. Broadcast fertilizer around the root system in early November. The Amur maple is an excellent and more valuable specimen in the landscape when pruned to multiple stems. It has few problems with pests.

ADDITIONAL INFORMATION

The Amur maple came to North America from its native habitats in China, Korea, Japan, and Siberia. Its leaves do not resemble those of "typical" maples; they are much longer and more pointed.

ADDITIONAL SPECIES, CULTIVARS, OR VARIETIES

Outstanding cultivars include 'Compactum' and 'Flame'. Although slightly taller than the Amur maple, some other maples recommended for their short stature include the hedge maple, *Acer campestre*. As its name suggests, the hedge maple makes an excellent formal hedge when heavily pruned. The paperbark maple, *Acer griseum*, has peeling bark that makes it especially pleasing to view during the winter. Paperbark maple is not reliably hardy in northern Indiana.

Bald Cypress

Taxodium distichum

Zones: 5, 6
Height: 50 to 100 feet
Type: Deciduous

Light Requirement:

The bald cypress is one of Indiana's most reliable native trees. It has short, soft, flat, feathery, needle-like leaves that give it a very fine texture. It is one of the few deciduous conifers (cone-bearing trees). It is best known to grow in swampy areas like the Florida Everglades where it produces knobby growths from the roots that are called "knees." The knees grow above the waterline near the swamp banks and help give those wet landscapes a haunting appearance. The leaves emerge light-green in spring and turn darker as summer passes. In the fall they turn coppery-brown before dropping to the ground where they disappear into the lawn or groundcover. Since it is a conifer, some people have mistaken the brown fall color for a sudden and premature death! When young, the tree has a more formal, pyramidal shape. As it ages, the bald cypress develops a broader and more open shape with a flatter top. It has no pest problems to speak of and makes a good street tree.

WHEN TO PLANT

Plant bald cypress in spring, preferably when the soil is dry enough to crumble in your hand, or fall. Summer planting should be avoided since bald cypress requires heavy watering when it is small.

WHERE TO PLANT

Plant bald cypress where quick shade is desired since it is a medium- to fast-growing tree when young. Even though its native habitat is in the swamps, bald cypress prefers a deep and well-drained sandy soil with plenty of organic matter. It will, however, naturally tolerate wet soils and sometimes grows well in heavy clay. The soil should be slightly acidic; bald cypress will yellow if the pH goes much above 7.5. It makes an excellent specimen tree but also provides a nice fine-textured background for smaller trees with coarse texture.

How to Plant

Plant balled-and-burlapped specimens by digging a hole 2 to 3 times as wide as the rootball. Place the tree in the hole so that the top of the rootball is level with the ground around it. Remove any twine or wire wrapped around the trunk. Cut away any burlap or wire basket to half the height of the rootball. Backfill the hole with the original soil and water deeply. Spread an organic mulch up to 3 inches deep.

Advice for Care

Bald cypress is one of the few carefree trees. Keep it watered with 1 to 1 1/2 inches of water per week, especially when young. Broadcast fertilizer around the root zone in early November, especially during the first 5 to 10 years after transplanting. Check the soil pH every few years if you know it to be alkaline in your area. Lower the pH by applying sulfur in early December at the rate of 3 to 4 pounds per 100 square feet of area around the tree. Prune to remove dead branches only.

Additional Information

Bald cypress has one of the hardest and most rot-resistant woods and is often used as mulch for landscaping purposes for this reason. The tree is also extremely tolerant of wind and makes a nice windbreak. Its closest relative is the dawn redwood, *Metasequoia glyptostroboides*, also known as the "Fossil Tree." Dawn redwoods were believed extinct until earlier this century. Bald cypress are reported to live up to 1300 years.

Additional Species, Cultivars, or Varieties

There are very few exceptional new varieties on the market. 'Monarch of Illinois' has branches that may spread 65 feet wide, so plant it with enough room to grow. 'Shawnee Brave' is narrower and more columnar; use it where space is tighter.

Beech

Fagus grandifolia

Other Name: American Beech **Zones:** 5, 6 **Height:** 50 to 70 feet **Type:** Deciduous	**Light Requirement:** 

*T*he sentimentally regarded American beech is one of our most outstanding native trees. It grows at least as wide as it is tall, so it is not a tree for small landscapes. Give it plenty of room and plenty of time because it grows slowly, too. In the landscape, beech trees generally have short trunks with smooth gray bark. The branches grow upward and spreading, giving the tree a nice broad shape when grown in the open. Its glossy green leaves turn orange-yellow in the fall before turning brown. Beech trees are easily spotted in the winter because they retain many of their lower leaves. Twigs grow in a distinctive zigzag shape and end with a pointy brown bud that will sometimes break the skin if you are careless.

WHEN TO PLANT

Plant beech in spring after the soil is dry. Like most other nut trees, they do not tolerate fall planting.

WHERE TO PLANT

Beech should be planted where it will have plenty of room to grow; it is perfect for big open spaces. The soil should be moist but well drained with high organic matter content. Beech does not grow well in heavy clay or compact soils that get a lot of foot traffic. It prefers soil with a slightly acidic pH. Beech is among the slowest growing landscape trees; we must plant them for the next generation.

HOW TO PLANT

Plant balled-and-burlapped specimens after digging a hole at least 2 to 3 times the width of the rootball. Dig the hole deep enough so that the top of the rootball is level with the ground around it after planting. The wider the planting hole, the easier and more quickly a beech will establish itself. Be sure to remove any twine or wire from around the trunk. Cut away any burlap or wire basket to half the height of the rootball. Return the original soil to the planting hole after amending it with organic matter. Water deeply and spread a 2- to 3-inch layer of mulch.

ADVICE FOR CARE
Maintain a 2- to 3-inch layer of mulch around the root zone. Beech has a very shallow root system that needs the protection and added moisture mulch provides. An established tree has such shallow roots that it is impossible to grow grass around it, so don't bother. Beech is considered a "bleeder," so prune any time after June to avoid excessive sap flow from the cut. Water deeply each week in summer to avoid drought stress. Broadcast fertilizer around the root zone in early November, especially during the first 10 to 20 years after transplanting.

ADDITIONAL INFORMATION
Beech will sucker from the roots and establish a small stand of trees over time. They are regarded sentimentally for the soft bark that we carved our names in as youngsters. Avoid this practice now—beech need as much protection as possible.

ADDITIONAL SPECIES, CULTIVARS, OR VARIETIES
American beech has very few named varieties, probably because the European beech, *Fagus sylvatica*, is a more reliable tree for landscaping purposes. Although similar in all respects to the American, it is more tolerant of poor soils and urban planting conditions. The copper or purple beech, *F. sylvatica* 'Purpurea', has beautiful purple leaves and is one of the most widely planted European varieties. *F. sylvatica* 'Pendula' , a weeping form, is a stunning specimen. *F. sylvatica* 'Tricolor' is a popular purple-leaved variety with rosy-white edges that will brown in summer if the soil dries out.

Bur Oak

Quercus macrocarpa

Zones: 5, 6
Height: 75 to 100 feet
Flowers: Insignificant; large acorns
  in the fall
Type: Deciduous

Light Requirement:

There is no larger, statelier, and more rugged tree that grows naturally in Indiana than the bur oak. Its massive trunk and sturdy limbs dwarf most other trees around it. The trunk has deep furrows and the twigs' cork-like ridges give them a rough and gnarled appearance. When given ample space, bur oak grows into an imposing, broadly spreading specimen. Its rugged appearance makes other trees look tame. Bur oaks are in the white oak family and have leaves with deep, rounded-edge, irregular lobes that are dark green all summer. The leaves turn a dull brown in late fall. Bur oak will tolerate wind and cold extremes and is found growing naturally in open fields. Specimens found in developed areas have probably been there a long time.

WHEN TO PLANT

Plant bur oak in the spring, after the soil dries. Nut trees like oak will not live if planted in the fall.

WHERE TO PLANT

Bur oak tolerates a wide range of soil conditions and growing environments, including pollution and other urban ills. It will grow as well in heavy clay as in sandy loam, but does best on deep prairie-type soils with good drainage. It tolerates both an acidic and alkaline pH range. Plant bur oaks in open spaces where it will have plenty of room to grow.

HOW TO PLANT

Plant balled-and-burlapped specimens in spring, after the ground dries out. Bur oak is notoriously difficult to transplant. Handle the tree carefully so as not to cause the soil to break away from the roots. Prepare a planting hole that is at least 2 to 3 times the width

of the rootball. Dig the hole deep enough so that the top of the rootball is level with the ground around it. Be sure to remove any twine
or wire from around the trunk. Cut away any burlap or wire basket
to half the height of the rootball. Backfill the hole with the original
soil and water deeply. Spread a 2- to 3-inch layer of organic mulch
over the planting area.

ADVICE FOR CARE

Bur oak grows very slowly, so don't despair. You are planting a
tree for your grandchildren to enjoy. Water the tree with 1 to 1^1/$_2$
inches of water per week, especially if it was recently transplanted;
older trees will tolerate drier conditions. Broadcast fertilizer in early
November to encourage growth, especially during the first 20 years
after transplanting. An established bur oak should not require much
fertilization. Prune out any deadwood. Bur oak should not have
many pest problems other than occasional oak galls. If you can
reach them, remove the galls with pruning shears.

ADDITIONAL INFORMATION

A favorite bur oak grows about five feet from the shoulder of a busy
thoroughfare in Indianapolis. It is obvious that the tree was spared
when the road was built, but it doesn't seem likely that this one will
survive. Though their rugged nature helps them withstand city conditions quite well, even a bur oak cannot survive having its roots
destroyed by construction and the repeated passing of automobiles.
Bur oaks are named for the coarse and hairy bristles on the rim of
the acorn cup.

ADDITIONAL SPECIES, CULTIVARS, OR VARIETIES

The swamp white oak, *Quercus bicolor*, is closely related to the bur
oak and will transplant more easily. As its name suggests, swamp
white oak tolerates damp soils. The red oak, *Quercus rubra*, is one
of the fastest growing oaks, but it sometimes yellow in alkaline soils.

TREES

Flowering Crab Apple

Malus spp.

Zones: 5, 6	**Light Requirement:**
Height: 15 to 25 feet	
Bloom Period: April, May; fruits in fall	
Flowers: Pink, red, white (fruit, red and yellow)	
Type: Deciduous	

*T*here is no tree more spectacular in spring than the flowering crab apple. With its dense display of cotton candy-like flowers, it's easy to understand why. Billowy clouds of pink and white blooms along city streets, in yards, parks, cemeteries, and other green spaces just say spring. Children frequently use the large fruit of the old crabs as ammunition during frequent neighborhood "battles." Fortunately, new hybrids with smaller and more colorful fruit are replacing the old varieties. Birds are also fond of the fruit display, so plant the trees close to the house to better see our feathered friends.

WHEN TO PLANT

Plant crab apple in spring, preferably before the leaves or flowers emerge. They can also be planted in the fall before the ground freezes.

WHERE TO PLANT

Crab apple should be planted in full sun to insure the maximum possible bloom. It prefers average to slightly acidic pH soils, but has been observed growing well in alkaline situations. The soil should be well drained. Plant crab apple along the street and under power lines where larger specimens would grow too tall.

HOW TO PLANT

Prepare a planting hole 4 times the width of the rootball. Gently slope the sides of the planting hole outward from the bottom up to ground level. Set the tree so that the top of the rootball is level with the ground around it. Cut away the burlap and wire from wire baskets up to half the height of the rootball. Be sure to remove any twine or wire from around the trunk. Backfill the hole with the original soil. Water deeply and spread a 2- to 3-inch layer of organic mulch around the planting area.

ADVICE FOR CARE

Keep flowering crabs watered with 1 to 1^{1}/$_{2}$ inches of water per week. Fertilize in early November, especially during the first 10 years after planting. Crab apples tend to sprout many stems around the trunk of the tree. These sprouts, called "suckers," are undesirable and can be pruned at any time of the year. Unfortunately, there is no way to prevent the suckers from growing back. Crab apples are prone to several diseases in Indiana. The most prevalent is called "apple scab." It causes yellow spots followed by gray-black scabs on the leaves and fruit. The most reliable way to control this disease is to plant a resistant variety. Old varieties of crabs are usually susceptible to apple scab and can drop more than half their leaves by midsummer as a result. A minimum of three fungicide sprays per year are necessary to control apple scab. Contact your County Extension Office for more information on pest control.

ADDITIONAL INFORMATION

Some crab apples have a tendency to bear flowers and fruit more heavily in alternating years. Most crab apples are grafted. A grafted crap apple's suckers should not be replanted since the new growth will not resemble the above-ground portion of the tree.

ADDITIONAL SPECIES, CULTIVARS, OR VARIETIES

The sargent crab, *Malus sargentii*, is a popular dwarf crab apple, rarely exceeding 10 feet tall. It may bear fruit in alternate years. Some of the best varieties that also have excellent disease resistance are 'Prairiefire', dark pink flowers with reddish-purple fruit; 'Donald Wyman', pink buds that open to white, with red fruit; 'Robinson', pink flowers with red fruit; 'Sugartyme', white flowers with red fruit; and 'Snow Magic', white flowers with wine-red fruit.

Flowering Pear

Pyrus calleryana

Other Name: Ornamental Pear **Zones:** 5, 6 **Height:** 25 to 40 feet **Bloom Period:** April (small fruit in summer and fall) **Flowers:** White (fruit, dull brown) **Type:** Deciduous	**Light Requirement:**

lowering pear is one of the largest and most beautiful blooming trees available. Along with serviceberry, it is one of our earliest bloomers and helps announce the arrival of spring. Flowering pear grows in a formal, pyramidal shape. The branches turn white with flowers which dot the landscape with teardrop-like clouds. When in bloom around the American Legion Mall in Indianapolis, they are statuesque. Glossy green leaves with undulated margins follow the blooms and last well into fall. Flowering pears turn scarlet red in October and November and are one of the last trees to shed their leaves. Fruit that rarely exceeds a half-inch in diameter turns a dull brown in late summer. Unlike flowering crab apple fruit, which sometimes makes a mess on the sidewalk, flowering pear fruit rarely causes a litter problem.

WHEN TO PLANT

Flowering pear recovers slowly after transplanting. Plant in early spring to enjoy the bloom and to give it the longest growing season possible the first year.

WHERE TO PLANT

This tree has been synonymous with the word "subdivision" since the 70s, when its versatility and season-long display were discovered. It prefers full sun and will grow in confined spaces, like easements along the street. It makes an excellent street tree and is planted in many new developments, too extensively in some instances. Flowering pear grows well in raised areas such as berms. Slightly acidic and well-drained soil is the best, but pears will also tolerate a soil with alkaline pH.

How to Plant

Plant a balled-and-burlapped specimen after digging a hole 4 times the width of the rootball. Dig the hole deep enough so that the top of the rootball is level with the ground around it. Remove any twine or wire from around the trunk. Cut away the burlap and any wire basket up to half the height of the rootball. Backfill the hole with the original soil and water deeply. Spread 2 to 3 inches of organic mulch over the planting area.

Advice for Care

Keep flowering pear watered in summer, especially in the first 5 years after planting. Maintain a 2- to 3-inch layer of organic mulch around the tree. Broadcast fertilizer around the root zone of the tree in early November, especially during the first 5 to 10 years after transplanting. Flowering pear has few pest and disease problems. Fire blight causes frequent branch dieback on its cousin, the fruiting pear, but rarely affects the ornamental pear. Prune in spring immediately after bloom. Prune carefully and leave the branches with the widest crotch angle. Some flowering pear varieties are notorious for having weak branches due to narrow crotch angles.

Additional Information

'Bradford Pear' is a variety of flowering pear that was introduced and widely popularized by landscapers. Unfortunately, Bradford proved to be a rather weak-wooded selection. When the original Bradfords turned 20 or 30 years old, their branches started breaking, especially during storms. It is not unusual to see older Bradfords that are almost split in two, or that have large gaps in the canopy due to limb breakage. Avoid using 'Bradford Pear' at all costs because of its weak branch angles.

Additional Species, Cultivars, or Varieties

There are several new varieties on the market that are easy to find and are superior to the popular predecessor, 'Bradford Pear'. 'Chanticleer', formerly known as 'Cleveland Select', is probably the best. It has sturdy limbs and its leaves color much earlier than 'Bradford Pear' in the fall. 'Autumn Blaze' has similar features and is also an excellent choice. 'Aristocrat' is broader at the base and is a fast grower. 'Capital' grows 15 feet wide and would be excellent in small spaces.

Ginkgo

Ginkgo biloba

Other Name: Maidenhair	**Light Requirement:**
Zones: 5, 6	
Height: 50 to 75 feet	
Type: Deciduous	

One of the most unusual-looking and trouble-free ornamental trees, a ginkgo is grown for the shade it provides as well as for its spectacular fall color. Because it tolerates pollution and the other stresses of "city life," ginkgo is often the tree of choice for dense urban centers. This ability to thrive in difficult planting sites makes it perfect for suburban or rural areas as well. In the fall, ginkgo leaves will often turn color all at once, going from a thick, medium green to bright yellow and then dropping from the tree within a few days. When young, before side branches have begun to fill out the canopy, ginkgo appears thin and spindly; the mature ginkgo has fork-like limbs that spread forty feet wide.

WHEN TO PLANT

Plant ginkgo in spring or fall when the soil is dry and crumbly. If planting in summer, be sure to provide 1 to 1¹/₂ inches of water per week.

WHERE TO PLANT

Ginkgo prefers moist but well-drained soil with a slightly acidic pH, but it will grow in very poor and alkaline soil as well. Give it full sun with plenty of room to grow. It makes an excellent street tree and grows well despite pollution and the heavy use of road salt.

HOW TO PLANT

Plant a balled-and-burlapped specimen by preparing a hole 4 times the width of the rootball. The wider the hole, the more quickly the tree will establish itself. Plant it deep enough so that the top of the rootball is level with the ground around it. Remove any twine or wire from around the trunk. Cut away any burlap or the remaining wire basket to half the height of the rootball. Backfill the hole with the original soil and water deeply. Spread an organic mulch 2 or 3 inches thick around the planting area to help conserve moisture.

ADVICE FOR CARE

Ginkgo takes a long time to recover from transplanting. Even after recovery they have only a medium to slow growth rate; this is a tree we plant for future generations. Ginkgo will develop more rapidly if you provide it with extra care. Broadcast an all-purpose fertilizer around the root zone in early November, especially during the first  10 to 20 years after transplanting. Water the tree throughout the summer with 1 to $1^1/_2$ inches per week. Maintain a 2- to 3-inch layer of organic mulch around the root zone. Prune the tree when young to help stimulate lateral branches. Shape the tree to encourage the ginkgo's strong central leader.

ADDITIONAL INFORMATION

Ginkgo is "dioecious," which means that there are male and female trees. The female tree will develop a fruit about the size of a tan cherry. A soft flesh, well known for its malodorous effect, covers the ginkgo seed inside the fruit. Even the birds won't eat them! Be sure to plant male specimens. Ginkgo is one of the oldest and most primitive cultivated trees; ginkgo fossils millions of years old have been found in North America. Ginkgo extract has recently been promoted for health reasons, but consult your physician before taking it.

ADDITIONAL SPECIES, CULTIVARS, OR VARIETIES

'Autumn Gold' is an improved variety with outstanding yellow fall color. Most of the other improved varieties are extremely columnar in shape and resemble the Lombardy poplar. Two good seedless varieties are 'Princeton Sentry' and 'Fastigiata'.

Green Ash

Fraxinus pennsylvanica

Zones: 5, 6 **Height:** 40 to 60 feet **Type:** Deciduous	**Light Requirement:**

There is hardly a more adaptable and fast-growing shade tree than the green ash; in this age of instant gratification, it is a good choice for "instant shade." Green ash is suitable for any Hoosier landscape and is widely used in the landscape industry. Like its cousin the white ash, the green ash is a native tree in Indiana. In its natural habitat, it grows near streams and rivers and other bottomland locations. In cultivation, green ash adapts to just about any growing condition including confined and urban areas. It develops a broadly spreading, rounded canopy; its glossy compound leaves emerge late in the spring and turn a bright yellow in fall occasionally tinged in purple. When mature, the green ash's bark is deeply fissured and forms irregular diamond shapes that help to identify it.

WHEN TO PLANT

Plant balled-and-burlapped green ash just about any time the soil is dry in spring, summer, or fall. If planting in summer, be sure to keep the soil moist after planting.

WHERE TO PLANT

Plant green ash where fast shade is desired. Give the tree some room to spread, as the crown can reach 30 feet wide. Rows of green ash create a nice avenue effect when planted along a street or driveway. Green ash prefer moist and well-drained soil but will tolerate other soil types.

HOW TO PLANT

Plant a balled-and-burlapped specimen by preparing a hole at least 4 times the width of the rootball. Dig the hole deep enough so the top of the rootball is level with the ground around it after planting. Remove any twine or wire from around the trunk. Cut away the burlap and any wire basket to half the height of the rootball.

Backfill the hole with the original soil and water deeply. Spread a 2- to 3-inch layer of organic mulch over the planting area. Bare-root specimens are much easier to handle because they don't have a heavy rootball. Examine the trunk where it joins the roots to find the soil line and plant the tree only as deep as it was growing in the field. Bare-root specimens will also have to be staked to prevent leaning.

ADVICE FOR CARE
Green ash are tough trees and require little attention, but they will grow more rapidly if you keep the soil moist and fertilized. Water with at least 1 to $1^{1}/_{2}$ inches per week, particularly in summer. Broadcast fertilizer around the root zone in early November, especially during the first 5 to 10 years after transplanting. Green ash tends to have weak wood and narrow crotch angles. Prune at a young age to develop a solid branching pattern. The ash borer will attack when the tree is under stress from drought or other environmental conditions. A spring foliar disease, called anthracnose, causes brown blotches on the leaf margins and near the veins. Temporary leaf drop may result, but the tree will recover.

ADDITIONAL INFORMATION
Although ash is reported to be drought tolerant, instances of stress have been observed in the hot and dry periods of recent summers. Ash is "dioecious," which means that there are male and female trees. Choose the male trees if possible since they will not produce the seeds that are a maintenance nuisance.

ADDITIONAL SPECIES, CULTIVARS, OR VARIETIES
'Marshall's Seedless', 'Patmore', and 'Summit' are all excellent seedless varieties. 'Cimmzam' or cimmaron ash has strong branch angles and develops purplish-bronze fall color instead of the typical yellow.

Hemlock

Tsuga canadensis

Other Name: Canada Hemlock

Zones: 5, 6

Height: 60 to 80 feet

Bloom Period: Small cones in fall

Flowers: Insignificant

Type: Evergreen

Light Requirement:

emlock, a native tree in Indiana, is one of the most useful evergreens you can plant here. When properly sheared, newly planted hemlocks make excellent hedges or dense screens. When trained into a hedge, they provide an excellent background for a perennial flower bed. At its mature height, the hemlock's pendulous, weeping branches create a solid backdrop for smaller flowering trees. Hemlock is easily identified by the silvery-white stripe on the underside of its short, flat needles. As with other evergreens, some of the needles are shed each year; in contrast to other evergreens, especially pines, hemlock needles are small enough to disappear into the lawn.

WHEN TO PLANT

Plant Canada hemlock in spring when the soil is dry enough to crumble, or *early* fall. If planting in fall, be sure to water the tree each week before the ground freezes or it may suffer winter damage. A good layer of organic mulch will also help prevent the needles from drying out.

WHERE TO PLANT

Hemlock prefers moist, well-drained soil that has a high organic matter content. It will not grow in waterlogged soils or exposed and windy sites that dry out during the heat of summer. The soil should be slightly acidic, though hemlocks grow in alkaline environments. It is one of the few conifers that tolerates shade, but it will not be as dense as those grown in full sun.

HOW TO PLANT

Prepare a hole 4 times the width of the rootball. Dig deep enough so that the top of the rootball is level with the ground around it. In

heavy soils where drainage is poor, the tree should be set so that it is a few inches higher than the soil around it. Remove all twine or wire from around the trunk. Cut away any burlap or wire basket to half the height of the rootball. Backfill the hole with the original soil and water deeply. Spread a 2- to 3-inch layer of organic mulch around the planting area.

ADVICE FOR CARE

Hemlock is sensitive to dry planting sites, so be sure to keep it watered with 1 to 1^1/$_2$ inches of water per week, especially in the first 5 years after planting. Evergreens do not require supplemental fertilization. To keep the soil pH slightly acidic, apply sulfur to the root zone after the grass goes dormant in the fall. Prune dead branches each spring. If using hemlock as a hedge, shear regularly because it grows rapidly in this situation. Hemlock has few serious pests in Indiana, but spider mites may cause problems in dry years. Use horticultural oil according to label directions for spider mite control.

ADDITIONAL INFORMATION

Hemlock is often mistakenly planted as a foundation plant near a house. It will quickly outgrow those sites. It has shallow roots, so surrounding turf or other ornamentals will need supplemental watering in the summer. A hemlock has a distinguished terminal branch which bends slightly and will help in identification. Mature trees produce thousands of inch-long brown cones.

ADDITIONAL SPECIES, CULTIVARS, OR VARIETIES

There are few named varieties of Canada hemlock readily available. 'Sargentii' is a weeping form that is much broader than it is tall and makes an outstanding specimen plant.

Japanese Black Pine

Pinus thunbergiana

Other Name: *Pinus thunbergii*
Zones: 5, 6
Height: 15 to 40 feet
Type: Evergreen

Light Requirement:

he Japanese black pine is uncommon in Indiana but worth asking your local nursery representative to find. Native to Japan and Korea, it has a scrubbier shape than most pines, with needles that grow to three or four inches long. Its irregular and open form makes it an excellent accent or specimen plant in the landscape. Unlike the white, red, and Austrian pines which are plagued with numerous problems and almost not worth the trouble, the Japanese black pine is virtually pest-free in the Hoosier state.

WHEN TO PLANT

Japanese black pine prefers spring planting before the leaves or needles emerge. The second-best time to plant is in the early fall, when the soil is still warm; this gives the roots a chance to establish themselves. If planting in the fall, water the tree deeply once a week until the ground freezes to help keep the needles from drying out.

WHERE TO PLANT

Plant Japanese black pine where it will have room to spread. It grows at least half as wide as tall, and looks best in its natural shape. It prefers moist but well-drained soil and is perfect for the sandier sites of southwest Indiana or up around Lake Michigan. Japanese black pine will not grow well in clay. For best results, plant in full sun where the soil is slightly acidic. Partly shaded sites will produce a spindlier tree.

HOW TO PLANT

Prepare a planting hole that is 4 times as wide as the rootball. Dig deep enough so that the top of the rootball is even with the ground around it after planting. Slope the sides of the hole outward from the bottom up to the surface grade. Remove any twine or wire that is wrapped around the trunk. This prevents girdling which could eventually kill your tree. Backfill the hole with the original soil and water deeply. Spread a 2- to 3-inch layer of organic mulch around the planting area.

ADVICE FOR CARE
Japanese black pine needs very little care. It tolerates dry soil and drought conditions very well. Despite its rugged nature, it will grow best if it receives from 1 to $1^1/2$ inches of water each week, especially during the height of summer. Maintain a 2- to 3-inch layer of organic mulch around the root zone to help preserve moisture and keep the roots cool. Pines and other evergreens do not require fertilization. Japanese black pine prefers an acidic soil pH; adjust the soil pH by adding sulfur in late fall after the grass goes dormant. Prune dead branches as needed.

ADDITIONAL INFORMATION
Japanese black pine will naturalize in sandy soils and is extremely tolerant of salt. For these reasons it is used to stabilize dunes on the east coast and other seashore locales. In extreme northern Indiana, Japanese black pine may develop tip burn from severe cold weather. Plants around Lake Michigan should not have this problem due to the water's warming effect. A note for the crafty sort: these pines are prolific cone producers.

ADDITIONAL SPECIES, CULTIVARS, OR VARIETIES
There are very few varieties which are hard to locate. 'Majestic Beauty' is tolerant of pollution, making it an attractive variety for urban planting. The eastern white pine, *Pinus strobus*, is a popular species of pine for Indiana. It is a relatively fast grower but for uncertain reasons suffers decline and sudden death in some locations. Austrian pine, *Pinus nigra*, is also very popular but extremely susceptible to diplodia tip blight, a common pine disease in the Midwest.

Japanese Maple

Acer palmatum

	Light Requirement:
Zones: 5, 6 **Height:** 10 to 25 feet **Type:** Deciduous	

*T*he Japanese maple is the "queen" of small trees in the garden. Its lacy leaves in a wide variety of colors have made it hugely popular. The colorful leaves lend interest to the garden at a time in the season when many perennials and flowering shrubs have taken a break from blooming. As its name suggests, this maple is native to Japan and Korea, where breeders have developed hundreds of different varieties which differ in height and growth habit, such as spreading branches vs. weeping, leaf color, and the degree to which the leaves are naturally cut or dissected. The Japanese maple should be planted as a specimen tree where the home owner can enjoy the beautiful leaves which subtly change color throughout the season. Japanese maple also works well in mixed-flower borders as an accent plant or background screen. Some varieties have brilliant red fall color. Japanese maple has a medium to slow growth rate.

WHEN TO PLANT

Plant the Japanese maple in either spring or fall. When planting in spring, wait until after the last expected frost in your area because the leaves can be sensitive to a late freeze. Although many small trees can withstand summer planting with proper care, avoid planting a Japanese maple during the heat of June, July, and August.

WHERE TO PLANT

Plant the Japanese maple in slightly acidic soil that has plenty of organic matter and good drainage. It prefers sunny to partly sunny locations but should not be subject to heavy winds; a partially sheltered location is ideal. Since many Japanese maple varieties require extra watering in the heat of Indiana summers, be sure to plant them in a part of the yard you can reach with the hose.

HOW TO PLANT

Prepare a planting hole 4 times the width of the rootball. Plant balled-and-burlapped or container-grown trees so that the bottom of the rootball is resting on the bottom of the hole. Remove any twine or wire wrapped around the trunk. Cut away burlap or wire baskets to half the height of the rootball. Amend the soil with plenty of peat, compost, or other organic matter, especially when planting container-grown stock. Replace the amended soil in the original planting hole. Water, using a soaker hose so that the water soaks deeply in to the ground. Spread a 2-inch layer of organic mulch around the tree at least as wide as the planting hole.

ADVICE FOR CARE

Keep Japanese maples moist throughout the summer. Water at least 1 to 1$^1/_2$ inches per week. Be sure to apply an organic mulch each season to help keep the roots cool and moist during hot and dry spells. Prune out dead branches. Fertilize around Thanksgiving with an all-purpose granular or an organic fertilizer. Japanese maples have few problems with pests. Container-grown Japanese maples need extensive protection in winter.

ADDITIONAL INFORMATION

Leaf color will change slightly according to sun exposure. Purple-leafed varieties retain more green in the leaf in shadier sites. For the adventurous, Japanese maples are good to try as bonsai. There are some Japanese maple bonsai specimens at the National Arboretum in Washington, D.C, that are hundreds of years old.

ADVICE FOR REGIONAL CARE

Select only varieties recommended as hardy to plant in Zones 5 and 6. Japanese maples are not reliably hardy in Zone 5A.

ADDITIONAL SPECIES, CULTIVARS, OR VARIETIES

The variety 'Bloodgood' has typical Japanese maple foliage with deep-red leaves. It is one of the best selections for Indiana gardens. 'Burgundy Lace', another red-leafed variety, has more finely dissected leaves. 'Crimson Queen' and 'Ornatum' have cascading and mound-like growth habits, and are excellent along pathways and in rock gardens.

Japanese Tree Lilac

Syringa reticulata

Zones: 5, 6
Height: 15 to 30 feet
Bloom Period: May to June
Flowers: Creamy white panicles
Type: Deciduous

Light Requirement:

*W*hen I first saw this impressive tree used effectively in the garden, I immediately recalled landscape design classes I had taken as a student. Landscape architects often talk about creating "rooms" in the landscape just as building architects create in the home. In this particular landscape, the tree lilacs were definitely functioning as the "walls." With their thick, dark-green leaves that closely resemble those of their cousin, the common lilac, tree lilacs make excellent screens or background plants. Their strong branches and reddish-brown bark make them enjoyable to look at even in winter. Tree lilacs grow more graceful with age as their branches arch outward toward the tips. Flowers are large, bold, creamy-white panicles up to eight inches long; they grow wide at the base and taper to a point. Their fragrance is different from the common lilac and is often described as closer to privet. Tree lilacs have a medium growth rate.

—T.T.

WHEN TO PLANT
Plant tree lilac in either spring or fall, when the ground is workable. When planting in summer, be sure to water well.

WHERE TO PLANT
Tree lilac tolerates wide ranges of pH and should grow well in just about any Indiana soil. It will reward the grower with more flowers when planted in full sun. Plant as a background screen in the flower border or around the corners of buildings to help soften the edges.

HOW TO PLANT
Plant balled-and-burlapped or container-grown specimens after digging a hole 4 times the width of the rootball. Gradually taper the sides of the hole outward from the bottom to the existing grade.

Plant the tree so that it rests at the bottom of the hole and the top of the rootball is level with the ground around it. Remove any twine or wire from around the trunk and cut away burlap and wire baskets to half the height of the rootball. Backfill the hole with the original soil and water deeply. Spread a 2-inch layer of organic mulch around the entire planting area.

ADVICE FOR CARE

The Japanese tree lilac requires very little maintenance. Prune dead flowers after they fade in June to encourage more blooms the following year. Remove any dead branches or prune to shape immediately after flowering as well. Broadcast an all-purpose fertilizer in early November, especially during the first 10 years after transplanting. Japanese tree lilac is only occasionally bothered by the powdery mildew that plagues the common lilac. Water the tree with 1 to $1^1/2$ inches of water per week in the summer, when it is setting buds for next year. This will ensure maximum bloom the following year.

ADDITIONAL INFORMATION

Seeds of the Japanese or "Giant" tree lilac were sent from Japan to America in 1876. Unlike some other introduced species, they don't "take over" and are relatively trouble free in Indiana. They can be pruned into a multi-stemmed form that is more interesting to observe in the winter garden. Like the common lilac, if this tree gets out of hand it can be rejuvenated by cutting it down to the ground. Tree lilacs make excellent street trees; some cities promote them for this purpose. They may prove hard to find at your local nursery or garden center, though most nurseries will find one for you if you order ahead.

ADDITIONAL SPECIES, CULTIVARS, OR VARIETIES

The most common variety is called 'Ivory Silk'. It grows to 20 feet but produces more flowers than other varieties. A similar variety called 'Summer Snow' is slower growing and shorter. 'Regent' is the fastest-growing variety.

Kousa Dogwood

Cornus kousa

Zones: 5, 6
Height: 20 to 30 feet
Bloom Period: May to June
Flowers: White
Type: Deciduous

Light Requirement:

Kousa dogwoods are often overlooked in favor of their more popular relatives, the native flowering dogwoods (*Cornus florida*). But Kousas are just as beautiful in bloom and have numerous other positive attributes as well. They bloom later in spring than the native dogwood; the flowers open well after the Kousa dogwood has set leaves, and when most other spring-blooming trees have finished. The blooms are extremely long lived, remaining on the tree for up to six weeks. Each Kousa dogwood flower has four pointed bracts; the leaves resemble the native flowering types and turn a dull, bronzy red in the fall. As the plant matures, it develops very distinguished, elegant horizontal branches and will sometimes grow as wide as it is tall. In late summer it produces an unusual-looking fruit that resembles a large raspberry. The Kousa dogwood is virtually trouble free and will prove to be more reliable than the native type, which may be troubled with disease and exposure problems.

WHEN TO PLANT

Plant Kousa dogwood in spring or fall, when the ground is easily worked. If planting in the summer, be sure to provide plenty of water as dogwood can be slightly sensitive to drought.

WHERE TO PLANT

The Kousa dogwood prefers soils with a slightly acidic pH. The soil should be moist but well drained and have plenty of organic matter. Kousa dogwood will reward the gardener with more blooms if planted in sunny locations, although they tolerate dappled shade. Plant them as background plants in the shrub or flower border, or in corners where nothing else seems to work.

HOW TO PLANT

Prepare a planting hole at least 2 to 3 times the size of the rootball. Dig the hole only deep enough so that when the base of the rootball is sitting on the bottom of the hole, the top of the rootball is level with the ground around it. Remove all the twine or wire from around the trunk. Cut away the burlap and wire baskets to half the height of the rootball. Backfill the hole with the original soil and water it deeply. Spread a 2-inch layer of organic mulch around the planting site. Plant Kousa dogwoods 10 to 15 feet apart to form a nice screen or background for the flower border.

ADVICE FOR CARE

Kousa dogwood, which requires minimal care, will reward the gardener with year-round satisfaction. Remove dead branches or prune to shape after the tree finishes blooming in late spring. This will ensure maximum flower production for the following year. Broadcast an all-purpose fertilizer in early November, especially during the first 5 to 10 years after transplanting. Maintain a 2- to 3-inch layer of organic mulch to help keep the roots cool and moist, especially in the heat of summer.

ADDITIONAL INFORMATION

After its flowers, the horizontal branching habit of the Kousa dogwood is its most attractive attribute. Use this tree to break up vertical lines at the corners of buildings. For maximum fruit production in the fall, plant at least two specimens. The Kousa dogwood is preferred over the flowering dogwood in today's land-scapes because the latter is extremely prone to disease, especially anthracnose, which is decimating native dogwood stands in the Northeastern and some Midwestern states.

ADDITIONAL SPECIES, CULTIVARS, OR VARIETIES

'China Girl' and 'Milky Way' are excellent white varieties of Kousa. 'Rosabella' has pink bracts. 'Gold Star' has variegated gold-and-green leaves with white bracts. 'Summer Stars' has been known to retain its bracts until late summer.

Littleleaf Linden

Tilia cordata

Zones: 5, 6
Height: 60 to 80 feet
Bloom Period: June
Flowers: Yellowish-green, very fragrant
Type: Deciduous

Light Requirement:

For those gardeners fond of fragrant plants, a littleleaf will become the backbone of the garden. This tree is the unusual exception to the rule that shade trees don't have interesting flowers. Lush, green, heart-shaped leaves emerge in spring and are followed by clusters of pendulous flowers that send a sweet scent into the June air. The blooms themselves, a rather dull yellow-green, are no match for a dogwood or crab apple, but what they lack in flash they easily make up for in fragrance. Littleleaf lindens also make excellent shade trees. Their dense, pyramidal canopy casts heavy shade on the ground around it. They have a medium to slow growth rate but will eventually reach an average height of seventy feet under ideal conditions. The littleleaf linden is a smaller European relative of the American linden, or basswood, *Tilia americana*. The basswood can reach heights of over 100 feet, as did the one in the landscape of my childhood home. It was so tall with branches so out-of-reach that I don't ever recall noticing the fragrance, which was probably lost in the wind—all the more reason to plant its smaller cousin, the littleleaf linden!

—T.T.

WHEN TO PLANT

Transplant balled-and-burlapped specimens in spring or fall when the ground is dry.

WHERE TO PLANT

Littleleaf linden prefers soil that is moist but well drained with plenty of organic matter. It does, however, tolerate compact soil and confined areas making it one of the most common street trees around. It also does well despite pollution and other urban ills, though leaf scorching has been noticed during the height of summer. Littleleaf linden has no preference for pH and will grow in either acidic or alkaline soil. In the home landscape, plant linden for an avenue effect along the driveway, or as a screen or specimen plant.

HOW TO PLANT

Prepare a hole 4 times the width of the rootball. Dig deep enough so that the top of the rootball is level with the ground around it after planting. Remove any twine or wire from around the trunk of the tree and cut away the burlap and wire basket to half the height of the rootball. Backfill the hole with the original soil and water deeply. Spread a 2- to 3-inch layer of organic mulch around the planting area.

ADVICE FOR CARE

Littleleaf linden requires average care, though regular watering and fertilization will help it grow more rapidly. Broadcast an all-purpose fertilizer in early November, especially during the first 5 to 10 years after transplanting. In summer, be sure to water the tree with 1 to 1^1/$_2$ inches of water per week, especially during dry spells. Soaker hoses help the water get directly to the roots. Prune dead branches; corrective pruning is not normally necessary. Linden's most notorious pest is the Japanese beetle, which seems to like this tree as much as it likes roses. Though the beetles cause much cosmetic damage by chewing the leaves, the long-term health of the tree is rarely jeopardized. Sunscald will sometimes injure linden in winter.

ADDITIONAL INFORMATION

Littleleaf linden adapts well to heavy shearing and would make an excellent tree for hedges in a more formal garden. It is very hardy and makes a good container tree for very large raised planters.

ADDITIONAL SPECIES, CULTIVARS, OR VARIETIES

The most common variety of littleleaf linden is 'Greenspire'. This variety is planted in the majority of landscapes that call for linden. 'Prestige' and 'Redmond' are both fast growers but are harder to find.

Redbud

Cercis canadensis

Zone: 5, 6
Height: 15 to 30 feet
Bloom Period: April
Flowers: Rose-pink, white
Type: Deciduous

Light Requirement:

*N*o tree symbolizes the arrival of spring in Indiana more than the redbud. It is one of our best-loved native trees. Redbud blooms with the spring flush of new leaves, usually at the same time as the dogwood. It grows on the edge of the forest, in old fence rows, and in suburban landscapes. Though it does best in its natural setting, redbud tolerates urban conditions quite well. Branches grow upright and spreading and give the tree a stately appearance when it is in bloom. The deep-red, almost purple, buds open to reveal rose-pink flowers held tightly to the branches. A close-up view of the flowers through a window is breathtaking. The heart-shaped leaves can reach five to six inches in length and give the tree a more rounded appearance. Fall color is a rather dull yellow.

WHEN TO PLANT

Plant redbud in spring or fall when the ground is workable. Redbud will tolerate summer planting if it is watered deeply on a weekly basis.

WHERE TO PLANT

Redbud prefers moist but well-drained soil that has plenty of organic matter. It tolerates acidic or alkaline soil pH and should adapt to just about any planting site in Indiana except heavy clay. It prefers full sun but will do well in a partly shaded location.

HOW TO PLANT

Prepare the site by digging a hole 4 times the width of the rootball. Dig deep enough so that the top of the rootball is level with the ground around it. Remove the planting container or cut away any twine or wire from around the trunk. If planting a balled-and-burlapped specimen, cut away the burlap and wire basket to half the height of the rootball. Backfill the hole with the original soil and water well. Spread a 2- to 3-inch layer of organic mulch around the planting site.

ADVICE FOR CARE

Prune away dead branches, or prune redbud to its natural shape in spring right after it has bloomed. Many redbuds grow in clump form with two or three trunks growing on the same root system. Prune to encourage this natural growth habit. Broadcast an all-purpose fertilizer around the root zone in early November, especially during the first 5 to 10 years after transplanting. Keep the redbud well watered in summer, especially during dry spells. Redbuds will occasionally suffer from a wilt or a canker-causing disease. The symptoms usually appear as sudden death of scattered branches on the tree. Over the years, wilt can be fatal to redbuds, but they reseed readily and sometimes sprout suckers that seem immune. There is no effective treatment to relieve the problem. Remove the dead branches and keep the tree free from stress to prolong its life.

ADDITIONAL INFORMATION

Redbuds produce seed in a flat pod that will provide the gardener with volunteer trees for years to come. Many a Hoosier gardener has brought seedling trees back from the farm or a country cabin to suburbia for planting. Redbud blooms are edible and will help brighten a dull green salad in spring.

ADDITIONAL SPECIES, CULTIVARS, OR VARIETIES

'Forest Pansy' produces bright-purple leaves after blooming. The leaf color will fade after May or June. It is hardy only in Zone 6 in Indiana. 'Flame' has double flowers and is a vigorous grower. 'Royal White' and 'Alba' are both white varieties; the former has larger flowers than 'Alba' and blooms longer.

Red Maple

Acer rubrum

Zones: 5, 6
Height: 40 to 60 feet
Type: Deciduous

Light Requirement:

*T*he red maple is a popular shade tree with a medium to fast growth rate. Native to Indiana, it grows well in most soils and tolerates the stress of urban areas. Red maple has an oval shape when mature and may grow to over 100 feet tall in its native habitat. Its leaves emerge from red buds that swell in late winter and announce the arrival of spring. Leaves have three to five lobes, or points, and are slightly smaller than other maple species. They remain a dark, glossy green throughout the summer. The red petiole, which attaches the leaf to the stem, helps distinguish the red maple from other maples. The red fall color can be outstanding. It is unfortunate that red maples were not planted years ago when all the silver maples were planted. Our fall landscapes would be more beautiful, and our pruning bills would be lower.

WHEN TO PLANT

Red maple is slow to grow new roots after transplanting. Plant a balled-and-burlapped specimen in early spring just as the new growth starts; this will give it the longest growing season possible in its first year. The second-best time to plant is in the fall after the leaves drop.

WHERE TO PLANT

Red maple prefers moist but well-drained loamy soil with a neutral to acidic pH. In alkaline soil, it may undergo a process called "chlorosis," in which a nutrient deficiency causes the leaves to turn yellow. Red maple tolerates heavy, wet soil and adapts well to low spots in the landscape. It makes a nice specimen tree in the yard or in a row along the driveway or property line. Red maple is popular in new housing developments and is excellent for planting along the street.

TREES

HOW TO PLANT
Plant balled-and-burlapped specimens by preparing a hole 4 times the width of the rootball. Dig the hole deep enough so that the top of the rootball when planted is level with the ground around it. Remove any twine or wire from around the trunk of the tree. Cut away the burlap and wire basket to half the height of the rootball. Any synthetic covering for the rootball such as plastic should be completely removed. Backfill the hole with the original soil and water well. Spread a 2-inch layer of organic mulch around the planting area.

ADVICE FOR CARE
Water the tree with 1 to 1^1/$_2$ inches of water each week, especially during the first five years after transplanting. Broadcast fertilizer around the root zone in early November to encourage faster growth. Maintain a 2- to 3-inch layer of mulch around the planting area. Prune dead branches any time, but prune to shape the tree in mid-summer or late fall. Like other maples, the red maple is a "bleeder" and will leak excessive sap from a pruning cut made in spring.

ADDITIONAL INFORMATION
Red maple has shallow roots and may cause the lawn to brown more quickly during dry spells. Fall color is not always as reliably "spectacular" as described. Be sure to choose varieties known for good coloration. There are no major pests that cause regular problems, but red maple is known to get sunscald in winter or leaf scorch in summer.

ADDITIONAL SPECIES, CULTIVARS, OR VARIETIES
'Red Sunset' is the most reliable and colorful variety. 'October Glory' is another excellent choice. 'Columnare' has a much narrower and more upright form that works well for more limited spaces. Avoid planting silver maple, *Acer saccharinum*, at all costs. It is a weedy, trashy, weak-wooded tree with a shallow root system that will invade drain tiles and septics.

River Birch

Betula nigra

Zones: 5, 6
Height: 50 to 70 feet
Type: Deciduous

Light Requirement:

*R*iver birch is a plant lover's tree; it changes each season to reveal another unique characteristic. Like other birches in late winter, the river birch develops male flowers called "catkins" which hang at least two inches from the branches. Following the flowers are pyramid-shaped river birch leaves of a dark, glossy green; the edges are highly serrated. The leaves turn bright yellow in the fall. Winter reveals a trunk and branches with beautiful beige bark. The outer layers of bark peel away to reveal lighter inner bark with a creamy color. On older trees, the bark tears off in large sheets. Plant this tree near an evergreen background with some spring daffodils at the base for an exquisite effect. River birch is also the solution for the gardener who has to have a fast-growing tree. It is an all-around outstanding landscape plant.

WHEN TO PLANT

River birch is slow to regenerate new roots after transplanting. Plant it in early spring for best results. The second-best time for planting is late fall.

WHERE TO PLANT

As the name suggests, river birch likes moisture and can tolerate low spots that hold a lot of water. It grows alongside stream banks in its native habitat but also tolerates drier soils. The ideal site should be moist but well-drained with high organic matter content. River birch does best in acidic soil and sometimes will develop chlorosis in alkaline planting conditions. Chlorosis causes the leaves to turn yellow while the leaf veins stay green. Plant river birch close to the patio for shade or near a window so you can enjoy the bark in winter.

How to Plant

Plant balled-and-burlapped specimens by preparing a planting hole 4 times the width of the rootball. Dig the hole deep enough so that the top of the rootball is level with the ground around it. Remove any twine or wire from around the trunk and cut away the burlap or wire basket to half the height of the rootball. Backfill with the original soil and water deeply. Spread a 2- to 3-inch layer of organic mulch around the planting area.

Advice for Care

River birch needs 1 to 1^1/$_2$ inches of water each week, especially in the heat of summer. During prolonged dry weather, random leaves will turn yellow and drop to the ground to protect the birch from drought. Broadcast an all-purpose fertilizer around the root zone in early November, especially during the first 5 to 10 years after transplanting. Prune to remove dead branches or shape in midsummer or late fall. River birch is resistant to the bronze birch borer, an insect responsible for the early demise of countless white birch trees each year.

Additional Information

The river birch is a native tree in Indiana and adapts to many growing conditions. It grows as a single stem or a multi-stem, clump-forming specimen. The multi-stem form is more interesting.

Additional Species, Cultivars, or Varieties

White birch, *Betula papyrifera*, is a popular tree in Indiana but only has a life expectancy of around 10 years due to borers. If you water the tree regularly in summer and keep it free from stress, you may avoid the dead stems and trunks commonly seen in white birch. Resist the temptation to plant a white, and plant 'Heritage' river birch instead. It is an outstanding variety and has the Pennsylvania Horticultural Society's Gold Medal award to prove it!

Serbian Spruce

Picea omorika

Zones: 5, 6	Light Requirement:
Height: 50 to 60 feet	
Type: Evergreen	

Though not as widely known as the Colorado blue or the Norway spruce, the Serbian spruce is far superior to both for this area. Spruce are native to more northerly climates than Indiana and it is surprising that any of them tolerate our hot and humid summers. While the Colorado and Norway spruce are bothered by spider mites, needlecast, and other problems, the Serbian spruce is not. It has few if any difficulties with our growing conditions, and will grow as tall as sixty or seventy feet, though the base usually grows to only twenty-five feet wide. The Serbian spruce's shape and texture define the word "graceful." Its branches droop outward from the trunk, but not too far, and turn slightly up at the tip as if to "curtsy" to neighboring trees. The upper surface of the needles are dark green; two whitish-blue stripes run the length of the underside.

WHEN TO PLANT

Plant the Serbian spruce in spring, preferably before new growth starts. The second-best time to plant is in early fall while the soil is still warm. If planting in the fall, help prevent the needles from drying in winter by watering the tree deeply once a week until the ground freezes.

WHERE TO PLANT

Serbian spruce prefers moist but well-drained organic soil. Unlike most evergreens, which prefer acidic soil, the Serbian spruce also grows well under alkaline conditions. It tolerates pollution and makes an excellent evergreen for the urban environment. Unlike the Norway spruce, which grows far too wide, or the Colorado blue, whose color dominates the landscape, the Serbian spruce can be planted closer to the house to soften corners. It shows its best when planted as a group in the corner of the yard, and makes an excellent screen at the same time. Spruce provide good cover for nesting birds.

How to Plant
Plant a balled-and-burlapped specimen in a hole that is 4 times the width of the rootball. Dig the hole deep enough so that the top of the rootball is level with the ground around it. Be sure to remove all twine and wire from around the trunk and cut away the burlap and wire basket to half the height of the rootball. Backfill the hole with the original soil and water well. Spread a 2- to 3-inch layer of organic mulch around the planting area.

Advice for Care
Serbian spruce is almost maintenance free. It is not necessary to fertilize evergreens such as spruce since they fend for themselves much better than their deciduous counterparts do. Keep them watered with 1 to 1¹/₂ inches of water each week. Prune only to remove dead or dying branches. Because the branches are so pendulous, don't shear Serbian spruce as is sometimes done with the Norway species.

Additional Information
It is especially important to keep newly planted spruce well watered into the very late fall. Evergreens continue to lose water through their needles when the temperature is above forty-five degrees. They need a steady supply of water in the soil to replace what is lost, or they may suffer tip burn during the winter. In Zone 5A in extreme northern Indiana the Serbian spruce may be more prone to tip burn than in other parts of the state.

Additional Species, Cultivars, or Varieties
'Pendula' is a shorter variety with a weeping habit. 'Nana' is a dwarf and rarely grows taller than 8 or 10 feet. The Norway spruce, *Picea abies*, and the Colorado blue spruce, *Picea pungens*, are good substitutes for the Serbian, but more prone to problems. The Norway spruce is a good windbreak in open areas.

TREES

Serviceberry

Amelanchier × grandiflora

Other Names: Shadblow, Juneberry,
   Apple Serviceberry
Zones: 5, 6
Height: 15 to 40 feet
Bloom Period: April (fruits in June)
Flowers: White (fruit, purplish-black)
Type: Deciduous

Light Requirement:

Serviceberry is a tree for year-round enjoyment. Its large white flower clusters are the first to open in spring along with the early daffodils. Native species of serviceberry are easily recognized blooming on the edge of the woods before anything else is ready. The plentiful fruit, which quickly follows in June, provides food for the birds. The smooth, shiny green leaves cast a touch of elegance on the garden as they shimmer in summer breezes. Fall color in serviceberry is a brilliant orange red that lasts for a few weeks. Plant serviceberry near the house to enjoy the smooth gray bark in winter; hang a feeder to enjoy both the birds and the bark.

When to Plant

Plant serviceberry in spring when the soil can be worked, or fall. If planting in summer, be sure to water deeply on a weekly basis.

Where to Plant

A native plant in Indiana, serviceberry will tolerate a wide range of soil types. Be sure the soil is moist but well drained with plenty of organic matter. Serviceberry prefers soils with an acidic pH but will grow in slightly alkaline soils as well. It is one of the few flowering trees that does well in a partly shaded environment. Windy and exposed sites are not recommended. Serviceberry makes an excellent small patio tree, so plant it around your outdoor sitting area.

How to Plant

Prepare a planting hole 4 times the width of the rootball. Dig the hole deep enough so that the top of the rootball is level with the ground around it. Remove any twine or wire from around the trunk and cut away the burlap or wire basket to half the height of the rootball. Backfill the hole with the original soil and water deeply. Spread a 2- to 3-inch layer of organic mulch around the planting site.

ADVICE FOR CARE
Serviceberry likes deep, moist soils, so maintain a mulch layer up to 2 or 3 inches thick. Keep the tree well watered during the predictable "hot and dry spells" we have each summer. A yearly application of sulfur after Thanksgiving will help keep the pH in the acidic range. *Amelanchier × grandiflora* is much less prone to some common problems that plague the native serviceberry such as rust, fire blight, or mites. Prune any deadwood and shape into the more interesting and valuable clump form. Broadcast an all-purpose fertilizer in early November, especially during the first 5 to 10 years after transplanting. Beware of Japanese beetles which sometimes make a meal of serviceberry. Knock them into a pot of boiling water to help reduce damage.

ADDITIONAL INFORMATION
Juneberries make wonderful pies and jams if you can beat the birds to the fruit. *Amelanchier × grandiflora* is a hybrid of two native species, *A. arborea* and *A. laevis*.

ADDITIONAL SPECIES, CULTIVARS, OR VARIETIES
'Autumn Brilliance', 'Cole's Select', and 'Princess Diana' all have spectacular fall color. 'Robin Hill' blooms before any other serviceberry on the market. *Amelanchier laevis* 'Cumulus' is a fast grower with upright form that makes a nice screen or background for the flower or shrub border. Its natural tendency to grow as a single trunk makes it useful as a street tree.

Shingle Oak

Quercus imbricaria

Zones: 5, 6	**Light Requirement:**
Height: 50 to 60 feet	
Bloom Period: Spring	
Flowers: Insignificant; acorns in fall	
Type: Deciduous	

Shingle oaks, like other oaks and large shade trees, form the foundation or "backbone" of the landscape. The shade cast by their massive canopies helps cool nearby buildings in summer, while the trees themselves serve as windbreaks in winter. The shingle oak's glossy-green, narrow leaves more closely resemble willow than they do the heavily lobed shapes of other oaks. The leaves turn a golden yellow in fall, then brown, and persist on the branches well into winter. Some gardeners find this distracting in the landscape, especially since the leaves gradually drop off in winter. However, the rustling of leaves on windy days brings some relief during the bitter cold of January and February. Shingle oak is a native tree in Indiana and has a medium growth rate.

WHEN TO PLANT

Plant shingle oak in spring, after the soil is dry enough to work in and preferably before the leaves emerge. Do not plant shingle oak or any oak in the fall. Shingle oak is typically easier to transplant than other oaks, which are sometimes slow to recover from transplant shock.

WHERE TO PLANT

Since shingle oak tolerates acidic or alkaline soil, it makes an excellent choice for all parts of the state. It prefers moist but well-drained soil with plenty of room to grow. Plant shingle oak as a screen or windbreak in wide open areas like parks or golf courses. It also makes a good street tree and tolerates city conditions quite well. Shingle oak responds well to shearing and will make a nice formal hedge when pruned in this way.

How to Plant

Prepare a planting hole 4 times the width of the rootball. Plant the shingle oak deep enough so that the top of the rootball is level with the ground around it after planting. Untie any twine or wire that is wrapped around the trunk and cut away the burlap or wire basket up to half the height of the rootball. With all oak species, be careful not to let the soil break away from the roots during planting. Backfill the hole with the original soil and water deeply. Spread a 2- to 3-inch layer of organic mulch over the planting area.

Advice for Care

A shingle oak has a medium growth rate but can be encouraged to grow faster with a little extra care. Water with 1 to 1^1/$_2$ inches of moisture each week during the growing season. Broadcast an all-purpose fertilizer in early November, especially during the first 10 to 20 years after transplanting. Prune dead branches in spring after the leaves emerge. Like many oaks, the shingle oak is occasionally bothered by galls. When the tree is young and the galls are easy to reach, removing them with pruning shears should not be a problem. Larger trees might be more of a challenge. Fortunately, the galls cause no long-term damage.

Additional Information

Shingle oak was used by the early settlers for roofing tiles. The Latin word *imbrex* means "tile." In this instance, it is easy to see how the tree was named *Quercus imbricaria*.

Additional Species, Cultivars, or Varieties

There are no improved varieties of shingle oak available. The shingle oak is often passed over in favor of the much overplanted pin oak, *Quercus palustris*. With age, pin oak becomes extremely sensitive to alkaline soil conditions and will develop yellow leaves which eventually turn brown. Shingle oak is an excellent substitute for pin oak and should be used in all situations where soil pH is unknown. Use the pin oak in acidic soils only.

Staghorn Sumac

Rhus typhina

Zones: 5, 6
Height: 15 to 25 feet
Bloom Period: June to July (fruits in fall through winter)
Flowers: Greenish-yellow (fruit, crimson)
Type: Deciduous

Light Requirement:

*S*taghorn sumac gets its name from the thick, velvety, upright branches left after the leaves drop in the fall; they resemble deer antlers. The flowers open in an erect, tightly packed, light-green panicle that turns deep red when mature. The bristly red fruit will last until early spring and provide great winter interest in the bleak Indiana landscape. The compound leaves of the staghorn sumac have leaflets eight inches long. They resemble a walnut leaf from a distance, but are much smaller and more delicate. Staghorn sumac's greatest attribute is perhaps the spectacular fiery red fall color of its leaves. In their natural environment they grow in large groupings that "light up" a hillside or bank. The deep-red fuzzy berries stand erect above the "flames."

WHEN TO PLANT

Staghorn sumac is tough and can be planted any time the soil is dry in spring, summer, or fall. If planting in the summer, be sure to water deeply on a weekly basis to reduce transplant shock.

WHERE TO PLANT

Plant staghorn sumac where it will receive plenty of sun. Related species are known as weed trees and will grow in the cracks of cement. Staghorn will also tolerate tough conditions, so plant it where nothing else seems to grow. It prefers well-drained to dry soil and suckers freely if given ample space. Plant where there is plenty of room along a creek bank, hillside, or anywhere you desire a natural, grove-like effect.

How to Plant

Transplant balled-and-burlapped or container specimens after digging a hole 4 times the width of the rootball. Place the tree in the planting hole so that the top of the rootball is level with the ground around it. Remove any twine or wire from around the trunk and cut away the burlap and wire basket to half the height of the rootball. Backfill with the original soil and water deeply. Spread an organic mulch to 3 inches deep around the planting area.

Advice for Care

Staghorn sumac requires very little care. Remove any deadwood down to the ground each spring. In smaller planting areas you may have to keep the suckers in check with regular pruning. Although staghorn is prone to a canker disease that causes some stems to die back each year, it quickly produces new canes to replace the dead ones. Once established, this tree should not require fertilizer or extra water.

Additional Information

Some still may consider this a weed tree. Named varieties used in the landscape may change your mind. Not only is the fuzzy fruit attractive while still on the tree, but staghorn sumac leaves also look great, even garish, in dried arrangements. Their red color makes them a perfect addition to holiday trees, wreaths, or garlands. In today's fast-paced society, the staghorn sumac fills the need for a "fast-growing" tree.

Additional Species, Cultivars, or Varieties

'Laciniata' makes an outstanding short specimen with highly dissected leaves. *Rhus glabra* is closely related to *R. typhina* and differs only by having smooth rather than velvety bark.

Sugar Maple

Acer saccharum

Other Name: Hard Maple	**Light Requirement:**
Zones: 5, 6	
Height: 60 to 80 feet	
Type: Deciduous	

Sugar maple is unmatched by any other tree for its brilliant fall color. Hordes of tourists flock to New England and Canada like pilgrims each fall to view the turning of the maple leaves. The reds, oranges, and yellows look like balls of fire in the landscape. In summer, the sugar maple's rounded to pyramidal canopy helps to keep nearby buildings much cooler. The tree casts very dense shade that makes it nearly impossible to grow grass beneath it. Sugar maple has a medium growth rate and develops coarsely furrowed gray bark when mature.

WHEN TO PLANT

Transplant balled-and-burlapped specimens of sugar maple in spring before the leaves emerge or in fall after the leaves drop. If transplanting in summer, be sure to provide adequate moisture.

WHERE TO PLANT

Sugar maple thrives in moist but well-drained high-organic soil not unlike its native soil. It prefers slightly acidic conditions and if planted in such will reward you with faster growth; but it also grows in alkaline environments and is commonly found throughout all soil types in Indiana. Plant it away from the house where you'll be able to observe the fall color in all its glory. Unlike red maples, sugar maple dislikes heavy or compact soil. It does not tolerate salts, so planting close to the street is not a wise choice in most cities. Sugar maple will grow well in full sun or partial shade.

HOW TO PLANT

Prepare a planting hole 4 times the width of the rootball. Gradually slope the sides of the hole outward from the bottom up to ground level. Plant the tree so that the top of the rootball is even with the ground around it. Remove any twine or wire from around the trunk to prevent girdling. Cut away the burlap and wire basket to half the height of the rootball. Backfill the hole with the original soil and water deeply. Spread a 2- to 3-inch layer of organic mulch over the planting area.

ADVICE FOR CARE

Sugar maple will grow faster if you provide it with a little extra care. Be sure to water the tree with at least 1 to $1^1/2$ inches of water per week during the growing season. This is especially important during the dry months of summer. Sugar maple will scorch around the leaf margins during long dry spells. Maintain a 2- to 3-inch layer of organic mulch around the tree to help preserve moisture and to keep the roots cool. Prune dead branches or prune to shape in June, or after leaves drop in the fall. Pruning in the spring will cause excessive amounts of sap to "bleed" from the pruning cut. Although this does not hurt the tree, it is unsightly.

ADDITIONAL INFORMATION

Sugar maple is one of the most beloved trees in Indiana and across the eastern part of North America. It is the "state tree" for four states and the national symbol of Canada. Many Boy Scouts, Girl Scouts, and would-be naturalists have tapped the sugar maple in late winter in search of sap for maple syrup.

ADDITIONAL SPECIES, CULTIVARS, OR VARIETIES

'Green Mountain' is the most common variety in Indiana and rightly so. It resists scorch from hot and dry weather better than any other variety. 'Legacy' has thick leaves and a dense canopy that is also very drought resistant. 'Commemoration' is a fast-growing cultivar that colors earlier than most other maples in the fall. For smaller planting sites, 'Goldspire' is an excellent choice for its narrow canopy, scorch resistance, and beautiful golden leaves in the fall.

Sweet Bay Magnolia

Magnolia virginiana

Zones: 5, 6	**Light Requirement:**
Height: 15 to 25 feet	
Bloom Period: May-June, sporadically during summer (fruits, summer to fall)	
Flowers: Creamy white (fruit, brown pods with bright-red seeds)	
Type: Deciduous	

Sweet bay magnolia blooms after the "spring rush" of early flowering trees like redbud and crab apple. It is a "quiet bloomer" that lacks the gaudiness of the related star and saucer magnolias. Its more subtle lavender-pink blooms open to three inches across after the leaves emerge, which helps to soften the tree's appearance. Sweet bay magnolias bloom off and on all summer, though not as heavily as they do in the spring. Their sweet fragrance will calm you after a bad day at the office and bring a smile to your face. It is a medium to fast grower, which helps satisfy the impatient gardener. Plant the native sweet bay magnolia near a patio, deck, or window so you can enjoy this wonderful attribute.

When to Plant

All magnolias are slow to regenerate new roots after transplanting. Plant balled-and-burlapped specimens in the early spring, before the leaves emerge, for best results. The second-best time to plant is in the fall after leaf drop.

Where to Plant

Plant sweet bay magnolia where it will get plenty of moisture. It dislikes dry sites and will not grow well there. Poorly drained, even swampy sites are preferable. Sweet bay magnolia must have a slightly acidic soil and will yellow in alkaline sites. If the soil pH is above 7.0, adjust it by adding sulfur. Magnolia prefers full sun but will also grow well in partly shaded sites. This variety makes a good screen or background plant for the flower border.

How to Plant

Prepare a planting hole 4 times as wide as the rootball. Slope the sides of the hole outward from the bottom up to ground level. Plant the tree deep enough so that the top of the rootball is even with the established grade. Remove any twine or wire from around the trunk to prevent girdling, which could kill the tree in subsequent years. Cut away the burlap or wire basket to half the height of the rootball and backfill the hole with the original soil. Water deeply and spread 2 to 3 inches of organic mulch around the planting site.

Advice for Care

Under proper growing conditions, sweet bay magnolia will thrive with few problems. Water during the growing season with 1 to $1^1/2$ inches of water per week, especially during hot and dry spells. Maintain a 2- to 3-inch layer of mulch around the root zone at all times to keep the moisture in the ground and to prevent drought stress. To encourage faster growth and overall good vigor, broadcast fertilizer around the root zone in early November. Prune dead branches when they become apparent. Sweet bay magnolia can be easily pruned into a multi-stemmed specimen.

Additional Information

Sweet bay magnolia may be partially evergreen in southern locations such as Evansville. In the coldest regions of Zone 5, in northern Indiana, it may not be reliably hardy. This tree was sometimes called 'Beaverwood' since it was the primary structural component in beaver dams.

Additional Species, Cultivars, or Varieties

There are few improved varieties of sweet bay magnolia, but 'Henry Hicks' is known to remain evergreen at temperatures well below zero. *Magnolia stellata*, the star magnolia, and *Magnolia × soulangiana*, the saucer magnolia, are more popular species in this area. However, their flowers are routinely killed by late spring freezes; as a result, the flowers become brown mush about 2 out of every 3 years. The sweet bay magnolia is a much better selection.

White Fir

Abies concolor

Other Name: Concolor Fir
Zones: 5, 6
Height: 40 to 60 feet
Type: Evergreen

Light Requirement:

hite fir has an erect and formal appearance in the landscape, and from a distance is very similar to the ubiquitous Colorado blue spruce. White fir needles have a pale blue cast but never turn quite as blue as the spruce. The needles will grow to two inches long and are flat, as is typical of the needles of most firs. They curve inward towards the tips and are much softer than spruce needles. White fir has a slow to medium growth rate, but it is worth planting. It is very adaptable to a wide variety of growing conditions and makes an outstanding specimen for Hoosier landscapes. White fir trees are pest-free and are popular nesting sites for birds.

WHEN TO PLANT

The best time to plant is early spring before the flush of new growth. The second-best time is in early fall when the soil is still warm. If planting in the fall be sure to water the white fir deeply once a week up until the time the ground freezes. This will help prevent winter desiccation.

WHERE TO PLANT

White fir tree grows to 30 feet wide and therefore adapts to more confined planting sites. It prefers moist but well-drained soil and does not tolerate clay. This fir grows in granite and rocky soils in its native habitat in the West. Here in the Midwest, it will tolerate drier and sandier sites than do other evergreens. Plant white fir near the corner of the house to soften the edges, or in groups as a screen. It does best in sunny sites but will also grow well in partial shade.

HOW TO PLANT

Prepare a planting hole up to 4 times as wide as the rootball. Dig deep enough so that after planting the top of the rootball is level

with the ground around it. Gently slope the sides of the planting hole outward from the bottom to the finished grade. Don't forget to remove any twine or wire that is wrapped around the trunk. This will prevent girdling, which could kill the tree in future years. Cut away the burlap and any wire basket to half the height of the rootball. Any plastic or other synthetic wrap around the rootball should be completely removed. Backfill the hole with the original soil and water deeply. Spread a 2- to 3-inch layer of organic mulch around the planting area.

ADVICE FOR CARE

White fir and other evergreens require very little care after planting. Although more tolerant of dry soil than other conifers, the most important task will be to ensure the tree receives 1 to $1^1/2$ inches of water each week during the growing season. It is especially important in late fall when the tree is preparing for winter. Maintain a 2- to 3-inch layer of organic mulch like wood chips around the root zone. This will help prevent moisture loss. No regular pruning is required. Remove dead branches as needed.

ADDITIONAL INFORMATION

In parts of the West, the white fir is a utilitarian tree. Its wood is a desirable source of lumber for general construction purposes. It is also a popular variety for Christmas trees.

ADDITIONAL SPECIES, CULTIVARS, OR VARIETIES

These varieties may be difficult to locate but are worth the search. The variety 'Candicans' has eye-catching silver-blue needles. 'Compacta' is a dwarf variety with good needle color. 'Conica' is a semi-dwarf with a very narrow spread.

Winter King Hawthorn

Crataegus viridis 'Winter King'

Zones: 5, 6 **Height:** 20 to 35 feet **Bloom Period:** May (fruits in fall through winter) **Flowers:** White (fruit, bright red) **Type:** Deciduous	**Light Requirement:** 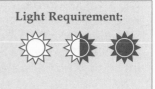

Winter King Hawthorn is one of the outstanding small trees that should be a part of any Hoosier landscape. Selected from the Simpson Orchard Co. in Vincennes, Indiana in 1955, it quickly gained popularity due to the year-round interest it provides as well as its ability to tolerate poor planting sites. The glossy green leaves emerge in April and are followed by clusters of creamy-white flowers in May. In "good years" the blooms will cover the canopy of the tree. Leaves turn scarlet-red in fall and look great when planted next to ornamental grasses. Known for larger fruit than other hawthorn species, the winter king's one-fourth inch-round berries, called "haws," follow the flowers and turn bright orange-red in the fall. Once viewed in the dead of winter, it is easy to understand how this hawthorn gained the name 'Winter King'. The haws persist on the branches well into late winter, that is, unless the birds find them first. The haws also make festive additions to wreaths and other holiday decorations. Winter king's light-gray bark contrasts well with the colorful fruit. When blanketed in snow, the combination of red haws and gray bark is stunning.

WHEN TO PLANT

Winter king hawthorn should be planted in early spring after the ground is dry. If planting in summer, be especially sure to water deeply every week.

WHERE TO PLANT

Plant a winter king hawthorn in soil that is well drained and slightly acidic. Winter king is a tough plant that tolerates poor planting sites and slightly alkaline soil as well. It is a good tree for screening or for softening the corners of houses and other buildings.

How to Plant

Plant balled-and-burlapped specimens by digging a hole 2 to 3 times as wide as the rootball. Dig deep enough so that the top of the rootball is at ground level. Remove all twine or wire from around the trunk and cut away the burlap or wire basket to half the height of the rootball. Backfill the hole with the original soil. Water deeply and spread a 2- to 3-inch layer of organic mulch to keep the roots cool and moist. Be wary of the thorns of this tree when handling as they can grow to 1 inch long.

Advice for Care

Because of its "tough composition," winter king hawthorn requires little care. Broadcast an all-purpose fertilizer in early November, especially during the first 5 to 10 years after transplanting. Keep it watered to protect from drought stress in summer. Maintain a 2- to 3-inch layer of mulch to help keep the roots moist. Prune occasionally to keep the natural shape of the tree, which is upright and spreading with a nice horizontal branching pattern. Winter king may be attacked by cedar hawthorn rust which is prevalent on all hawthorns, though much less so on this variety. After the leaves drop in fall, prune out the branch tips that are swollen with the dark brown cankers that harbor this fungus.

Additional Information

When the tree matures, the bark will peel to reveal a rust-colored inner bark. The thorns of winter king, though fewer than other hawthorns, are fierce. It would be best to choose another tree if you have young children.

Additional Species, Cultivars, or Varieties

Crataegus phaenopyrum, the Washington hawthorn, has slightly smaller fruit and may be more prone to rust than winter king. *C. phaenopyrum* 'Fastigiata' has a columnar growth habit. 'Princeton Sentry' is shaped like a narrow pyramid and is practically thornless.

CHAPTER ELEVEN

Vines

A physician can bury his mistakes, but the architect can only advise his clients to plant vines.

—Frank Lloyd Wright, architect

*I*NDEED, VINES COVER A MULTITUDE OF SINS IN THE landscape as they climb, cling, mound, or ramble. They also have practical uses. Fast-growing annual or perennial vines form summer screens to shade or provide privacy for a porch. A vine mounding over a stump in the yard provides an interesting contour of foliage or flowers. Vines add beauty through color, texture, foliage, bark, flowers, and fruit.

Although vines are natural climbers, they may require some training. Weave them through fences or provide string bridges to get them started; this will train the vines to cover surfaces horizontally as well as vertically. Because they are heavy and have a natural tendency to fall away from the trellis or wall, it may sometimes be necessary to tie vines to a support. Be careful not to restrict their growth when doing this.

Use caution when allowing vines to climb wood or masonry houses, fences, or other structures. At best, the plants may mar or stain the surfaces; at worst, the vines could cause already weakened mortar joints to deteriorate. Plant vines several inches from the support or wall on which they are to grow. There may be large clumps of concrete around fence posts, lampposts, and mailboxes that make digging there difficult. Move a foot or so away from the post, and train the vine with a string bridge, wire or wooden stakes placed at a slant toward the structure.

Vines planted under eaves, trees or other areas sheltered from the rain will benefit from an occasional supplemental soaking.

Chapter Eleven

Vines need pruning to give them shape and to stimulate growth, so don't be afraid to cut them back. Prune out large branches down to the vine's base every few years to keep the plant's growth balanced. If you trim back only the top, growth will be focused there and the bottom will become sparse.

Vines that bloom on new growth should be pruned in late winter or early spring, while those that bloom on year-old growth should be pruned immediately after they flower. Clematis, which is discussed in this chapter, has fairly specific pruning needs. Here are a few basics:

- Clematis varieties in the Jackman Group have large flowers and include the popular 'Jackmanii', with purple, white, or red flowers in July and August. 'Comtesse de Bouchard' has pink flowers from June through October. 'Perle d'Azur' has sky-blue flowers in summer. 'Star of India' has reddish-plum flowers with red stripes from July through September. The members of this group usually bloom on new growth. Prune them severely in late winter or early spring, when the buds begin to swell. You can cut the vines back to six to twelve inches above the ground.
- Clematis varieties in the Lanuginosa Group have large flowers and include 'Elsa Spath', with blue flowers; 'Henryi', with white flowers; and 'Nelly Moser', with pink flowers that have darker pink stripes. Prune back two-thirds of the vine in late winter or early spring. Many of the clematis vines in this group will flower on the old growth near the bottom of the plant in June, and on the new growth at the top later in the summer.
- Clematis varieties in the Patens Group have large flowers and include 'Lincoln Star', which has white flowers with raspberry-red stripes from May through September; 'The President', with dark-violet flowers; and 'Mrs. N. Thompson', which has violet-blue flowers with scarlet stripes from May through September. Members of this group bloom on last year's growth, so prune them immediately after they flower.

Boston Ivy

Parthenocissus tricuspidata

Other Names: Japanese Creeper, Japanese Vine, Woodbine **Zones:** 5, 6 **Height:** 40 to 50 feet **Type:** Deciduous	**Light Requirement:** 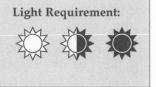

*T*his is the plant that gave Ivy League colleges the name. Boston ivy forms disk-like root clusters that help it climb and cling to masonry or wood walls or buildings. Its flowers are insignificant and occur only on mature growth. The flowers may be followed by dark-blue berries. The three-lobed leaves are a shiny green and form a dense screen when growing on a wall. Each leaf has three points and hence the species name *tricuspidata*. They turn red or bright orange in fall before they drop to the ground, revealing a woody vine.

WHEN TO PLANT

Container-grown transplants may be planted in early spring as soon as the soil can be worked.

WHERE TO PLANT

Plant in sun or shade. This ivy seems to prefer a northern or eastern exposure. It does best in a well-drained, moist spot that has been amended with compost or organic material.

HOW TO PLANT

Plant container-grown transplants at the same depth they were growing in their pots. Water them well.

ADVICE FOR CARE

Boston ivy tolerates average soil. Pruning usually isn't necessary except to keep the plant under control and away from windows, doors, gutters, and downspouts. Some of the foliage or parts of the vine may suffer winterkill, but Boston ivy usually recovers without any effort on the gardener's part. The leaves may be hit by mildew or Japanese beetles. Good air circulation and environmental controls should help with the mildew problem. To control the beetles—try hoping that your neighbor installs a Japanese beetle trap. The problem with beetle traps or lures is that they work only too well, sending out "calling all beetle" signals far and wide, bringing the pesky creatures to the yard. This is why it's best the neighbors have one, so the beetles will go over there!

ADDITIONAL INFORMATION
Despite its Boston moniker, this plant is from Asia. It is related to Virginia creeper, which is a native plant of North America. Boston ivy is good for urban settings because it tolerates pollution, shade, and average soil.

ADDITIONAL SPECIES, CULTIVARS, OR VARIETIES
Parthenocissus tricuspidata 'Lowii', or Low's Japanese creeper, has smaller leaves; 'Veitchii' turns purple in fall; 'Robusta' is considered very hardy.

Clematis

Clematis spp.

Other Name: Virgin's Bower	**Light Requirement:**
Zones: 5, 6	
Bloom Period: various	
Flower: Pink, white, lavender, purple	
Height: 4 to 40 feet	
Type: Perennial	

The versatility and long-lasting flowers of clematis make this vine a worthy addition to any landscape. Clematis climbs posts, twists up trees, or scampers along the soil to make an unusual groundcover. You can cut the flowers (some are fragrant) for indoor floral arrangements, or leave them to dry on the vine, where they exhibit feathery or spidery seedheads that complement the dark-green leaves. There are more than 250 native clematis species in cold and temperate zones: *Clematis virginiana* is from North America; *C. montana* from India; *C. patens* from Japan; and *C. lanuginosa* from China, to name a few. Clematis has two basic types of flowers: small and large. Within the two types, however, are dozens of classifications and varieties, all of which seem to have different pruning requirements. Many gardeners find this confusing. Also confusing is how to pronounce the name: CLEM-a-tis or Cle-MA-tis. The British and many horticulture professionals use the former, while most of the rest of the population uses the latter. Either way, it's beautiful and delightful for the home garden.

WHEN TO PLANT

Plant container-grown transplants in the early spring as soon as you can work the soil.

WHERE TO PLANT

As a basic rule, clematis vines like hot heads and cool feet. The most important factor is a sunny, well-drained spot that is moderately moist but not wet. Clematis thrives in the alkaline soils found throughout most of Indiana.

How to Plant

Dig a hole about 1 foot deep and 1 foot wide. Amend the soil with compost, a couple handfuls of sand, peat moss, finely chopped leaves, or other organic material. Replace soil in the hole so that the plant's crown will be 2 to 3 inches below ground level; this is deeper than it was growing in its container. Space plants about 18 inches apart. Water them well, and mulch.

Advice for Care

Apply an all-purpose granular fertilizer in the spring, when new growth appears, or spread a layer of compost around the plants in the spring and fall. Supplement rainfall by watering as needed during the blooming period. You can use a water-soluble, all-purpose fertilizer or compost tea throughout the growing season.

Additional Information

The blooming period of clematis determines when you should prune it. Keep this in mind when selecting which varieties you want to plant as well as where you want to plant them. Please refer to the introduction of this chapter for specific pruning instructions regarding clematis.

Additional Species, Cultivars, or Varieties

Clematis maximowicziana (*C. paniculata*, *C. dioscoreifolia*, *C. terniflora*) is sweet autumn clematis, a wonderfully rambling plant that quickly covers fences. If not kept in check, it will shroud nearby trees and shrubs, but will not otherwise harm them. Sweet autumn clematis has small, fragrant, star-shaped white flowers that bloom from late July through fall. For best results, cut it back hard in late winter or early summer—or allow it to ramble without doing anything. It frequently reseeds itself, providing starts you can give to friends and neighbors. *Clematis montana*, sometimes called anemone clematis, is among the earliest to bloom in May. Although frequently said to be hardy in Zone 5, it is a safer bet for Zone 6. *C. montana* 'Rubens' has red flowers; 'Elizabeth' has slightly fragrant, pink flowers; and 'Alexander' has white, sweet-smelling flowers. These can be vigorous growers; prune to tame them immediately after they flower. *Clematis tangutica*, or golden clematis, has yellow, lantern-like flowers that bloom on new growth in early summer; in the fall it produces silky seedpods. Prune golden clematis hard in late winter or early spring. It is hardy to Zone 5.

Climbing Black-Eyed Susan

Thunbergia alata

Zones: 5, 6
Height: 6 feet
Bloom Period: Summer
Flower: Orange, yellow, white
Type: Annual

Light Requirement:

A tender perennial native to Africa, the climbing black-eyed Susan is a charming summer annual. Climbing black-eyed Susan can be used as a summer groundcover, in a hanging basket or pot, or it can be trained to cover a fence. It also looks good in rock gardens. The most common varieties have orange, yellow, or cream-colored trumpet-like one-and-one-fourth-inch-wide flowers with dark throats. Its small flowers are never ostentatious. The pointed green leaves are soft and a bit hairy. *Thunbergia alata* is named for Carl Peter Thunberg, a Swedish botanical author.

WHEN TO PLANT

Plant container-grown transplants in the spring after the danger of frost has passed. Start seeds indoors in March or April.

WHERE TO PLANT

Plant in full sun or dappled shade in well-drained soil. If it gets too hot, climbing black-eyed Susan may slow down or stop flowering, so a little protection from hot afternoon sun would be best.

HOW TO PLANT

Plant container-grown transplants at the same depth they were growing in their containers. Plant about 12 inches apart and water well. If you are planting seeds, sow 2 or 3 seeds about 1/4 inch deep in 3-inch peat pots that are filled with soilless mix. Water gently and place indoors in a warm, bright spot that is out of direct sunlight. For best results, grow them under fluorescent lights until they are large enough for transplanting. Germination may take up to 3 weeks. Snip off the weakest seedling with scissors and transplant the remaining seedling peat pot and all. Break off any part of the peat pot that sticks out above the ground.

ADVICE FOR CARE

Climbing black-eyed Susan prefers moist soil. Pruning is not required. Fertilize regularly throughout the growing season. Use a balanced, slow-release fertilizer.

ADDITIONAL INFORMATION

Climbing black-eyed Susan provides a fast summer cover for a tree stump, rock, or other shape in the yard. It also makes a good houseplant. You can winter it over in a bright window out of direct sun, then move it outdoors in the spring. Every time you move it, you will need to acclimate it slowly to its new environment.

ADDITIONAL SPECIES, CULTIVARS, OR VARIETIES

T. alata 'Suzy Mixed' has yellow, orange, and white flowers. *T. fragrans* 'Angel Wings' has 2-inch-wide white flowers that bloom 16 weeks after the seed is sown. The vine may reach a length of 8 feet; despite the plant's botanical name, the flowers are only mildly fragrant. *T. grandiflora* has $2^{1}/_{2}$-inch-wide light-blue flowers. Another native of South Africa, *T. gregorii* (*T. gibsonii*), is sometimes called orange clockvine. The flowers are bright-orange tubes about $1^{1}/_{2}$ inches wide and $1^{3}/_{4}$ inches long; the color may clash with other flowers. This vine will reach a length of 20 feet.

Climbing Hydrangea

Hydrangea anomala spp. *petiolaris*

Zones: 5, 6
Height: 50 feet or more
Bloom Period: June
Flower: White
Type: Perennial

Light Requirement:

*Y*es, hydrangea is a shrub with large white, blue, pink, or green flowers, but this variety is a beautiful vine that is not used nearly enough. The leaves are glossy, dark green, and heart shaped; airy clusters of white flowers bloom for about two weeks in June before turning a warm, light brown. These remain on the vine until Christmas or beyond, and along with the peeling cinnamon- or red-dish-brown bark, add winter interest to the landscape. Climbing hydrangea readily clings to flat surfaces, or can be used as a ground-cover. This plant was formerly known as *Hydrangea petiolaris*.

WHEN TO PLANT
Plant container-grown transplants in the spring as soon as you can work the soil.

WHERE TO PLANT
Climbing hydrangea is one of our most adapatable vines, thriving in both full sun and full shade, when allowed plenty of room to climb or wander. Choose well-drained soil.

HOW TO PLANT
Dig a hole that is as deep as the container the plant has been growing in and twice as wide. Amend the soil with organic material. Don't plant the transplant any deeper than it was growing in its pot. Firm soil around the plant, water well, and mulch.

ADVICE FOR CARE
Apply an all-purpose granular fertilizer in the spring, when new growth appears, and then again in fall; or spread a layer of compost

around the base of the plant in spring and fall. Pruning is usually not necessary, but if you need to keep the plant looking tidy, prune it after it blooms.

ADDITIONAL INFORMATION

Be sure climbing hydrangea has adequate support. The plant is slow to get started; it frequently will not flower for 3 or more years after transplanting. Climbing hydrangea benefits from regular feeding and watering while establishing itself; otherwise, it requires very little maintenance.

ADDITIONAL SPECIES, CULTIVARS, OR VARIETIES

Hydrangea anomala has small flowers and longer, more pointed leaves than *Hydrangea anomala* spp. *petiolaris*; it is attractive in June and July. It should be hardy to Zone 5, but may not be as hardy as *H. anomola* ssp. *petiolaris*.

Cup-and-Saucer Vine

Cobaea scandens

Other Names: Cathedral Bells, Mexican Ivy
Zones: 5, 6
Height: 15 to 20 feet
Bloom Period: Summer
Flower: Pale-green to purple
Type: Annual

Light Requirement:

Cobaea scandens is named for Father Cobo, a seventeenth-century Jesuit missionary and naturalist from Spain who lived and worked in Central America for almost forty years until his death in 1659. Cup-and-saucer vine grows as a rambling perennial in Central America, but in Indiana it is an annual vine that offers a very unusual flower for a trellis, arbor, or other support. The name "cup-and-saucer" describes the flowers, which start as pale-green buds that turn purple as they open into two-inch-long "cups" and eventually form greenish "saucers." The leaves are pointed, and grow almost four inches in length. The plant uses tendrils from branch tips to hold onto its support.

WHEN TO PLANT

Plant container-grown transplants in the spring after the danger of frost has passed. Start seeds indoors 6 or 8 weeks before the last frost.

WHERE TO PLANT

Plant cup-and-saucer vine in full sun or light shade. Choose well-drained soil, and amend it with compost or other organic material.

HOW TO PLANT

Plant container-grown plants 24 to 30 inches apart at the same depth they were growing in their containers and water well. If you are starting from seed, nick seeds with a knife before sowing. Place two or three seeds in 3-inch peat pots that are filled with soilless potting mix. Barely cover the seeds. Moisten and place pots in a warm spot out of direct sunlight. For best results indoors, grow *Cobaea* under fluorescent or grow lights until large enough to transplant. Germination may take a month. Snip off the weakest seedlings with scissors then plant the vine, pot and all. Water them well.

ADVICE FOR CARE

Cobaea scandens prefers moist soil. Protect it from the afternoon sun and you will prolong its blooms. You may pinch it for branching and shape. Apply a water-soluble fertilizer or compost tea regularly throughout the growing season.

ADDITIONAL INFORMATION

Cup-and-saucer vine's flowers smell bad when they first appear and may attract flies. Once they open, however, the flowers acquire a more pleasant smell and may attract bees. Cup-and-saucer vine has been grown in conservatories and greenhouses for more than 100 years.

ADDITIONAL SPECIES, CULTIVARS, OR VARIETIES

Cobaea scandens 'Flore Albo', or 'Alba', has white flowers.

Honeysuckle

Lonicera spp.

Zones: 5, 6
Height: 10 to 40 feet
Bloom Period: Spring, summer
Flower: White, red, orange, purple
Type: Perennial

Light Requirement:

There's nothing like the fragrant honey or lemon scent of honeysuckle in early summer. Birds love the red or black honeysuckle berries, and even unscented varieties of this vine may attract hummingbirds. Though most honeysuckle varieties lose their leaves in the fall, some plants are almost semi-evergreen, keeping their leaves well into winter.

WHEN TO PLANT

Plant container-grown transplants in the spring as soon as you can work the soil.

WHERE TO PLANT

Honeysuckle prefers full sun but will tolerate partial shade. Choose a well-drained location. Honeysuckle will climb fences, trellises, and other supports, or it can be left to ramble along the ground.

HOW TO PLANT

Honeysuckle is not picky about soil quality, but if you want it to last a long time in the landscape, give it a good place to grow. Amend the planting hole with organic material and plant transplants as deep as they were growing in their containers. Space them at least 24 inches apart. Water them well and mulch lightly.

ADVICE FOR CARE

Prune honeysuckle immediately after it flowers. Apply an all-purpose granular fertilizer in the spring when new growth begins, or spread a layer of compost around the base of the plant in the spring and fall.

ADDITIONAL INFORMATION

Several varieties need to be kept under control or they will take over the yard. If a honeysuckle vine becomes too large, cut it back to the ground; the plant will send up new shoots.

ADDITIONAL SPECIES, CULTIVARS, OR VARIETIES

Lonicera japonica 'Halliana' is commonly available at garden centers and through mail-order catalogs. It has black fruit and white, incredibly fragrant, trumpet-like flowers that turn golden yellow. This variety can be a nuisance in the backyard because birds eat the fruit and deposit the seeds elsewhere. *Lonicera × heckrotti* is frequently called goldflame or everblooming honeysuckle; it may be semi-evergreen, depending on the severity of winter weather. The fragrant flowers are carmine, open to show yellow inside, and fade to pink. The vine grows 10 to 20 feet high or long. *Lonicera sempervirens*, or trumpet honeysuckle, has orange-red flowers that are yellow inside. Four to 6 flowers develop in a cluster, or whorl, along the vine. Trumpet honeysuckle starts leafing out in early spring; in April, it begins to bloom on last year's growth, and continues to produce flowers in this way for about 3 months. It then blooms on new growth throughout the rest of the summer. The beautiful flowers are not fragrant, but they do attract hummingbirds. This variety is native to the eastern United States. 'Sulphurea' or 'Flava' has yellow flowers in April. 'Magnifica' has red flowers. 'Dropmore Scarlet', a hybrid between *L. hirsuta* and *L. sempervirens*, blooms all summer long and is one of the best honeysuckles available. *L. maackii*, the amur honeysuckle, has escaped cultivation and naturalized itself in woodland areas. It is threatening the ecology of the forest because of its aggressive nature. It is a medium-sized shrub that stays evergreen into late fall and early winter. It is easily identified at this time in the forest understory.

Hyacinth Bean

Dolichos lablab

<table>
<tr><td>Other Names: Lablab or Indian, Egyptian, Seim, Bonavista, or Lubia Bean
Zones: 5, 6
Height: 15 to 30 feet
Bloom Period: Mid- to late summer
Flower: Purple or white
Type: Annual</td><td>Light Requirement:</td></tr>
</table>

Hyacinth bean, a tropical plant native to North America, is a woody vine that quickly twines up a trellis or fence to make a dense, green summer screen. It has six-inch, heart-shaped, purplish-green leaves. The fragrant flowers are purple or white and resemble sweet peas; they are one-inch long and stand six inches from the foliage. The flowers are followed by decorative, purple seedpods that grow two to two-and-one-half inches long. The pod is eaten in the tropics. *Dolichos* is a Greek word for bean.

WHEN TO PLANT

Hyacinth bean does not transplant well, so you may not be able to buy container-grown plants. If transplants are available, plant in the spring after all danger of frost has passed. Sow seeds indoors 6 to 8 weeks before the last frost in the spring. Otherwise, direct plant seeds in the garden after the last frost.

WHERE TO PLANT

For best results, plant in loamy, moist, well-drained soil in full sun or light shade. Plant hyacinth bean where there is a support for it to climb, near a trellis or fence.

HOW TO PLANT

Plant container-grown transplants no deeper than they were growing in their pots. Amend the soil with compost or other organic material and plant transplants about 1 foot apart. Water them well. If you are planting from seed, soak the seeds in water for a day before sowing. Sow 2 or 3 seeds in a 3-inch peat pot that is filled with soilless potting mix; barely cover the seeds. Moisten and place the pots in a warm, bright location, indoors, out of direct sunlight. Germination may take a month. For best results, grow them under fluorescent lights until large enough to transplant outdoors. Snip off the weakest seedlings, then plant the vine, peat pot and all, outdoors when the threat of frost has passed. Water them well.

ADVICE FOR CARE

The hotter the better for hyacinth bean, which thrives in the humid weather of southern Indiana. Be sure to keep the vine moist. Frost will kill the hyacinth bean.

ADDITIONAL INFORMATION

Hyacinth bean is difficult to transplant, which is why peat pots are recommended. These pots allow you to plant transplants without disturbing the roots. The pots decompose in the ground. Once you plant a hyacinth bean, you'll be rewarded year after year as the seed is easily saved. Harvest dried and shriveled seed pods and store in a cool, dry place until the following spring.

ADDITIONAL SPECIES, CULTIVARS, OR VARIETIES

Hyacinth bean is sometimes referred to as *Dipogon lablab*. *Dolichos lablab* 'Darkness' has purple flowers. 'Daylight' has white flowers.

Moonflower

Calonyction aculeatum

Zones: 5, 6	**Light Requirement:**
Height: 20 to 40 feet	
Bloom Period: Mid- to late summer	
Flowers: White	
Type: Annual	

*P*eople often confuse this night bloomer with morning glory (*Ipomoea*) which is discussed elsewhere in this chapter. Though they look similar, *Calonyction* is a different species. Both are tropical vines, but moonflower puts on a spectacular show at night, when the six-inch, satiny, white flowers unfurl and release their sweet scent. Moonflowers are grown from seed and flower late in the growing season.

WHEN TO PLANT

You are unlikely to find transplants of moonflowers at garden centers. In the spring, sow seeds directly outdoors after the danger of frost has passed. For flowers earlier in the season, sow seeds indoors 4 to 6 weeks before the last frost.

WHERE TO PLANT

Moonflowers need a support to climb. Plant in full sun; choose well-drained, loamy soil that has been amended with compost or other organic material. Avoid planting these plants where they can climb, take over, or strangle nearby plantings—or train them to vine where you want them to grow.

HOW TO PLANT

For best results, nick seeds with a knife, or scrape with a file, and soak them overnight before sowing. Outdoors, sow seeds about $1/2$-inch deep in moistened soil directly where you want them to grow. Indoors, sow 2 or 3 seeds $1/2$-inch deep in 3-inch peat pots that are filled with a moistened soilless mix. Germination may take 2 to 3 weeks. Place in a warm location indoors, out of direct sunlight. For best results indoors, grow them under fluorescent lights until they are large enough to transplant outdoors. Snip off the weakest seedlings with scissors and transplant the vine, peat pot and all, to a hole in a prepared spot.

ADVICE FOR CARE
You can pinch shoots to contain growth or to train the vine to a trellis. Water during dry spells.

ADDITIONAL INFORMATION
Moonflowers do not like to be transplanted. You can grow them in hanging baskets or other containers. Because they flower and emit their scent at night, plant them where they can be seen or smelled, such as near a porch, bedroom window, patio, or deck.

ADDITIONAL SPECIES, CULTIVARS, OR VARIETIES
Moonflower is sometimes listed as *Ipomoea alba* or *Ipomoea bona-nox*.

Morning Glory

Ipomoea purpurea

Other Name: Cardinal Climber **Zones:** 5, 6 **Height:** 8 to 20 feet **Bloom Period:** Mid- to late summer **Flowers:** Various **Type:** Annual	**Light Requirement:**

This vining annual has historic roots in the American landscape as a symbol of home on the homestead, covering fenceposts and porches as pioneers moved west. These are late bloomers. They don't live up to their name until mid- to late summer when blue, pink, white, red, or bicolored trumpet-shaped flowers appear. They are a welcome addition to the garden at a time when there isn't a lot else going on. Morning glories bloom in the morning, closing by afternoon. Many varieties will stay open on cloudy days. Morning glories readily self-sow, a habit that may make them invasive in some gardens. To keep them under control, remove the flowers as they wilt and dry but before they can release their seeds.

WHEN TO PLANT

Transplants of morning glories will probably not be available from garden centers. Sow seeds directly where they will grow outdoors in spring after all danger of frost has past. For flowers earlier in the season, sow seeds indoors 4 to 6 weeks before the last frost.

WHERE TO PLANT

A morning glory vine needs some support such as a fence or trellis, or you can allow it to ramble over the woodpile, a stump, or other structure in the landscape as a summer groundcover. Avoid planting where it can climb, take over, or strangle nearby plantings, or train it to vine where you want it. Plant in full sun in a well-drained, loamy soil that has been amended with compost or other organic material. Morning glories can also be grown in hanging baskets or other containers.

How to Plant

For best results, nick morning glory seeds with a knife or scrape them with a file and soak them overnight before sowing. Sow seeds about $1/2$ inch deep in moistened soil directly where they will grow outdoors. Indoors, sow 2 or 3 seeds $1/2$ inch deep in 3-inch peat pots filled with a moistened soilless mix. Germination may take 3 weeks. Place in a warm location but out of the direct sun. For best results, grow them under fluorescent lights until they are large enough to transplant outdoors. Snip off the weakest seedlings with scissors. Transplant vine, peat pot and all, into a hole in a prepared spot.

Additional Information

Morning glories resent being transplanted, as do many annual vines, which is why starting them in peat pots is recommended if you want to start seeds early. Don't plant the vines any deeper than they were growing in their pots. Too much water and too much nitrogen fertilizer will cause more foliage than flowers. When it comes to temperature: the hotter the better.

Additional Species, Cultivars, or Varieties

Ipomoea purpurea (sometimes *I. nil*) 'Heavenly Blue' has 4-inch-diameter flowers; 'Scarlet O'Hara' has wine-red 4-inch flowers; 'Pearly Gates' has 4-inch white flowers. 'Scarlet O'Hara' and 'Pearly Gates' are All-America Selections, which have been grown from seeds in trial gardens all over the United States and judged by seed merchants and growers to be excellent performers. *I. × multifida* has arrow-like leaves and bright-red flowers—it is said to look like the logo for Chrysler Corporation. *Calonyction aculeatum*, or moonflower, is sometimes confused with *Ipomoea alba*. Moonflower is discussed elsewhere in this chapter.

Porcelain Berry

Ampelopsis brevipedunculata

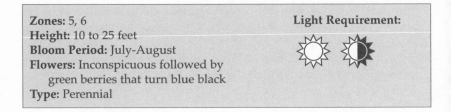

Zones: 5, 6
Height: 10 to 25 feet
Bloom Period: July-August
Flowers: Inconspicuous followed by
   green berries that turn blue black
Type: Perennial

Light Requirement:

*P*orcelain berry is a fast-growing import from Asia that is prized for its fruit rather than for its foliage or flowers. The leaves are dark green and deeply cut, but provide no fall color; inconspicuous green flowers appear in July and August. Ah, but the berries! One-fourth to one-third inch in diameter, they are originally cream, yellow, or pale lavender, and change in late summer or early fall to green, bright blue, and black. Because of its fast growing habit, porcelain berry can quickly provide shade or a screen by covering a fence or trellis. It can also sprawl along the ground.

WHEN TO PLANT

Plant container-grown transplants in the spring as soon as you can work the soil.

WHERE TO PLANT

Porcelain berry does best in full sun and well-drained soil. You should plant it in an area where the roots will be restricted; this is reported to improve fruit production. The vine should have something on which to climb.

HOW TO PLANT

Prepare a hole as deep as and about twice as wide as the container the transplants were growing. Amend the soil with organic material. Plant transplants at the same depth they were growing in their pots. Firm soil around the plant, water well, and mulch lightly.

ADVICE FOR CARE
Apply an all-purpose granular fertilizer when new growth appears in the spring or spread a layer of compost around the base of the plant in spring and fall. Porcelain berry may require periodic pruning during the growing season to keep it under control.

ADDITIONAL INFORMATION
Porcelain berry may be cut back to the ground in late winter or early spring to keep it under control. It will grow, flower, and set fruit in a growing season. Japanese beetles like this plant and can make it disappear almost as quickly as it grew. Wasps hover around this plant in late summer and fall, feeding off the sweet sap.

ADDITIONAL SPECIES, CULTIVARS, OR VARIETIES
Ampelopsis brevipedunculata 'Elegans' has smaller, variegated leaves; it may be suitable for spots where the species would be too invasive. *Ampelopsis aconitifolia,* or monkshood vine, starts slowly, but by the third year it will flower and bear small fruit that turn from yellow to blue. Monkshood vine can climb to 20 feet, so prune annually to keep it under control.

Trumpet Vine

Campsis radicans

Other Name: Trumpet Creeper,
  Hummingbird Vine
Zones: 5, 6
Height: 30 to 40 feet
Bloom Period: Summer
Flowers: Reddish-orange, yellow
Type: Perennial

Light Requirement:

This vine is native to the eastern United States and will climb up or creep over whatever is in its path. Trumpet vine produces clusters of six or more reddish-orange, trumpet-shaped, three-inch-long flowers from June through September. The colors may vary from plant to plant, but that doesn't matter to hummingbirds, who love trumpet vine. It climbs by aerial roots, and has dark-green, serrated leaves that may not appear until mid- to late May. The vine retains its woody seedpods into cold weather, giving it an interesting appearance in winter.

WHEN TO PLANT

Plant container-grown transplants in the spring as soon as you can work the soil.

WHERE TO PLANT

Trumpet vine does best in full sun but will tolerate partial shade. Give it something to climb on, but do not let it attach itself to your house; the vine can creep into downspouts, gutters, windows, or any other crack or crevice. It is very aggressive.

HOW TO PLANT

Trumpet vine is not picky about soil, but all plants do best when you start them out in a well-prepared site. Dig the hole the same depth as the container the plant is growing in and about twice as wide. Amend the soil with organic material. Plant trumpet vine no deeper than it was growing in the container; space plants 2 feet or more apart. Firm soil around the plant, water well, and mulch lightly.

ADVICE FOR CARE

Apply a water-soluble fertilizer or compost tea throughout the growing season for the first year or two. Later, apply an all-purpose granular fertilizer in the spring, or spread a layer of compost around the base of the plant in the spring and fall. Cut back to shorten stems, or thin the plant as needed. Growth tips can be pinched out during the summer to help shape the plant and fill in gaps.

ADDITIONAL INFORMATION

This plant needs to be kept in check and given substantial support. It can damage houses and other structures. Trim back the top each year, especially if there is little growth at the bottom. This will keep the flowers low enough so that you can see the hummingbirds visit.

ADDITIONAL SPECIES, CULTIVARS, OR VARIETIES

'Flava' has yellow or orange-yellow flowers. 'Crimson Trumpet' has red flowers. 'Praecox' has red flowers that appear earlier in the season. 'Madam Galen' (*Campsis* × *tagliabuana*) is a showy hybrid that may be less reliably hardy in Zone 5; it should be fine in Zone 6.

Virginia Creeper

Parthenocissus quinquefolia

Other Names: Woodbine **Zones:** 5, 6 **Height:** 30 to 50 feet **Type:** Deciduous	**Light Requirement:** 

$\mathcal{V}$irginia creeper is a relative of Boston ivy (*Parthenocissus tricuspidata*) that often decorates the ivy-covered walls of colleges and universities. Virginia creeper is native to the eastern United States and is grown for its foliage, which is reddish when new and dark green in the summer. It turns brilliant purple or crimson in autumn before falling to the ground and revealing one-fourth- to one-half-inch-wide blue-black fruit. This vine is a woody climber that needs strong support. It can be shaped into a hedge or allowed to grow along the ground. It will also climb trees. Virginia creeper has an open growth pattern; you can see the structure or wall on which it is growing.

WHEN TO PLANT

Plant container-grown transplants in the spring, as soon as you can work the soil. Virginia creeper can also be planted in the fall.

WHERE TO PLANT

Virginia creeper prefers average soil that drains well.

HOW TO PLANT

Prepare a hole that is as deep as and twice as wide as the container the vine was growing in; add organic material. Don't plant Virginia creeper any deeper than it was growing in its container. Firm the soil around the plant and water well.

ADVICE FOR CARE

Apply an all-purpose granular fertilizer when new growth appears in the spring or spread a layer of compost around the plant in spring and fall.

ADDITIONAL INFORMATION

Pruning usually isn't necessary, but may be done in early spring if desired.

ADDITIONAL SPECIES, CULTIVARS, OR VARIETIES

Parthenocissus quinquefolia englemannii has smaller leaves that are more dense and more leathery than *P. quinquefolia* leaves. *P. quinquefolia saint-paulli* leaves are also smaller, and the vine may cling better.

CHAPTER TWELVE

Water Garden Plants

ATER CAN BE MORE THAN AN ELEMENT OF THE garden. It can be the garden. Water gardening is a fast growing landscaping trend and consumers don't need a lake in the backyard to dive in.

For those without their own natural or man-made body of water, manufacturers make kits to create them. They may be as simple as a half-whiskey barrel, or more complex to include preformed molds and liners that are buried in the soil and outfitted with streams, waterfalls or fountains.

In Indiana water gardens, more than the garden is in a container. The plants also are grown in containers for several reasons, not the least of which is most will have to be brought indoors to be wintered over. Container ponds don't have muddy bottoms, which means plants have no place to root. Many specimens are invasive, so pots keep them under control. There are containers, liners and soil mixes specially made for water gardening. One needs to be careful in selecting materials that don't leach chemicals or other contaminants into the pond.

Many plants, or aquatics, sold for water gardens are winter hardy in Indiana, but that assumes their crowns grow or can be sunk well below the ice that will form on the pond. The smaller container gardens and ponds are apt to freeze solid, killing any plants that remain, which is why most water garden plants are brought indoors to winter over or treated as annuals and discarded at the end of the season.

Tropical water garden plants are those that are not winter hardy here, no matter how deeply they are planted. These are usually treated as annuals and discarded at the end of the growing season.

Shelves can be made in the ponds from concrete blocks or other materials so plants can be placed at various heights, according to their planting needs and light requirements.

Chapter Twelve

Aquatics have a specific depth they need to grow. That depth is measured from the plant's crown, or point where growth comes from the soil in a container, to the top of the water surface. A plant required to grow three inches deep means its growing point is that far below the water surface when in the container.

Plants are oxygenators, marginals, floaters, deep water or bog lovers. Oxygenators are fast growing and help clean the pond, including removing certain mineral salts that allow algae to thrive. These plants are necessary if fish are in the pond. Marginals live on the edges, or margins, of ponds, usually in shallow water. They provide cover for wildlife; some varieties may provide oxygen to the water.

Deep-water aquatics are planted a foot or more below the water surface and floaters do what they say. There also are bog- and moisture-loving plants that thrive near the edges of ponds or in very wet areas, but usually not directly in the water. However, many marginal and bog plants may survive in each other's environment, so it's all right to experiment.

Use the largest container possible for the site. The soil should be heavy, loamy and free of chemicals. Slow-release fertilizer tablets or granules specially made for water gardens may be mixed with the soil when planting aquatics.

Place balls, logs or other material on the pond in fall to keep the pressure from building up when the water freezes and prevent the pond from cracking or splitting. A pump or heater in the water also keeps it from freezing, depending on the depth.

Cut back plants when removing them for winter storage. Store in their containers. Place the container in a plastic bag to help retain moisture and store in a cool area that will not freeze.

Arrow Arum

Peltandra virginica, Peltandra undulata

Other Name: Tuckahoe **Zones:** 5, 6 **Height:** 15 to 20 inches **Bloom Period:** Early to midsummer **Flowers:** Greenish-white	**Light Requirement:**

A native North American plant, arrow arum has rich, green, heavily veined leaves that grow eighteen inches long. It grows in clumps near the edge of standing or shallow water. The flower, called a spathe, is small and insignificant, but green-bronze berries develop along the stalk as the growing season continues. The berries contain seeds. Native Americans harvested the roots, steamed them to get rid of poisonous materials, dried them, and ground them into meal.

WHEN TO PLANT

Plant container-grown transplants in the spring. You can also divide arrow arum at this time.

WHERE TO PLANT

Arrow arum prefers full sun, but will tolerate light shade. Plant along the margins, or edges, of ponds.

HOW TO PLANT

Plant in a large, deep container. Place the base of the plant about 3 inches below the water surface.

ADVICE FOR CARE

If left outdoors, arrow arum must spend the winter below the pond's anticipated ice level. If your water garden is small and/or shallow, either bring the plant indoors during the winter or treat it as an annual and discard it. If you choose to bring it indoors, do so before the first frost.

ADDITIONAL INFORMATION

Arrow arum is easy to divide. It is sometimes confused with arrow-head (*Sagittaria*).

ADDITIONAL SPECIES, CULTIVARS, OR VARIETIES

Peltandra sagittaefolia is native from the Carolinas to Mississippi, where it is called spoon or white arum. Its flower is edged in white and its berries are red.

Arrowhead

Sagittaria sagittifolia

Other Name: Duck Potato
Zone: 6
Height: 18 to 24 inches
Bloom Period: Mid- to late summer
Flowers: White

Light Requirement:

*A*rrowhead grows on the water's edges, or margins. It gets its name from the shape of its three-pointed leaves, and because it was a food used by many Native American tribes. The tubers, or roots, were harvested in fall, then dried and stored for winter. Native Americans boiled the tubers for food; they can also be eaten raw, baked, or roasted. Cooking sweetens the tubers, which are otherwise fairly bitter. The plant has dark-green leaves that can reach two feet. It grows in a cluster, or clump; the stems ooze a white, milky substance when broken. The white flowers have dark centers and grow on stems that shoot from the plant. *Sagittaria* can be invasive when planted directly in the bottom of a pond, so growing it in a container is recommended.

WHEN TO PLANT
Transplant container-grown plants from March through July. You can divide arrowhead during that same period.

WHERE TO PLANT
Plant arrowhead in full sun on the edge of a pond, lake, or slow-moving stream.

HOW TO PLANT
Plant in a large container. *Sagittaria* needs to grow 2 to 5 inches below the water surface.

ADVICE FOR CARE
In late fall, sink the container about a foot deep, or at the bottom of the pond—well below the ice line during the winter. Return it to its shelf in the spring.

ADDITIONAL INFORMATION

For best growth, plant *Sagittaria* in a large container. In Zone 5 *Sagittaria* is an annual since it is not hardy.

ADDITIONAL SPECIES, CULTIVARS, OR VARIETIES

Sagittaria japonica has white flowers with yellow centers. *Sagittaria japonica* 'Flora plena' is a slow-spreading plant with double, white flowers, which are small and short-lived. *Sagittaria latifolia* is better known for its decorative foliage than for its small, white flowers.

Blue Flag Iris

Iris versicolor

Other Names: American Blue Flag,
  Fleur-de-lis
Zones: 5, 6
Height: 24 to 30 inches
Bloom Period: Early to midsummer
Flowers: Blue

Light Requirement:

*M*any irises are as at home in dry soil as they are in the margins of ponds. Blue flag iris is a native plant that is hardy from Newfoundland to Virginia, where it adapts readily in various sites, including shallow water and wet soil. The plant has narrow leaves and purple-blue flowers with gold flecks. It forms large, dense clumps at the edges of shallow ponds. It gets about two to three feet tall and is more refined than its European sister, *pseudacorus*, making it more adaptable to smaller ponds. Native Americans used blue flag for medicinal purposes. It reportedly was a remedy for thyroid growths and for getting rid of tapeworms.

WHEN TO PLANT
Plant container-grown transplants in the spring.

WHERE TO PLANT
Plant blue flag in full sun or light shade at the edge of the water. *Iris versicolor* prefers moist soil but may tolerate drier soil.

HOW TO PLANT
Iris versicolor should be planted 2 to 4 inches below the water surface in a large container.

ADVICE FOR CARE
If you want to leave *Iris versicolor* outdoors during the winter, you will have to place the container below the ice line in the pond. If the pond is shallow, bring the iris indoors to winter it over. Otherwise, sink the pot in the garden and mulch well. Remove it the following spring when the ground softens.

ADDITIONAL SPECIES, CULTIVARS, OR VARIETIES

Iris versicolor 'Kermesina' has plum flowers and green leaves. Yellow flag or flag iris (*Iris pseudacorus*) is a European native with yellow flowers and green foliage; it grows 4 feet tall. Although attractive, it may be too large for smaller ponds. *I. pseudacorus* 'Bastardii', or 'Sulphur Queen', has pale-yellow flowers; 'Golden Queen' has golden-yellow flowers. *I. pseudacorus* 'Variegatus' has white-and-green foliage with yellow flowers that fade to pale green. *Iris pseudacorus* does best in water 2 to 4 inches deep. *Iris laevigata*, or Japanese water iris, has blue flowers. *I. laevigata* 'Colchesteri' has white-and-violet flowers; 'Alba', white; 'Rose Queen', pink; 'Snowdrift', white with a streak of yellow and lilac; and 'Midnight' has deep-blue flowers with a yellow stripe. *I. laevigata* 'Variegata' has green-and-white foliage and lilac flowers.

WATER GARDEN PLANTS

Pickerel

Pontederia cordata

Other Names: Pickerel Weed,
   Pickerel Rush
Zones: 5, 6
Height: 18 to 30 inches
Bloom Period: Late summer
Flowers: Blue

Light Requirement:

*P*ickerel is a native plant that grows along the muddy margins of lakes, ponds, and slow-moving rivers from Minnesota to South Carolina. Native Americans made cereal out of its nut-like seeds, or ground them for bread. Pickerel is easy to grow, blooms late in the season, and, unlike many water plants, is not considered invasive. It is among the hardiest plants for water gardening. Depending on the depth of your water garden, you can sink pickerel's container and leave it outdoors during the winter. Pickerel has shiny olive-green leaves that are sometimes said to resemble an arrowhead or heart. The blue flowers cluster along two-foot-tall spikes from July into September.

WHEN TO PLANT
Plant container-grown transplants in the spring. You can also divide pickerel at this time.

WHERE TO PLANT
Plant pickerel in full sun on the margins of ponds or water gardens.

HOW TO PLANT
Pickerel must be 3 to 6 inches below water during the growing season. In summer, transplant into a container with room to grow.

ADVICE FOR CARE
If left outdoors, pickerel must spend the winter below the pond's anticipated ice level. In late fall, place it in the bottom of the pond. Return it to its shelf in the spring.

ADDITIONAL INFORMATION

Divide the plants by separating, splitting, or cutting rhizomes and repotting them.

ADDITIONAL SPECIES, CULTIVARS, OR VARIETIES

Pontederia lanceolata grows up to 4 feet tall and has lance-shaped leaves and blue flowers; it may be less hardy in Indiana. *P. cordata* 'Alba' has white flowers, and may also be less hardy in Indiana. *Pontederia paniculata* has a violet-blue flower. Some varieties may be difficult to find.

Water Lily

Nymphaea spp.

Zones: 5, 6
Spread: 6 inches to 5 feet or more
Bloom Period: June through September
Flowers: Various

Light Requirement:

*L*ily ponds, lily pads, and water lilies call to mind fairy tale images of floating exotic flowers and frogs resting on green, rounded leaves. Water lilies are deep-growing plants that send up leaves and flowers from the bottom of the pond. Large ones grow from a depth of three feet and spread to five feet or more; the flowers can achieve widths of ten inches. Given the right conditions—warm water temperatures, little competition, and sunny days—water lilies can quickly take over, so opt for smaller rather than larger plants. Water lilies are frequently the focal point or main feature of a water garden, so selecting the right variety is important. *Nymphaea* species and hybrids come in four types: *dwarf*, with a planting depth of four to six inches; *small*, at six to eighteen inches; *medium*, two feet; and *vigorous*, with a planting depth of three feet. The deeper the plant needs to be, the wider it will spread; therefore, dwarf and small varieties are recommended for container ponds or other shallow water gardens.

WHEN TO PLANT

Plant container-grown hardy water lilies in mid-spring through late summer. You can also divide water lilies in the spring. Do not plant tropicals until after the last spring frost.

WHERE TO PLANT

Water lilies do best in full sun in still, open water.

HOW TO PLANT

Plant in containers that are at least 6 inches deep and 12 inches wide. Set the containers in the pond or water garden.

ADVICE FOR CARE

Insert a slow-release tablet of fertilizer into the container about every 6 weeks. If the pond is deep and the water lily is growing below the expected ice or freeze level, the plant can stay outdoors for the winter. If the pond is shallow, you will need to bring the hardy water lilies indoors.

ADDITIONAL INFORMATION

There are hardy and tropical water lilies, the latter adding fragrance and night bloomers to the mix. Hardy water lilies are native to North America while others come from Asia and Europe. They may be able to withstand Hoosier winters, depending on the depth of the pond. Treat tropical water lilies like annuals; discard them at the end of the growing season.

ADDITIONAL SPECIES, CULTIVARS, OR VARIETIES

Nymphaea 'Chromatella' is a good water lily for beginners because it produces many yellow flowers, even when planted in a small pond under less-than-ideal conditions. *Nymphaea* 'Laydekeri' hybrids are recommended for container gardens and pools. They prefer to be planted 30 inches below the water surface, but will tolerate 24 inches. There are several other cultivars that are recommended for container water gardens. 'Froebeli' has red flowers and olive-green leaves. 'James Brydon' has red flowers, purple foliage, and the ability to adapt to lightly shady spots. Several water lilies are known as "changeables": 'Aurora', with mottled, purple-green leaves and cream flowers that turn to yellow, orange, and red; 'Sioux' or 'Comanche', with flowers that change from buff to pink to copper; and 'Indiana', with purple-spotted leaves and flowers that turn from peach to copper-orange with red stains. Tropical water lilies to consider are 'Missouri', a night-bloomer with white flowers; 'Mrs. George C. Hitchcock', another night-bloomer with pink flowers; and 'Daubeniana', which has small blue flowers. Tropical water lilies are usually hardy only to Zone 8.

SOURCES

Mail-Order Sources

The following listing includes sources for a variety of plant materials suitable for the home gardener. Inclusion in the list should not be considered an endorsement nor should exclusion be viewed as disapproval. Information was deemed correct at the time of publication.

Beaver Creek Nursery
P.O. Box 18243
Knoxville, TN 37928
(615) 922-8561
Unusual Trees and Shrubs

Bluestone Perennials
7211 Middle Ridge Road
Madison, OH 44057
(800) 852-5243
Perennial Flowers

Daffodil Mart
7463 Heath Trail
Gloucester, VA 23061
(800) All-Bulb
Hardy and Tender Bulbs

Dutch Gardens
P.O. Box 200
Adelphia, NJ 07710-0200
(800) 818-3861
Bulbs

Forest Farm
990 Tetherow Rd.
Williams, OR 97544-9599
(541) 846-7269
Trees, Shrubs, Perennials

Hortico, Inc.
723 Robson Road, R.R. #1
Waterdown, ON, Canada
LOR 2H1
(905) 689-6984
Roses, Trees, Shrubs

Indiana Division of Forestry
Jasper-Pulaski Nursery
R.R. #1 Box 241
Medaryville, IN 47957
(219) 843-4827
Seedlings Trees and Shrubs for Conservation Purposes

Mellinger's, Inc.
2310 W. South Range Road
North Lima, OH 44452-9731
(216) 549-9861
Perennials

Nor'East Miniature Roses, Inc.
58 Hammond Street
Rowley, MA 01969
(617) 948-7964
Miniature Roses

Park Seed
Geo. W. Park Seed Co., Inc.
1 Parkton Ave.
Greenwood, SC 29647-0001
(864) 223-7333
Flower and Vegetable Seeds; Perennial Plants

Perry's
P.O. Box 442
Carpinteria, CA 93013
(805) 684-5468
Groundcovers

Sources

Pinetree Garden Seeds
Box 300
New Gloucester, ME 04260
(207) 926-3400
*Flower and Vegetable Seed; Unusual
Plants*

Prairie Nursery
P.O. Box 306
Westfield, WI 53964
(608) 296-3679
*Wildflowers and Native Grasses,
Plants and Seed*

Seed Saver's Exchange
3076 North Winn Rd.
Decorah, IA 52101
*Heirloom Vegetable and
Flower Seeds*

Seeds of Change
P.O. Box 15700
Sante Fe, NM 87506-5700
(888) 762-7333
*Vegetable and Flower Seeds,
Organically Grown*

Shady Oaks Nursery
700 19th Ave. NE
Waseca, MN 56093
*Shade-loving Perennials, Trees and
Shrubs*

Shepherd's Garden Seeds
30 Irene Street
Torrington, CT 06790-6658
(860) 482-3638
Flower, Vegetable, and Herb Seeds

Stonehurst Rare Plants
1 Stonehurst Court
Pomona, NY 10970
(914) 354-4049
Dwarf and Unusual Conifers

Thompson and Morgan
P.O. Box 1308
Jackson, NJ 08527-0308
(800) 274-7333
*Flower, Vegetable, Tree, and Shrub
Seeds; Exotic Seeds*

Vallonia Nursery
2782 West Co. Road 540 South
Vallonia, IN 47281
(812) 358-3621
*Tree and Shrub Seedlings for
Conservation Purposes*

W. Atlee Burpee & Co.
300 Park Ave.
Warminster, PA 18974
(215) 674-4915
Flower and Vegetable Seeds; Plants

White Flower Farm
Plantsmen
P.O. Box 50
Litchfield, CT 06759-9988
(800) 411-6159
Perennial Flowers, Bulbs, Shrubs

Public Gardens and Horticultural Attractions

Indiana is fortunate to have many public parks and gardens to enjoy and visit for inspiration. Although the following operating schedules are believed to be correct, visitors should call ahead to verify schedules to avoid disappointment.

Cool Creek Park and Nature Center
2000-1 E. 151st Street
Fishers, IN 46038
(317) 848-0576

A recent addition to the Hamilton County Parks system, the Nature Center at Cool Creek Park in Fishers features a greenhouse with over 1,000 butterflies in various stages of metamorphosis. The butterflies live on more than fifty species of plants and flowers maintained by a dedicated staff of volunteers. Outdoor gardens designed for butterflies surround the greenhouse and are a great way to get ideas to bring home to your yard! Open Wednesday to Saturday, 10 a.m. to 5 p.m., and Sunday, 1 p.m. to 5 p.m., the butterfly sanctuary and nature center conducts regularly scheduled activities for families, and group tours by request.

The Display Garden
Allen County Extension Office
4001 Crescent Ave.
Fort Wayne, IN 46815-4590
(219) 481-6826

This display garden features more than 13 theme gardens highlighting butterfly and hummingbird plants, herbs, prairie plants, ornamental grasses, woodland plants and wildflowers, vegetables, cottage garden plants, and a children's garden. Maintained by dedicated Master Gardener volunteers, a visit to this garden is an educational opportunity for both beginning and advanced gardeners.

E. G. Hill Memorial Rose Garden
Richmond All-American Rose Garden
Friendship Rose Garden
Glen Miller Park, 828 Promenade
Richmond, IN 47374

Three gardens with more than 2,200 roses are open to the public during park hours. The Hill Memorial Garden was founded in 1937 and is the most

Sources

formal, featuring about 200 plants. The All-American Rose Garden was started in 1987 and has about 2,000 plants. Friendship Garden opened in 1992 and is a sister garden to Richmond's sister city, Zweibruken, Germany. Some of the 120 roses are the same as those that grow in the German garden. The Richmond Parks & Recreation Department takes care of the Hill Memorial Garden; the other two are overseen by volunteers and the Richmond Rose Garden Board of Directors.

Eli Lilly Botanical Gardens
Indianapolis Museum of Art
1200 W. 38th Street
Indianapolis, IN 46208-4196
(317) 923-1331

The Eli Lilly Botanical Gardens surround the centerpiece, the Indianapolis Museum of Art, on West 38th Street in Indianapolis. The grounds include Oldfields, the 26-acre estate and former home of Hugh McK. Landon and, later, J. K. Lilly, Jr. The Oldfields landscape has been restored in the original style of the '20s, when it was designed by the Olmsted Brothers of Brookline, Massachusetts. Impeccably maintained by a dedicated staff of horticulturists, the gardens are a wonderful place to escape the hectic pace of city life. There are numerous smaller gardens within the larger grounds, where it is easy to lose oneself exploring the unique collection of plants. Areas include a woodland garden, a formal garden, an herb garden, a rock garden, a garden for everyone, and a dwarf conifer collection. Plants are well labeled, and self-guided or guided tours of the grounds are available from staff or volunteers. One of the focal points of the grounds is the Madeline F. Elder Greenhouse. Dedicated in 1995 after a major renovation, the greenhouse sells unique tropical, bedding, and perennial plants, as well as other gardening gifts.

Foellinger-Freimann Botanical Conservatory
1100 South Calhoun Street
Ft. Wayne, IN 46802
(219) 427-6440

Managed by Fort Wayne Parks and Recreation, the Foellinger-Freimann Botanical Conservatory is a natural oasis in the middle of an urban jungle. The 3 glass-domed conservatories house collections of tropical plants with distinctly different environments. The Showcase area has seasonal displays of flowers for 6 different occasions throughout the year, including a fall

411

mum show, poinsettia show, spring bulbs, and more. The Tropical House is a jungle of exotic flowering and foliage plants maintained in a humid environment and includes a wonderful cascading waterfall and sparkling stream. The Desert House is home to plants from dry and desert environments and features the massive saguaro and barrel cactus and many others. The Conservatory is host to numerous lectures, events, and educational programs throughout the year. The Tulip Tree Gift Shop features unique plants and botanical gifts. Group tours are available. Regular hours of the Conservatory are Monday to Saturday, 10 a.m. to 5 p.m., and Sundays from noon to 4 p.m. Admission is $2.50 for adults, $2 for students grade 6 through college, and $1.25 for children age 4 through grade 5.

Garfield Park Conservatory and Sunken Gardens
2450 South Shelby Street
Indianapolis, IN 46203
(317) 327-7184

Garfield Park is among the oldest parks in Indianapolis, and the Conservatory and Victorian-era Sunken Gardens have a long botanical history. Having recently completed a full-scale renovation, the Conservatory houses an Amazon River region rainforest environment with extensive displays of bromeliads and numerous other tropical plants in a natural setting. Various seasonal floral shows are exhibited in the Conservatory throughout the year, including a fall mum show, holiday poinsettia show, and a spring bulb show. A variety of plants are for sale in the gift shop. The historic Sunken Gardens, which are being renovated, are just west of the Conservatory and have beautifully patterned brick pathways among the flower beds. The Conservatory is open from 10 a.m. to 5 p.m., Tuesday through Sunday; admission is $2 for adults, $1.50 for seniors, and $1.00 for children. The Sunken Gardens are open during regular park hours.

Hayes Regional Arboretum
801 Elks Rd.
Richmond, IN 47374
(765) 962-3745

The Hayes Regional Arboretum sits on 285 acres of land acquired by railroad official and inventor Stanley W. Hayes. As a regional arboretum, plant collections have been deliberately limited to those that are native to the Whitewater Drainage Basin, which encompasses 14 counties in east-central Indiana and west-central Ohio. The arboretum borders U.S. 40 and is

Sources

located on the eastern edge of Richmond. It can be enjoyed while on foot as well as on a 3.5-mile tour by automobile. Attractions abound, including the Mabelle Hayes Fern Garden, the Native Woody Plant Preserve, the Wildflower Display Garden, and a 40-acre original beech maple forest. Activities and information revolve around the Nature Center, which schedules numerous seasonal programs and events throughout the year. These include, but are not limited to, hosting group tours, summer classes for kids of all ages, an Arbor Day Tree Giveaway, and specially scheduled gardening and environmental workshops. The arboretum is a relaxing and beautiful escape as well as an educational opportunity not to be missed. It is free and open to the public for touring 9 a.m. to 5 p.m., Tuesday through Saturday, and 1 p.m. to 5 p.m. on Sunday.

Holcomb Gardens and Butler Prairie
Butler University
4600 Sunset Ave.
Indianapolis, IN 46208
(317) 283-9413

Holcomb Gardens offers a nice display of annuals and perennials in well-manicured grounds along the Indianapolis Water Company Canal immediately north of the Butler University campus. Rectangular beds of peonies, iris, and daylilies greet the many dog-walkers and strollers who visit the gardens, and are replaced with a good collection of popular annuals later in the season. Holcomb gardens once boasted a collection of 101 different varieties of lilac, a favorite spring-blooming shrub with heavenly fragrance. Although not as extensive, remnants of those shrubs still bloom today. Scattered throughout the grounds are sitting areas and statuary with pensive quotes from famous American authors and figureheads.

Tall-grass prairies covered 15 percent of Indiana before the settlers transformed the land for agricultural use. In an effort to create the original prairie environment found in west central and northwest Indiana, the Butler University Biology Department established the Butler University prairie in 1987. Located west of campus, across the Indianapolis Water Company Canal and adjacent to the Butler playing fields, the several-acre prairie is used as an outdoor laboratory for Biology courses, as a public education resource, and for wildlife living along the nearby White River. The area combines elements of several different prairie types including tall- and short-grass species. More than 30 different plant species were sown to make up the Butler prairie. Only a short 10-minute drive from the heart of downtown, the Butler prairie is a natural hidden treasure in the midst of urban sprawl.

Sources

Jerry E. Clegg Foundation Botanical Gardens
1782 North 400 East
Lafayette, IN 47905
(765) 423-1325

Due east of Lafayette, the Jerry E. Clegg Botanical Garden is a short distance from I-65 and overlooks beautiful Wildcat Creek. After Clegg's death in 1963, his family summer home and grounds were turned into a memorial. Five different trails traverse the sometimes steep and wooded terrain that is home to hundreds of species of woodland wildflowers collected by the Clegg family and their friends. The display of Shooting Star, a native wild-flower, is considered one of the finest in the state. There are at least 44 different species of trees that are well labeled in the garden, a favorite for school children making leaf collections. One of the most popular spots in the garden is Lookout Point, which gives a sweeping, breathtaking view of the Wildcat Valley below. The garden is open from 10 a.m. to sunset daily; admission is free. Group tours are available by calling the County Naturalist or Garden Manager.

Oakhurst Gardens
1200 North Minnetrista Parkway
Muncie, IN 47303
765-282-4848
1-800-CULTURE

Opened in May 1995, the 6.5-acre Oakhurst Gardens is part of the Minnetrista Cultural Center and the former home of George and Frances Ball and their daughter Elisabeth. The mission of Oakhurst is to create awareness, understanding, and appreciation of our natural environment. Built in 1895 and restored with the 1995 opening, Oakhurst includes a sunken garden, formal gardens, and a woodlands wildflower meadow. A visit to Discovery Cabin, a hands-on center, will teach visitors more about nature and its many wonders.

Sources

Gene Stratton-Porter State Historic Site
Wildflower Woods
1205 Pleasant Point
Rome City, IN 46784
(219) 854-3790
    and
Limberlost State Historic Site
P.O. Box 356
Geneva, IN 46740
(219) 368-7428

The state has taken over both Noble County homesites of the famous
Hoosier writer, Gene Stratton-Porter (1863-1924), author of *Girl of the
Limberlost* and other nature books. The homesites are now being restored,
including the swampland at Limberlost and Wildflower Woods. Stratton-
Porter grew up near Geneva on about 25,000 acres of swampland that served
as a personal laboratory for her interest in natural history and botany. When
the land was drained in 1913 she moved to Rome City, bringing with her
hundreds of native plants she salvaged from the swamps and woods. Many
of the plants she rescued have taken root at Wildflower Woods, where the
public gardens are open dusk to dawn. Tours of Stratton-Porter's 16-room
cabin are available. The peak time to visit is in late April and early May
when hundreds of wildflowers are in bloom. There's also a 1-acre formal
garden that includes several plots laid out by Stratton-Porter.

Purdue University Horticulture Gardens
1165 Horticulture Building
Purdue University
W. Lafayette, IN 47907-1165
(765) 494-1298

The Horticulture Gardens are a bright spot on the south end of the Purdue
campus, just outside the Horticulture Building on Marstellar Street. The
gardens feature a broad, well-maintained collection of herbaceous annuals
and some perennials that have been tastefully planted in large curving beds.
Visiting the gardens is an educational adventure since most of the plants
have won awards or are new varieties for the market. The plants are all
well labeled and referenced in a guide that is provided for visitors at the
entrance to the garden. The Purdue Horticulture Department and Master
Gardeners host the annual Purdue Garden Day in the horticulture gardens
on a Saturday in July. The event features tours of the gardens and lectures
by experts. Check with your County Extension Office for the date each year.

Sources

T.C. Steele State Historic Site
4220 S. T.C. Steele Road
Nashville, IN 47448
(812) 988-2785

More than 200 acres nestled in the hills of beautiful Brown County, the
summer retreat of Hoosier impressionist painter T.C. Steele and his wife,
Selma Neubacher Steele, is a nature-lover's paradise. The grounds and natural areas around the estate were often the subject or the inspiration for
many of Steele's paintings. Managed by the Indiana Department of Natural
Resources, the property has partially restored lily ponds, a formal garden,
and hillside and perennial gardens, as well as the 92-acre Selma Steele State
Nature Preserve. Dedicated in 1990, the preserve remains a "tribute to natural beauty," as requested by Mrs. Steele, and is crisscrossed by five hiking
trails. The nature preserve is a favorite among wildflower lovers and is host
to a "Wildflower Foray" each spring. Numerous other events are scheduled
every year as well as educational outreach and summer programs.

White River Gardens *(Opening Spring of 1999)*
1200 W. Washington Street
P.O.Box 22309
Indianapolis, IN 46222-0309
(317) 630-2045

The Indianapolis Zoological Society has announced the opening of the
White River Gardens in Spring 1999. It will encompass 2 acres of exterior
display gardens surrounding a 5,000-square-foot glass-enclosed conservatory. Separate but situated at the east end of the Indianapolis Zoo and
overlooking the White River, the gardens will feature intimate spaces where
you can relax, be inspired, and gather ideas for your own backyard.
Outdoor display areas will include a wedding garden, a water garden, a formal garden, and numerous seasonal "theme" gardens, all with practical
ideas for visitors to take home. A resource center will give visitors the
opportunity to ask questions and have their home gardening problems
answered. Recently accredited as a botanical garden, the existing grounds of
the Zoo are already a great "green" escape a short walk across the restored
Old Washington Street Bridge from the heart of downtown Indianapolis.
The White River Gardens are an eagerly anticipated addition to the renais-
sance and beautification of downtown.

SOURCES

Bibliography

Allison, James. *Water in the Garden*. Salamander Books, 1991.

Archibald, David and Mary Patton. *Firefly Gardener's Guide: Water Gardens*. Firefly Books, 1996.

Armitage, Allan; Heffernan, Maureen; Kleiber, Chela; and Shimizu, Holly. *Burpee Complete Gardener*. Macmillan Inc., 1995.

Armitage, Allan. *Herbaceous Perennial Plants: A Treatise on Their Identification, Culture, and Garden Attributes*. Varsity Press Inc., 1989.

Ball, Jeff and Liz. *Flower Garden Problem Solver*. Rodale Press, 1990.

Beard, James B. *Turfgrass Science and Culture*. Prentice Hall Inc., 1973.

Better Homes and Gardens: Bulbs For All Seasons. Better Homes and Gardens Books, 1994.

Boerner Botanical Gardens. *Rose Gardening*. Pantheon Books, 1995.

Brady, Fern Marshall, editor. *Gardening with Perennials*. Rodale Press, 1996.

Brickell, Christopher, Elvin McDonald, and Trevor Cole. *The American Horticultural Society Encyclopedia of Gardening*. Dorling Kindersley, 1993.

Bryan, John E. *Hearst Garden Guides: Bulbs*. Hearst Books, 1992.

Burns, Russell M. and Barbara H. Honkala. *Silvics of North America Volume I. Conifers*. U.S. Forest Service, 1990.

Bush-Brown, Louise and James. *America's Garden Book*. Revised edition by Howard S. Irwin with the assistance of the Brooklyn Botanic Garden. Macmillan Inc., 1996.

Clausen, Ruth Rogers and Nicolas H. Ekstrom. *Perennials for American Gardens*. Random House Inc., 1989.

Coats, Alice M. *Garden Shrubs and Their Histories*. Simon and Schuster, 1992.

Cox, Jeff and Marilyn. *The Perennial Garden: Color Harmonies Through the Seasons*. Rodale Press, 1985.

Crandall, Chuck and Barbara. *Flowering, Fruiting & Foliage Vines: A Gardener's Guide*. Sterling Publishing Co., 1995.

Cutler, Karan Davis, editor. *A Harrowsmith Gardener's Guide: Vines*. Camden House Publishing Inc., 1992.

417

Sources

Damrosch, Barbara. *The Garden Primer*. Workman Publishing, 1988.

Dana, Michael N. *Ornamental Grasses for Indiana Landscapes*. Purdue University Department of Horticulture Cooperative Extension Home Yard and Garden Series, 1994.

—. *Cooperative Extension Trees and Landscaping Publications*. Purdue University Department of Horticulture.

Deam, Charles C. *Shrubs of Indiana, Second Edition*. Historic Hoosier Hills Woodland Committee, 1932.

Dirr, Michael A. *Manual of Woody Landscape Plants, Fourth Edition*. Stipes Publishing Co., 1990.

Druse, Ken. *The Natural Garden*. Clarkson N. Potter Inc., 1989.

Ernst, Ruth Shaw. *The Naturalist's Garden*. Globe Pequot Press, 1993.

Ellis, Barbara W. and Fern Marshall Bradley, editors. *The Organic Gardener's Handbook of Natural Insect and Disease Control*. Rodale Press, 1992.

Flint, Harrison. *Landscape Plants for Eastern North America*. John Wiley and Sons, 1997.

Glattstein, Judy. *The American Gardener's World of Bulbs*. Little, Brown and Co., 1994.

Glattstein, Judy. *Waterscaping*. Garden Way Publishing, 1994.

Glimn-Lacy, Janice. *What Flowers When with Hints on Home Landscaping*. The Flower and the Leaf Press, 1995.

Greenlee, John. *The Encyclopedia of Ornamental Grasses*. Michael Friedman Publishing Group, 1992.

Grehold, Lacasse and Wandell. *Street Tree Fact Sheets*. Pennsylvania State University Press, 1993.

Griffiths, Trevor. *The Book of Classic Old Roses*. Michael Joseph Limited, 1987.

Haggard, Ezra. *Perennials for the Lower Midwest*. Indiana University Press, 1996.

Halpin, Anne. *Foolproof Planting*. Rodale Press, 1990.

Heath, Brent and Becky. *Daffodils for American Gardens*. Elliott & Clark Publishing, 1995.

Sources

Hendrickson, Robert. *Ladybugs, Tiger Lilies & Wallflowers: A Gardener's Book of Words*. Prentice-Hall General Reference, 1993.

Heriteau, Jacqueline and Marc Cathey. *The National Arboretum Book of Outstanding Garden Plants*. Simon and Schuster, 1990.

Hessayon, D.G. *The Bulb Expert*. Expert Books, 1995.

Hill, Lewis and Nancy. *Bulbs: Four Seasons of Beautiful Blooms*. Garden Way Publishing, 1994.

—. *Successful Perennial Gardening: A Practical Guide*. Garden Way Publishing, 1988.

Hull, George. *The Language of Gardening: An Informal Dictionary*. World Publishing Co., 1967.

Indianapolis Rose Society. *Successful Rose Growing in Indiana*.

Jacobsen, Arthur Lee. *North American Landscape Trees*. Ten Speed Press, 1996.

Karnok, Keith. *Certified Turfgrass Professional*. University of Georgia and the Georgia Center for Continuing Education, 1994.

Lacy, Allen. *Gardening with Groundcovers and Vines*. Harper Collins, 1993.

Lathrop, Norma Jean. *Herbs: How to Select, Grow and Enjoy*. HP Books, 1981.

Lawn Care Series. Purdue University Department of Agronomy.

Lerner, B. R. *Roses*. Purdue Department of Horticulture Home Yard and Garden Series. Purdue University Press, 1988.

Loewer, Peter. *Rodale's Annual Garden*. Wings Books, 1992.

MacCaskey, Michael. *Lawns and Ground Covers: How to Select, Grow and Enjoy*. HP Books, 1982.

McClure, Susan. *The Herb Gardener: A Guide for All Seasons*. Garden Way Publishing, 1996.

McDonald, Elvin. *Rose Gardening*. Meredith Books, 1995.

Mathew, Brian and Philip Swindells. *The Complete Book of Bulbs, Corms, Tubers, and Rhizomes*. Reader's Digest Books, 1994.

McKeon, Judith. *The Encyclopedia of Roses*. Rodale Press, 1995.

Sources

Morgan, Hal. *The Mail Order Gardener*. Harper and Row, 1988.

Morrisey, Sharon Irwin and F. A. Giles. *Dwarf Flowering Shrubs for the Midwest*. University of Illinois at Urbana-Champaign, College of Agriculture Special Publication 60, 1980.

—. *Large Flowering Shrubs for the Midwest*. University of Illinois at Urbana-Champaign, College of Agriculture Special Publication 74.

Nash, Helen. *The Pond Doctor: Planning & Maintaining a Healthy Water Garden*. Sterling Publishing Co., 1994.

Oakes, A. J. *Ornamental Grasses and Grasslike Plants*. Van Nostrand Reinhold, 1990.

Osborne, Robert and Beth Powning. *Hardy Roses*. Storey Communications Inc., 1991.

Ottesen, Carole. *Ornamental Grasses, The Amber Wave*. McGraw Hill, 1989.

Phillips, Roger and Martyn Rix. *The Random House Book of Perennials, Vol. 1 and 2*. Random House, 1991.

Poor, Janet M., Editor and Nancy Peterson Brewster. *Plants that Merit Attention: Volume I, Trees*. Timber Press, 1984.

—. *Plants That Merit Attention: Volume II, Shrubs*. Timber Press, 1996.

Powell, Eileen. *From Seed to Bloom*. Garden Way Publishing, 1995.

Reader's Digest Handbooks: Herbs. Reader's Digest, 1990.

Redell, Rayford Clayton. *Rose Bible*.

Rice, Graham. *The Complete Book of Perennials*. Reader's Digest, 1996.

Ritter, Frances, Editor. *Shrubs and Climbers*. DK Publishing, 1996.

Robinson, Peter. *Wayside Gardens Collection: The Water Garden*. Sterling Publishing Co., 1995.

Rodale's Chemical-Free Yard & Garden. Rodale Press Inc., 1991.

Rose, Peter Q. *Climbers and Wall Plants*. Blandford, 1990.

—. *Ivies*. Blandford, 1990.

Sala, Orietta. *The World's Best Roses*. Prentice Hall, 1990.

Scaniello, Stephen and Tanya Bayard. *Climbing Roses*. Hall, 1994.

Schulz, Warren. *The Chemical Free Lawn*. Rodale Press, 1983.

Sources

Scott, O. M. and Sons. *Scotts Information Manual for Lawns*. O. M. Scott and Sons Company, 1979.

Sternberg, Guy and Jim Wilson. *Landscaping With Native Trees*. Chapters Publishing Limited, 1995.

Stokes, Donald and Lillian. *The Wildflower Book East of the Rockies*. Little, Brown and Co., 1992.

Swindells, Philip. *Planning and Planting Water Gardens*. Ward Lock Books, 1996.

Taylor's Master Guide to Gardening. Houghton Mifflin Co., 1994.

Thomas, R. William. *Trees and Shrubs*. Hearst Books, 1992.

Turgeon, A. J. *Turfgrass Management*. Reston Publishing Company, Inc., 1980.

Wyman, Donald. *Shrubs and Vines for American Gardens*. Macmillan Inc., 1969.

INDEX

Index

Index

Index

Index

Index

Index

Index

Index

ABOUT THE AUTHORS

*T*OM TYLER is an Extension Educator and horticulturist for the Purdue Cooperative Extension Service in Indianapolis. Each Thursday he answers gardening questions during the "Lawn and Garden Show" on WMYS Radio, and makes frequent appearances on local television. He also reaches gardeners through numerous gardening lectures, workshops, newsletters and other community projects while coordinating urban gardening efforts in the county. Tyler received a BS in Horticulture from Clemson University and an MS in Agronomy from Purdue University. He spent several years in Niger as a research associate and Peace Corps Volunteer and currently serves as President of the American Community Gardening Association. He lives and gardens in Indianapolis with Buffy and Jody, his cats.

*J*O ELLEN MEYERS SHARP writes a garden column in *The Indianapolis Star* on Sundays, and for Web-19, an internet magazine. After more than 16 years as a reporter at *The Indianapolis Star and News,* she recently left the newspapers to found Jemstone Communications, a freelance writing and communications business. Before that, she was a reporter in Southern Indiana and Louisville, Kentucky, for *The Courier-Journal* and *The Louisville Times.* She has a bachelor's degree in education from Indiana University-Purdue University at Indianapolis. A Master Gardener, she lives in her native Indianapolis, where she gardens in an urban yard in spite of her dogs, Moon and Penn.

INDIANA GARDENING
ONLINE

432